Dan Gookin's Guide to Underground DOS 6.0

Dan Gookin's
Guide to Underground DOS 6.0

Dan Gookin

BANTAM BOOKS
NEW YORK • TORONTO • LONDON • SYDNEY • AUCKLAND

Dan Gookin's Guide to Underground DOS 6.0
A Bantam Book / April 1993

All rights reserved.
Copyright © 1993 by Dan Gookin
Cover design Copyright © 1993 by Bantam Books
Interior design by Nancy Sugihara
Produced by The LeBlond Group

*No part of this book may be reproduced or transmitted
in any form or by any means, electronic or mechanical,
including photocopying, recording, or by any information
storage and retrieval system, without permission in writing from
the publisher.*
For information address: Bantam Books

*Throughout this book, tradenames and trademarks of some companies
and products have been used, and no such uses are intended to convey
endorsement of or other affiliations with the book.*

ISBN 0-553-37097-9

Published simultaneously in the United States and Canada

Bantam Books are published by Bantam Books, a division of Bantam Doubleday Dell Publishing Group, Inc. Its trademark, consisting of the words "Bantam Books" and the portrayal of a rooster, is Registered in U.S. Patent and Trademark Office and in other countries. Marca Registrada, Bantam Books, 1540 Broadway, New York, New York 10036.

PRINTED IN THE UNITED STATES OF AMERICA

0   9   8   7   6   5   4   3   2   1

Contents

Introduction   xiii

Part I Useful Things To Know   1

1 Booting the PC   3
To Boot a PC   3
The Cold Boot   4
The Warm Boot   5
The Psychological Effects of Booting   5
What Goes on When You Flip the Big Red Switch   7
Booting with DEBUG   7
The DOS Boot Process   10

2 All about CONFIG.SYS   15
How It All Works   15
Editing CONFIG.SYS   19
Creating the Best CONFIG.SYS File   21
Configuration Commands   22
   BREAK   22
   BUFFERS   23
   COUNTRY   24
   DEVICE   25
   DEVICEHIGH   27
   DOS   29
   DRIVPARM   30

FCBS 31
FILES 31
INSTALL 33
LASTDRIVE 33
NUMLOCK 34
REM 34
SET 35
SHELL 35
STACKS 35
SWITCHES 36
New CONFIG.SYS Stuff for DOS 6.0 37
The Best Configuration Is Sometimes No Configuration 38
Configuration Menu Commands 39

3 All about COMMAND.COM 43

The Command Interpreter 43
The Multiple Personalities of COMMAND.COM 44
COMMAND.COM the Transient 45
Specifying the Command Interpreter 48
COMMAND.COM's Secret Format 50
COMMAND.COM the Program 51
The Shell Game 52
COMMAND.COM's Command Line Format 54
Running a DOS Window in Windows 55
Using the Mysterious, New /K Switch 57
Running a DOS Window in DESQview 58

4 All about AUTOEXEC.BAT 63

How COMMAND.COM Runs AUTOEXEC.BAT 63
Things to Do in an AUTOEXEC.BAT File 65
Create a Beautiful PROMPT 67
Set a Proper PATH 69
Create Environment Variables 72
Configure the System 74
Set the Date and Time? 75
Load Startup Programs 76
Start Your First Program or Menu System 78

Extra Fun with SUBST 79
   The Major Caveats 80

5   DOS the Device Master 83

DOS's Devices 83
   The Basic Devices 84
   The Interesting NUL Device 85
   Other Devices 87
Devices and I/O Redirection 88
   From Here to There 89
   Redirecting Output 91
   Redirecting Input 95
   Using the Pipe 96
Using Filters 97
   How Filters Work 98
   The MORE Filter 99
   The SORT Filter 101
   The FIND Filter 101

6   Keyboard Control 103

All about ASCII 103
   The Mysterious Control Characters 104
   Entering the Escape Character 105
   The Extended ASCII Character Set 108
   The Alt-Keypad Trick 108
Using ANSI.SYS 109
   Modifying the Keyboard 110
   Reversing the Process 111
   Using Keyboard Scan Codes 112
   Using ANSI Commands with the DOS Editor 113
   Using ANSI Commands with DEBUG 115
   Using ANSI Commands at the DOS Prompt 117
Command Line Editing 121
Using DOSKEY for Command Line Editing 122
   Editing with DOSKEY 122
   The Command History 122
Abbreviating DOS Commands with DOSKEY 124

Part II Spelunking With DEBUG 127

7 All about DEBUG 129
What Is This Thing, This DEBUG? 129
Why Is There DEBUG? 130
What You Can Do with DEBUG 130
Running DEBUG 132
Using DEBUG 134
Quitting DEBUG 136
Learning More about DEBUG 136

8 Removing the Hex from Hexadecimal 137
Counting Systems 137
The Binary Counting System 139
Making Binary Easier to Read 140
The Hexadecimal Counting System 141
From Binary to Hex, and Finally to Decimal 143
Bits and Bytes 144
Looking at Hexadecimal Numbers 146
Diving into DEBUG 147
Using DEBUG's H Command 148

9 The Ugly Truth about PC Memory 151
A Look at Memory 151
The PC Memory Map 152
RAM and ROM 154
Finding a Byte in Memory 156
The PC's 16-bit, 64K Limitation 156
That Awful Segmented Architecture 156
Locating a Byte in Memory 159
One Byte, Many Addresses 160
Really Weird Stuff 163

10 Working with Memory 167
Peeking at Memory 167
DEBUG's Memory Display 168
Using the D Command 170

Contents ix

  Manipulating Memory 173
    Changing Memory 173
    Changing a Lotta Memory 176
    Copying Blocks of Memory 177
    Comparing Memory 180
    Searching Memory 182

11 Disks and DEBUG 185
  Working with Files 185
    Saving Memory to Disk 186
    Loading a File from Disk 191
    Saving and Restoring the Screen 192
  Raw Disk Action 197
    Reading Your Disk Directly 197
    Writing Raw Sectors to Disk 200

12 Peeling the Lid off the Microprocessor Chip 205
  Anatomy of a Microprocessor 205
    The Microprocessor's Registers 206
    Different Registers for Different Purposes 207
  A Look at the Registers in DEBUG 208
    Using the R Command 209
    The Accumulator Registers 210
    Working with Files and the CX Register 210
    Specific Accumulator Register Tasks 212
    Split Personalities 213
  Special Purpose Registers 214
    The Index Registers 214
    The Segment Registers 217
    The Flags Register 219

13 How the Microprocessor Works 221
  The Art of Programming 221
    Seven Paragraphs on Programming Languages 222
    Telling The Microprocessor What To Do 223
  The Mini-Assembler 226
    Building the Program 226
    Running the Program a Step at a Time 228

Go for It with the G Command 229
Saving Your Program to Disk 231
Jumping, Looping, Interrupting 231
Loading the Instruction Pointer 232
Labels in Assembly Language 234
How the Stack Pointer Works 236
Two Stack Examples 239
Call and Return Instructions 242
Calling DOS 243

Part III The Interesting, Curious, and Exotic 247

14 Ugly Memory Stuff 249

The Program Segment Prefix 249
How Programs Run under DOS 250
The COM File Format 250
The EXE File Format 251
The PSP Up Close and in Person 254
The SAY Program 258
Know Thyself by Reading Thy ROM 262
The BIOS Data Area 263
The Various BIOSs Found in Upper Memory 269

15 More Ugly Memory Stuff 273

DOS and Memory Blocks 273
How DOS Allocates Memory 274
The Memory Block "Arena Header" 275
Finding Blocks with the MEM Command 277
The Environment Memory Block 278
Video Memory 280
Peeking and Poking through Video Memory 280
All about Attribute Bytes 284
CGA Video Pages 288
Video Character Sets 292

Contents   xi

16 Disks, Files, and Stuff   297

The Wondrous Boot Sector   297
   Looking at the Boot Sector   298
   Changing the Boot Message   306
   The Hard Disk Partition Table   308
The File Allocation Table   309
   Walking the FAT   311
   Using the CHKDSK Command   314
The Truth about the Directory   314
   What a Directory Listing Really Looks Like   315
   Finding a Subdirectory   320

17 File Editing in DEBUG   325

Hard-Core File Editing   325
   Editing a Program File   326
   Patching COMMAND.COM   330
Document Rescue and Recovery   331

18 Programming in DEBUG   337

Hip Deep in Scripts   337
   Creating the Program   338
   Script Strategy   342
   Creating an E Script   343
   Creating an A Script   344
   Testing the Script   348
Programs under DOS   350
   A Good Greeting   350
   The ASK Program   352
   Which CPU Is This?   353
   Making the PC Sing   354
   Where to go Next?   357

Appendix A   ASCII Table   359
Appendix B   Line Drawing Characters   371
Appendix C   ANSI Commands   375

Appendix D Counting Systems 379
Appendix E Common DOS Function Calls 381
Appendix F Keyboard Scan Codes 393

Index 397

Introduction

What Is "Underground DOS?"

Underground DOS is the good stuff, the solid information you need to be productive with your personal computer (PC) and to understand how and why it works. It's not hidden information or the nefarious "undocumented" commands. Most of DOS, the reliable part, is documented. It's just done in such a muddled manner that no one with an IQ less than one bazillion will ever figure it out.

Now I don't have an IQ that high, and you probably don't either. Lucky for both of us, since we have to interact with other humans on this planet. I haven't read all of the DOS manual, but the parts I do understand — the stuff I consider worthy and important — is all covered in this book. That's the first part of underground DOS — it's knowing how to get the most from your PC: how to start your computer properly, and what beneficial things you can do with it once it's up and running.

The second part of underground DOS is more fun: exploration. The personal computer is one of the most amazing devices. It's like Idaho in a way: the PC is full of fun and interesting little spots that will amaze you, yet they are highly neglected. The many interesting spots and gizmos inside your PC are ignored for things like "running a word processor" or "doing a spreadsheet." A PC is much more than that.

Your computer can be entertaining, and not only for playing games with you. I had a blast in the early days of the personal computer. Exploring my PC back then was a hobby, a fun trip. Okay, so I lacked a social life. Each night, armed with a handy "snooping" tool, I explored the bowels of the computer like an adventurer from Jules Verne's "Journey to the Center of RAM." (Those guys were pretty nerdy too, if you remember.)

Is Underground DOS for You?

Quite possibly, yes. You could be just starting out, intimidated and afraid of "the box." Be prepared to have your eyes opened. Intermediate and advanced users will enjoy the casual exploration and the deep dive into the darkness inside their

PC. This book will quench your curiosity about such things as DEBUG and its cryptic script files. You'll learn how the microprocessor works and what role it plays, how characters appear on the screen, and how to control everything using the DOS prompt.

The language this book uses is light and nonthreatening; it's written for everyone and assumes nothing. I try to inform and entertain at the same time, so be prepared to dazzle yourself while exploring the depths. It's really easy, once you know how.

The bulk of this book covers what some have called "the most frightening DOS command of them all!" It's DEBUG, which is an ugly word — especially to insects. DEBUG can really be warm, melting putty in your hand, and I'll prove it to you. It's the handiest tool I can think of, too long neglected and way too powerful to be ignored.

This book will train you to use DEBUG in a painless and entertaining way. Soon you'll be using that tool to see how the computer works and to tell it exactly what you want it to do. No math is required. No brainwork here! Everything is geared toward exploring your PC and enjoying yourself.

Exploration Utilities

The only tools you need for this book are your computer, DOS, and your brain. Your computer should have come with DOS, and your head came with a brain. How you use your brain is up to you. How you use DOS and your computer is covered in this book.

Instead of being "frightening," DEBUG is the "handiest" utility, and it comes with DOS. Other cool utilities worth having can be located through various sources: user groups, national on-line services, shareware "warehouses," and mail order companies — the usual places.

I don't recommend very many utilities. At the top of my list are SemWare's QEdit text editor, Vern Buerg's LIST, the "Baker's Dozen" utilities, the ZANSI.SYS replacement driver for DOS's ANSI.SYS, and a good hexadecimal-decimal calculator, like HexCalc or the Windows' Calculator program. I can't list a single source for these, but you can find them all over. CompuServe is a good place to go file hunting, although buying six disks for $20 from a mail-order shareware place often leads to some interesting finds; select from the "utilities" or "batch file helpers" disk categories.

Conventions Used in This Book

This is an active book! Crack it open, break the spine, and sit it flat in your lap. Poise yourself at the keyboard and start typing away. I always assume you have a PC right in front of you as you read.

Read and do! Consider this book your road map — or treasure map — to all the goodies that lurk inside the beast computer before you. But, a fair warning: You should take breaks every so often. Sometimes, exploring your PC can be too much fun. Keep an eye on the clock, get up and do some proper stretching exercises every so often, or you'll be supporting your local chiropractor!

Introduction XV

✎ ***Note:*** Interesting notes or asides will appear like this in the text. This is a "note."

▶ ***Tip:*** This is a "tip." It contains additional helpful information or a collection of tips about the topics at hand. I also use these to summarize things so that you can find them quickly when you use the book as a reference. (I never write a book I wouldn't want to use myself.)

During the course of your reading, you'll encounter the following DOS prompt:

```
C:\>
```

That's the example prompt I'm using in this book, although it may not appear exactly that way on your screen. If you're ever directed to type something in, do so as shown below:

```
C:\> DEBUG
```

This command starts DEBUG. You don't have to be "in drive C" to issue this command. In fact, creating a special work directory for this book would be a great idea.

I've assumed that you automatically will press Enter after each command, including those in DEBUG, as follows:

```
-D100 L80
```

Press Enter after typing this example. Only if the text tells you to wait should you do so. And nothing I direct you to type in will harm your PC (contrary to what "they" have been telling you). But just to be safe, double-check everything.

Where to Begin?

This book is divided into three parts: Part I contains general information about how your PC works, how DOS works, and how the three of you can learn to get along famously. I've written the chapters in Part I to be read in order: Chapter 1 is about booting your PC, followed by "what happens next" in Chapter 2, then "what happens after that" in Chapter 3, and so on. But you can really start reading anywhere.

Part II offers an introduction to using DEBUG and trains you on the finer points of 'BUG etiquette. This is required if you're unfamiliar with DEBUG, and recommended for everyone (even the "advanced" readers).

Part III releases the brakes and takes the car underground for some detailed and grimy exploration of your PC's most sensitive circuits. I recommend reading Part II (or at least Chapters 7 through 13 on subjects new to you), before reading Part III. Otherwise, everything in Part III (Chapters 14 through 18) can be read in any order.

Several interesting and useful appendixes have been tossed in at the end, just because they're things I always look up and I've always wanted a book where they were all in one place. (I'd add more, but the book is already four months past due and way too big.)

This is a fun, active book. I've really enjoyed writing it, and am certain that you will enjoy reading it, taking advantage of the numerous useful tips contained here, and getting to know more about your PC and its innermost secrets. Happy spelunking!

Part I

Useful Things to Know

There's no use exploring underground DOS if you lack a few basic DOS fundamentals. Some people may refer to these chestnuts as "advanced." Yeah, right. Nothing is advanced if it's already in the DOS manual. Instead, I think of it as "barely documented." Granted, the DOS manual doesn't scream out these things, and it will never tell you how to make them work for you. That's the purpose of this part of the book. You'll find the following information nestled in the next six chapters:

- Booting the PC "behind the scenes"
- Information on what should happen in your CONFIG.SYS file
- Understanding COMMAND.COM and how to use it to its full abilities
- Information on AUTOEXEC.BAT and what should happen there
- Cool stuff about DOS and how it deals with *devices*
- Everything you want to know about your keyboard and how to get more control over it.

These chapters cover what I call DOS fundamentals for PC spelunkers. You won't find a tutorial for the editor or DOS Shell here, nor will you waste any time learning about the COPY command's concatenation feature. Instead, this material touches upon some interesting and useful stuff you may not already know — or may know about, but have not yet considered how to apply it.

1

Booting the PC

Booting a PC is more than just turning it on. There are two major types of boot: the "cold" boot and the "warm" boot. These are nice human terms that, as usual, have nothing to do with what they represent. This chapter covers these terms and everything else that goes on when you boot your computer.

To Boot a PC

The term *boot* comes from *bootstrap loader*, which is a program that starts a computer. The "loader" represents the part of the program that puts itself into memory, allowing the program to take control. "Bootstrap" refers to the loops on either side of a boot — bootstraps. They help you pull on a boot. The old computer adage, used over and over, is that a computer is "pulling itself up by its bootstraps." Yawn. I prefer an older, archaic version of the verb *boot*, which meant "to put on one's boots." So you can imagine someone in Shakespeare's day saying, "Help booteth thy father, he be'th late for work." It works for computers, too.

In computer parlance, *to boot* means to start or restart (reset) the computer. Essentially, when you boot you start over from the beginning, whether the computer was already on or not. This is necessary for the following reasons:

- To "unlock" a hopelessly "hung" computer
- To assert changes made in CONFIG.SYS or AUTOEXEC.BAT
- To reset your hardware
- Just because.

Obviously, if the computer is unresponsive — which happens a lot when you learn to program — you'll need to reset. Programs lock up, things fail, and computers run amok. In desperate instances, rebooting the computer brings it back to life.

Another reason for rebooting is that certain things in your computer require you to start over before they can start working. Since the CONFIG.SYS and AUTOEXEC.BAT startup files only run when you start the PC, you'll need to reboot to make any changes take effect. Most people boot their computer once a day when they turn it on. Or, if you're like me and leave the system on all the time, you can boot occasionally just because it makes you feel good and reminds the computer of who's ultimately in charge.

> ***Note:*** Should you keep your computer on all the time? Most experts say yes. The reasons are varied, but two compelling ones usually surface: The first is that turning the system on sends a stressful jolt of electricity through its components. When you leave the PC on all the time, there is no stress. The second is that turning the system off and on cycles the temperature from hot to cold. That strains the solder joints, causing them to become brittle and crack. On some systems, the heat change actually causes chips to bulge out of their sockets.

The major argument against leaving the computer on all the time is that it wears the bearings in your constantly spinning hard drive. While that's true, it's not as big an issue as the damage caused by turning the PC on and off once a day. My advice is to leave the computer on all the time — even over the weekend.

The Cold Boot

A cold boot is a reset involving the power switch; it can be anytime you first turn the system on. The hard-core tech weenies refer to this as a "power cycle": you must turn off the computer if it's on, wait for everything to "power down," then turn the system on again. That's the only way to cold boot. Even if your PC has a reset button, pressing it is not the same as a true cold boot.

Why wait before turning the computer on again? Two reasons: the most important is that you need to make sure your hard drives stop spinning. This takes about 15 seconds for most hard drives, seeing how well greased their bearings are and that they spin faster than 3,600 RPMs. If you just punch off the power then quickly flip it back on, you could fry the drive controller mechanism — or anything else in the system — by the sudden surge of energy. (I know this firsthand; the power company dropped power for two seconds — long enough for me to lose a 90M hard drive.)

The second reason for waiting is to ensure that your hardware fully resets. I can't figure this one out, but it's true: some electrical components need to "drain" themselves before they're fully reset. Some self-configuring PC expansion cards react this way. You need to perform a cold boot so that they "forget" their configurations. A simple reset doesn't do the job.

The Warm Boot

You don't always need to cold boot to reset a computer. Most of the time, only a warm boot is necessary. There are two conventional ways to do this:

1. The computer's reset button (if present)
2. Ctrl-Alt-Delete

Pressing the Ctrl (control), Alt, and Delete keys all at the same time is known as the "three-finger reset button" or my favorite, "the Vulcan nerve pinch." This is the traditional way to warm boot a computer, traditional because the first IBM computers and their clones lacked reset buttons.

Note: On some computers, pressing the reset button is more drastic than Ctrl-Alt-Delete. For example, when you press Ctrl-Alt-Delete, the computer usually skips its warm-up calisthenics — the memory test and self-diagnostics — and just starts over again. Pressing the reset button, on the other hand, forces the computer to truly start over. Still, keep in mind this is not the same as a cold boot.

Unlike a cold boot, a warm boot doesn't reset all of your hardware. In fact, most computers will skip their memory tests and other self-diagnostics during a warm boot. This means you can reset the computer faster than having to turn it off, wait, then turn it on again. It also makes the warm boot more practical when making changes to CONFIG.SYS or AUTOEXEC.BAT and to get out of lockups.

The Psychological Effects of Booting

When to boot is almost as important as how you boot. This isn't a time-sensitive issue. "When to boot" means that you should really only boot your computer when it's not doing anything else. For example, the worst time to boot is when your disk drives are in action. *Never boot your PC when the drive light is on!* The best time is when you're at the DOS prompt:

```
C:\>
```

When the cursor is just sitting there waiting for your input, you can freely reset. Of course, you should take care to make sure you've properly exited from any environments, such as Windows or *DESQview*, before you reset. They'll catch Ctrl-Alt-Delete, but not a press of the reset button or a cold boot.

▬▶ *Tip:* To make sure you're not in a Windows or *DESQview* DOS "window," type EXIT at the DOS prompt and press Enter. If that doesn't close the window, then press Alt-Esc to return to Windows or press and release the Alt key to see *DESQview's* DESQ menu.

It's very bad to reset instead of quitting an application. At most businesses and nearly all government bureaucracies this is the preferred method of exiting *1-2-3* or *WordPerfect*. The person doing the on-the-job training states, "When you're done here, just push this big red button. . . ." Wrong! That's what keeps the majority of the $45/hour computer consultants employed. Never boot the computer to get out of a program unless the program is stuck in a loop or hopelessly hung; always properly quit your applications.

When you do reset in the middle of something, it's not the end of the world. Most of the time, the computer really couldn't care less. But in some cases programs will leave little pieces of themselves all over the hard drive — part of the emotional leftovers of being shattered by a warm boot. Those pieces of files are referred to as "unallocated clusters" or "lost file chains." (What clusters are and how they work is covered in Chapter 12, "Underground Disk Stuff.")

As unwitting users continue to reset their PCs, more lost clusters accumulate and hard disk performance eventually drops. The cure is to run the CHKDSK program after you've had to reset in the middle of something. As soon as you see the DOS prompt again, type the following:

```
C:\> CHKDSK
```

If you have any lost clusters, you'll see something like the following in CHKDSK's output:

```
Errors found, F parameter not specified
Corrections will not be written to disk

  25 lost allocation units found in 3 chains.
   51200 bytes disk space would be freed
```

When this happens, run CHKDSK again and specify the /F switch. This will remove the lost chains and clean up the hard drive. It should be done on each of your hard drives — and before you run *DESQview*, Windows or any menu program:

```
C:\> CHKDSK D: /F
```

Above, CHKDSK, is run on drive D. The /F switch directs CHKDSK to fix any lost clusters it finds. CHKDSK does this by writing the lost clusters to files in the root directory. Each file is given the name FILE*xxxx*.CHK, where the *xxxx* starts with 0000 and increments by one for each lost cluster found.

The instructions in the DOS manual claim that you can examine the files once they've been recovered, changing their names as necessary if you want to keep the data. but let's be honest: The file fragments contain junk you don't need; feel free to delete them after their recovery:

```
C:\> DEL \FILE*.CHK
```

Another side effect of booting your computer is that you lose the contents of your RAM drives. If you store only temporary files there, no problem. But if you're using the RAM drive for any other purpose, it goes bye-bye. The reason is that RAM, specifically the Dynamic RAM or DRAM in all PCs, requires a constant flow of electricity to remain active. A cold boot shuts off power, so the RAM is lost anyway. A warm boot unloads the RAM drive software — which is then rerun when the system initializes again and memory is "reformatted." Either way, you lose your RAM drive.

What Goes on When You Flip the Big Red Switch

There are three things that make booting possible on a PC: the power switch, the microprocessor, and ROM, Read-Only Memory. The power switch supplies the electricity, the microprocessor is the brains, and ROM tells the microprocessor what to do next.

When you flip on the power switch, you supply electricity to the computer's *power* supply. That's a big metal box inside the PC's case that translates the 120 volt 60 cycle (MHz) alternating current into 5 and 12 volt direct current for the computer's electronics. (The volt-cycle/MHz values are different outside the United States.) While this sounds like a brainless thing to do, the power supply actually has some smarts to it. It won't send juice out to the rest of the system if the power coming from the wall isn't high enough. This is why your PC won't run during a brownout, even though other appliances may be duped into functioning.

After the juice flows from the power supply, it energizes every part of the computer. When the microprocessor receives power, it does a little self-test to make sure it's working and then — just as it's wiping the last bit of sleep from its eyes — it starts executing instructions at a specific memory location inside the computer. Keep in mind that the microprocessor doesn't know anything; it looks for instructions elsewhere to tell it what to do.

Specifically, each microprocessor does things a little differently when it starts. But for the purposes of booting DOS, all of them act similarly to the 8088, the microprocessor in the first PC. That chip would begin looking for instructions at memory location FFFF:0000. All its descendants — the 80286, the 386 family, the i486, and beyond — follow suit as far as all DOS users are concerned. (Information on reading memory locations in the above format is covered in Chapter 7, "All About DEBUG.")

When your PC's microprocessor looks at location FFFF:0000 when it boots, it sees ROM — the third element of booting a PC. The ROM at location FFFF:0000 is your computer's BIOS, the Basic Input/Output System. The microprocessor instruction at FFFF:0000 varies depending on the computer and who made the BIOS. For just about everyone, however, the instruction is a "jump" into the bootstrap loader routine located elsewhere.

Booting with DEBUG

DEBUG is a handy tool, and you'll be using it heavily throughout this book. To start with, you can use DEBUG to look at your PC's BIOS and see the same instructions the microprocessor sees when it starts your computer. To do this, pull your stool up tight to the computer and make sure you're looking at a DOS prompt. Further, make sure you're not using an environment like Windows or *DESQview*. You need raw DOS for DEBUG stuff. To start DEBUG:

```
C:\> DOS DEBUG
-
```

I'll describe the details of DEBUG and what it does in the second part of this book. For now, consider it your headlamp as you explore the lower caverns of DOS. To display memory location FFFF:0000, type in the D command followed by that address:

```
-D FFFF:0000
```

You can use upper- or lowercase; DEBUG isn't picky. What you see on your screen will look similar to that shown in Figure 1-1. You'll see eight lines of text in three columns: memory addresses, hexadecimal data, and the text or ASCII representation of that data. The top line is what concerns you here. The first byte, at memory location FFFF:0000, will be EA. That's followed by four additional bytes that tell the microprocessor where to jump — the location of the bootstrap loader. These bytes vary from system to system, as will the copyright date of the BIOS, which you can also see in Figure 1-1. To exit DEBUG all you have to do is to type Q.

Note: If you have DOS's HIMEM.SYS or similar XMS device driver installed, the bottom seven lines you see on the screen are actually *extended* memory. That's the first part of the HMA which an XMS device driver creates for DOS. On any machine running DOS's RAM drive software, you'll probably see "VDISK 3.3" as shown in Figure 1-1.

You can take an additional peek at the ROM instructions by using DEBUG's U, unassembled, command. Type in U followed by FFFF:0000:

```
-U FFFF:0000
```

Tip: As long as you haven't typed anything else in DEBUG, type in U then press F3. This displays *u ffff:0000* since DOS's command line editing keys are still active in DEBUG. (But note that DOSKEY won't be active; it only works at the DOS prompt.)

```
FFFF:0000   EA BF 05 7E 02 30 31 2F-31 35 2F 38 38 FF FC 00   ...~.01/15/88...
FFFF:0010   00 00 00 56 44 49 53 4B-33 2E 33 80 00 01 01 00   ...VDISK3.3.....
FFFF:0020   01 40 00 00 02 FE 06 00-08 00 01 00 00 00 40 04   .@............@.
FFFF:0030   70 00 2E 8E 06 30 00 BF-E0 06 B9 04 00 AB 47 47   p....0........GG
FFFF:0040   E2 FB CB 56 50 51 52 57-55 1E 06 53 8B EC 8B 76   ...VPQRWU..S...v
FFFF:0050   12 2E 8E 1E 30 00 8B 44-02 A2 21 00 88 26 E7 04   ....0..D..!..&..
FFFF:0060   8B 34 C4 1E 12 00 26 8A-47 01 26 8A 67 0D 26 8B   .4....&.G.&.g.&.
FFFF:0070   4F 12 26 8B 57 14 81 FE-A2 04 75 17 C7 06 2B 05   O.&.W.....u...+.
```

Figure 1-1 Here are the first ROM instructions the microprocessor sees after a boot

Booting the PC   9

You'll see a bunch of Assembly language code displayed after typing in the above command. The first line is the only important thing. It's a *jmp* or jump instruction to some address in the computer. That address is what's presently handling any boot commands.

You're just one step away from resetting the computer using DEBUG. The G command is used to run a program in memory. G, meaning *go,* is followed by the memory location of the routine you want to run. Since the routine at FFFF:0000 boots the computer, you can type in the following to reset your PC:

```
-G FFFF:0000
```

Press Enter and you've just reset. (Or press G, F3, then Enter.) You can combine these commands into a batch file that feeds the necessary instructions into DEBUG. The program RESET.BAT is shown in Figure 1-2. Feel free to type it in using your favorite text editor (DOS's EDIT program will do nicely) and save it to disk as RESET.BAT. The line numbers are for reference only; don't type them in.

The program feeds itself into DEBUG — which is disgusting to think about and ugly on the screen — but it works. Lines 3 through 7 contain the DEBUG instructions. These are skipped over in line 1, which jumps to the BEGIN label at line 9. The batch file is then force-fed into DEBUG at line 10 using *I/O redirection* (covered in Chapter 5). Note that you should use the full pathname to this batch file; in line 10 I put C:\UTIL\RESET.BAT, which is where it is on my system.

When DEBUG runs, it chokes horribly on line 1 of the batch file. This produces an error because DEBUG doesn't know the GOTO BEGIN command:

```
-goto begin
 ^ Error
```

The blank line (2) skips over the error and the real DEBUG instructions begin on line 3. Essentially the program sets up the same thing accomplished with the *g ffff:0000* command: RCS sets the *code segment* to FFFF in lines 3 and 4, RIP sets the *instruction pointer* to zero in lines 5 and 6, and finally the G command is used in line 7. Klunk! Your system is reset.

```
 1: GOTO BEGIN
 2:
 3: RCS
 4: FFFF
 5: RIP
 6: 0000
 7: G
 8:
 9: :BEGIN
10: DEBUG   C:\UTIL\RESET.BAT
```

Figure 1-2 Here is the code for RESET.BAT

```
 1: GOTO BEGIN
 2:
 3: E 40:72 34 12
 4: RCS
 5: FFFF
 6: RIP
 7: 0000
 8: G
 9:
10: :BEGIN
11: DEBUG   C:UTIL\REBOOT.BAT
```

Figure 1-3 Here is the code for REBOOT.BAT

The type of reset RESET.BAT does is generally a hard reset; most computers will just start over, performing a memory test and startup diagnostics. There's a way to avoid this, and the time lag it causes, by adding one line to the code. Figure 1-3 shows a second batch file, REBOOT.BAT. This program is quicker on the rest than RESET.BAT because it uses a simple trick to tell the PC to skip the memory check and diagnostics — the "startup calisthenics."

Two lines are different between REBOOT.BAT and RESET.BAT. An extra line (line 3 in Figure 1-3) uses DEBUG's E command to change two bytes in memory. At memory location 40:72 the bytes 34 and 12 are *poked* into that memory location using the E, enter, command. Everything else is the same as RESET.BAT, save for the name change in line 11 to REBOOT.BAT.

Putting the two bytes 1234 at memory location 40:72 tells DOS to skip the memory test and diagnostics when it boots. This is what the Ctrl-Alt-Delete routine does. Aside from that, there's no difference between the two routines.

The DOS Boot Process

After the microprocessor jumps up to FFFF:0000 and starts reading your PC's ROMs, the following things happen:

1. The Power-On Self Test, or POST, is performed.

    The POST includes the memory test, self-diagnostics, and an inventory of all the PC's hardware. Some adapter cards, such as hard drives and graphics cards, will also perform their own tests.

2. The operating system load: step 1, the boot sector.

    The last desperate act of the ROM bootstrap loader is to hunt for an operating system to load from disk. First it checks for a disk in drive A, then it looks to the hard drive C. If a disk is found, the first 512 bytes of that disk are loaded into memory. That part of the disk contains a small program and the microprocessor is told to execute it.

Booting the PC   11

If a disk isn't found, you'll see some type of error message. The message text you see depends on your computer. It'll be something like "Insert boot disk and press any key." This is bound to cause distress — especially if your system is supposed to have a hard disk inside.

Note: On some computers, you might see a version of the BASIC programming language, ROM BASIC. This happened on most of the early PCs. Some modern systems may display a detailed error message or cute "insert the disk" graphics. Either way, if you wanted to boot from a hard disk this isn't what you were expecting.

For the hard disk, the first 512 bytes loaded are actually the *partition table*. The partition table contains a small program that locates the start of the first *logical* hard drive and loads its first 512 bytes. This extra step allows many logical drives to be on a single physical drive, as well as the ability to store several operating systems on a single hard drive.

Note: A single physical hard drive is composed of one or more logical hard drives. It's the partition table that knows where everything is. The partition table also contains a program that tells DOS where to locate the logical drive C. Once there, DOS continues booting the computer.

3. The boot sector program is executed.

If the disk isn't a DOS disk, the boot sector program displays a simple two-line message:

```
Non-System disk or disk error
Replace and press any key when ready
```

It then waits for you to press any key, at which time step 2 repeats.

When you have a real DOS disk, the boot sector program looks for the file named IO.SYS on disk and loads it. With some versions of DOS, the file is named IBMBIO.COM.

4. IO.SYS and SysInit.

The IO.SYS program is DOS's first boot file. It's a hidden file, sitting in the root directory of every boot disk. IO.SYS contains basic input/output functions that take care of communications between your individual computer's BIOS and hardware and DOS itself. These are actually a series of special device drivers called *resident drivers* that are loaded low into memory.

You can see the resident drivers in your system using the MEM command with the /DEBUG or /D switch. Figure 1-4 shows a partial listing of MEM /DEBUG's output. There are 12 device drivers shown in the IO area; these are the 12 low-level communications drives set up by IO.SYS when the computer boots.

✎ **Note:** Additional device drivers to control other, nonstandard devices are loaded in your CONFIG.SYS file, which is covered in Chapter 2.

After the resident drivers are loaded into low memory, IO.SYS carries out the SysInit, or system initialization, procedure. SysInit controls the rest of the boot process, which starts by locating and loading the program named MSDOS.SYS, which may also be called IBMDOS.COM in some versions of DOS.

5. MSDOS.SYS, the kernel.

The MSDOS.SYS program is the core of the MS-DOS operating system, called the *kernel*. It contains all the instructions for working with disks, loading and executing programs, memory management, interdevice communications, and so on. The only thing lacking is the actual "user interface," which is supplied later.

6. System configuration and CONFIG.SYS.

After SysInit loads MSDOS.SYS, it looks for a file named DBLSPACE.BIN in the root directory of the boot disk. This is the DoubleSpace device driver, used to mount DOS's compressed drives. DBLSPACE.BIN needs to be loaded first in order to mount any compressed drive C that may, in turn, contain the rest of DOS's boot files.

If DBLSPACE.BIN isn't found, or if drive C isn't a DoubleSpace drive, then SysInit looks for CONFIG.SYS. (Even if DBLSPACE.BIN is found, the compressed

```
C:\> MEM /DEBUG

Conventional Memory Detail:

 Segment            Total            Name           Type
 -------            -----            ----           ----
 00000              1039    (1K)                    Interrupt Vector
 00040               271    (0K)                    ROM Communication Area
 00050               527    (1K)                    DOS Communication Area
 00070              2656    (3K)     IO             System Data
                                     CON            System Device Driver
                                     AUX            System Device Driver
                                     PRN            System Device Driver
                                     CLOCK$         System Device Driver
                                     A: - C:        System Device Driver
                                     COM1           System Device Driver
                                     LPT1           System Device Driver
                                     LPT2           System Device Driver
                                     LPT3           System Device Driver
                                     COM2           System Device Driver
                                     COM3           System Device Driver
                                     COM4           System Device Driver
(etc.)
```

Figure 1-4 A partial listing of MEM /D showing IO.SYS's device drivers

drive C would be "mounted" and then startup would continue with CONFIG.SYS as before — but from the compressed drive.) If a CONFIG.SYS file is found, SysInit executes the commands and instructions contained in that file. Those commands fall into two categories: system configuration commands and device drivers. These are both discussed fully in Chapter 2.

If CONFIG.SYS is missing, then SysInit makes some assumptions about setting up your system and configures your system based on those assumptions. Usually, those assumptions are wrong, which is why it's best to write a proper CONFIG.SYS file for your system.

One assumption made if CONFIG.SYS isn't found is that the command interpreter — the user interface for DOS — is named COMMAND.COM, and it is in the root directory of the boot disk. This is what you'd normally expect, however, it's possible to relocate COMMAND.COM, or specify another command interpreter, by using the SHELL configuration command in CONFIG.SYS.

7. The command interpreter.

The command interpreter is DOS's user interface, the shell program, COMMAND.COM. This is what you see when you use DOS, the ugly DOS prompt, obtuse commands, all that. (Although a great deal of the commands exist as external files on disk, DOS holds about 30 or so inside COMMAND.COM itself. You'll see them in Chapter 3.)

If another command interpreter has been selected in CONFIG.SYS, it will be run here as well, offering DOS a method of communicating with the user other than COMMAND.COM. Two popular alternatives to COMMAND.COM are J.P. Software's 4DOS and Norton's NDOS, which are enhanced command interpreters with several additional commands and functions. If you really want to make a dedicated computer, you could specify another DOS program as the command interpreter. For example, the following line in CONFIG.SYS causes *WordPerfect* to be a command interpreter:

```
SHELL=C:\WP51\WP.EXE
```

Of course, this means you don't have access to any file commands other than those in *WordPerfect*. And if you quit *WordPerfect,* you'll see the message "Bad or missing Command Interpreter." Still, it's an interesting trick, useful in a few circumstances.

It's at this point that the SysInit procedure gives up the ghost. There is, however, one more step in the boot process: the startup program.

8. AUTOEXEC.BAT, the startup program.

AUTOEXEC.BAT is the batch file your computer will execute automatically at startup — providing the file exists and that you've done the proper things to COMMAND.COM.

When COMMAND.COM is in the root directory of the boot disk, it naturally looks for a file named AUTOEXEC.BAT. It then runs that batch file, which means all the lines in the file — which are simple DOS commands — are executed. This allows you to further configure the computer, customize the command interpreter, or run startup programs or TSRs.

If COMMAND.COM is in another location, such as a subdirectory specified by the SHELL configuration command, then you must specify its /P switch for AUTOEXEC.BAT to run. For example:

```
SHELL=C:\DOS\COMMAND.COM C:\DOS /E:512 /P
```

COMMAND.COM is run from the DOS subdirectory. The C:\DOS after the filename tells the system always to load COMMAND.COM from that directory. (Technically speaking, it sets the COMSPEC variable in the environment to that location.)

The /E switch sets DOS's environment size to 512 bytes, and /P makes COMMAND.COM permanent and runs AUTOEXEC.BAT. Making the command interpreter permanent means you can't use the EXIT command to quit DOS. More information on setting up COMMAND.COM and what its switches do is covered in Chapters 2 and 3.

> ***Tip:*** The /P switch can also be used in *DESQview* or Windows to set up an unclosable DOS window. This does present some problems, however, since AUTOEXEC.BAT will run in that window and attempt to load some programs twice. Rewriting AUTOEXEC.BAT, or giving it the ability to detect whether *DESQview* or Windows is running is possible, but time-consuming.

From this point on, your system has booted and you're ready to work. IO.SYS is still in there, along with its resident device drivers. You'll also find MSDOS.SYS hanging around, as well as numerous copies of COMMAND.COM. The next chapter elaborates on CONFIG.SYS's role in your computer's setup, gives some tips on how you can customize DOS right in the middle of the boot process, and describes some interesting and undocumented stuff.

2

All about CONFIG.SYS

You may have heard all about CONFIG.SYS: what the commands do, which ones you need, and — this is obvious — how CONFIG.SYS helps to configure your system. This chapter discusses all of these again, along with the *reasons* for why things work the way the do, whether you need a command, and how it all works.

How It All Works

CONFIG.SYS must do three things:

1. Configure DOS, setting aside memory and *buffers* for use in disk operations, controlling internal settings and memory management.

2. Load device drivers, which allow DOS and your applications to interface with nonstandard hardware.

3. Be easy to control.

To make CONFIG.SYS easy, the wizards of DOS elected to make it a text file any DOS yahoo can modify using a text editor. Given the importance of CONFIG.SYS, this was necessary. However, given its complexity, many users neglect to do everything they should in CONFIG.SYS.

The story of CONFIG.SYS starts with IO.SYS, also called IBMBIO.COM on some systems. IO.SYS begins the SysInit process, which is the program that loads the rest of DOS from disk. SysInit sits high in memory after loading. That way it can stick IO.SYS and its companion file, MSDOS.SYS (aka IBMDOS.COM), into low memory.

After MSDOS.SYS is loaded, SysInit looks for a file named CONFIG.SYS in the root directory of the boot disk, in either drive C or drive A. That file is read from disk and placed high into memory. CONFIG.SYS's text is loaded, converted into uppercase, and stored into high memory where SysInit reads the commands and carries out the instructions.

Since IO.SYS contains SysInit, you can use the DEBUG command to peek into IO.SYS and get a good idea of where CONFIG.SYS is and what its internal commands are. If you have a third-party file peeker, such as Vernon Beurg's *List* program, I recommend using it instead. However, things work just fine with DEBUG. (The full tutorial and documentation for DEBUG starts in Part Two of this book.)

Note: To use *List*, type the following at the DOS prompt

```
LIST C:\IO.SYS
```

First use the W command to wrap long lines of text on the screen. Then type the F command to find the text *config.sys*. The command list should appear right below the first instance of CONFIG.SYS.

Start DEBUG at the DOS prompt, loading IO.SYS from drive C or any DOS boot disk:

```
C:\> DEBUG C:\IO.SYS
-
```

IO.SYS is a hidden system file, yet DEBUG can still load it and scrutinize its vitals. There are two parts of IO.SYS, as discussed in the previous chapter. The first part of the file contains the basic DOS device drivers, the *resident* drivers. The second part of IO.SYS is the SysInit procedure.

You can use DEBUG to look at all the *machine language* instructions for starting DOS if you like. However, these instructions are only palatable by the microprocessor and a few true DOS zanies that understand raw hex data (and they don't get outside much). To bring meaning to this exercise, you should use DEBUG's search command to quickly find what we're looking for, "CONFIG.SYS." Type S followed by 100, A000 (A-thousand), then CONFIG.SYS in double quotes:

```
-S 100 A000 "CONFIG.SYS"
```

This command will locate several instances of the text "CONFIG.SYS" inside the IO.SYS file. Make sure you type CONFIG.SYS as all caps, even though DEBUG is not case-sensitive. You'll see something like this:

```
1F5B:7E8B
1F5B:81D4
1F5B:832B
1F5B:8345
-
```

All about CONFIG.SYS 17

These represent four *memory* addresses — locations in IO.SYS where CONFIG.SYS is mentioned by name. The numbers you see on your screen will probably be different. However, whichever address showed up first is probably the one worth looking at. Use the last four digits of that address with the D, display, command. For example, in the list above the digits are 7E8B. You would use them with the D command as follows:

```
-D 7E8B L 170
```

Note that D is followed by the four-digit address, and the L command tells DEBUG to display 170 hexadecimal bytes, which is about 23 lines on the screen. You'll see something like Figure 2-1 displayed. You'll be reading about DEBUG and what all this means starting in Chapter 7. For now, look at the listing, specifically the text in the right-hand column. Locate the word CONFIG.SYS, which is probably split between two lines as in the figure.

CONFIG.SYS is specified twice in Figure 2-1 (which is taken from the IO.SYS file in DOS 5.0, dated 4-9-91). On your screen, it may look different. The second CONFIG.SYS is preceded by A:\, which is how DOS locates CONFIG.SYS on drive A. That's followed by a lot of empty space (the zeros), the word COUNTRY, and then \COMMAND.COM. This is how SysInit locates COMMAND.COM on the boot disk — unless another location has been specified.

Positioned toward the bottom of your screen, you should see the 17 configuration commands, which are also shown in Table 2-1. This is the CONFIG.SYS *internal* command list. This figure includes the 14 standard CONFIG.SYS commands included with DOS 5.0 — plus two commands added with DOS 6.0 — NUMLOCK and SET. You may find several other commands nestled in the command list. For example, there are the five configuration menu commands in DOS 6.0: INCLUDE, MENUCOLOR, MENUDEFAULT, MENUITEM, and SUBMENU.

```
1F5B:7E80                               43 4F 4E 46 49        CONFI
1F5B:7E90   47 2E 53 59 53 00 41 3A-5C 43 4F 55 4E 54 52 59   G.SYS.A:\COUNTRY
1F5B:7EA0   2E 53 59 53 00 00 00 00-00 00 00 00 00 00 00 00   .SYS............
1F5B:7EB0   00 00 00 00 00 00 00 00-00 00 00 00 00 00 00 00   ................
1F5B:7EC0   00 00 00 00 00 00 00 00-00 00 00 00 00 00 00 00   ................
1F5B:7ED0   00 00 00 00 00 00 00 00-00 FF 43 4F 55 4E 54 52   ..........COUNTR
1F5B:7EE0   59 00 00 5C 43 4F 4D 4D-41 4E 44 2E 43 4F 4D 00   Y..\COMMAND.COM.
1F5B:7EF0   00 00 00 00 00 00 00 00-00 00 00 00 00 00 00 00   ................
1F5B:7F00   00 00 00 00 00 00 00 00-00 00 00 00 00 00 00 00   ................
1F5B:7F10   00 00 00 00 00 00 00 00-00 00 00 00 00 00 00 00   ................
1F5B:7F20   00 00 00 00 00 00 00 00-00 00 00 00 00 00 00 00   ................
1F5B:7F30   00 00 00 00 00 00 00 00-00 00 00 00 00 00 00 00   ................
1F5B:7F40   00 00 00 00 00 00 00 00-00 00 00 00 00 00 00 00   ................
1F5B:7F50   00 00 00 00 00 00 00 00-00 00 00 00 00 00 00 00   ................
1F5B:7F60   00 00 00 07 42 55 46 46-45 52 53 42 05 42 52 45   ....BUFFERSB.BRE
1F5B:7F70   41 4B 43 06 44 45 56 49-43 45 44 0A 44 45 56 49   AKC.DEVICED.DEVI
1F5B:7F80   43 45 48 49 47 48 55 05-46 49 4C 45 53 46 04 46   CEHIGHU.FILESF.F
1F5B:7F90   43 42 53 58 09 4C 41 53-54 44 52 49 56 45 4C 0A   CBSX.LASTDRIVEL.
1F5B:7FA0   4D 55 4C 54 49 54 52 41-43 4B 4D 08 44 52 49 56   MULTITRACKM.DRIV
1F5B:7FB0   50 41 52 4D 50 06 53 54-41 43 4B 53 4B 07 43 4F   PARMP.STACKSK.CO
1F5B:7FC0   55 4E 54 52 59 51 05 53-48 45 4C 4C 53 07 49 4E   UNTRYQ.SHELLS.IN
1F5B:7FD0   53 54 41 4C 4C 49 07 43-4F 4D 4D 45 4E 54 59 03   STALLI.COMMENTY.
1F5B:7FE0   52 45 4D 30 08 53 57 49-54 43 48 45 53 31 03 44   REM0.SWITCHES1.D
1F5B:7FF0   4F 53 48 00 00 02 00 00-50 00 00                  OSH.....P..
-
```

Figure 2-1 CONFIG.SYS and its commands are located in IO.SYS

Table 2-1 Configuration Commands

Command	Description
BREAK	Controls Ctrl-C monitoring
BUFFERS	Sets aside space for file I/O buffers
COUNTRY	International support information
DEVICE	Loads a device driver
DEVICEHIGH	Loads a device driver into upper memory
DOS	Loads DOS into the HMA
DRIVPARM	Configures a disk drive or similar storage device
FCBS	Sets aside space for file control blocks
FILES	Reserves a number of file handles for file access
INSTALL	Loads a memory resident program (TSR)
LASTDRIVE	Sets the highest available drive letter
NUMLOCK	Deactivates the numeric keypad
REM	Allows remarks to be inserted into CONFIG.SYS (you can also use a semicolon)
SET	Uses CONFIG.SYS to create environment variables, such as PATH, PROMPT, etc. (normally done in AUTOEXEC.BAT)
SHELL	Specifies the name and location of the command interpreter
STACKS	Sets aside space for DOS's internal stacks
SWITCHES	Miscellaneous stuff

There may also be some undocumented commands, including COMMENT, MULTITRACK, and INSTALLHIGH. I telephoned Microsoft about the undocumented commands and, much to my shock, they had never heard of them. I found this to be very strange; therefore, I won't say anything further on the subject.

Each command that appears in the list is surrounded by two bytes, as shown in Figure 2-2. The first byte is a *count byte* that specifies the length of the command. This is followed by the command itself, which is listed in all caps. The final byte is a *token value*, probably representing the location of the command's instructions stored in a "table" elsewhere in IO.SYS. The tokens start with the letter *B*, seen after BUFFERS, and increment one letter of the alphabet for each configuration command. (This leads to some humorous results: LASTDRIVEL, DOSH, and so on.)

SysInit reads CONFIG.SYS one line at a time. If the line is blank, it's skipped and the next line is read. If the line contains text, then the first part of the line is compared with each word in the internal command list. The count byte tells SysInit how much of the command to compare. So if the first seven letters of the line aren't "BUFFERS," then the first five letters are compared with "BREAK" and so on down the list. When a match is made, that command is carried out according to

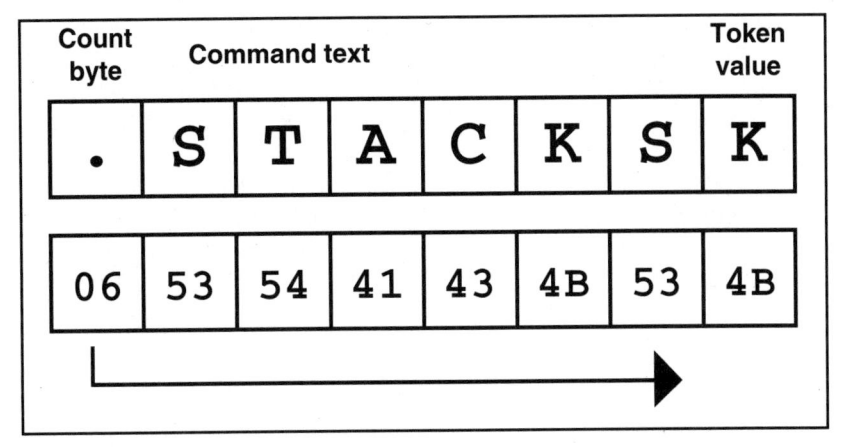

```
                Count                                    Token
                byte    Command text                     value
               ┌─────┬─────┬─────┬─────┬─────┬─────┬─────┬─────┐
               │  .  │  S  │  T  │  A  │  C  │  K  │  S  │  K  │
               └─────┴─────┴─────┴─────┴─────┴─────┴─────┴─────┘

               ┌─────┬─────┬─────┬─────┬─────┬─────┬─────┬─────┐
               │ 06  │ 53  │ 54  │ 41  │ 43  │ 4B  │ 53  │ 4B  │
               └─────┴─────┴─────┴─────┴─────┴─────┴─────┴─────┘
                  └──────────────────────────────────▶
```

Figure 2-2 The format for CONFIG.SYS's internal command list

the token value (and to figure out how that works would require a more detailed analysis of SysInit than this book has space for).

If no match is made, then SysInit generates an error message for CONFIG.SYS. The text for the error messages is just a little bit down in the IO.SYS file. If you're using DEBUG, type in the D command three or four times. Eventually you'll see the error messages, one of which will be "Unrecognized command in CONFIG.SYS." Press D a few more times to see the rest of the error messages.

Note: If you're using LIST, press the PgDn key to see the error messages.

There are several error messages in IO.SYS, many of which are related to startup problems. The ones specific to CONFIG.SYS are shown below, though this may not be a complete list:

```
Unrecognized command in CONFIG.SYS
Bad or missing device driver
Configuration too large for memory
Incorrect order in CONFIG.SYS
Error in CONFIG.SYS line xxx
```

The error message "WARNING! Logical drives past Z: exist and will be ignored$" marks the end of the IO.SYS file. Everything else in there is best left alone. Carefully type Q and press Enter to exit DEBUG. If you've been using LIST to peek into IO.SYS, press the Esc key to return to DOS.

Editing CONFIG.SYS

CONFIG.SYS is a text file, which allows you to review, edit, and change it using any text editor or word processor. Text editors are best, since their native mode is editing only text files, of which CONFIG.SYS is one. Word processors present a few problems, but are still workable. The big deal is that you're essentially using a chain saw to do the work of a kitchen knife (or vice versa).

DOS comes with two text editors: EDLIN, which everyone detests, and the new EDIT program, which is actually the editing mode of the QBASIC interpreter shipped with DOS 5.0 and later. Either one will do for editing CONFIG.SYS, though EDIT is a full screen editor and a more logical choice. Third-party editors will also work. I prefer SemWare's QEdit program, which can be found in a demo version on many on-line services or mail-order software houses. Or you can order a legit copy from SemWare itself, 4343 Shallowford Road, Marietta, GA 30062-5003, (404) 641-9002.

Here are the rules for editing CONFIG.SYS:

- Each command in CONFIG.SYS must be on a line by itself.

  You cannot split commands between two lines, which means you should turn off the "word wrap" feature if you're using a word processor. Set the left margin at 255 characters or columns, or use any number greater than 128. (Some magazines and books with narrow margins or smaller column formats may split long configuration commands between two lines. That cannot be done in CONFIG.SYS.)

- Blank lines between commands are okay.

  I use blank lines to clean up the display in my CONFIG.SYS files; commands are organized by category and separated by blank lines. This makes the file much easier to read, along with plenty of comments using the REM command.

- CONFIG.SYS must be saved as a plain text or ASCII file.

  All text editors, including EDLIN, EDIT, and *QEdit,* save in the plain text mode. Word processors, however, must be told to save in the plain text mode. For example, in *WordPerfect* you save a file in the "DOS Text" mode by pressing Ctrl-F5, T for DOS Text, then S to save.

- CONFIG.SYS must be in the root directory of the boot drive.

  There's no way to change the file's location. The root directory is where SysInit expects to find CONFIG.SYS.

- You must reboot the PC for changes in CONFIG.SYS to take effect.

Since CONFIG.SYS is only loaded once at boot time, you need to reset your computer to activate any changes. This also holds true for any editing changes made to AUTOEXEC.BAT: Edit the file, save it to disk, return to DOS, then reset for the changes to take place.

▶ *Tip:* If you're using Microsoft Windows you can use a secret, undocumented program called SysEdit to quickly edit CONFIG.SYS, AUTOEXEC.BAT, or the two central Windows INI files — WIN.INI and SYSTEM.INI. Use the File Manager to run SysEdit, which is in your WINDOWS\SYSTEM directory, or you can add SysEdit to the Program Manager using the New menu item. Note that you must exit Windows and reset for any changes to take effect.

Creating the Best CONFIG.SYS File

There are only 17 (documented) commands you can put in your CONFIG.SYS file, and no one needs all of them. No problem. However, multiply 50 million PCs by the different types of hardware and software available and you have an endless variety of configurations. There is no single CONFIG.SYS file for everyone, which is both good and bad: It's good because DOS is flexible and allows you to custom configure your PC to get the most from it. Yet it's bad because getting that custom configuration isn't that obvious.

For older versions of DOS, CONFIG.SYS was ignored. The old SELECT program didn't create a CONFIG.SYS file and if one did exist on your PC, it might contain the FILES and BUFFERS commands, required for database users, and the DEVICE command as needed for various device drivers. But DOS offered no standard, manufacturer's suggested CONFIG.SYS file. That changed with DOS 5, where the standard "DOS configuration," as shown in Figure 2-3, was installed on most computers.

The manufacturer's suggested CONFIG.SYS file isn't that bad. It does three of the four things all CONFIG.SYS files should do, as shown in the following categories:

Category 1: It sets up basic memory management.

This is done for all PCs with an 80286 or 386-family microprocessor. Specifically, the HIMEM.SYS device driver and the DOS=HIGH command will use any extended memory to improve DOS's memory usage. This also sets up the XMS, or extended memory specification, which allows some DOS programs and Windows to use extended memory.

Category 2: It configures the file system.

The FILES=10 command is okay, but not perfect. The BUFFERS command is as necessary as FILES in many cases. Also the value of 10 is a bit low for most people's needs (see the FILES section below).

Category 3: It sets up DOS internals.

The SHELL configuration command locates COMMAND.COM and sets its various options. This is really unnecessary since DOS also copies COMMAND.COM to the root directory of the boot drive. (I suppose they added it to make a safety net for those few neophytes who accidentally delete COMMAND.COM from their root directories.)

```
DEVICE=C:\DOS\HIMEM.SYS
DOS=HIGH
FILES=10
SHELL=C:\DOS\COMMAND.COM C:\DOS /p
STACKS=0,0
```

Figure 2-3 The manufacturer's suggested CONFIG.SYS file

The STACKS=0,0 command saves most PC users about a kilobyte of precious low memory. Since the "stacks" aren't used in most PC configurations, this command is rather smart.

There's one additional thing CONFIG.SYS needs to do:

Category 4: Load necessary device drivers

Since the device drivers on your system are unique, DOS could never guess what they are or how you use them (although it will meld the manufacturer's suggested CONFIG.SYS with your own if you already have one).

Over all, device drivers are the biggest variable in CONFIG.SYS. They present the most problems for memory management software, and since each device driver has its own set of options and particulars, it presents the biggest challenge to writing a good CONFIG.SYS file.

Configuration Commands

The following sections discuss CONFIG.SYS's configuration commands. This isn't as complete documentation as you may find in the DOS manual. Instead, these are my suggestions for using the commands, along with comments and hints on what they do and how they work.

All configuration commands use the same format:

```
command=value
```

There can be spaces on either side of the equal sign. In fact, the equal sign itself is optional and can be replaced by one or more spaces, a tab, or the comma (,) or semicolon (;) characters. For consistency's sake, however, this book will keep with the standard equal sign.

BREAK

DOS's universal cancel key is Ctrl-C or Ctrl-Break. Pressing either key combination generates a special *interrupt* inside the PC (Interrupt 23h if you're curious). That interrupt tells a DOS program to stop executing and "quit at once!"

Applications programs generally ignore the Ctrl-C key combination. Pressing Ctrl-C in *WordPerfect,* for example, puts a ^C on the screen — the symbol for the Control-C character. Even in DOS, the only time Ctrl-C is effective is when characters are written to or read from the screen, keyboard, printer or serial port. Those activities are referred to as DOS *character* I/O (Input/Output).

If DOS is performing character I/O, say the TYPE command is displaying a file, pressing Ctrl-C cancels the operation. However, if DOS is writing information to disk, or some other time-consuming process is taking place, the Ctrl-C will be ignored until character I/O happens. Then the program will cancel. This explains why Ctrl-C seems to be such an inconsistent cancel key at times.

You can force DOS to pay closer attention to Ctrl-C by using the BREAK configuration command — or the counterpart BREAK command at the DOS prompt:

```
          COLES BOOK STORES
          SOUTHCENTRE MALL
       100 ANDERSON RD. S.E.
       GST-FED #: 101048478

SALE    000745 0076 003 00002 06284
            93/09/29          16:11

COMPUTERS 0553370979 41 1 @      31.95
    07.0% GST - FED              2.24
       TOTAL SALE               34.19
       VISA                     34.19
757622    9407 4523910525093

            THANK YOU

          CUSTOMER COPY
```

```
BREAK=ON
```

This configuration command falls into category 3, DOS internals. This activates extra Ctrl-C checking in CONFIG.SYS. DOS monitors the Ctrl-C key press even when it's not doing character I/O. There is a minor speed penalty for specifying BREAK=ON, but this is negligible on some of the faster PCs.

I recommend setting BREAK=ON only if you've ever been frustrated when trying to cancel a DOS command (such as FORMAT). However, note that you can turn BREAK on or off using the BREAK command at the DOS prompt. This makes it easy to stick BREAK ON into a batch file, then put BREAK OFF before the batch file quits.

Typing BREAK by itself at the DOS prompt tells you the current status of the BREAK command's setting:

```
C:\> BREAK
BREAK is off
```

BUFFERS

Most people get confused about the BUFFERS command. It's easily associated with the FILES configuration command, although the two are only related in that they configure elements of DOS's file system. Basically, BUFFERS controls a small disk cache DOS uses to speed up disk access.

BUFFERS sets aside space used to store information read from or written to disk. Each buffer is a chunk of memory about 534 bytes long (just a hair over one *sector* of disk information). This raises a concern that too many buffers use up too much conventional memory. For example, BUFFERS=15 sets aside 7.8K of precious memory for disk access. CONFIG.SYS's DOS=HIGH command will load the buffers "high"; see the section on "DOS" in this chapter. But if you're not using that command, or are using a previous version of DOS, then the buffers will eat up conventional memory.

The odd thing about the BUFFERS command is that it really isn't necessary; DOS sets aside space for disk buffers whether or not you use the BUFFERS configuration command in CONFIG.SYS. The number of buffers your PC has assigned to it depends on how much memory you have. Since most PCs have 640K, you get 15 buffers — more than enough. On the other hand, leaving buffers equal to that value may not help system performance. And setting buffers too high will definitely degrade performance. There is, however, a happy medium.

There are two ways to judge how many buffers you need. The first depends on the size of your hard drive and the number of subdirectories you have. Table 2-2 shows the number of buffers you should specify for a given size hard drive. Just look up your hard disk size and plug in the proper value. For example, I have a 200M hard drive so I could use this command in CONFIG.SYS:

```
BUFFERS=50
```

Table 2-2 Amount of Buffers to Specify Based on Your Hard Disk Size

Hard Drive Size	BUFFERS=
Up to 40M	20
Greater than 40M	30
Greater than 80M	40
Greater than 120M	50

If you have an even larger hard drive, you can specify a higher value for BUFFERS; valid numbers range from one all the way up to 99. Unless you have an extremely larger hard drive, there's never a need to specify a value that high.

The actual format for the BUFFERS command is:

`BUFFERS=buffers,cache`

The *cache* value species how many disk sectors DOS can read ahead into memory, from 1 through 8. This can greatly improve performance, especially when a value of 8 is used (what I recommend). For example, if you had a 80M hard drive you could specify the following in CONFIG.SYS:

`BUFFERS=40,8`

There's one more limitation to the BUFFERS command — and an important one at that. If you're using any disk-caching software, such as DOS's SMARTDrive, you only need to specify 20 buffers maximum (some even claim 15 will do you). The reason is that SMARTDrive improves disk access in a much better way than DOS does with its buffers. Therefore, there's no use wasting memory on the BUFFERS command when you're using a disk cache. I recommend the following setting:

`BUFFERS=20`

If you ever remove the disk cache, set BUFFERS according to your hard drive size and add on the *cache* or "read-ahead" option.

▶ ***Tip:*** If you're using SMARTDrive, I recommend setting a cache size from a minimum of 256K up through 1,024K, all depending on how much memory you have in your system. I also recommend putting the cache in extended memory if you have it. If you have the memory to spare, a 2M cache (2,048K) is desirable, but anything above that is a waste of memory; SMARTDrive starts to lose its efficiency when the cache gets larger than 2M. Other, third-party disk caches may be different; refer to their manuals for information.

COUNTRY

The COUNTRY command is the first of many steps required to give yourself an international flavor PC. This is an internal configuration command used to set the alphabetic sorting order, time and date formats, and currency symbol, and to allow access to foreign language character sets. Most foreign versions of DOS configure themselves to work in other languages using this command. For the United States, however, it remains a curiosity.

Personally, I detest the COUNTRY command, as well as all the related "code page" commands. They're confusing, complicated, and a true bother to set up. To properly configure the COUNTRY command for, say, Brazil, you need to know the country code (055) and code page code (850 or 437). Then you use the COUNTRY command as follows:

```
COUNTRY=055,850,C:\DOS\COUNTRY.SYS
```

The COUNTRY.SYS file, usually found in your DOS subdirectory, contains the information the COUNTRY configuration command needs to operate. That's all there is; however, DOS has four additional commands that work toward international and foreign language support, as well as the dreaded code page switching

- The CHCP command is used to switch between two code pages, as allowed for the country you selected in CONFIG.SYS

- The KEYB command is used to select different keyboard arrangements, giving you access to special foreign language characters. (This can be used by itself if, say, you wanted to type a letter and have access to Portuguese characters.)

- The MODE *device* CODEPAGE command is used to set the code pages for certain devices.

- The NLSFUNC command can also be used at the DOS prompt, or in CONFIG.SYS via the INSTALL command, to configure your PC for international use. Primarily NLSFUNC lets you configure all the devices at once, as opposed to the MODE command, which only changes one device at a time.

The pages, codes, and numbers are all listed in the DOS manual if you're interested in messing with all this. Quite frankly, if you're already in a foreign country, this has been done for you. If not, then those bold enough to play with this can suffer through it on their own.

DEVICE

DEVICE is a heavy hitter in CONFIG.SYS, the only configuration command aside from REM that can be used more than once. This command loads device drivers into memory. The device drivers allow your computer to communicate with nonstandard devices. Just about anything created for a PC since 1981 is considered a nonstandard device. This includes:

- RAM drive software

- Disk caches

- Memory managers

- External drives (Bernoullis, CD-ROMs, tape drives, and so on)

- Computer mouse hardware
- Scanners
- Multimedia equipment (Sound cards, MIDI, video hookups)

The list is really endless. For every device there is a device driver. DOS even comes with several, including: RAMDrive, RAM disk software; SMARTDrive, a disk cache; the ANSI screen and keyboard enhancement program; HIMEM and EMM386 memory managers; and various other device drivers. All of them are listed in Table 2-3.

Note: SMARTDrive was distributed as a device driver, SMARTDRV.SYS, with Windows through version 3.0 and in DOS 5.0. Starting with the release of Windows 3.1 and DOS 6.0 Microsoft revamped SMARTDrive as a memory resident program, SMARTDRV.EXE, which is now loaded in AUTOEXEC.BAT.

Most device drivers will end with a SYS extension, but this is not a hard and fast rule. Some drivers can end in EXE and a few end in COM. (A SYS file is basically a specially formatted COM file anyway.) Even so, watch out for some SYS files that are not device drivers. DOS has three of them: KEYBOARD.SYS, COUNTRY.SYS and, of course, CONFIG.SYS. Don't ever use any of these with the DEVICE configuration command.

Table 2-3 DOS's Device Drivers

Device Driver	Function
ANSI.SYS	Enhanced screen and keyboard control
DISPLAY.SYS	Provides support for hardware code pages on certain displays
DBLSPACE.SYS	Creates DoubleSpace or "compressed" drives
DRIVER.SYS	Creates "logical" floppy drives
EGA.SYS	Provides EGA display support for Windows and DOS Shell
EMM386.EXE	386 system expanded memory device driver
HIMEM.SYS	Extended memory (XMS) device driver (80286 and 386 only)
PRINTER.SYS	Controls IBM printers and code pages (discontinued with DOS 6.0)
RAMDRIVE.SYS	RAM disk software (can be used more than once to create multiple RAM drives)
SETVER.EXE	DOS version-fooling utility
SMARTDRV.SYS	Disk-caching software (now SMARTDRV.EXE with DOS 6.0)

To use the DEVICE command, follow it by an equal sign plus the *full* pathname of the device driver — including the drive letter. This is very important. DOS doesn't have a "search path" yet, so you must be specific about the driver's location. For example:

`DEVICE=C:\DOS\HIMEM.SYS`

Note that HIMEM.SYS is loaded from the DOS subdirectory on drive C. The drive letter, colon, and pathname all make the full pathname. Any additional options after the driver's name follow it in CONFIG.SYS. Note that many device drivers don't bother with the DOS convention of using the slash character (/). For example:

`DEVICE=C:\DOS\EMM386.EXE NOEMS`

Sometimes I'll accidentally type in /NOEMS (with a slash). Either way it's okay here, but many device drivers dispense with the slash.

As far as an order for your device drivers, I recommend the following:

1. Start with any hard disk drivers, drivers that set up the SCSI device if you have any SCSI drives, partitioning software, external drive device drivers, and so on. An exception here is the *Stacker* disk doubling device driver, which should always be last (according to the *Stacker* manual).

2. Follow with memory management device drivers. If you're using DOS, that's HIMEM.SYS followed by EMM386.EXE on 386 systems. Otherwise, specify your third-party memory manager, which usually takes only one line in CONFIG.SYS.

3. Load other device drivers after the memory management drivers. This includes RAM drives, disk caches, mouse drivers, and other hardware drivers as required by your system. This allows those device drivers to be loaded high, and gives you more conventional memory.

4. Make sure device drivers that request to be loaded last are loaded last. The only one I can think of is *Stacker*.

The other configuration commands can be sprinkled around the device drivers as necessary. For example, some people put all their DOS and file system configuration commands first, and then load all the device drivers. Others may put them last. Still others may opt for a haphazard arrangement. Whatever works.

DEVICEHIGH

DEVICEHIGH is nothing more than a specialized version of the DEVICE command. It's used with DOS's 386 memory management tools to load device drivers into upper memory as opposed to precious conventional memory. This frees up conventional memory, making more room for memory-hungry applications as well as environments such as Windows or *DESQview*.

The format for DEVICEHIGH is nearly identical to DEVICE. In fact, you simply need to edit CONFIG.SYS, search and replace DEVICE for DEVICEHIGH, and you've done the job (providing that you've activated the 386 memory management abilities).

28   *Dan Gookin's Guide to Underground DOS 6.0*

✎ ***Note:*** DOS's 386 memory management abilities require a 386 or compatible microprocessor with at least 1M of extended memory (a minimum of 2M total memory). Three commands are required in CONFIG.SYS before you can use DEVICEHIGH:

```
DEVICE=C:\DOS\HIMEM.SYS
DOS=HIGH,UMB
DEVICE=C:\DOS\EMM386.EXE NOEMS
```

EMM386 needs either the NOEMS or RAM option in order to create the *upper* memory blocks, which allow DEVICEHIGH to work. The DOS configuration command must also have its UMB option specified.

```
DEVICEHIGH=C:\MOUSE\MOUSE.SYS
```

Above, DEVICEHIGH attempts to load the Mouse device driver into upper memory as best it can. If it fails, the driver is loaded low.

First, to verify that drivers are being loaded high, you use the MEM command with its /C or /CLASSIFY switch. I pipe the output through the MORE filter so that the display pauses after a screenful. (The MORE filter is covered in Chapter 5.)

```
C:\> MEM /C | MORE
```

With DOS 6.0, the MEM command has a handy /P switch — the same as the DIR command's /P — which pauses the display every screen or so. This is a lot handier than typing | *MORE* (or remembering how that works). For example:

```
C:\> MEM /C /P
```

The output is divided into two large and informative, but somewhat baffling, sections. The first is *Modules using memory below 1MB*, which includes almost every program, device driver, and TSR loaded under DOS. The second is *Memory Summary*, a detailed table of how much memory is available, used, and free in three areas of your PC: Conventional, Upper, and ROM, plus any Extended or Expanded memory available. Figure 2-4 shows a sample of the MEM command's output on my test computer.

The MEM /C command's output is complex, but there is a secret to reading it. In the first part of the display, look for the zeros. If the zero after a program's name is in the Conventional column, then that program has been loaded into upper memory. If the zero is in the Upper Memory column, the program has been loaded low.

▶ ***Tip:*** DOS isn't as smart as third-party memory managers about loading things high. Occasionally you'll see lots of upper memory available via the MEM /C command, yet DOS refuses to load some device drivers high. The solution lies in the order of your device drivers. DOS is better able to load larger drivers first and smaller drivers last. To do this, look at MEM /C's output, figure out which device drivers are biggest, and then load them first. Remember, CONFIG.SYS is read from top to bottom, so put the larger drivers "higher" than the smaller ones.

All about CONFIG.SYS 29

```
Modules using memory below 1 MB:

 Name          Total        =  Conventional    +   Upper Memory
 ----          -----           ------------        ------------
 MSDOS         12429  (12K)    12429   (12K)           0    (0K)
 SETVER          624   (1K)      624    (1K)           0    (0K)
 HIMEM          1104   (1K)     1104    (1K)           0    (0K)
 EMM386         3072   (3K)     3072    (3K)           0    (0K)
 COMMAND        2912   (3K)     2912    (3K)           0    (0K)
 MOUSE         15152  (15K)    15152   (15K)           0    (0K)
 SMARTDRV      26832  (26K)    10432   (10K)       16400   (16K)
 RAMDRIVE       1200   (1K)        0    (0K)        1200    (1K)
 ANSI           4208   (4K)        0    (0K)        4208    (4K)
 STACKER       28432  (28K)        0    (0K)       28432   (28K)
 DOSKEY         4144   (4K)        0    (0K)        4144    (4K)
 Free         615824 (601K)   609664  (595K)        6160    (6K)

Memory Summary:

 Type of Memory        Size         =     Used        +      Free
 --------------        ----              ----               ----

 Conventional          655360 (640K)     45696  (45K)     609664  (595K)
 Upper                  60544  (59K)     54384  (53K)       6160    (6K)
 Adapter RAM/ROM       332672 (325K)    332672 (325K)          0    (0K)
 Extended (XMS)       3145728 (3072K)  2375680 (2320K)    770048  (752K)
 --------------        ----              ----               ----
 Total memory         4194304 (4096K)  2808432 (2743K)   1385872 (1353K)

 Total under 1 MB      715904 (699K)    100080  (98K)     615824  (601K)

 EMS is active.
 Largest executable program size        609568  (595K)
 Largest free upper memory block          6032    (6K)
 MS-DOS is resident in the high memory area.
```

Figure 2-4 The output of the MEM /C command

DOS

The DOS configuration command falls into both the memory management and DOS internals category. It has two purposes in life: to load DOS into the High Memory Area (HMA), which is created by the HIMEM.SYS, or into the compatible XMS, device driver. The DOS configuration command also lets DOS (the operating system) know about the upper memory blocks (UMBs), which can be used by the DEVICEHIGH configuration command and the LOADHIGH command.

This command is really easy to figure out. You just need to ask yourself two questions:

1. Are you using an 80286 or greater microprocessor in your PC?

    If yes, then you can stick the following into CONFIG.SYS:

    DOS=HIGH

This loads DOS's two internal programs, IO.SYS and MSDOS.SYS, into the HMA. The end result is that you get a bonus 40K of conventional memory, which really helps. To make it work, however, you must load the HIMEM.SYS device driver, or a similar memory manager that creates the HMA. The order in CONFIG.SYS isn't important; DOS=HIGH can come before or after HIMEM.SYS. Traditionally, most users put it after HIMEM.SYS.

2. Are you using a 386 variety of PC and do you want to load device drivers and memory resident programs high?

If yes, then you need to create upper memory blocks. That's done by the EMM386.EXE device driver with either its NOEMS or RAM option. But to make it happen, you need to specify the DOS configuration command's UMB option, typically:

```
DOS=HIGH,UMB
```

Note: If you're using a third-party memory manager, then you don't need the UMB option. You should still load DOS high with DOS=HIGH, however.

DRIVPARM

This is the most horrid of all the configuration commands. DRIVPARM is not a cute term, nor is it polite to say it aloud in mixed company. Quite simply, this is a command that controls external disk drives (what the manual calls block devices) for use with DOS.

Okay. Let me give you another clue: it's an IBM command. IBM thought of it. They created it and stuck it in here. When you buy an IBM external drive, tape backup system, or read/write optical disk, you'll probably use this command to set it up. Anyone else's hardware will come with its own, smartly named device driver. End of story.

Suppose, however, you need to use DRIVPARM. If so, it will probably tell you what to do in the manual that came with that piece of hardware. This isn't something you need to futz with otherwise.

Note: There seems to be a lot of confusion between DRIVPARM and the DRIVER.SYS device driver. This should clear things up:

DRIVER.SYS creates *logical* floppy drives using any existing floppy drives you have. For example, if you have an internal 1.4M drive, you can use DRIVER.SYS to make that drive also act like an external 1.4M (or 720K) drive D — or whichever logical letter is next highest in the list. DRIVER.SYS only works with floppy drives.

DRIVPARM is used to let DOS know about any external storage devices on your system: floppy drives, hard disks, tape drivers, and optical disks. DRIVPARM can define any external or additional drives, whereas DRIVER.SYS only defines floppy drives. If this command is required, you'll read about it in the external storage device's manual.

FCBS

This is one of DOS's more confusing configuration commands. It's a file system command, since FCBS stands for File Control BlockS. For most users, this command is wholly unnecessary. Only two groups of users will need it:

1. Network users.
2. Multitasking environment users who have loaded the SHARE.EXE program.

If you don't fit into either category, then you don't need the FCBS command in your CONFIG.SYS file.

FCBS is used on network systems to help control how DOS accesses files. It helps the networking software control who has access to what files, preventing mishaps that occur when several programs attempt to change a single file at once. Your networking software may set the FCBS command as required during installation. For example, LANtastic puts the following FCBS command into the CONFIG.SYS file of its network workstations and file servers:

```
FCBS=16,8
```

(I've also seen FCBS=20,8; it depends on the size of the hard drive.) The first value, 16 above, specifies the number of file control blocks DOS can have open at a time. Values range from 1 through 255, with 4 as the default. The second value, which they stopped documenting with DOS 5.0, tells DOS how many files it can't automatically close. In the example, when the number of open files hits 16, DOS can close all but 8 of them.

If you're using a multitasking environment, such as Windows or *DESQview*, you may have the SHARE program installed. That prevents two programs (running at the same time) from trying to modify a single file. SHARE is really optional under most circumstances; you can run Windows or *DESQview* without it. If you do use it, the FCBS command will tell SHARE how many files you can have open at a time and how many not to close.

▶ ***Tip:*** I don't recommend using SHARE unless you have a network installed. SHARE blocks some file utilities and other data recovery programs. It just isn't worth the hassle on a nonnetwork machine. And since you're not using SHARE, there's no point in bothering with FCBS either.

FILES

The FILES configuration command helps set up DOS's file system. This command lets DOS know how many files it's allowed to open at a time. That sounds silly: DOS should be able to open as many files as it wants. Yet, each one of those files requires space in memory, so an unlimited number would eat up too much RAM. This is why the FILES command exists, to let you tell DOS how much memory to set aside for the maximum number of files you'll have open at any given time.

Every time you open a file, or an application opens a file, it requires a DOS file handle. That's a special ID number programs use to identify files after they're opened. (The files are opened using the filename, but from then on the handle ID number is used.)

Right off the bat, the first five file handles are used by DOS, as shown in Table 2-4. If you don't specify the FILES command in CONFIG.SYS, DOS gives you room for an additional three handles, making the standard value 8. But most of the time you'll want a value higher than that. For example, suppose you're running WordPerfect. Opening that program file (WP.EXE) requires another file handle, plus a handle for the document you're editing. In addition, WordPerfect opens temporary files, bringing the total up to 3 or 4. Open a second document and the number goes higher. (In fact, WordPerfect won't even run if you have FILES set to a value less than 11.)

A good value to set FILES equal to is 20. It can go as high as 255, though the most I've ever seen is FILES=50, and that was on a file server. Anything more than that without a good excuse is a waste of RAM. For most PCs, the best value is 30:

```
FILES=30
```

That won't eat up too much RAM, and it should allow for enough open files to keep the system running. By the way, if you set the FILES value too low, you'll see the following error message:

```
Too many open files
```

That's a good sign that you need to set the FILES value higher in CONFIG.SYS.

▶ *Tip:* If you're using the *QEMM* or *QRAM* memory management packages, you can use their FILES.COM program to reduce the amount of RAM the file handles occupy. The idea is to set FILES=10 in CONFIG.SYS, then use the FILES.COM program in AUTOEXEC.BAT to reset the value higher. For example:

```
C:\QEMM\FILES.COM 50
```

Above, FILES.COM brings the total number of handles up to 50. This is handy to know, but it's not that obvious in the manual.

Table 2-4 DOS's First Five File Handles

Handle No.	Device	Description
0	CON	Standard input device, the keyboard
1	CON	Standard output device, the screen
2	CON	Standard error device, the screen (used to display error messages)
3	AUX	First serial port (COM1)
4	PRN	Printer port (LPT1)

INSTALL

The INSTALL configuration command is peculiar and, at first blush, unnecessary. It allows you to load a memory resident program — a TSR — in CONFIG.SYS. Normally that's done in AUTOEXEC.BAT. In fact, there's no driving force behind using INSTALL in CONFIG.SYS over loading the same program in AUTOEXEC.BAT. The only difference is a minor memory savings.

I've seen INSTALL commonly used in two ways. The first is to load the FASTOPEN.EXE program. (I don't like FASTOPEN and recommend against its use.) The second is to load the SHARE.EXE program for a networked PC. For example:

```
INSTALL=C:\DOS\SHARE.EXE /L:200 /F:2048
```

Above, the SHARE.EXE program is loaded into memory in CONFIG.SYS. This saves a few bytes over loading the program in AUTOEXEC.BAT. (The extra bytes are used by DOS's environment, which is stuck between TSRs like a pat of butter between two pancakes in a stack.) You can also load the same program in AUTOEXEC.BAT — or at the DOS prompt — by typing the line without the initial "INSTALL=":

```
C:\DOS SHARE.EXE /L:200 /F:2048
```

Before you let your imagination run away with this, the memory savings aren't that lush. Also, some TSRs — specifically the pop-up variety and other programs, such as DOSKEY — require that COMMAND.COM be loaded first. Since that doesn't happen until after CONFIG.SYS runs, it's a good idea to specify only those programs that claim they work with the INSTALL configuration command. That's a short list.

LASTDRIVE

This command configures DOS's file system, letting the operating system know how many drive letters it can use. As with FILES, the purpose here is to set aside only as many drive letters as you need, which saves on RAM. However, the savings is only slight, so I recommend the following setting for everyone:

```
LASTDRIVE=Z
```

This sets LASTDRIVE equal to drive Z, which is the highest possible drive letter under DOS.

Without LASTDRIVE, the highest letter DOS allows is E. That's unless you have a hard drive higher than drive E, or when you create RAM drives. Either way, the highest letter DOS allows will be equal to the last hard drive or RAM drive in your system. (So, to make a long story short, you don't need to use the LASTDRIVE command if you have six hard drives and three RAM drives.)

LASTDRIVE was introduced with DOS 3.0, which led many users to believe it was a network-only command. Wrong! While you do need to set LASTDRIVE if you're going to access network drives higher than drive E, any DOS user can specify LASTDRIVE. For example, you need it if you have a CD-ROM drive in your

PC; DOS won't recognize the drive unless LASTDRIVE is set high enough to include the drive letter. Setting LASTDRIVE equal to Z fixes this problem, no sweat.

> ***Tip:*** If you're using the *QEMM* or *QRAM* memory management packages, you can use the LASTDRIV.COM program to reduce the amount of RAM LASTDRIVE uses to store its drive letters. Just set LASTDRIVE equal to your highest hard drive or RAM drive letter in CONFIG.SYS, say LASTDRIVE=E. Then use LASTDRIV.COM in AUTOEXEC.BAT to set it equal to drive Z:
>
> ```
> C:\QEMM\LASTDRIV.COM Z
> ```
>
> Above, LASTDRIV.COM brings the total number of available drive letters up to Z.

NUMLOCK

The NUMLOCK command was added with DOS 6.0. It serves the valued function of shutting off your keyboard's numeric keypad. It also turns off the annoying little light which lets you know that by pressing your cursor keys, you will fill your screen with a long number instead of doing what you want. I recommend that you add the following command to CONFIG.SYS:

```
NUMLOCK=OFF
```

The DOS manual tells you to put this command in a menu configuration block. Don't bother! NUMLOCK can go anywhere. You'll know it's working; immediately after you see *Starting MS-DOS...* on your screen, the Num Lock light will go off.

REM

This handy command allows you to insert comments into your CONFIG.SYS file. The idea is that everything after REM (plus a space) is ignored when the SysInit process reads CONFIG.SYS. For example:

```
REM Gateway 2000, 486/33 Windows System
REM CONFIG.SYS file, 10/19/92
```

Above, the REM commands are used in CONFIG.SYS to tell you which system it was written for as well as the date it was created or updated.

Since everything after the REM command is ignored, you can also use it temporarily to disable some commands without deleting them outright. For example, say you were duped into using the SHARE.EXE program with *DESQview*. You later discovered, as a single user, it was easier to be careful than to put up with file sharing violations. So you did the following:

```
REM INSTALL=C:\DOS\SHARE.EXE /L:200 /F:2048
```

The REM command disables the INSTALL configuration command's loading of SHARE.EXE. If you ever want the command back, just edit CONFIG.SYS, and delete the REM.

✏️ *Note:* In DOS 6.0 and later versions, you can use a single semicolon (;) to replace the REM command. Anything following the semicolon is ignored. (This is Microsoft's first attempt to make CONFIG.SYS more like a Windows INI file — watch out!)

SET

SET is a DOS command, typically used in AUTOEXEC.BAT to create environment variables. You can still use it there; in fact I recommend it. If you feel overly anxious about creating environment variables, you can do so in CONFIG.SYS as well.

The format for the SET command is the same in CONFIG.SYS as it is in AUTOEXEC.BAT. For example:

```
SET PATH=C:\DOS;C:\BATCH
```

Above, the SET command creates a DOS search path in CONFIG.SYS.

The primary reason for including the SET command was to match up with DOS's new configuration menu system, where you can select multiple configurations when CONFIG.SYS starts. I'll blab on about this at length toward the end of this chapter.

SHELL

The SHELL configuration command identifies the command interpreter. It can be used in two ways: first, to load a command interpreter besides COMMAND.COM, and second, to specify a location for COMMAND.COM other than the root directory.

As long as COMMAND.COM is in the root directory of your boot disk, there's no need for the SHELL command. DOS finds COMMAND.COM all by itself (see Figure 2-1; "\COMMAND.COM" is listed inside IO.SYS). But suppose you're using Norton's NDOS.COM, or J.P. Software's 4DOS (basically they're the same thing). You can then specify it as your command interpreter as follows in CONFIG.SYS:

```
SHELL=C:\NORTON\NDOS.COM /E:512 /P /S:X
```

Above, NDOS.COM is specified as the command interpreter. DOS will load it from the NORTON subdirectory on drive C. Any necessary options after NDOS are specified at the end of the line, which also holds true for COMMAND.COM (see Chapter 3).

I recommend using SHELL because it allows you to configure COMMAND.COM as it's loaded. You can set the environment size, as well as some other special options only by loading COMMAND.COM in this manner. (Refer to Chapter 3 for more information on COMMAND.COM and its options.)

STACKS

This is an interesting DOS internal configuration command. Right away I can recommend you set this as follows in CONFIG.SYS (this is for everyone!):

```
STACKS=0,0
```

That's the preferred setting for the majority of DOS computers. This tells DOS to reserve no (zip, zero, none) memory for its internal "stacks." Without that line in CONFIG.SYS, DOS may squander away over 1K of memory for something you don't even need. (I know — 1K ain't much, but it's 1K you don't have otherwise.)

If you experience any problems with the above command, specifically you see an error message along the lines of "Internal stack overflow," then delete that line in CONFIG.SYS. Sure, it gobbles back up the 1K of storage, but it also prevents similar errors from happening in the future.

The biggest problem with the STACKS command is understanding what the stacks are and how they work. Stack of what? you may ask. Technically speaking, the "stack" is an internal storage place used by the microprocessor. Using the STACKS command, you can tell DOS how many internal stacks it can use and how big each one can be. Without a STACKS command in CONFIG.SYS, DOS sets up 9 stacks each 128 bytes in size. (9 x 128 = 1,125 bytes.) This is equivalent to the following STACKS configuration command:

```
STACKS=9,128
```

By setting STACKS=0,0, you're giving DOS zero room for extra stacks. Fortunately, that's fine for most PCs. However, if you experience a system crash due to a "stack overflow," then eliminate STACKS=0,0 in CONFIG.SYS and you'll be fine. There's no reason to mess with any other settings of this command.

SWITCHES

This is an oddball, throw-away configuration command that falls (loosely) into the DOS internals category. SWITCHES is like the MODE command, which does several unrelated, yet necessary, things. SWITCHES does two interesting yet unrelated things: it fools DOS into thinking an enhanced keyboard works like the older PC keyboards, and it allows the WINA20.386 file to be moved out of the root directory.

Suppose, for some reason, you had an older PC program that refused to work with your new — and standard — 101 key "enhanced" keyboard. For example, the program doesn't understand the nonnumeric keypad arrow keys or any key in that area between the typewriter keys and the numeric keypad. If so, add the following to CONFIG.SYS:

```
SWITCHES=/K
```

That will clear up the problem. In addition to this, if you're loading the ANSI.SYS screen and keyboard enhancement driver, you'll need to specify a /K after it as well:

```
DEVICE=C:\DOS\ANSI.SYS /K
```

In the second world of SWITCHES, suppose you're bothered by that pesky WINA20.386 file in your root directory. That file allows both Windows and DOS to share the HMA, so you need it if you're running Windows in the 386 Enhanced mode under DOS. You can, however, move it out of the way. This requires the following command in CONFIG.SYS:

```
SWITCHES=/W
```

Further, you need to edit your SYSTEM.INI file in the WINDOWS directory. In that file, look for the "[386Enh]" section, and under it add the following:

```
device=pathname\WINA20.386
```

The *pathname* indicates the full pathname, drive, and directories, where the WINA20.386 file has been moved. You need to make this change, save SYSTEM.INI, then reset your PC for it to work. Only by changing both CONFIG.SYS and SYSTEM.INI can you move the file.

▶ *Tip:* If you're not using Windows in the 386 Enhanced mode, or if you've upgraded to Windows version 3.1 or later, then you can delete the WINA20.386 file. Note that this file is read-only. To delete it, use the following command first:

```
ATTRIB -R C:\WINA20.386
```

Then use DEL to delete it.

If you need to use both options with the SWITCHES configuration command, you can specify both:

```
SWITCHES=/K /W
```

As usual, there's no need to mess with this if either of the above situations don't apply to you.

With DOS 6.0, you can use the SWITCHES=/N command to disable the F5 and F8 key presses when the Starting MS-DOS... message initially appears. This prevents someone from pressing the F5 key to skip CONFIG.SYS and AUTOEXEC.BAT completely, or pressing the F8 key to selectively pick and choose configuration commands. It's a security measure. (These two key commands are covered in the next section.)

You can mix and match the switches all on a single line if you like:

```
SWITCHES=/K/N
```

Above, the Switches command provides keyboard compatibility and disables the F5 and F8 tricks.

And, if you're in a hurry, you can use the /F option. SWITCHES=/F directs DOS to dispense with the initial two-second pause after the *Starting MS-DOS...* message is displayed.

New CONFIG.SYS Stuff for DOS 6.0

More than any other version of DOS, DOS 6.0 offers unique and interesting new configuration commands. Apparently, someone in Microsoft listened. Not all of these are suitable to everyone, athough you may find some new tricks you can use. If you don't yet have DOS 6.0 or a later version, then you may skip onward to Chapter 3.

The Best Configuration Is Sometimes No Configuration

The computer starts, it thinks, it beeps. Then you see:

```
Starting MS-DOS...
```

At this point you have three options:

1. Do nothing. CONFIG.SYS will load and your computer will start as normal.
2. Press the F5 key. DOS skips over both CONFIG.SYS and AUTOEXEC.BAT, dumping you down to the boring old DOS prompt. This is the no-brainer boot, the "naked" boot, the minimum system configuration. It's ideal when something is wrong and your PC won't start because of a nasty command in CONFIG.SYS or AUTOEXEC.BAT. Reset, wait, press F5, and then use the EDIT program to patch up the error.
3. Press the F8 key. This causes DOS to stop and present you with a prompt for each command in CONFIG.SYS. For example:

```
DEVICE=C:\DOS\HIMEM.SYS [Y/N]?
```

Press Y to run the command, N to skip it. If you press Y, the command instructions are carried out. Press N and it was never there. Either way, the next line in CONFIG.SYS is displayed with the same yes-or-no prompt. If you tire of this, press F1 to run the lot of them. Otherwise, you'll eventually see:

```
Process AUTOEXEC.BAT [Y/N]?
```

Press Y if you want to run AUTOEXEC.BAT; N skips it.

The F5 and F8 keys present marvelous ways of skirting around certain startup commands. An even better solution is to employ DOS 6.0's *query* configuration command. It works like this: stick a question mark immediately after the configuration command you want to yes-or-no on startup. For example:

```
DEVICE?=C:\DOS\CRASH.SYS /BOOM
```

Whether or not you press F8, DOS will always display the following prompt for the above command:

```
DEVICE=C:\DOS\CRASH.SYS /BOOM [Y/N]?
```

This way you can turn on or shut off single commands that may not be necessary each time you boot or which may conflict with other commands. You can use the question mark/query command anywhere in CONFIG.SYS; just stick it right after the configuration command.

Configuration Menu Commands

There are five special commands used in DOS 6.0 to generate a menu of configuration choices when the computer first starts. You can pick and choose the commands that will configure your system. This comes in handy when you have incompatible drivers or different situations that require many CONFIG.SYS files at the ready.

To begin, I have a bit of advice: only mess with the multiple configuration commands if you truly need them. How can you tell? If you have several files on your system for startup and must constantly rename and reset in order to use your computer, you're a prime candidate. For example, suppose you have the following CONFIG.SYS files:

CONFIG.WIN, which configures the PC specifically for Windows
CONFIG.DOS, a generic DOS configuration file
CONFIG.NET, a version of CONFIG.SYS that's network-friendly

If you're using Windows and want to access the network, you need to rename CONFIG.SYS to CONFIG.WIN; then rename CONFIG.NET to CONFIG.SYS and reset. This smells of monumental pain, athough the situation is easily fixed using DOS 6.0's menu configuration commands.

You should bother with this only if your situation is described above. I don't make this warning casually. The truth is that many programs and disk utilities count on a solid, unchanging CONFIG.SYS file. DOS's MEMMAKER, QEMM's Optimize, and other memory management utilities will wreck havoc in a multiconfiguration CONFIG.SYS file. So only consider this solution if your pain level is high.

The five new menu configuration commands are listed in Table 2-5. The most popular will be the MENUITEM command, which is used to identify various configuration blocks you've created in CONFIG.SYS.

Just for fun, suppose we are looking at two of your CONFIG.SYS files. The first one is used for Windows.

Table 2-5 Configuration Menu Commands

Command	Function
INCLUDE	Directs CONFIG.SYS to use commands from another menu block in the current block
MENUCOLOR	Sets the foreground and background color of the menu's startup screen
MENUDEFAULT	Specifies the default menu item and an optional timeout, after which that item is selected
MENUITEM	Defines a configuration block that appears in the configuration menu
SUBMENU	Defines a submenu of configuration choices

```
REM I use this to start Windows
DEVICE=C:\DOS\HIMEM.SYS
DOS=HIGH,UMB
DEVICE=C:\DOS\EMM386.EXE NOEMS
FILES=30
```

This one is used for DOS:

```
REM I use this to start DOS
DEVICE=C:\DOS\HIMEM.SYS
DOS=HIGH,UMB
DEVICE=C:\DOS\EMM386.EXE RAM
FILES=30
DEVICEHIGH=C:\MOUSE.SYS
```

Rather than juggle these two files, you can create a configuration menu system in a single CONFIG.SYS file, as shown in Figure 2-5.

A CONFIG.SYS file with a menu system starts with the [MENU] configuration block. This is the only place the five menu commands can be used. The two MENUITEM commands in Figure 2-5 specify the two different configurations, Windows and DOS. Notice how each is followed exactly by the configuration block titles, each of which sits before its group of commands.

When the computer starts, you'll be presented with the two choices: "Windows" and "DOS." You are then allowed to select between them. Additional menu blocks, each appearing after a block title in square brackets, can also be added. Each menu block needs its own MENUITEM command in the main [Menu] block.

```
[Menu]
MENUITEM=Windows
MENUITEM=DOS

[Windows]
DEVICE=C:\DOS\HIMEM.SYS
DOS=HIGH,UMB
DEVICE=C:\DOS\EMM386.EXE NOEMS
FILES=30

[DOS]
DEVICE=C:\DOS\HIMEM.SYS
DOS=HIGH,UMB
DEVICE=C:\DOS\EMM386.EXE RAM
FILES=30
DEVICEHIGH=C:\MOUSE.SYS
```

Figure 2-5 A CONFIG.SYS file with configuration menu commands

This is a valid and highly useful approach to managing multiple configurations. If you're adept with batch files, you can continue the modification in AUTOEXEC.BAT using the CONFIG environment variable which is set equal to the configuration block you've selected in CONFIG.SYS. However, with sub-menus and "includes" this can become quite involved. So, I only recommend the configuration menu system in the most dire of circumstances.

3

All about COMMAND.COM

COMMAND.COM is only one of three programs that make up DOS, yet it's the most visible. You rely on COMMAND.COM as your base of operations and use its internal commands to manage the file system. Without COMMAND.COM, the system won't start (ever see that cheery "Bad or missing command interpreter" message?). This chapter discusses COMMAND.COM, how it starts, its options, and tips on using it with environments such as *DESQview* and Windows.

The Command Interpreter

Once the SysInit procedure loads MSDOS.SYS (or its IBMDOS.COM counterpart), DOS is loaded and ready to run on your computer. What's missing is the command interpreter, DOS's user interface. That's supplied with DOS via COMMAND.COM, perhaps the most ugly and traditional computer interface out there.

It is true that you can run your computer without the command interpreter. You can use the SHELL configuration command to specify some program's COM or EXE file as a "command interpreter." For example, if you only wanted your system to run *WordPerfect*, you could specify WP.EXE as your command interpreter in CONFIG.SYS:

```
SHELL=C:\WP51\WP.EXE
```

I do not recommend doing this, however. When *WordPerfect* (or whichever program you've specified with the SHELL configuration command) quits, you'll get a "Bad or missing command interpreter" error. You'll see the same error if the program just doesn't cut it with the SHELL command, e.g., Windows. Those programs just aren't designed to fill the role of command processor. Further, without COMMAND.COM (or a similar command interpreter) you won't be able to run batch files, use the DOS prompt, or set up your system with AUTOEXEC.BAT. Therefore, stick with COMMAND.COM, Norton's NDOS, J.P. Software's 4DOS, or whatever, as your command interpreter.

> ***Tip:*** Okay, you could load some TSRs in CONFIG.SYS using the INSTALL configuration command. However, I don't recommend using the SHELL command to load anything other than a true command interpreter. If you have a compelling reason to do otherwise and it works, great. But you're on your own.

Looking back to Figure 2-1, you'll see how COMMAND.COM is listed in the SysInit part of IO.SYS. If the SHELL command isn't in CONFIG.SYS, then SysInit uses "\COMMAND.COM" as specified in IO.SYS to load the command interpreter. It's loaded from the root directory of the boot disk. If the SHELL command is used, then SysInit uses the command interpreter listed, loading it into memory as well. Either way, COMMAND.COM behaves the same once its loaded into memory and run by SysInit. (For this book, I'll assume the command interpreter is COMMAND.COM, although other work-alikes can behave similarly.)

The Multiple Personalities of COMMAND.COM

COMMAND.COM has three different parts or modules: The initialization module, and then the resident and transient portions. The reason behind this is to give you as much memory as possible. By itself, COMMAND.COM is a big program: almost 50K in size for DOS 5. However, in memory COMMAND.COM uses only 3.5K — or less. To prove it you can use the MEM command as follows:

```
C:\> MEM /C | FIND /I "COMMAND"
    COMMAND       2928    ( 2.9K)     B70
```

You may see more than one copy of COMMAND.COM in memory; it depends on whether you've "shelled" from an application or are running an environment such as Windows or *DESQview*. And the size you see will vary as well; above it's 2.9K, but I've seen as little as 2.6K. Where did the rest of it go?

You can see how COMMAND.COM deals with its three parts in Figure 3-1. The whole program is loaded into memory first. The main part is the *resident portion*, shown at the bottom of the memory maplike figure in Figure 3-1. The resident portion contains the guts of COMMAND.COM: the program-loading routines, the routines called when a program quits, and critical error handling routines. It's also responsible for reloading the *transient* portion back into memory — but more on that in a moment.

The *initialization* module has several interesting, albeit brief, tasks. When COMMAND.COM is first loaded, the resident portion (which is always in charge) calls the initialization module. It then does three things:

1. The initialization module takes the *transient* portion and loads it as high as possible into conventional memory. (This overwrites the SysInit program, which was previously sitting high in memory.)
2. It processes any optional switches specified after COMMAND.COM in CONFIG.SYS. This is only if the SHELL configuration command was used to load COMMAND.COM, or when COMMAND.COM is run as a program at the DOS prompt.
3. It looks for and runs the AUTOEXEC.BAT file found in the root directory of the boot disk. This is done automatically when the computer first starts. However, if you run COMMAND.COM a second time, or if the SHELL command loads COMMAND.COM, you must specify the /P switch for AUTOEXEC.BAT to be run.

After doing those three things, the initialization process frees up the memory it used, giving you more conventional memory for your programs. Control passes back to the resident portion, which volleys control up to the transient portion high in memory. It's the transient portion that displays the DOS prompt and processes all DOS internal and external commands, program files, and batch files.

COMMAND.COM the Transient

The transient portion of COMMAND.COM sits high in memory, which is weird, so I'm going to elaborate on it. It's been loaded as high as possible in memory ever since the first version of DOS. Even more so back then, when 128K was the standard, memory on a PC was tight.

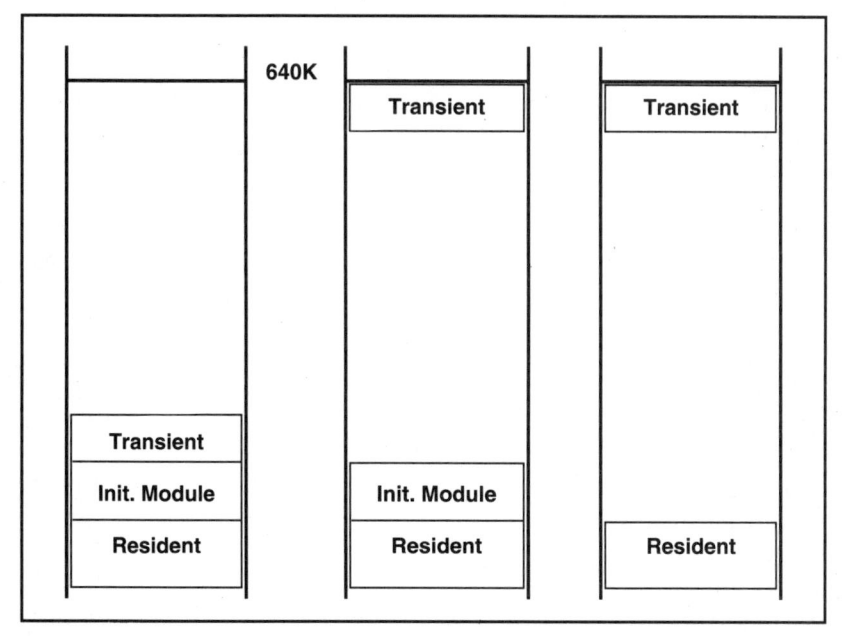

Figure 3-1 How COMMAND.COM sets itself up in memory

Since the transient portion isn't protected, any DOS program can stomp all over it. This doesn't pose a problem for any application; the information in the transient portion of COMMAND.COM isn't accessible to a program running under DOS. And if your application wanted to run a DOS command, say COPY or RD, then DOS runs another copy of COMMAND.COM and the transient area is rebuilt. (They thought of everything, didn't they?)

Whether or not the transient portion survives, when a program quits, control returns to the resident portion of COMMAND.COM. It locates where it last left the transient portion and does a quick checksum on the bytes there. If everything is intact, then COMMAND.COM pops right back up again. Otherwise, the resident portion attempts to reload COMMAND.COM from disk. It does this by first looking for the COMSPEC environment variable, then by checking the root directory of the boot disk for COMMAND.COM.

The COMSPEC variable is created by the initialization module when COMMAND.COM first starts. Under DOS 5, this information is obtained from a special command line option used when COMMAND.COM is started in CONFIG.SYS using the SHELL command. If that's not there, then COMSPEC is set equal to C:\COMMAND.COM, regardless of where COMMAND.COM is actually located on disk. (After all, since SHELL didn't load COMMAND.COM, it must be in the root directory.) To prove this, use the SET command on your computer to see where COMMAND.COM sits:

```
C:\> SET
COMSPEC=C:\DOS\COMMAND.COM
PROMPT ($P)
PATH C:\DOS;C:\UTIL;C:\WINDOWS
TEMP=D:
NET=OFF
```

You can see that COMSPEC is set equal to C:\DOS\COMMAND.COM, which is where the resident portion of COMMAND.COM will fetch the transient portion should it be needed.

Tip: You can change the COMSPEC variable at any time using the SET command. Prior to DOS 5, this was required if you were using SHELL in CONFIG.SYS to relocate COMMAND.COM and it wasn't in the root directory of the boot disk.

COMSPEC, along with PATH, are the only two environment variables found at boot time. Everything else was added manually, most likely in AUTOEXEC.BAT.

If the resident portion can't locate COMMAND.COM on your disk, you'll see the following error message:

```
Cannot load COMMAND, system halted
```

This message may also appear if the transient portion, for whatever reason, cannot be rebuilt. You must reset to get out of it.

So where is the transient part of COMMAND.COM? It depends on how much memory your system has, as well as the DOS version and on other things in memory. (For example, virus infected computers may have a virus riding high — and protected — in conventional memory, which brings the transient portion down 2K or so.)

On a typical 640K machine, the transient portion sits in the middle of bank 9 (about the 608K mark). It takes up about 32K of memory. If you like, hop on into DEBUG for a look-see:

```
C:\> DEBUG
-D9800:0 L400
```

After starting DEBUG (type DEBUG at the DOS prompt), the D command displays 1K of memory starting at location 9800:0 — the middle of bank 9 where the transient portion of COMMAND.COM waits. There isn't much to see there, but since the DOS command list is kept high, you can find and view it using the S, search, command. Type in the following:

```
-S9800:0 L8000 "CALL"
9800:5F81
9800:6CEB
```

The CALL command is located twice in COMMAND.COM's transient portion (that's for DOS 5, and your output may vary). The first find under DOS 5 is the CALL command's help information — what you see when you type "CALL /?" at the DOS prompt. The second find is in the command list. In the example that's 6CEB. To see the list, replace the last two digits with zeros, then use the number with the D command as follows:

```
-D9800:6C00 L100
```

Replacing the last two digits of 6CEB yields 6C00. That's used with the D command to list (or "dump") 128 bytes of memory. If everything goes as planned, you'll see the first part of the internal command list, stored high in the memory in the transient portion of COMMAND.COM. If you like, type the D command (by itself) a few more times to page through the command list.

> *Note:* The command list you see is DOS's *internal command list*. DOS commands fall into two categories: internal and external. Internal commands are part of COMMAND.COM and do not need to be loaded from disk. External commands, like other DOS applications, are program files on disk.

DOS has the following internal commands, listed in the same order as they appear in memory:

NOT	DATE	PROMPT
ERRORLEVEL	TIME	PATH
EXIST	VER	EXIT
DIR	VOL	CTTY
CALL	CD	ECHO
CHCP	CHDIR	GOTO
RENAME	MD	SHIFT
REN	MKDIR	IF
ERASE	RD	FOR
DEL	RMDIR	CLS
TYPE	BREAK	TRUENAME
REM	VERIFY	LOADHIGH
COPY	SET	LH
PAUSE		

The list ends with some program-processing routines. Specifically, you'll see the text that allows programs with the COM, EXE, or BAT extension to be run at the DOS prompt:

```
.'Yp...COM.EXE.B
AT?VBAPWRHSvDANE
```

There's nothing else to see, at least nothing else worth jumping up and down about, so you can quit DEBUG by typing Q, and return to the DOS prompt. As you do so, keep in mind that the following is happening: You're passing control to the resident portion of COMMAND.COM, which handles DEBUG's quit function. Then the resident portion is checking the transient portion, reloading it if necessary, and passing control to it where the DOS prompt is displayed.

Specifying the Command Interpreter

DOS comes with COMMAND.COM ready and able as your command interpreter. It's built that way: \COMMAND.COM is a part of IO.SYS and the SysInit process will look hard for it on the boot drive. To specify another command interpreter, or to tuck COMMAND.COM away in a subdirectory, you use the SHELL configuration command in CONFIG.SYS.

Here is the command used by DOS 5 to load the command interpreter, as part of its manufacturer's suggested CONFIG.SYS file:

```
SHELL=C:\DOS\COMMAND.COM C:\DOS /p
```

(Refer to Figure 2-3 if you want to see the full "manufacturer's suggested" CONFIG.SYS file; refer to the section on the SHELL configuration command in Chapter 2 for more information on it.)

The purpose of the SHELL command is merely to specify a command interpreter. Its job stops with the pathname of the command interpreter you specify. Above, SHELL only cares about C:\DOS\COMMAND.COM. The rest of the line is handled by COMMAND.COM itself. Here's what each part does:

`C:\DOS\COMMAND.COM`

This is the name of the command interpreter and its location on disk. True, you can specify C:\COMMAND.COM. No problem with that; it allows you to list important options after COMMAND.COM that wouldn't otherwise be executed.

`C:\DOS`

This option sets the COMSPEC variable. The manual refers to this as the *dos-drive:dos-path*, where COMMAND.COM is located. I'll admit this sounds dorky: the first part of the command lists the full pathname for COMMAND.COM. However, a DOS program doesn't always know where it's located each time it runs. Therefore this option helps COMMAND.COM's initialization module set the COMSPEC properly.

`/P`

The /P switch makes COMMAND.COM *permanent*; you cannot type EXIT to quit. It's also required to run AUTOEXEC.BAT. While you may assume that's done automatically, when you use the SHELL command it isn't the case.

If there's a SHELL command in your PC's CONFIG.SYS, it may have these same options: the full path for COMMAND.COM and the /P switch. It may also have the /E switch, which sets the size of DOS's environment.

The environment is a scratch pad for DOS — a storage place where environment variables (like COMSPEC) are placed, along with the variable's contents. COMMAND.COM creates a 256-byte environment each time it starts. You can select a different size by specifying the /E switch. For example:

`SHELL=C:\COMMAND.COM C:\ /E:512 /P`

Above, /E sets aside 512 bytes for environment storage. Further information on using this switch is covered in the next section.

Using SHELL to load COMMAND.COM is important, and I recommend it. Without a SHELL command in CONFIG.SYS, COMMAND.COM would start up with its default values, which isn't what you want.

On the other hand, using SHELL to move COMMAND.COM to another directory may not be a hot idea. In the second SHELL example in this section, COMMAND.COM was located in the root directory. That's perfectly fine — it allows you to specify COMMAND.COM's options.

▬▶ *Tip:* Why not move COMMAND.COM to a subdirectory? You may accidentally delete it or move it during major disk reorganization. I've done that several times. Also, the popular *Stacker* disk doubler requires extra effort when the SHELL command specifies another location for COMMAND.COM. My advice: Keep it in the root directory, but still use the SHELL configuration command.

COMMAND.COM's Secret Format

Not all of COMMAND.COM's format is secret (though there are some undocumented switches). Here is the command format for COMMAND.COM as used in the SHELL configuration command:

```
SHELL=[path]COMMAND.COM [d:path] [device] [/e:n] [/p]
[/msg]
```

Everything after COMMAND.COM is optional. Before COMMAND.COM should be its full *path*, including the drive letter and colon. After COMMAND.COM you can specify any of the following options:

D:PATH — This is a simple echo of the *path*; the location of COMMAND.COM. Always specify this option so that the COMSPEC will be properly set and COMMAND.COM will know where to reload itself should the transient portion be trashed.

DEVICE — This option allows you to specify a DOS device COMMAND.COM will use for input and output. It can safely be ignored.

✎ ***Note:*** Normally the CON (console) device is used for DOS I/O and the *device* option isn't specified with COMMAND.COM. The only other device that could be used is the AUX port, and that only works if you have an external terminal hooked up. Further, only DOS commands and DOS I/O will work on that terminal; all other applications remain local. This remains a mystifying option.

/E:*N* — You can set the environment to any size *n*, from 160 to 32,768 bytes in length. All values are rounded to the nearest multiple of 16. For most users, the default of 256 bytes is big enough for the environment. I use 512 on my system because I have a lot of variables. If your situation is similar, set the value higher. If you don't have many variables, set the value lower. Setting *n* too high can really waste a lot of RAM.

/P — This is a required switch if you're loading COMMAND.COM with the SHELL configuration command. It makes COMMAND.COM permanent; you cannot type EXIT to "quit." Further, it directs the initialization module to load AUTOEXEC.BAT.

▶ ***Tip:*** The only other time you should use the /P switch is when running COMMAND.COM as a DOS window in either Windows or *DESQview*. That subject is raked over the coals in the last two sections of this chapter.

/MSG — Do you have a hard drive? If yes, you can ignore this option. If you have only a floppy disk system, then specifying /MSG loads DOS's detailed error messages into the resident portion of COM-

MAND.COM. This prevents the limited messages that appear otherwise, since the disk with COMMAND.COM may or may not be in your floppy drive. For a hard drive system, this isn't a problem. (And specifying /MSG on that system wastes memory.)

Note: If you specify /MSG you must also specify /P.

COMMAND.COM has one additional option not covered here: The /C switch is used to send COMMAND.COM a message, usually the name of a program to run. This is covered in the next section on COMMAND.COM, the program.

COMMAND.COM the Program

COMMAND.COM is also a program you can run at the DOS prompt. Technically, running COMMAND.COM is referred to as generating another "shell," and it happens more often than you think.

To demonstrate the shell, you can run COMMAND.COM by itself. Just type COMMAND at the DOS prompt:

```
C:\> COMMAND
```

You'll see the DOS copyright notice displayed, then another DOS prompt. Big deal! (In fact, I once found an ancient computer book that said you could type in COMMAND to see the DOS copyright notice. You'll see why that's not fully correct in a moment.)

Now use the MEM command to take a look at what's in memory:

```
C:\> MEM /D /P
```

The /D debug switch displays more memory detail than the standard Mem command and displays much more than the /C switch. The /P pauses the Mem command's output after a full screen; this is similar to the way the /P switch works with the Dir command. (If you have DOS 5.0 or an earlier version, pipe the output of MEM /D through the More filter: *mem /d | more.*)

In your output, look for part of the listing that resembles Figure 3-2. You should see seven sets of COMMAND items, which indicate two copies of COMMAND.COM in memory; the first you were already in and the second is the shell you just started. Additional copies of COMMAND may appear in low memory, especially if you're running a multitasking environment, the DOS Shell, Windows, *DESQview*, or have shelled from another program.

```
004CB      2640    (3K)    COMMAND     Program
00575       272    (0K)    COMMAND     Environment
009A7       160    (0K)    COMMAND     Data
009B1      2640    (3K)    COMMAND     Program
00A56       272    (0K)    COMMAND     Environment
```

Figure 3-2 Multiple copies of COMMAND.COM in memory

The reason COMMAND appears a few times is for each of the memory blocks COMMAND.COM creates in RAM. The first block contains 128 bytes that describe the program that's running, COMMAND.COM in this case. The second block contains the program data itself. The third block contains a copy of the environment. This size will vary on each computer, depending on the size of your environment set in CONFIG.SYS. In Figure 3-2, the environment block is 272 bytes long.

Every copy of COMMAND.COM you run has its own environment block attached to it. It's actually a copy of the *master environment block*, held low in memory. In fact, changing the environment is one way to ensure you're in a shell. Type the following:

```
C:\> PROMPT (In a shell)
```

That changes the DOS prompt to read "(In a shell)". But don't worry about changing it back. Instead, quit the shell by typing EXIT:

```
(In a shell) EXIT
C:\>
```

The EXIT command is what cancels COMMAND.COM; the "quit" command, if you will. The reason it doesn't work for the main copy of COMMAND.COM is that /P switch you add in CONFIG.SYS. If not, when the SysInit process loads COMMAND.COM, it's made permanent automatically. And keep in mind that /P prevents you from typing EXIT any time after that. For example:

```
C:\> COMMAND /P
```

Don't type that in! If you do, you'll run a second copy of COMMAND.COM that you will be unable to remove from memory. Instantly you'll lose 3K of conventional memory — not much, but pretty dumb just the same.

The Shell Game

Shell is simply a computerese term for a user interface. DOS "the program" is actually in the IO.SYS and MSDOS.SYS files already in memory when COMMAND.COM is run. So COMMAND.COM supplies you with the shell — the insulating case that protects you from the raw and hostile operating system.

Normally, there's no reason to run COMMAND.COM at the DOS prompt. However, many programs have a "shell" feature, one that lets you exit the program, run another program, then return to the original — just as was done above with COMMAND.COM. This involves some cute terminology:

- The first program you run is the parent.
- The program run — or "shelled" — is the child.

For example, suppose you're in *1-2-3*. The Shell command is /S (slash, then S). The S means system. What it does is to run a second copy of COMMAND.COM. After typing /S you'll be dumped out to the DOS prompt. To return, type EXIT.

(This is an amazing trick to novice *1-2-3* users who stumble over /S on their way to save a worksheet.)

What happens in *1-2-3* is that a special DOS function, EXEC, is used to run a second, child program. The parent program is *1-2-3*. The child in this case is COMMAND.COM — which *1-2-3* locates via the COMSPEC environment variable. A better example is provided in *WordPerfect*.

To run a child program from *WordPerfect* you use the Shell command. Pressing Ctrl-F1 displays a brief menu at the bottom of the screen:

```
1 Go to DOS; 2 DOS Command:
```

Here you're given an option: Select 1 or G and you run COMMAND.COM. Selecting 2 or C provides another prompt where you can enter a DOS command, program name, or a full command line. This works just like COMMAND.COM, but the program that's run is specified at a prompt — it's not COMMAND.COM.

Doing all this — running one program from another — is referred to as "shelling." If you run COMMAND.COM, then you're "shelling out to DOS." When you run another program, such as *1-2-3*, you're "shelling out" to it. Yet, while it's true that both programs are in memory, only one of them can run at a time. Figure 3-3 illustrates how this looks with programs as blocks in memory.

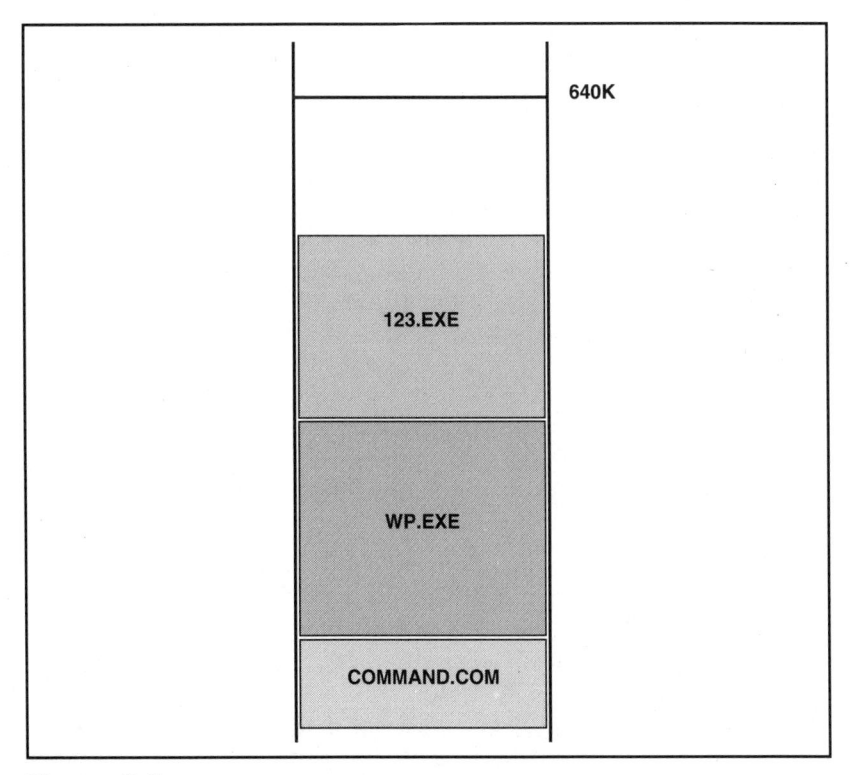

Figure 3-3 *WordPerfect* has shelled out to *1-2-3*

When one program quits, it's removed from memory. Its parent program then picks up where it left off. This is important to remember: Shelling to another program is not the same as a TSR or multitasking; the parent program lays dormant in memory until you quit the child program.

▶ *Tip:* Sometimes not every program will fit. That situation produces an "out of memory" error, and your child program won't run. If that bugs you, consider using a program like DOS Shell that allows you to switch between several programs, swapping them in and out of memory to disk. More splash is offered with *DESQview*, which lets the programs you're not working on continue to run — even when you don't see them. That's true multitasking — but only on an 80386 compatible PC.

COMMAND.COM's Command Line Format

The following is the format for COMMAND.COM as used at the DOS prompt:

```
COMMAND.COM [/p] [/c message] [/k message]
```

The only two switches you'll want to specify are /P or /C, and they would be used independently of each other. All other options are unnecessary — and counterproductive — at the DOS prompt.

The /P Switch

The /P switch makes the copy of COMMAND.COM permanent and directs it to run AUTOEXEC.BAT. Obviously, this isn't a sane choice if you've just shelled from another program; you'll never be able to type EXIT and quit the shell. Therefore, using /P is only recommended to create unclosable DOS windows in *DESQview* or Windows (which is conveniently discussed in the next two sections).

The /C switch is used to pass a line of text to the new copy of COMMAND.COM. This is the same thing as running COMMAND.COM, typing in the command or *message*, then typing EXIT. For example:

```
COMMAND /C DIR
```

The above command runs another copy of COMMAND.COM, executes the DIR command, then returns to the current copy of COMMAND.COM. It's the same as the three commands COMMAND, DIR, and EXIT.

There is only one real reason to use the /C switch with COMMAND: to run or shell to a program that requires a second copy of the command interpreter. The biggest example of this type of program is a batch file. But since DOS 3.3, the CALL command has allowed you to run batch files without COMMAND /C. So the only other compelling reason is to use I/O redirection with a batch file, which is impossible otherwise.

For example, suppose you had a batch file that scanned for files to backup on all your hard drives. Call it CHKBAK.BAT. If you wanted to save the output of that file, you might think I/O redirection would help, but think again:

```
C:\> CHKBAK > COUNT.DAT
```

This looks like the output from CHKBAK will be sent to a file named COUNT.DAT. But since CHKBAK is a batch file, COUNT.DAT will be empty (a null file, actually). Traditionalists will claim that you need to stick a *COUNT.DAT* to the end of each command in CHKBAK.BAT for this to work. The real solution is to use COMMAND /C:

```
C:\> COMMAND /C CHKBAK > COUNT.DAT
```

This isn't the same as the previous DOS command. What's happening here is that COMMAND.COM is running the CHKBAK program. It's not running "*chkbak > count.dat.*" Instead, the output from *COMMAND.COM* is being redirected to COUNT.DAT. Since the batch file runs under COMMAND.COM, its output is also sent to the file.

Other uses for COMMAND /C include running batch files from some menu systems that don't allow it. Although I can't think of any applications offhand, suppose you encountered a program that could only shell to COM or EXE programs. In that case, you can run a batch file by specifying COMMAND /C followed by the batch filename. (Using the CALL command may also work, though COMMAND /C is guaranteed.)

Running a DOS Window in Windows

Since COMMAND.COM is a program, you can run it as a shell or a menu option in a menu program. You can also run it under Windows as a "DOS prompt." The merits of this are questionable, since Windows is designed to insulate you from the ugly DOS prompt. But it can be done, right or wrong.

Windows sets itself up with a DOS Prompt icon. That's hooked up to a Windows PIF (Program Information File) that simply tells Windows to run COMMAND.COM. This got sophisticated with Windows version 3.1. When Windows sees COMMAND.COM being run it displays an interesting "hello" banner, as shown in Figure 3-4. This is part of Windows, not COMMAND.COM.

As with any DOS program under Windows, you can press Alt-Enter to zap it into a graphic window screen. Press Alt-Enter again and it's back to a full text screen. (This only works in the 386 Enhanced mode.) Since you're running DOS, I

```
┌─────────────────────────────────────────────────────────────────┐
│  ■ Type EXIT and press ENTER to quit this MS-DOS prompt and    │
│    return to Windows.                                           │
│  ■ Press ALT+TAB to switch to Windows or another application.  │
│  ■ Press ALT+ENTER to switch this MS-DOS Prompt between a      │
│    window and full screen.                                      │
└─────────────────────────────────────────────────────────────────┘

Microsoft(R) MS-DOS(R) Version 6
         (C)Copyright Microsoft Corp 1981-1993.

(C:\WINDOWS)
```

Figure 3-4   Here is how Windows runs COMMAND.COM

recommend keeping COMMAND.COM, or whichever DOS program you're running, in the normal text screen mode. This makes the program run faster and presents the display the way the developer intended. It also lets you use the mouse if the DOS program supports it.

In the graphical window, you can use the Windows mouse to cut and paste blocks from the screen: Click in the screen, then drag to select information. The hyphen menu's "Edit" item allows you to copy or paste information. So much for the Windows mini-lecture.

Instead of specifying COMMAND.COM directly, I use a special batch file on my Windows system. The program is RUNDOS.BAT, and it's shown in Figure 3-5. The graphic text window was created using the characters shown in Table 3-1. (A full list of these line drawing characters is shown in Appendix B.)

Before giving this batch file a resounding "big deal," consider what it does. RUNDOS.BAT will not display the same box you see when running COMMAND.COM straight. Therefore, this batch file contains its own informative box. (See how the EXIT item isn't included in my batch file as it was in Figure 3-4? The DOS prompt takes care of that information.)

The RUNDOS batch file runs DOSKEY and the MOUSE.COM device driver. DOSKEY gives you command line editing and MOUSE gives you a mouse for any DOS programs you run. Sticking those two TSRs here means they're not wasted in low memory *before* Windows runs. And after you quit COMMAND.COM, they'll be removed from memory.

▶ **Tip:** There's no need to run DOSKEY or the MOUSE device driver in AUTOEXEC.BAT or CONFIG.SYS on a Windows system. Since Windows isn't a command line environment, you don't need DOSKEY, and it also supplies its own mouse driver. Therefore, by not running them at startup you save about 20K (or more) of memory.

If you run a DOS prompt, such as with RUNDOS, you can then start these memory resident programs. They'll be removed from memory when you type EXIT to return to Windows. An exception is the MOUSE device driver. If your DOS programs need it under Windows, then it must be loaded before you start Windows.

Finally, RUNDOS changes the DOS prompt so that you constantly know you're in Windows. The prompt looks like this:

```
@echo off
DOSKEY /INSERT
MOUSE
echo
echo    You're now in a Windows DOS shell
echo    Type Alt-Enter to make this a graphic window.
echo    'EXIT' closes this window
echo
echo.
prompt In Windows; type EXIT to return$_($P)
command
```

Figure 3-5 RUNDOS.BAT is a better way to run COMMAND.COM in Windows

Table 3-1 Here Are the Line Drawing Characters Used in RUNDOS.BAT

Symbol	Code
┌	2-0-1
─	2-0-5
┐	1-8-7
│	1-8-6
└	2-0-0
┘	1-8-8

To enter the character code, press and hold the Alt key, and type the code number on the numeric keypad. Release the Alt key and the symbol will appear. This trick works in EDLIN, EDIT, and *QEdit* and in some word processors.

```
In Windows; type EXIT to return
(C:\)
```

This way you'll remember you're in Windows long after you start the DOS window.

As with any other program, you must quit COMMAND.COM to close the DOS window. Typing EXIT at the DOS prompt does this, returning you to Windows. This is all provided that you didn't specify /P when you started the DOS window. If you did, then AUTOEXEC.BAT will run and, in most cases, will attempt to restart memory resident programs that will crash Windows. Though Windows doesn't grind to a halt, the system is corrupted; you'll need to reset to restore system integrity.

> *Tip:* Don't specify the /P switch when running COMMAND.COM under Windows. You'll never be able to close the DOS window — unless you're insistent, at which point Windows will recommend that you reboot to recover.

Using the Mysterious, New /K Switch

DOS 6.0 includes a new switch to COMMAND.COM, /K. The new /K switch is a sort of combination /C and /P switch. It works like /P because it's designed to be used when COMMAND.COM first starts, such as with a DOS session in Windows as previously discussed. But it also works like the /C switch in that you specify the name of a command or program to run after /K. This makes /K ideal for setting up DOS sessions in multiple program environments.

To see how this works, pretend that your PC is already started and your main AUTOEXEC.BAT program has already run. You're running a multitasking environment, something like Windows or *DESQview*. And in that environment you want to start another DOS session. The technique you use to configure the DOS session, either dual AUTOEXEC.BAT files, multiple decisions in AUTOEXEC.BAT, or special startup files, is covered in the next section. With DOS 6.0. you would specify your startup configuration file as follows:

```
COMMAND /K C:\STARTUP.BAT
```

The above command starts a new version of COMMAND.COM — a DOS session. The /K switch directs COMMAND.COM to immediately run the following command, just as if it were the first thing typed after COMMAND.COM starts. Above, that's the file C:\STARTUP.BAT. In Windows, that file may contain special startup commands for the Windows DOS session, as discussed in the previous section. In *DESQview*, it may configure the system prompt, run a startup program, or whatever. The point is, it isn't AUTOEXEC.BAT but it acts like AUTOEXEC.BAT.

If you would have used the /P switch instead, then AUTOEXEC.BAT itself would have run. This brings up all sorts of issues, which are covered in the section that follows. It also makes COMMAND.COM permanent, meaning you can't type exit to close the DOS session or DOS program window. With /K, the Exit command still works.

Running a DOS Window in *DESQview*

Unlike Windows, *DESQview* is a multitasking DOS environment for text-based programs. When you run COMMAND.COM in *DESQview*, you're creating a DOS "window," which may be one of several programs running simultaneously on the same computer.

Normally COMMAND.COM is run under *DESQview* without any options. But you may want to change, primarily by adding the /P switch. That has a big plus in that it creates a DOS window you can't close by typing the EXIT command. The big minus is that AUTOEXEC.BAT runs again, which is probably not what you want. Thanks to batch files, however, there are ways around this. (More information on AUTOEXEC.BAT is provided in Chapter 4.)

Before getting into it, you need to be fairly convinced that adding /P to COMMAND.COM is worth it. After all, what harm is there in running COMMAND.COM without it? Nothing is different, other than EXIT closes the window. However, there may be times when you want to run a startup batch file. AUTOEXEC.BAT is ideal, but must be modified to run twice; once at startup and again when a *DESQview* DOS window appears.

▶ ***Tip:*** What you do in a special *DESQview* startup AUTOEXEC.BAT file is up to you. You may want to run the DVANSI program for ANSI capability, run a mouse driver or DOSKEY — which would keep those programs out of memory before you start *DESQview* — or any number of tricks.

What you don't want to do when you run AUTOEXEC.BAT again is reload some TSRs, restart your network connections, or rerun *DESQview* again. This dual-booting AUTOEXEC.BAT file handles those situations most deftly.

```
@echo off
echo Running DESQview . . .
echo DESQview is active  %TEMP%\DVACTIVE
c:
cd \system\dv
break off
dv %1 %2 %3 %4 %5
del %TEMP%\DVACTIVE
cd \
:END
```

Figure 3-6 A batch file to start *DESQview*

The first solution is to create a temporary file or environment variable that AUTOEXEC.BAT can examine to see if *DESQview* is running. For example, the batch file in Figure 3-6 could be used to start *DESQview*. Note the third line down. It creates a file named DVACTIVE in the temporary directory, as specified by the TEMP environment variable. AUTOEXEC.BAT — or any other batch file — can then check to see if *DESQview* is active by checking for this variable:

```
IF EXIST %TEMP%\DVACTIVE GOTO BOOT
REM Startup DESQview here
 . . .
GOTO END
:BOOT
REM Startup DOS here
 . . .
END
```

In the example AUTOEXEC.BAT file, the file DVACTIVE is checked out in the first line using IF-EXIST. If the file doesn't exist, it's safe to assume that *DESQview* isn't active; batch file execution goes to the BOOT label and DOS is started as normal. If DVACTIVE is detected, then the special *DESQview* startup sequence is engaged and the DOS sequence is skipped.

The second method works the same way, but uses an environment variable instead of a temporary file on disk. Figure 3-7 shows the modified DV.BAT file used to start DESQview. The AUTOEXEC.BAT file would then use the following test instead of IF-EXIST:

```
IF NOT "%DVACTIVE%"=="TRUE" GOTO BOOT
```

If the variable DVACTIVE is equal to *TRUE*, then *DESQview* is active. In the example, if *DESQview* isn't active (DVACTIVE doesn't equal anything) then AUTOEXEC.BAT does its standard boot sequence.

The environment variable method is better than the temporary file method. For example, if your machine crashes, the temporary file will still exist, forcing the

```
@echo off
echo Running DESQview . . .
set DVACTIVE=TRUE
c:
cd \system\dv
break off
dv %1 %2 %3 %4 %5
set DVACTIVE=
cd \
```

Figure 3-7 A second batch file to start *DESQview*

wrong part of AUTOEXEC.BAT to execute. That doesn't happen with the environment variable, since it's erased after a crash.

In either method, the temporary file or environment variable is removed after DESQview runs. In Figure 3-6, the temporary file is deleted after DESQview quits; in Figure 3-7, the DVACTIVE environment variable is reset by the SET DVACTIVE= command.

A third way of testing to see if DESQview is active involves some programming. You can write a small COM program in DEBUG that tests to see if DESQview is running or not. Figure 3-8 contains a DEBUG script, DVACTIVE.SCR, which creates the DVACTIVE.COM file. You can enter this script into a text editor, then save it as DVACTIVE.SCR. Note the blank line; it's necessary after the line with the INT 21 instruction. To create DVACTIVE.COM, use the following DOS command:

```
C:\> DEBUG < DVACTIVE.SCR
```

```
A
MOV     AX,1022
MOV     BX,0000
INT     15
MOV     AL,BL
MOV     AH,4C
INT     21

RCX
E
N DVACTIVE.COM
W
Q
```

Figure 3-8 The DVACTIVE.SCR script file for DEBUG

The commands held in DVACTIVE.SCR are fed into DEBUG, which creates the DVACTIVE.COM program file. This file can then be used in AUTOEXEC.BAT — or in any batch file — to see if *DESQview* is currently running.

DVACTIVE.COM works by returning an ERRORLEVEL value if *DESQview* is running. An ERRORLEVEL of zero means that *DESQview* isn't running. Any other value indicates *DESQview* is on. (The actual value returned is *DESQview's* major release number.) To make this work in AUTOEXEC.BAT, you would use the following:

```
C:\UTIL\DVACTIVE
IF NOT ERRORLEVEL 1 GOTO BOOT
```

It's assumed DVACTIVE.COM is in the C:\UTIL directory above. After it runs, an ERRORLEVEL of 1 is returned when *DESQview* is active. The NOT ERRORLEVEL 1 command is true when *DESQview* isn't active, and therefore batch file execution branches to the BOOT label. Otherwise *DESQview* is on and the instructions following the IF-NOT-ERRORLEVEL test are executed.

Remember, there are two reasons you would want to specify /P for a DOS window in *DESQview*: to prevent EXIT from closing the window, and to allow a custom startup file — part of AUTOEXEC.BAT — to be executed. If that's not your situation, then there's no reason to mess with the /P and no reason to modify AUTOEXEC.BAT.

> ***Tip:*** To close the DOS window you need to activate the DESQ menu and manually close it. The key sequence is Alt (the DESQ key), C, and Y for "yes" to close the window.

4

All about AUTOEXEC.BAT

AUTOEXEC.BAT is the last startup file that configures your system. Like CONFIG.SYS, it's a text file you have direct control over. Unlike CONFIG.SYS, AUTOEXEC.BAT is about configuring the DOS prompt and running special startup programs. (Although some system configuration is done in AUTOEXEC.BAT, it's not as direct as in CONFIG.SYS.)

This chapter takes the same approach with AUTOEXEC.BAT as Chapter 2 did with CONFIG.SYS; here you'll learn why things work the way they do in AUTOEXEC.BAT, what can be done, and what to avoid. Because AUTOEXEC.BAT lacks a set list of commands, the job here isn't as clear cut. So instead of listing recommended dosages, this chapter concentrates on helping you create the best startup file to configure your own PC.

How COMMAND.COM Runs AUTOEXEC.BAT

AUTOEXEC.BAT isn't part of the DOS startup sequence. Actually, DOS is loaded and stops starting itself after it executes CONFIG.SYS. Beyond that, a series of accidents causes COMMAND.COM and then AUTOEXEC.BAT to be executed.

The previous chapter discussed how COMMAND.COM starts. In summary, there are two methods: either by specifying COMMAND.COM using the SHELL configuration command in CONFIG.SYS, or by not doing anything, in which case DOS's SysInit process will hunt down COMMAND.COM in your root directory. COMMAND.COM takes a similar approach when dealing with AUTOEXEC.BAT.

If COMMAND.COM starts by accident (meaning you didn't use SHELL in CONFIG.SYS), then it looks for and executes a batch file named AUTOEXEC.BAT in the root directory of the startup disk. If you start COMMAND.COM using the SHELL command and specify the /P switch, then AUTOEXEC.BAT will again be executed. But note that if the /P switch is missing, AUTOEXEC.BAT will be skipped.

> ***Tip:*** Anytime you run COMMAND.COM and specify the /P switch, a batch file named AUTOEXEC.BAT—which must be in the root directory of the boot drive—will be run.

AUTOEXEC.BAT is embedded in COMMAND.COM's psyche, which means there's really no way to change it, to call it by another name, or to move AUTOEXEC.BAT to another location. You can see this by using DEBUG to peer into COMMAND.COM and hunt down AUTOEXEC.BAT. Enter DEBUG and then use the S, Search, command to scan for the text "AUTOEXEC" as follows:

```
C:\> DEBUG C:\COMMAND.COM
-S100 FFFF "AUTOEXEC"
```

Above, it's assumed COMMAND.COM is in the root directory. If not, then specify the proper path after DEBUG. Also, note that AUTOEXEC must be typed in uppercase, otherwise DEBUG cannot find the text. After entering the above command, you'll see a segment and offset value, something like this:

```
xxxx:20C0
```

(If you see more than one line, use the first line.) The first four digits differ from system to system. The last four hex digits give you the offset of AUTOEXEC.BAT (the text) in COMMAND.COM. To view that location, use the last four digits you see on your screen and use them after the D command. For example:

```
-D 20C0
```

The value 20C0 is used above. The D command will display (or "dump") 128 bytes of information at that location, which allows you to see AUTOEXEC.BAT as stored inside COMMAND.COM. What you see on your screen will look similar to Figure 4-1.

After COMMAND.COM is loaded and its transient and resident parts split up and are ready to go, it looks for AUTOEXEC.BAT. If it can't find it, COMMAND.COM asks you to enter the current date and time. Then the DOS copyright notice is

```
1F7D:1E70  41 55 54 4F 45 58 45 43-2E 42 41 54 00 0D 00 3A   AUTOEXEC.BAT...:
1F7D:1E80  5C 4B 41 55 54 4F 45 58-45 2E 42 41 54 00 0D FF   \KAUTOEXE.BAT...
1F7D:1E90  00 00 00 00 FF 4F 00 00-B9 2D 00 00 00 50 41 54   .....O...-...PAT
1F7D:1EA0  48 3D 00 43 4F 4D 53 50-45 43 3D 5C 43 4F 4D 4D   H=.COMSPEC=\COMM
1F7D:1EB0  41 4E 44 2E 43 4F 4D 00-3D 61 7A 20 43 41 00 00   AND.COM.=az CA..
1F7D:1EC0  00 00 00 00 00 00 00 00-00 00 FB 4F 00 00 00 00   ...........O....
1F7D:1ED0  00 00 00 00 00 00 D9 1E-00 00 02 EF 1E EF 1E 07   ................
1F7D:1EE0  F8 1E 04 1F 10 1F 1C 1F-35 1F 41 1F 4F 1F 00 01   ........5.A.O...
```

Figure 4-1 AUTOEXEC.BAT is nestled inside COMMAND.COM

```
Current date is Sun 04-05-1992
Enter new date (mm-dd-yy):
Current time is  4:41:32.11p
Enter new time:


Microsoft(R) MS-DOS(R) Version 6
           (C)Copyright Microsoft Corp 1981-1993.


C:\>
```

Figure 4-2 DOS's boring startup screen without AUTOEXEC.BAT

displayed, along with the default system prompt. An example of this startup is depicted in Figure 4-2.

> *Note:* You're only prompted for the date and time when COMMAND.COM first starts. If you run COMMAND.COM again, as a program for example, then you'll see only the copyright notice.

What is life without AUTOEXEC.BAT? In fact, entering the date and time is an anachronism from way back before all PCs came with internal clocks. And the vanilla DOS prompt—sheesh! This just begs for an AUTOEXEC.BAT file to be written. First, you want to get rid of the gauche date and time prompts. Second, something must be done about the DOS prompt. And finally, you need to take advantage of the power AUTOEXEC.BAT gives you to run DOS commands to further configure your system, as well as to run startup programs.

Things to Do in an AUTOEXEC.BAT File

AUTOEXEC.BAT is a batch file. That's a combination text file and DOS program file. Batch files contain commands as you would type them at the DOS prompt, basically lines of text. They're all stuffed one after the other into a text file, which DOS reads a line at a time as if you were typing each of the commands at the prompt. In short, that's how a batch file works.

The idea behind AUTOEXEC.BAT is to take care of all those commands you would normally type each time your start your computer. For example, suppose you have no AUTOEXEC.BAT file and your PC starts every day out looking like Figure 4-2. If so, you may type in the following three things:

1. The PROMPT command, to create a more interesting system prompt.

2. The PATH command, allowing DOS to hunt down programs anywhere in your system.

3. The name of the first program you run during the day: Windows, WordPerfect, *1-2-3*, and so on.

These three items form the basis of any AUTOEXEC.BAT program. Other items include configuring the system, starting the network, running memory resident or

"TSR" programs, and so on. The longer you use your computer, the longer your AUTOEXEC.BAT file will be.

As an example of a general-purpose AUTOEXEC.BAT file, consider the one created by the DOS 5.0 SETUP program, as shown in Figure 4-3. Each of its four lines does the following:

1. The @ECHO OFF command turns off the batch file echo. This means the batch file will run without displaying information on the screen (save for those commands that send information to the screen on purpose). This is the traditional way all batch files start.

2. The PROMPT command creates the standard system prompt: the drive letter, colon, and the current path (subdirectory). This is followed by a greater-than sign:

    C:\>

3. The PATH command tells DOS where to look for program files. Since DOS's SETUP program doesn't know how you've organized your hard drive, it simply puts DOS's own subdirectory "on the path."

4. The SET command creates the TEMP, temporary, environment variable. This tells DOS where to store its temporary files. (Other programs, such as Windows, will also use the TEMP variable.)

The DOS example is basic—stupid almost. It's better than nothing—a step in the right direction—but not as good as things could be for your own system. The following sections elaborate on things you can do in AUTOEXEC.BAT. You don't need to do all of them, and there are definitely more things that can be accomplished in AUTOEXEC.BAT than can be listed in a single chapter.

- Create a beautiful PROMPT
- Set a proper PATH
- Create environment variables
- Configure the system
- Set the date and time
- Load startup programs
- Start your first program or menu system

```
@ECHO OFF
PROMPT $p$g
PATH C:\DOS
SET TEMP=C:\DOS
```

Figure 4-3 The manufacturer's suggested AUTOEXEC.BAT file

These things can be done in any order, although the last item (starting your first program or a menu system) should obviously be last all the time. My personal preference is to do things in the above order, though some Master DOS Guru probably has a million reasons not to; basically do what makes you happy. Remember that everything starts with the first command as follows:

```
@ECHO OFF
```

After that, you're on your own.

Create a Beautiful PROMPT

Nothing is more boring than having "C>" as the DOS prompt. Ugh. DOS comes with a PROMPT command that has 14 optional subcommands, or *meta-characters*, you can use to create a custom prompt. These are all listed in Table 4-1. They can be entered using either upper- or lowercase letters.

In addition to the meta-character commands, you can specify any text as part of the DOS prompt (except for the characters $, |, > and <, which are supplied via the meta-characters). The prompt created by the PROMPT command is stored in DOS's environment. From there, DOS reads the special PROMPT command and customizes its prompt on the screen. (More information about the environment is presented later in this chapter.)

Table 4-1 The PROMPT Command's Meta-Characters

Meta-Character	Displays
$$	A dollar sign ($)
$_	Carriage return/line feed (new line)
$a	Null character (undocumented)
$b	A pipe character (|)
$d	The current date (Sun 04-05-1992)
$e	Escape character (used with ANSI commands)
$g	Greater-than character (>)
$h	Backspace and erase
$l	Less-than character (<)
$n	Current drive letter (no colon)
$p	Current directory
$q	Equal sign character (=)
$t	The current time (10:14:52.66)
$v	DOS name and version number (MS-DOS version 5.00)

The object to all this is to be brief and informative, which is why the following is the most popular PROMPT command to stick into an AUTOEXEC.BAT file:

```
PROMPT $P$G
```

This creates a prompt that contains the current drive, directory, plus the traditional greater-than symbol. Here's a nifty variation on this:

```
PROMPT $P$G $A
```

This command sticks a space after the greater-than character. The $A, an undocumented meta-character that represents a "null," holds the space to the end of the PROMPT. This is a minor difference, but I feel it cleans up the display a bit.

Variations on the standard prompt include adding the date and time ($D and $T), which are usually put on a line by themselves. The $_ meta-character produces a new line in the display. And if you want to get fancy, you can use the $E command (the Escape character) in conjunction with the ANSI.SYS driver to create all sorts of interesting and complex prompts. Needless to say, this leads away a bit from being practical.

> **Tip:** If you start getting creative with the DOS prompt, consider writing a special batch file that just sets the prompt. That batch file would contain the single PROMPT command that builds the DOS prompt for your system. You can then change the prompt by entering the name of the batch file, or by calling it from another batch file like AUTOEXEC.BAT:
>
> ```
> CALL SETPROM
> ```
>
> This names the batch file SETPROM.BAT. Remember, you cannot name the batch file PROMPT.BAT; since PROMPT is an internal DOS command, it will always be executed first over a program named PROMPT on disk.

If you work with several different systems you can create different prompts for each of them. One approach is to use the system's network name in addition to the standard PG prompt:

```
PROMPT Mail Server$_$P$G $A
```

This command creates the following prompt:

```
Mail Server
C:\>
```

Each system would have an individual prompt this way, which helps remind you which computer you're using. (It works better than the tacky punch-letter tape used at my old office.) This idea can also be applied to one computer if you use it in several different "modes." For example, you could have one prompt set for programming, another for your database, and so on. Small batch files can be written to change the prompt, or the new PROMPT commands can be embedded in other batch files that configure your system.

Here's a popular variation on the standard DOS prompt:

All about AUTOEXEC.BAT 69

```
PROMPT ($P) $A
```

This command displays the current drive and path inside parentheses (or you can use square brackets, angle brackets, or curly braces):

```
(C:\)
```

This prompt was actually the standard prompt for the old OS/2 1.0, way back in 1987. I use this prompt on my Windows system in a DOS window. On my *DESQview* system I use the following prompt:

```
PROMPT [$P] $A
```

This creates a similar prompt, but different enough to distinguish between the two systems. (Okay, they're really similar. But if I needed them any more different, I could make them so. You get the idea.)

Set a Proper PATH

Next to creating an interesting DOS prompt, the most common thing to do in an AUTOEXEC.BAT file is to build a proper search path. The search path is a list of subdirectories in which DOS will look for programs. This is created by the PATH command and, like PROMPT, it's placed into DOS's environment storage.

> ***Tip:*** The APPEND command works similarly to the PATH command, though it hunts down data files instead of programs. APPEND can be set in AUTO-EXEC.BAT just like the PATH command, however I strongly recommend against using it. APPEND has some deadly side effects that make it risky—especially to those beginners it purportedly tries to help the most.

When you type a command at the prompt, DOS looks for it in three places. First, the internal command list stored in the transient area of COMMAND.COM is scanned. If a match isn't found, then DOS starts hunting for a file with the command's name plus either a COM, EXE or BAT extension. First the current directory is scanned for such a program, then all the directories listed on the path are scanned. Only after all the possible locations have been searched does DOS return with a "Bad command or file name" error. Figure 4-4 illustrates how this works using the common computer metaphor, the flow chart.

Obviously, putting directories on the path means that you don't have to do a lot of typing at the DOS prompt; DOS can find the programs you want to run from anywhere on your disk system, thanks to the PATH command. What a time-saver! But what isn't obvious is that the longer the path, the more inefficient your system becomes.

The more directories you have on the search path, the longer it takes DOS to hunt for files. In fact, many people feel discouraged over the 124-character limit on items in the path. Bah! Why litter the search path with directories that contain only one program you may run occasionally? It's impractical. My advice is to put four or fewer subdirectories on the path. For example:

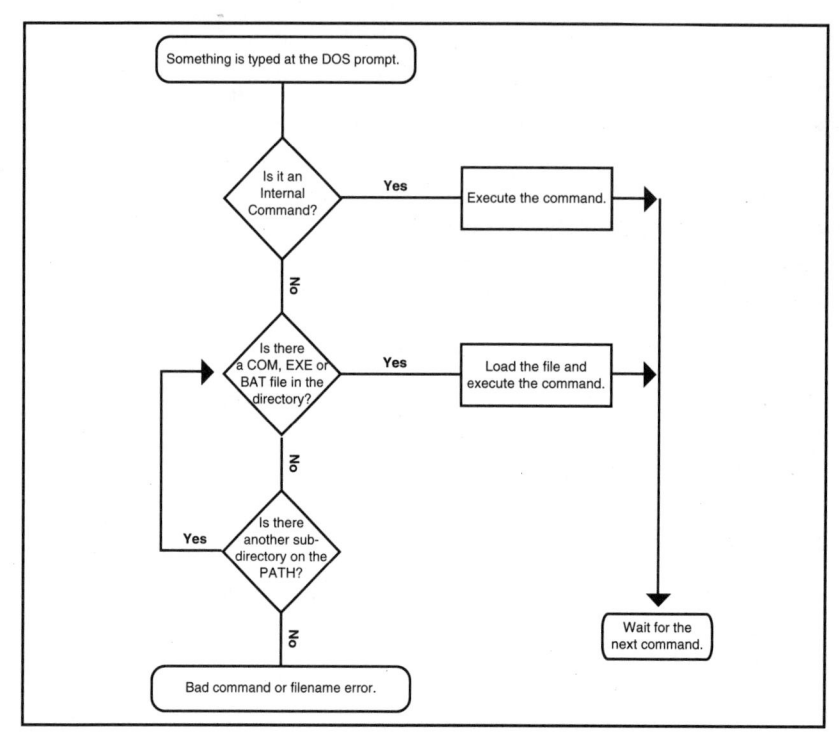

Figure 4-4 How DOS executes a command or program

```
PATH=C:\DOS;C:\UTIL;C:\BATCH
```

Then, the PATH command places three subdirectories on the path. Each of those subdirectories contains lots of commonly used programs. Especially note the batch subdirectory, which contains batch files that run various other programs in other directories on the system. Of course, what you stick into your path will vary. Just don't be tempted to place *all* your popular program directories on the path!

✏️ *Note:* This issue causes more heated debates than anything. As a curious aside, the DOS "beta" testers demanded a longer search path as a new feature more than anything. This means there are arguments going both ways as to whether a long path is justified or not.

While a shorter path is better, and I can insist upon it all day, there are a few legitimate reasons for having more than three or four directories on the path. Some programs just won't run if their directory isn't listed. Also, some people use their computers in a variety of different "modes." They need a long path to satisfy the different ways they use the PC.

A solution to the long path dilemma is to juggle several different paths using a single PATH statement and several similar environment variables. This keeps the path statement short and gives you the ability to access many subdirectories (although not all at once).

For example, suppose you need different paths for the different ways you use your PC. You create a unique path for each of those ways using the SET command in AUTOEXEC.BAT. SET will create several pathlike environment variables, one for each of your computer's modes:

```
SET APATH=C:\DOS;C:\WIN
SET BPATH=C:\DOS;C:\UTIL;C:\WP
SET CPATH=C:\DOS;C:\TURBOC;C:\TD
```

Note how each variable is set up like a PATH variable: subdirectories are listed with the drive letters and separated by semicolons. To switch between these paths, you can use something like the following in a batch file:

```
SET PATH=%APATH%
```

This sets or resets the path to the predefined environment variable (and it only works in a batch file, not at the DOS prompt). It also allows you to keep several directories on the path without creating an overly long PATH command.

Another way to modify the path is to create a temporary variable, append the path, then restore everything. This can handily be done in a batch file that runs a program (or sets a mode) for your computer.

For example, Windows programs are big on the path. Consider the following batch file:

```
@ECHO OFF
REM Run MS Windows
SET OLDPATH=%PATH%
PATH=%PATH%;C:\WINDOWS;C:\EXCEL
WIN
PATH=%OLDPATH%
SET OLDPATH=
```

This allows the batch file to run Windows. It also saves the old path in the OLDPATH variable. Then the path is appended with the C:\WINDOWS and C:\EXCEL directories—which is what Windows (and *Excel*) wants. Windows is run, then afterwards the path is restored. Note how the OLDPATH variable is removed on the last line to free up environment space.

▶ *Tip:* You don't have to mess with an "OLDPATH" variable if you create a copycat PATH variable in AUTOEXEC.BAT:

```
SET PATH=C:\DOS;C:\UTIL;C:\BATCH
SET PATHCOPY=%PATH%
```

With the PATHCOPY or similar variable you can always restore your original path in a batch file—no matter how tweaked it gets. Use the following:

```
PATH=%PATHCOPY%
```

Remember that you can only use this syntax (with the percent signs) inside a batch file. At the DOS prompt you need to type everything out.

Create Environment Variables

DOS uses the environment as a special storage place for information. Only two values are kept there when the computer first starts: the PATH and the COMSPEC variable. The PATH is originally set to nothing and COMSPEC is set to the location of COMMAND.COM, either in the root directory or wherever else you've placed it, providing you've used the SHELL command properly. (Refer to Chapter 3, "All about COMMAND.COM.")

If you look back to Figure 4-1, you can see DOS's two basic environment variables as they sit inside COMMAND.COM (before deployment). PATH is reset to zero (the null byte, 00), and the COMSPEC is presupposing \COMMAND.COM is where it's supposed to be.

The only other variable users traditionally stuck into the environment in AUTOEXEC.BAT was PROMPT. (PROMPT is an environment variable like PATH and COMSPEC). However, over the past few years more and more applications use their own environment variables, making AUTOEXEC.BAT an ideal place to set them. The most popular new addition is the TEMP variable.

The TEMP variable specifies a location for storing temporary files. It began life with Windows (which for some reason still sticks temporary files all over the hard drive, regardless), and is now used by DOS and several other programs. I recommend setting this variable in AUTOEXEC.BAT, pointing it to your TEMP or JUNK directory. Better still, set TEMP equal to a large RAM drive (512K or more). This should improve some operations a tad.

Beyond the programs that require or suggest environment variables, you can stick in a few of your own. For example, I use the environment to hold variables that tell me whether or not I'm using *DESQview*, Windows, or logged into my network. The environment on my system, as viewed by the SET command, is shown in Figure 4-5.

```
COMSPEC=C:\DOS\COMMAND.COM
DVACTIVE=TRUE
NETWORK=FALSE
PROMPT=[$P] $A
TEMP=L:
PATH=I:\;J:\;K:\
APATH=I:\;J:\;K:\
UTIL=J:\
PCTOOLS=F:\PCTOOLS
```

Figure 4-5 A busy environment, as set up by AUTOEXEC.BAT

You can stick anything into the environment using the SET command. The format is SET followed by the variable and its data. The variable and data are separated by an equal sign *and no spaces*. It's important not to buffer the equal sign with spaces, otherwise they become part of the variable and its data.

```
SET NETWORK=TRUE
```

In this example, the SET command sets the variable NETWORK to the value TRUE. DOS will stick that string into the environment verbatim. The only change that's made is that the variable name itself will be converted to uppercase.

To examine a variable's contents in a batch file, the following form is used:

```
IF %VARIABLE%!==contents! . . .
```

The variable name is surrounded by percent signs. What you're comparing it with is listed on the other side of the double equal signs. To avoid a syntax error (in case the variable isn't equal to anything), both the variable and its contents end with an exclamation point. A popular alternative is to enclose both in quotes, such as:

```
IF "%VARIABLE%"=="contents" . . .
```

When DOS sees a variable surrounded by percentage signs in a batch file, it *expands* it out to equal its contents. For example:

```
ECHO Network status is %NETWORK%
```

Here, the batch file displays the network status by echoing the contents of the variable NETWORK:

```
Network status is TRUE
```

If network doesn't equal anything, then nothing is displayed. Keep in mind that this double percent sign trick only works in a batch file; you cannot expand environment variables at the DOS prompt (although you can use the SET command by itself to view them all).

> ***Tip:*** Batch files "eat" percent signs. They use them to determine if a word is an environment variable and, if so, will expand the variable. Because of this, you need to be careful when using percent signs in a batch file. For example, if a filename starts with or contains a percent sign, you need to specify it twice in a batch file: ROYALTY%.XLS should be specified as ROYALTY%%.XLS in a batch file.

You can remove variables from the environment using the SET command followed by the variable name, an equal sign, and nothing:

```
SET NETWORK=
```

This destroys the environment variable in memory, and makes that memory available to other environment variables.

The only sticky point about using variables is that the environment is a finite area. While DOS gives you 256 bytes for the environment (only 160 with versions prior to DOS 5.0), you may want more. This is done using the SHELL configuration command in CONFIG.SYS. There you can specify COMMAND.COM's /E switch to set the environment. For example:

```
SHELL=C:\COMMAND.COM C:\ /E:512 /P
```

where an environment size of 512 bytes is specified. Any value from 160 to 32,767 bytes can be specified. DOS rounds the value to the nearest multiple of 16. (If you need more information on this format, see Chapter 3, "All about COMMAND.COM.")

Make sure you have a good reason to create a larger environment. Extra bytes mean less conventional memory for DOS. Also, because duplicate copies of the environment are created between programs, memory disappears quickly when the environment is too big.

Configure the System

One of the more traditional tasks done in AUTOEXEC.BAT is to take care of any extra system configuration that hasn't been done in CONFIG.SYS. This type of configuration falls into three categories: configuring the screen, printer, and serial ports.

Most of the time, these tasks are handled by the software you use. For example, *WordPerfect* can print to a serial printer without any configuration at the DOS prompt. In fact, most serial and printer port configuration is best done in applications that deal with those ports, for example, communications software programs the serial port much more efficiently than DOS does.

Beyond the hardware configuration, you can help set up your disk system. The following tasks are ideal to put into AUTOEXEC.BAT.

Scan for viruses. Along with the many diseases of the nineties comes computer viruses—much more of a real threat than they were just a few years back. Some virus scanning software works in CONFIG.SYS, but most work in AUTO-EXEC.BAT. Running a virus scanner—or any other type of security software—every time you start your system is a good idea. DOS 6.0's MSAV is a good example.

Set up your RAM drives. RAM drives are created in CONFIG.SYS and are ready for action by the time AUTOEXEC.BAT is run. If you're putting any programs on your RAM drives, now is the time to copy them there. The same holds for data files, batch files, or anything else you use your RAM drive for. DOS 6.0's MSAV is a good example.

On my computer, I have three RAM drives. The first one holds batch files (32K), the second holds utilities (1024K), and the third I use to hold two dozen-or-so popular DOS commands (740K). (The whole DOS regatta of files takes up some three megabytes—too much to waste RAM on.) I copy the necessary files to the proper RAM drives in AUTOEXEC.BAT, then I put the three RAM drive letters on the path (see the PATH line in the environment, Figure 4-5). The end result? A very, very fast system, with near instantaneous response for those programs on the RAM drives.

You can set up other drives as well, prompting to mount external drives, copying files from network drives, and so on.

General file management. If you're not shuffling files to a RAM drive, consider other file management chores you may want to perform in AUTOEXEC.BAT: globally deleting all your old BAK or "junk" files, copying files to special directories, creating backups of important files at the start of the day or performing a mini-backup, running a disk optimization program, updating log files, and so on.

Set the Date and Time?

Without AUTOEXEC.BAT, DOS prompts you for the date and time when you first start your computer. Because of this, it used to be the fashion to include the DATE and TIME commands in your AUTOEXEC.BAT file. This seemed to be suggested, even though 95 percent of the computers sold since 1988 have come with their own clocks, eliminating the need for those two drain-clogging commands at startup.

If you have an older computer, then you may still need the DATE and TIME prompts to set DOS's date and time. I recommend this, since all the files saved to disk will reflect the proper dates and times, which makes managing them easier. (Without setting the date and time, it will look like all the work you've ever done was on Tuesday, January 1, 1980, in the wee hours of the morning!)

The computers that started sporting the new internal clocks, making setting the date and time redundant, came with a new annoyance: they start up by setting the NumLock switch to on. This means the numeric keypad behaves like a numeric keypad—not the arrow keys most users expect. If you want the arrow keys, you're required to punch the NumLock key each time you start your PC. Or, if you want to take advantage of AUTOEXEC.BAT, you can create the NUMOFF.COM program using DEBUG. (Detailed information about using DEBUG is provided starting in Chapter 7.)

▶ ***Tip:*** If you have MS-DOS 6.0 or a later version, you can switch off the numeric keypad using the NUMLOCK=OFF command in CONFIG.SYS. The NUMOFF.COM utility, created with the instructions below, still does the job — and is necessary for earlier versions of DOS.

Start DEBUG then enter the *assembly* mode with the A command:

```
C:\> DEBUG
A
xxxx:0100
```

You'll see a memory address displayed, similar to that above. The first four digits vary from system to system, but the second four digits will always be 0100 when the A command is given by itself. Type in the following five lines as listed below, pressing Enter after each one:

```
MOV AX,0000
MOV DS,AX
MOV BX,0417
MOV BYTE PTR [BX],80
INT 20
```

After the file instruction, INT 20, press Enter on a line by itself. Then enter the following instructions at DEBUG's hyphen prompt:

```
-N NUMOFF.COM
-RCX
CX 0000
:D
```

The RCX command will prompt you to enter a value. Type the letter D, as shown above. (Yup, D is a "value" in hexadecimal, which is DEBUG's chosen counting base.)

The final command you need to enter is W, which writes the program you've just created to disk:

```
-W
Writing 0000D bytes
```

Type Q and press Enter to exit DEBUG.

You can test NUMOFF by pressing the NumLock key on your keyboard. With the NumLock light on, type NUMLOCK at the DOS prompt. The light will go off and, lo, the numeric keypad is a cursor keypad.

Save or copy NUMOFF.COM to your utility subdirectory. Then put the NUMOFF command into your AUTOEXEC.BAT file. This will automatically turn off the NumLock every time when your PC starts.

Load Startup Programs

So many people concentrate on system configuration in AUTOEXEC.BAT that they forget it's the ideal place to run startup programs. These include memory resident programs, or TSRs, which will modify your system, run startup, calendar, or reminder programs, and so on.

One type of startup program is the one that may start your network. On some systems this may include running several programs (or CALLing a STARTNET.BAT or similar batch file). The programs load your PC's networking software, place you on the network or log you into the file server, and then make network driver and printer connections.

Note: If your network startup includes running the SHARE program, refer to the TIP about SHARE in Chapter 2.

A great example of another type of startup program is the DOSKEY keyboard enhancer program included with DOS 5. AUTOEXEC.BAT is a great place to set that up:

```
DOSKEY /INSERT
```

Above, the DOSKEY program is loaded into memory. Command line editing is now possible in the "insert" mode. This beats the old function key command line editing, plus it gives you the ability to recall previously typed commands by pressing the up arrow key. (Other things DOSKEY can do are elaborated on in Chapter 6.)

Other startup programs—to-do lists, memory resident programs, pop-up calculators, and any non-CONFIG.SYS device drivers—can be scattered through AUTOEXEC.BAT as necessary. There are few rules about the order for these startup programs. Some, such as Borland's *SideKick*, insist that they be loaded last (toward the bottom of AUTOEXEC.BAT).

As a suggestion, it's a good idea to load these programs after using the PATH command. Without a search path you would have to specify the full pathname to each program file. Setting a path cuts down on your typing.

Calling batch files from AUTOEXEC.BAT. Some startup files can be other batch files that are called from AUTOEXEC.BAT. A good example is the command to start your network. If that batch file were called STARTNET.BAT, then it could be called from AUTOEXEC.BAT as follows:

```
CALL STARTNET.BAT
```

This keeps the commands that start the network separate from AUTOEXEC.BAT, cutting down on its size and making updating the file easier. In addition to starting the network, you might also consider starting other types of configuration commands from a separate batch file, for example, the many commands necessary to set up a multimedia PC.

Using the ASK command. A common tactic to take when loading quite a few memory resident programs or a network is to ask users whether or not they want certain items started. This allows you to customize your system as it starts while still keeping all the commands in AUTOEXEC.BAT. For example:

```
ASK Start network (Y/N)?
IF ERRORLEVEL 1 GOTO RESUME
CALL C:\LANTASTI\STARTNET.BAT
:RESUME
```

The ASK command displays a question and waits for a Y or N key press. If N is pressed, an ERRORLEVEL of 1 is returned; Y produces an ERRORLEVEL of zero. The IF command evaluates what was pressed, and if N was pressed, then the line that starts the network is skipped. A similar approach can be taken for memory resident programs as well as batch files that configure the system in some way. (Creating the ASK program in DEBUG is covered in Chapter 18.)

Using the Choice command. The Choice command is a new batch file command introduced with DOS 6.0. Where ASK is more specific, Choice gives you a, well, choice. For example:

```
CHOICE /C:YN Start Network
IF ERRORLEVEL 2 GOTO RESUME
CALL C:\LANTASTI\STARTNET.BAT
:RESUME
```

This is very similar to the ASK command you can (and will) create using Debug. The difference is that Choice displays its own Y/N prompt and it also produces ERRORLEVEL values starting with one, not zero. The above snippet of batch file code produces the following output:

```
Start network[Y/N]?
```

The Choice command also has timeout values. For example:

```
CHOICE /C:YN /T:N,10 Start Network
```

The /T switch is followed by the default choice and the number of seconds of indecision you're allowed. After 10 seconds N would be the key generated for the Choice command.

Loading memory resident programs "high." DOS 5.0 officially ushered in the era of memory management under DOS. Using the LOADHIGH command, you can load memory resident programs in upper memory, making more conventional memory available to your programs. This is a boon, especially if you have a lot of memory resident software.

Unlike CONFIG.SYS with its DEVICEHIGH command, the LOADHIGH command has no other options. Just stick LOADHIGH, or its abbreviated form LH, in front of a memory resident program to load it high. Note that this can only be done if you've started DOS's memory management abilities in CONFIG.SYS. And if you're using a third-party memory manager, then you'll be using its own version of the LOADHIGH command.

Start Your First Program or Menu System

The last thing AUTOEXEC.BAT should do is the first thing you do when you start your computer. For example, suppose you've created this marvelously intricate AUTOEXEC.BAT file. Your system really hums. Then every day, after AUTOEXEC.BAT runs, you type WP at the first DOS prompt and press Enter. Ding-ding-ding! What's wrong with this picture?

If you always start your computer with the same command, then why not stick it at the end of your AUTOEXEC.BAT file? If you run Windows, then have WIN as the last item in AUTOEXEC.BAT. If you dive right into *WordPerfect*, then end AUTOEXEC.BAT with WP. Or if you start your day with a menu program, put the MENU command right there in AUTOEXEC.BAT. This is the perfect ending to the smooth start of your computer.

Extra Fun with SUBST

The SUBST command takes a subdirectory and converts it into a disk drive. The subdirectory then becomes the root directory of the new drive. Accessing the drive is then the same as logging into that subdirectory. Here's the format of the SUBST command:

```
SUBST d: pathname
```

The first item is an available drive letter, not currently being used by a disk drive. The second item, *pathname*, is the full pathname of the subdirectory.

To make this work, you need to have available drive letters in your system. That's done by using the LASTDRIVE configuration command in CONFIG.SYS. If you've followed the suggestion in Chapter 2, then LASTDRIVE should be set to Z, which means you have 26 drive letters available, minus any already used by floppy drives, hard drives, RAM drives, *Stacker* drives, external drives, network drives, and so on. You can only use an unassigned drive letter with SUBST.

▶ *Tip:* By using SUBST, you can replace long CD commands with shorter drive letter commands. For example:

```
CD \WP\WORD\NOVEL\WAR&PEAC
```

where the directory, after being SUBST'd with drive W, can be accessed using the following command:

```
W:
```

Here's the SUBST command to do that:

```
SUBST W: C:\WP\WORD\NOVEL\WAR&PEAC
```

A highly useful example of using SUBST is to assign drive letters to the popular subdirectories on your system. The best directories to choose are those on the path. For example, suppose your path looks like this:

```
PATH=C:\DOS;C:\UTIL;C:\BATCH
```

You have hard drives C and D, plus a RAM drive E. This gives you drive letters F through Z to use with the SUBST command (providing you have LASTDRIVE=Z in CONFIG.SYS). You can use the SUBST command as follows in AUTOEXEC.BAT:

```
SUBST F: C:\DOS
SUBST G: C:\UTIL
SUBST H: C:\BATCH
```

This assigns drive letters F through H to your three most popular subdirectories. The advantage here is that it shortens your path:

```
PATH=F:\;G:\;H:\
```

While I don't recommend it, if you want to squeeze more directories on your path, you only need to use SUBST and pack the path with drive letters.

After the SUBST operation, you'll have extra drive letters on your system and quick access to special subdirectories. These subdirectories will then become the root directories of the hard drive. Any subdirectories of these directories will be subdirectories on the new hard drive as well. Note that nothing is duplicated on your system; you've just created a new way to access files you already have.

As long as there are available drive letters, you can assign subdirectories to them using SUBST. Keep in mind that letters of the alphabet allow you to get creative. Consider the following:

```
SUBST L: C:\123
SUBST U: C:\UTIL
SUBST W: D:\WINDOWS
```

Drive L is "Lotus," drive U is for utilities, and drive W is where Windows lives. While these aren't real drives on your system, they are easy to remember.

Always keep in mind that a SUBST'd drive letter is not a real disk drive. There are some things you cannot and should not attempt with the new drive (these are covered in the section "The Major Caveats"). Also, SUBST'ing a subdirectory does not restrict your access to it; the subdirectory still exists and you can use it as you did before. SUBST just gives you a new, quicker way to access the subdirectory via a drive letter.

To disable a SUBST'd drive, you use the following format:

```
SUBST d: /D
```

The drive letter is *d:*, above. This doesn't delete anything from your disk. It only removes the drive letter reference to your subdirectory.

The Major Caveats

During my travels I've found that some disk utilities have problems with drives that are SUBST'd. When you think about this, it's logical; SUBST creates new directories where none existed before. There's some overlap involved, which may not crash a disk utility but will confuse it (for example, finding duplicate files).

Table 4-2 lists DOS commands that won't work with or shouldn't be used on SUBST'd drives. This all makes sense if you keep in mind that the drives aren't real, they're "faked." For example, you shouldn't use the LABEL command on a drive that isn't there. (Duh.)

The list of third-party utilities that can understand and deal with SUBST is growing. However, there are certain categories of programs that don't make sense on a SUBST'd drive. The biggest offenders are disk optimizers or programs that defragment your hard drive. There's no point in running such a utility on a SUBST'd drive.

Disk caches don't pose a problem with SUBST'd drives; there is no need to use them on the extra drives, however. For example, a SUBST'd drive is really a subdirectory on another drive. Instead of caching the SUBST'd drive, cache the drive that subdirectory is on. This will cache both "drives" and it cuts down on overhead, making the cache more efficient.

Table 4-2 Commands that Refuse to Work with SUBST'd Drives

ASSIGN	FORMAT
BACKUP	LABEL
CHKDSK	MIRROR
DISKCOMP	RECOVER
DISKCOPY	RESTORE
FDISK	SYS

> *Tip:* The FASTOPEN command is also a type of disk cache you don't need to use on a SUBST'd drive. Nevertheless, I don't recommend using FASTOPEN at all.

Windows is compatible with drives you've SUBST'd. However, you should not use the SUBST command in a DOS window while Windows is running. Instead, make your drive substitutions before running Windows (in AUTOEXEC.BAT, for example).

The main problem some disk utilities have with SUBST'd drives is that there are too many files for them to deal with. Using SUBST isn't all that common, so few utilities check DOS's internals to see if it's running. When they don't, they just assume you have that many extra hard drives and soon they run out of memory scanning for files or they just crash outright. The solution in that case is to notify the developer and, until a fix is ready, stop using the SUBST command or just be selective about the drives on which you run the utility.

5

DOS the Device Master

At the core of everything in a computer is input and output, or I/O. You see this all over: The BIOS is the Basic *Input/Output* System, accessing your disk drives is often referred to as "disk I/O," and using the serial ports is "serial I/O." Everything is input and output in a computer, which you probably understand by now, so I won't continue beating you over the head with it. What you may not understand is that all input and output under DOS is done via *devices*.

This chapter explains the concept of devices and how they're used for input and output. The thing most users overlook is that DOS treats all devices equally. For example, the disk drive, keyboard, printer, serial port, and just about every other basic resource in your computer are looked upon in the same manner by DOS. This can be weird, but it has many advantages.

DOS's Devices

As far as DOS is concerned, all the basic components of your computer are kept on an even par with the disk drives. Older operating systems used to "hard wire" the disk drives, printer, screen, and keyboard. Limited commands let you deal with each individually. But under DOS, you can do similar things with all of them. DOS makes this distinction because it sees everything in the computer as a *device*. So what is a device?

A device is something capable of input, output, or both. An input device is something that supplies information to the computer. An output device is one that handles the computer's output. The most obvious device here is the disk drive. When you load a file from disk, you're creating input. Files on your disk drive store the computer's output. This makes the disk an obvious input/output device. What isn't obvious is that the keyboard, screen, printer and so on — other DOS devices — all can be treated the same way as a disk drive by DOS.

The Basic Devices

There are three basic DOS devices, as shown in Table 5-1. These devices are also used as the first five file *handles* DOS assigns for its basic tasks (refer to Table 2-4). Hint: Devices are treated like disk drives as far as DOS is concerned.

The CON device has a split personality. It's both an input and output device, although the input and output are split between the two parts of your console: The screen is DOS's output device and the keyboard is the input device.

Note: You may see from Table 2-4 that CON is also the "standard error" device. This is an independent device that is always connected to the screen. The standard output CON device is what you can manipulate using the CON device name under DOS; there's no way to redirect or otherwise mess with the standard error CON device.

The PRN device is DOS's standard printer. If you have more than one printer hooked up to your system, then the first printer (LPT1) is the PRN device. In addition to that, PRN can also be redirected to a serial printer attached to a serial port on your computer. This way, all DOS's basic printing chores can be handled through the common PRN device.

The AUX device handles DOS's serial communications. This is done through the first serial (or RS-232) port, also known as COM1. Unlike the printer port, information travels both to and fro in the serial world, making AUX a totally I/O device.

PRN is the only one of the three basic devices that performs output only. This makes sense because the printer produces only output and never sends information back to DOS. If you attempt to use the printer for input, it behaves similarly to the mysterious NUL device, which is elaborated upon in the following section.

Table 5-1 Three of DOS's Basic Devices

Device Name	Description	Input?	Output?
CON	Console device, the keyboard	Yes	—
CON	Console device, the screen	—	Yes
PRN	Printer port	—	Yes
AUX	Serial port	Yes	Yes

> **Note:** While it's true the printer isn't an input device, it does talk with DOS. Information sent from the printer includes "I'm busy" and "Out of paper" messages, but lacks the type of input the other devices can provide. In the world of I/O, the printer is an O device only.

The Interesting NUL Device

A fourth basic device is DOS's NUL device, the electronic equivalent of the hereafter as far as the computer is concerned. NUL is a legitimate I/O device, capable of swallowing output and generating input, but the output is saved nowhere and the input comes from the ether as well.

NUL is nothing. It's "null," as the name implies. Sending output to the NUL device goes nowhere. Input from the NUL device consists of an immediate end-of-file marker. Before shaking your head and muttering what good is it, try the following two tests.

For the first test, you're going to create a file and save it to the NUL device. Remember, DOS treats all devices just like disk drives, so you can save a file to any device. Use the DOS EDIT program and type in a few worthless lines of text. (The MS-DOS Editor is the best program to use because it doesn't insist upon a filename when it starts, unlike EDLIN or other text editors.)

Save your text to a file on disk named NUL. Type Alt-F, S, then enter NUL in the box. Press Enter. The Editor will snap back at you with the message "File already exists, overwrite?" (See Figure 5-1.) No, there isn't a file already on disk named NUL. DOS is just telling you that NUL is an existing device. Go ahead and overwrite it; press Enter.

Exit the editor with Alt-F, X. You can use the DIR command to hunt down the file you just created, but — never mind — it's not there. The file was saved to the NUL device, which means it was sent nowhere. The operation succeeds, and the

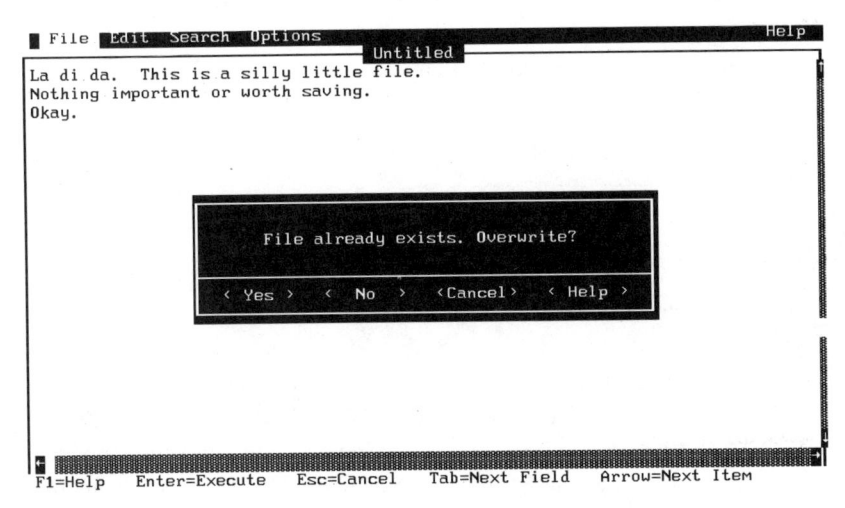

Figure 5-1 The file named NUL is saved in the MS-DOS Editor

Editor assumes the file was saved, even though the NUL device isn't capable of storing anything.

The second test is for input. Type the following at the DOS prompt:

```
C:\> TYPE NUL
```

This causes the "file" NUL to be displayed. Technically speaking, the TYPE command looks for input from the NUL device just as it would read input from a file on disk. None is generated, save for the end-of-file marker, so you don't see anything on your display. A more technical look at what's happening can be made with the following command:

```
C:\> TYPE NUL > TEST
```

This command redirects the output to the file named TEST on disk. (Output redirection is discussed in detail later in this chapter.) After the above command, you can type in DIR TEST to check out what NUL created — but don't get too excited. You'll discover that TEST has a file size of zero bytes. Although NUL did produce output, it was "nothing," and that's what was saved in the file named TEST. At this point the existential computer users start contemplating a long sea voyage.

And now for something useful. Unless you want to create zero-length files, the NUL device is quite unproductive. In fact, the DOS manual claims it can be used to "test" some things. Uh-huh. Seriously, a common problem many batch file programmers encounter is how to tell if a subdirectory already exists. You can use the NUL device to meet this end as follows:

```
IF EXIST subdir\NUL . . .
```

Here, the IF-EXIST test is used to test for the existence of the subdirectory named *subdir*. That's followed by a backslash and the filename NUL. If the directory exists, then the IF test passes. If there is no such directory, the test fails. This is the only way to conduct such a test in a batch file; testing for a filename — even the dot or *.* entries — is unreliable (especially if the directory is empty).

```
IF EXIST C:\BLORF\NUL GOTO SKIP
MD C:\BLORF
:SKIP
```

The above snippet of code could be part of an installation program. If the C:\BLORF directory exists the program skips over the MD C:\BLORF command.

▶ *Tip:* You can actually use any of DOS's device names for the IF-EXIST trick. NUL is the most common, but CON, PRN, and AUX also work as well. As a humorous aside, if you specify a device name when using some file-finding disk utilities, they'll report a CON, PRN, AUX, or NUL file in *all* of your subdirectories!

Other Devices

In addition to the three basic devices, CON, PRN, AUX, and the oddball NUL device, DOS has seven other devices (or device names) plus 26 letters of the alphabet for the potential 26 disk drives on your system. Table 5-2 lists everything.

The AUX and COM1 devices are the same, as are PRN and LPT1. Also, these are only DOS's basic devices. Your system may have more serial ports or printer ports; DOS only allows for three printers and four serial ports, so it only provides official device names for them.

All these devices are set up by DOS when it boots. Specifically, these items are called *system device drivers*, and they're loaded low into memory by IO.SYS's SysInit process. You can see how the drivers sit in memory using the MEM /DEBUG command. The following format of MEM /DEBUG shows only the DOS device drivers in memory:

```
C:\> MEM /D | FIND "System Device Driver"
```

You must type "System Device Driver" in mixed-case. (The FIND command won't locate the drivers without it.) Your output will look similar to Figure 5-2.

Table 5-2 All DOS's Devices

Device Name	Description	Input?	Output?
NUL	Null device, goes nowhere, does nothing	Yes	Yes
CON	Console device, the keyboard	Yes	—
CON	Console device, the screen	—	Yes
PRN	Printer port	—	Yes
AUX	Serial port	Yes	Yes
LPT1	First printer port (PRN)	—	Yes
LPT2	Second printer port	—	Yes
LPT3	Third printer port	—	Yes
COM1	First serial port (AUX)	Yes	Yes
COM2	Second serial port	Yes	Yes
COM3	Third serial port	Yes	Yes
COM4	Fourth serial port	Yes	Yes
A:	First floppy drive	Yes	Yes
B:	Second floppy drive	Yes	Yes
C:	First hard drive	Yes	Yes
D: - Y:	Additional drives	Yes	Yes
Z:	Last drive	Yes	Yes

```
CON            System Device Driver
AUX            System Device Driver
PRN            System Device Driver
CLOCK$         System Device Driver
A: - H:        System Device Driver
COM1           System Device Driver
LPT1           System Device Driver
LPT2           System Device Driver
LPT3           System Device Driver
COM2           System Device Driver
COM3           System Device Driver
COM4           System Device Driver
```

Figure 5-2 The basic DOS device drivers as they sit low in memory

Note the peculiar CLOCK$ device, as seen in Figure 5-2. This is the low-level device driver that controls DOS's system clock. It's *not* an I/O device. Don't use CLOCK$ as you would other I/O devices; it will lock up your system real tight. (It doesn't damage anything; it just locks up the PC.)

The drive letters listed in low memory are those available when you first start the computer. They don't include any RAM drives, external drives, CD-ROM drives, or network drives added later in CONFIG.SYS or AUTOEXEC.BAT. Note that the drives are all physical drives in your system, whereas DOS always installs COM1 through COM3 and up to LPT4 even if you don't have those devices.

> *Tip:* All device names can be followed by an optional colon. The colon is required only when citing the disk drives, when the colon helps identify the letter of the alphabet as a disk drive and not a single-character filename. And while other device names can be followed with an optional colon, that's it! If you try to use a path or filename after a device other than a disk drive, you'll get a "Too many parameters" error.

Devices and I/O Redirection

Input and output flows to and from DOS's various devices. But the CON device is the object of most of DOS's affections. CON is dubbed the "standard I/O device." Standard input is information that comes from the keyboard and standard output is information that DOS sends to the screen. All DOS commands expect their input from the keyboard and, naturally, send output to the screen. But since DOS is device oriented, it doesn't always have to be that way.

DOS treats all its devices identically. Because of this, you can send standard output — stuff that usually goes to the screen — to another device. This is called *redirected output* and it's done with the > symbol. *Redirected input* happens when input comes from a device other than the keyboard. That's made possible with the < symbol.

Another example of this device independence comes when manipulating files with the COPY command. COPY is a device command, moving information from one device to another. Normally the device is a disk drive and the information is held in a file. Yet, since all devices are treated equally, you can copy information to and from any device capable of input or output.

The following sections elaborate on the idea of devices and I/O redirection. This includes some material you may be familiar with, plus some new tricks to try.

From Here to There

The COPY command has a lot of depth. Its purpose is to move information from one place to another, usually in the form of a file. But COPY has many options and unusual parameters that make it capable of much more than many users think. Type in the following:

```
C:\> COPY CON TEST
```

This command tells DOS to copy information from one device to another. The source device is CON, the console or keyboard. The destination is a file named TEST on the current disk. COPY CON, as it's called, is used to create quick-and-dirty text files. Type in a line of text:

```
This is a test
```

Note: COPY CON reads in text a line at a time.

Each line can be no more than 127 characters in length (or the PC beeps at you).

There is no word wrap.

DOS command line editing keys are available: F1 to display the next character from the previous line, F2 to search, F3 to redisplay and edit the previous line, and F4 to search and delete.

DOSKEY's editing power is not available with COPY CON. The third-party program NDOSEDIT will work, however.

To end the "file" you're creating, type Ctrl-Z, DOS's end-of-file marker. This can also be done by pressing the F6 key under DOS:

```
^Z
```

Advanced users like COPY CON because it's fast; no need to mess with an editor. However, it lacks editing commands. Specifically, once you press Enter you cannot reedit a line of text. After the entire operation, you'll see the "1 file(s) copied" message. Since you've used the COPY command, DOS is telling you that the operation was successful. (To cancel COPY CON, or any COPY command, press Ctrl-C.)

To view the file, use the COPY command in the following format:

```
C:\> COPY TEST CON
```

Here, the source is the file TEST and the destination is the CON device, the screen in this case. This has the same effect as the TYPE command.

The COPY command can be used between any of DOS's devices. The following allows you to print a file:

```
C:\> COPY TEST PRN
```

PRN is the printer device. In the example, you're copying the file TEST to the printer.

> *Tip:* If you need to eject the page, which is required with a laser printer to see the output, then type in the following command:
>
> ```
> ECHO ^L > PRN
> ```
>
> That's the Ctrl-L character redirected to the printer device. Ctrl-L is the "eject paper" command for all printers.

The following command is the "DOS typewriter:"

```
C:\> COPY CON PRN
```

This copies information from the screen to the printer. It works similarly to those advanced electric typewriters that display one line of text at a time. You have some editing capability, but for the most part it's primitive.

> *Note:* Text appears on your printer only after you press Ctrl-Z or Ctrl-L to eject a page.

Try the following:

```
C:\> COPY CON CON
```

This copies information from the CON device (keyboard) to the CON device (screen), and it also clues you in to how this all works. You'll notice that you can type in several hundred characters, and only until Ctrl-Z is pressed will the file be copied to the display. (There is an upper limit on the number of characters you type, depending on how much free memory you have.)

One of the most ignored parts of the COPY command is its *concatenation* feature. This allows you to stick several text files together, for example:

```
C:\> COPY CHAP01+CHAP02+CHAP03 NOVEL
CHAP01
CHAP02
CHAP03
    1 file(s) copied
```

Chapters 1 through 3 are all stuck together (or "concatenated") into a final file, NOVEL. Here is the abbreviated format:

```
C:\> COPY CHAP* NOVEL
```

The CHAP* wildcard represents all of the chapter files, which are combined to create the NOVEL file. (This is one of those weird aspects of the COPY command that will blow you away if you're not careful.)

Even though concatenation only works with text files, this feature can be exploited in other ways. Consider this:

```
C:\> COPY TEST+CON TEST2
```

The CON device can't be appended to a file, but you can use this format to append information to a text file. Assuming that a file named TEST exists in the current directory and you enter this command, you'll see the following displayed:

```
TEST
CON
this stuff here is appended.^Z
    1 file(s) copied
```

First the COPY command lists both "files" you're copying: TEST, the original file, and the CON device. It then awaits your input — just like COPY CON. When you're done, press Ctrl-Z and the new file is created — and appended. To append information to the same file without creating a new file, use this format:

```
C:\> COPY TEST+CON TEST
```

Doing this also changes the file's date and time "stamp." However, another oddball format of the COPY command allows you to change a file's date and time without specifying anything else. Try this on:

```
C:\> COPY TEST+,, TEST
```

The two commas act as placeholders. The file is actually copied onto itself with only the date and time changed. To make the date and time current for all files in a directory, you must use this format:

```
C:\> FOR %A IN (*.*) DO COPY %A+,, %A
```

The FOR command must be used here. Without it, the command would look like this:

```
COPY *.*+,, *.*
```

This doesn't work (although it is one hell of a cryptic-looking command). COPY will delete the first file in the current directory then abandon the copy operation. The only way to update all the files is to use the FOR command as shown above.

Redirecting Output

Unless other instructions are received, DOS directs all its output to the standard output device, CON, or the screen. This is true for all DOS commands plus those few programs that use DOS. The secret is following the command with the symbol and the name of a device to which output will be redirected.

✎ **Note:** Most applications ignore DOS's standard output. Instead, they read the much faster BIOS or use their own output routines. So keep in mind that the following tricks only work with DOS commands and a handful of utilities that use DOS's standard output.

```
C:\> DIR > PRN
```

The highly useful command above redirects the output of the DIR command to the printer. This is the best way to get a hard copy of the files on disk — better than using Print Screen and more reliable than using Ctrl-P.

▶ **Tip:** DOS has a secret echo-to-printer command, Ctrl-P. Press Ctrl-P once, and all information on the screen is echoed to the printer. Press Ctrl-P again to turn it off. I call this trick unreliable because it always seems to take me several tries at Ctrl-P to make it work right.

After it's sent to the printer, you may need to eject the page. This is actually the only way you'll ever see the text on a laser printer. To do so, use the following:

```
C:\> ECHO ^L > PRN
```

The ECHO command displays the Ctrl-L character (not the ^ and L characters). This is the page-eject command for all popular printers, which is then sent to the printer via I/O redirection. (You can try the command without the " PRN" part if you like. You'll see the female character (♀), which is the symbol assigned to the Ctrl-L code.)

▶ **Tip:** You can print files using the TYPE *filename* > PRN command, but using COPY is more efficient.

Aside from the printer, you can also send a DOS command's output to any file on disk. Instead of a device name, follow the > with a drive letter, pathname, and filename:

```
C:\> DIR > DIRLIST.TXT
```

In the example, the output of the DIR command is saved in a file on disk, DIRLIST. This can be done with the output of any DOS command. From that point you can use a text editor to edit the file, or just save it for whatever reason.

One major drawback to this trick is that it doesn't work with batch files. Suppose CHKBAK is a batch file and you want its output. The following generates an empty file:

```
C:\> CHKBAK > DATA
```

DATA will be created, but the output of the CHKBAK batch file won't be sent there. In order to capture the batch file's output, you must run it as a *program* using COMMAND.COM. Here is the proper format:

```
C:\> COMMAND /C CHKBAK > DATA
```

DOS the Device Master   93

This works because you're actually getting the output from the COMMAND.COM program, not the CHKBAK batch file. DOS reads in command from left to right, first scanning for I/O redirection symbols. Above, it sees and runs COMMAND.COM first. When CHKBAK is run by COMMAND.COM, its output is incidentally sent to the DATA file.

Here's another batch file trick, this time using the "useless" NUL device:

```
COPY *.* A: > NUL
```

Nothing is copied to the NUL device above. Instead, any output from the COPY command that would normally be sent to the standard output device is suppressed. The output is sent to NUL device, which means you won't see anything on the screen at all. This is a handy trick to make batch files look less tacky.

When you send standard output to a file, the > symbol creates a new file if one doesn't already exist. If a file does exist, then it's obliterated and replaced by the redirected output. There's no way around this. However, if you want to append information to a file, you can use the output redirection symbol twice. For example:

```
C:\> ECHO This is the start of the log. > LOGFILE

C:\> ECHO Day one: >> LOGFILE
```

The first ECHO command is coupled with I/O redirection to create the file LOGFILE. The second ECHO command appends its text to the LOGFILE. And a handy trick here is putting the current date and time into the LOGFILE, which is covered in the section "Using the Pipe," later in this chapter.)

Saving output from a DOS program, or sending it off to the printer, is standard. Yet, sending output to a modem hooked up to a serial port is also possible. If you have a modem hooked up to your first serial port, the following two DOS commands will initialize it:

```
C:\> MODE COM1:2400,N,8,1
```

You must use COM1, not AUX, with the MODE command. Above, MODE sets up the serial port for 2400 BPS (bits per second) action, no parity, 8-bit words and one stop bit. (Slower, 1200 BPS modem users should use 1200 instead of 2400 above.) If all goes well, your serial port's status will be echoed back at you: *COM1: 2400,n,8,1,-.*

The ATZ command resets most Hayes-compatible modems. You can send that to the modem using the ECHO command. Make sure your modem is on before you enter this command (otherwise you'll get a timeout or write fault error):

```
C:\> ECHO ATZ > COM1
```

Note: This won't work under some circumstances: specifically, when other programs are controlling the modem, or sometimes when running in environments such as *DESQview* or Windows.

Figure 5-3 takes this to the ultimate extreme: It's a batch file that can be used to dial a phone number. This works only if the modem attached to COM1 is also

```
 1: @ECHO OFF
 2: IF "%1"=="" GOTO ERROR
 3: ECHO Make sure your modem is on, then
 4: PAUSE
 5: MODE COM1:2400,N,8,1  NUL
 6: ECHO Dialing %1
 7: ECHO ATDT%1   COM1
 8: ECHO Wait for the phone to ring, then
 9: PAUSE
10: ECHO AT   COM1
11: GOTO END
12: :ERROR
13: ECHO Format: DIAL number
14: :END
```

Figure 5-3 This is the DIAL.BAT phone dialing batch file

connected to your phone. You type DIAL and a phone number at the DOS prompt, then follow the instructions on the screen. After the phone rings, pick up your phone's handset, and press Enter. The batch file will hang up the modem, and you can continue with the conversation.

The line numbers in Figure 5-3 are for reference only; do not enter them when creating the batch file. The following is a technical description of what's going on.

Line 1 turns the echo off, making the batch file run "silently." Line 2 tests for an optional parameter, the phone number to dial. If it isn't found, then execution branches to the ERROR label at line 12.

Line 3 displays the message "Make sure your modem is on, then." This is followed by the PAUSE command at line 4, which completes the sentence with "Press any key to continue . . .".

Line 5 uses the MODE command to configure your serial port. The output is redirected to the NUL device, suppressing the "COM1: 2400,n,8,1,-" message that would otherwise be displayed.

Line 6 displays "Dialing" followed by the number entered, %1. Line 7 uses the ECHO command to send the Hayes modem dialing command, ATDT, followed by the phone number to the serial port. This dials the phone number.

After the number is dialed, line 8 prompts with "Wait for the phone to ring, then," and it's quickly followed by the PROMPT command's pause in line 9. After a key is pressed, line 10 sends "AT" to the modem, which hangs it up. Line 11 skips to the END label at line 14.

Line 12 is the ERROR label, branched to from line 2 when a phone number isn't entered. Line 13 displays a formatting message, instructing the user to enter a phone number after the DIAL command.

Redirecting Input

DOS's standard input device is the keyboard, the input half of the CON device. DOS expects all its input to come from the keyboard unless otherwise redirected. The symbol to redirect input is <, the less-than character. That's followed by the device from which DOS will expect input.

Redirecting input can be tricky. When you redirect input, DOS expects all input to come from that device and not the keyboard. If a character is missing, or unexpected input is requested, your system will sit and wait until it gets the proper input. If that doesn't happen, you'll have to reset. This is why redirecting input requires more care than redirecting output.

Of DOS's devices that supply input, only one is practical for redirected input: a file on disk. If you store all the keystrokes necessary in a file, you can then feed that file into a DOS program and watch it run auto"magically." Setting up the file requires an advanced knowledge of the required keystrokes.

As an example, create a file that contains a single press of the Enter key. Use COPY CON to do this:

```
C:\> COPY CON ENTER.DAT
```

After pressing Enter above, press Enter a second time — making a blank line below the command. Then press F6 to end input. This creates the file ENTER.DAT on disk.

The DATE and TIME commands display the current date or time, then ask for a new date or time to be entered. Pressing Enter completes the operation. With the ENTER.DAT file in the current directory, type the following command:

```
C:\> DATE < ENTER.DAT
```

This tells DOS to run the DATE command, but suspend input from the keyboard and read it instead from the device (file on disk) ENTER.DAT. Since ENTER.DAT contains the Enter key DATE needs, everything runs smoothly and you'll find yourself at another DOS prompt.

The most common place you'll see input redirection used is for DEBUG "scripts." These are lists of keystrokes required in DEBUG to carry out some task or create a little program. The script is nothing more than a collection of DEBUG commands stored on disk. These are fed into DEBUG using the following format:

```
DEBUG < SCRIPT.TXT
```

Magazines use this format to keep "innocent" users from meddling with DEBUG. Part Two of this book goes into intricate detail on DEBUG, which will permanently remove your fear of it. Instead of typing in script files, you'll be entering the commands directly. This may be more "dangerous," but it's what the input redirection does anyway, so you're saving a step.

To demonstrate this, you can create a text file with the exact same contents as shown in Figure 5-4. Check your work, making sure all the numbers match. (I know there's a lot to type, but using a text editor's copy and paste functions will reduce overall input time.) Save the file to disk as 2UPPER.SCR.

```
N 2UPPER.COM
E100 E8 57 00 3C 61 7C 06 3C
E108 7A 7F 02 24 5F E8 09 00
E110 3C 1A 75 EC B8 00 4C CD
E118 21 2E A2 76 01 BB 01 00
E120 B9 01 00 BA 76 01 B4 40
E128 CD 21 73 13 5B BA 94 01
E130 B9 9C FF BB 02 00 B4 40
E138 CD 21 B8 01 4C CD 21 3D
E140 00 00 2E A0 76 01 74 01
E148 C3 3C 1A 74 FB BA 77 01
E150 B4 09 CD 21 5B B8 01 4C
E158 CD 21 BB 00 00 B9 01 00
E160 BA 76 01 B4 3F CD 21 3D
E168 00 00 74 05 2E A0 76 01
E170 C3 72 B9 B0 1A C3 00 0D
E178 0A 07
E17A "Insufficient disk space"
E191 0A 0A 24 0D 0A 07
E197 "Some kind of error!"
E1AA 0D 0A
RCX
AB
W
Q
```

Figure 5-4 The contents of 2UPPER.SCR

At the DOS prompt, feed 2UPPER.SCR into DEBUG using the following command:

`C:\> DEBUG < 2UPPER.SCR`

This creates the file named 2UPPER.COM, which is a filter program you'll be using later in this chapter.

Using the Pipe

The final I/O redirection character is the pipe (|), the vertical bar character on your keyboard that really isn't much good for anything else (other than line drawing in your word processor). Unlike < and >, the pipe doesn't mess with devices at all. Instead, it's used to channel standard output into standard input. Try the following:

`C:\> ECHO. | DATE`

The ECHO. command displays a blank line — the Enter character, essentially. The output of that command is channeled to the input of the DATE command using the pipe character. This has the same effect as the DATE < ENTER.DAT command in the previous section.

✎ **Note:** Information can only start out or end up at a device. To modify information by sending it to another DOS command, you must use the pipe character.

The pipe must also be used in special circumstances when I/O redirection would normally fail. For example, if you want to scan the MEM command's output for special text, you can use the FIND command with a PIPE:

```
C:\> MEM /D | FIND "System Device Driver"
```

The output of the MEM command is fed to the FIND command. This is the only way FIND can scan a DOS command's output.

You can stack multiple commands at the DOS prompt using the pipe. But the only advantage is if each command takes the output of the first command, uses it, and produces output for the following command. The best example is the following convoluted method of producing the current date in a batch file:

```
C:\> ECHO. | DATE | FIND "Current"
```

The ECHO command produces the Enter key press for DATE. Then the output of the DATE command is fed to the FIND command, which locates and displays the line containing "Current." The output looks something like this:

```
Current date is Sat 04-12-1994.
```

The same can be done with the TIME command, but note that "Current" must be in mixed-case.

The pipe's main purpose in life is to modify the output of DOS commands through filters. DOS comes with three filters, which are each discussed in the following section.

Using Filters

A filter is a program that modifies standard input and produces standard output. By itself this is rather lame. But when a filter is used with I/O redirection, you can redirect the input or output of a DOS command or file, pump it through a filter, and get something else.

DOS comes with three filter programs, as shown in Table 5-3. If you created the 2UPPER.COM file from earlier in this chapter, then you have a fourth filter available:

Table 5-3 DOS's Filter Programs

Filter	Function
FIND	Locates text
MORE	Displays "more" message and waits for a key press after a screenful of text
SORT	Sorts information

2UPPER converts lowercase letters to uppercase — not truly impressive, but it's used here as a simple type of filter for the examples.

How Filters Work

There are two formats for using a filter in DOS:

```
program | filter
```

In this format, the filter takes the standard output of a DOS program, modifies it, then displays the modified output.

```
filter < filename
```

In this format, the filter receives its input from a text file on disk. The output is again sent through standard output.

You can add a second filter to further modify the output, or use the > symbol to redirect output to a device other than the console or to a file on disk. The basic idea here is that the filter modifies standard input and produces standard output. How you get the information there is up to you.

Internally, filters are very simple programs. The basic flow chart for a filter is shown in Figure 5-5. All filters operate this way, with only the center, "machine" part of the filter changing. For example, in the FIND filter the machine locates text; in the 2UPPER filter it converts lowercase letters to uppercase, and so on. Everything fits between two main routines: PUT and GET, which read a character from standard input and write a character back out, respectively.

The best way to see how this works is to use the simple 2UPPER filter created earlier in this chapter. 2UPPER has an advantage over DOS's filters in that its feedback is immediate. For practice, type 2UPPER at the DOS prompt:

```
C:\> 2UPPER
```

When you "run" a filter like this, it's modifying standard input and spitting standard output back at you. It's the same as typing 2UPPER < CON > CON; nothing is saved to disk, which is why filters are generally used with I/O redirection. Type in a line of text:

```
July 4th is here!
```

That's a short sentence that contains mixed-case letters plus nonalphabet characters. Press Enter and you'll see:

```
JULY 4TH IS HERE!
```

Feedback for the 2UPPER filter isn't immediate; it waits for you to press Enter, and then it spits back the modified line. Keep typing if you like, or press Ctrl-Z to end the "file" and return to the DOS prompt. Then type the following:

```
C:\> MEM | 2UPPER
```

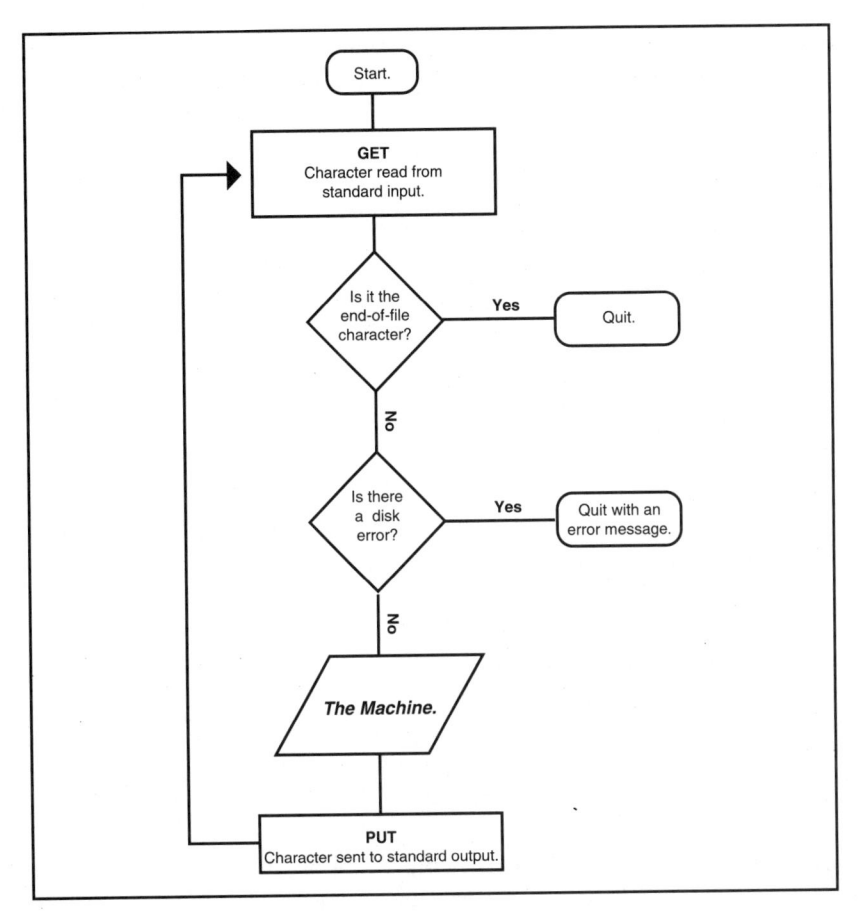

```
                    ┌─────────┐
                    │  Start. │
                    └────┬────┘
                         │
              ┌──────────▼──────────┐
    ┌────────▶│         GET         │
    │         │ Character read from │
    │         │   standard input.   │
    │         └──────────┬──────────┘
    │                    │
    │              ╱─────▼─────╲
    │            ╱   Is it the   ╲    Yes      ┌──────────┐
    │           ╱  end-of-file    ╲───────────▶│  Quit.   │
    │           ╲   character?    ╱            └──────────┘
    │            ╲               ╱
    │              ╲─────┬─────╱
    │                  No│
    │              ╱─────▼─────╲
    │            ╱   Is there    ╲   Yes    ┌──────────────┐
    │           ╱    a disk       ╲────────▶│ Quit with an │
    │           ╲    error?       ╱         │ error message│
    │            ╲               ╱          └──────────────┘
    │              ╲─────┬─────╱
    │                  No│
    │              ┌─────▼──────┐
    │             ╱              ╲
    │            ╱  The Machine.  ╲
    │            ╲                ╱
    │             ╲              ╱
    │              └─────┬──────┘
    │                    │
    │         ┌──────────▼──────────┐
    │         │         PUT         │
    └─────────┤Character sent to    │
              │  standard output.   │
              └─────────────────────┘
```

Figure 5-5 How a filter works

This time 2UPPER modifies the output of the MEM command, changing everything to uppercase. This is a more traditional use of a filter: to modify standard output. The DOS filters do a much better job of this than 2UPPER.

> **Tip:** To make playing with the filters more fun, create a text file using the following DOS command:
>
>   C:\> MEM /D > FILE.TXT
>
> This creates a long text file, FILE.TXT, which will be used in demonstrations throughout the rest of this chapter.

The MORE Filter

The MORE filter is used to pause output. After a screenful of text is displayed, MORE displays the message "-- More --" at the bottom of the screen. Press any key to see the next screen of text; press Ctrl-C to stop.

Note: Starting with DOS 5.0, MORE has gotten a lot smarter. When the ANSI.SYS device driver is loaded and the screen size is changed, MORE recognizes this and displays its message after the proper number of lines have been displayed.

How do you create a larger screen size? With ANSI.SYS loaded (from CONFIG.SYS), use the MODE command. Follow MODE with the word LINES, and equal sign, and the number of lines you want on the screen: 25, 43, or 50. For example:

```
MODE LINES=50
```

That will give you a 50-line display under DOS, providing you have ANSI.SYS loaded and your VGA display supports the 50-line mode. (Other modes are also possible, depending on the software that controls your video system.)

Normally the MORE filter is used with the piped output. For example:

```
C:\> TYPE FILE.TXT | MORE
```

The TYPE command displays the file, and the output is piped through the MORE filter. A better way to do this is:

```
C:\> MORE < FILE.TXT
```

The MORE filter needs only standard input, which is supplied as a filename above. This method is faster for displaying text files than using the pipe.

Tip: You should really only use the pipe symbol when modifying the output of a DOS command. Using the pipe symbol requires DOS to create two temporary files on disk, which adds overhead. To see these files, pipe the DIR command through the MORE (or 2UPPER) filter; the files will be displayed last and have a size of zero bytes. (They're deleted after the command has been executed.)

If you're stacking two or more filters at the DOS prompt, then the MORE filter should be the last filter you use. For example:

```
C:\> TYPE FILE.TXT | 2UPPER | MORE
```

In this example, the contents of FILE.TXT are run through the 2UPPER filter and then through the MORE filter. (Note that this command will run slowly, since 2UPPER is not the most efficient filter.) Another way to do this would be:

```
C:\> 2UPPER < FILE.TXT | MORE
```

This is a bit more efficient. Keep in mind, however, that this method only works with text files; you must use the pipe when modifying the output of a DOS command, for example, 2UPPER < DIR doesn't work because DOS would look for a file named "DIR" instead of running the DIR command.

The SORT Filter

The SORT filter is used to sort lines of text. It sorts alphabetically, forward or backward, although internally SORT sorts according to a character's ASCII value. (Refer to the ASCII table in Appendix A.) You can also sort at certain "columns" of text. Type the following:

```
C:\> SORT
```

When run by itself, SORT (like all filters) takes standard input and produces sorted standard output. Type the following list:

SUPERMAN
SPIDERMAN
BATMAN
MIGHTY MOUSE
UNDERDOG
ADAM ANT

Unlike the 2UPPER filter, SORT waits for a complete file before sorting. Press Ctrl-Z (or F6) and you'll see the sorted list.

Using the /R switch, SORT is forced to sort in reverse order. The /+ switch directs sort to order the lines of text at a certain column offset. For example, if you were sorting a list of presidents by their political parties, and that information was at column 30, you would use the following:

```
SORT /+30 < PRESIDNT.DAT
```

As with other filters, SORT can be used with I/O redirection. The pipe symbol must be used if your sorting output from a DOS command.

The FIND Filter

The FIND filter is used to locate text in a file. If found, FIND displays the line containing the matching text (the whole line). This is very useful, but it could be better: The FIND filter doesn't return any ERRORLEVEL codes, which makes it impractical for batch files.

In a way, FIND is more than a filter. You can specify a filename with FIND, and it will scan for text in that file:

```
C:\> FIND /I "SYSTEM DEVICE DRIVER" FILE.TXT
```

In this example, FIND scans for the text "system device driver" in FILE.TXT. The /I switch directs FIND to ignore the differences between upper- and lowercase letters. You could also use this format:

```
C:\> FIND /I "SYSTEM DEVICE DRIVERS" < FILE.TXT
```

Here, the contents of FILE.TXT are supplied as standard input. The advantage here is a cleaner display; when used with a filename, FIND displays ten hyphens, the filename, and the lines containing matching text. That junks up the display.

```
C:\> FIND /I "SYSTEM DEVICE DRIVERS" < FILE.TXT | SORT
```

Here, the output is piped through the sort filter. You can get even more carried away if you like:

```
C:\> FIND /I "SYSTEM DEVICE DRIVERS" < FILE.TXT | SORT
     | 2UPPER
```

Here the whole thing is piped through the SORT and then the 2UPPER filters. Yup, it all still works: standard output is always being modified.

When FIND is used with DOS commands, you must pipe the output:

```
C:\> MEM /D | FIND /I "SYSTEM DEVICE DRIVER"
```

One final quirky thing about FIND is that it cannot work with multiple files at a time. Instead, you must rely on the FOR command to feed the multiple files one at a time to the FIND filter. Here is the format:

```
FOR %F IN (filename...) DO FIND "text" %F
```

Put the names of files or wildcards between the parentheses, as well as the text to scan for between the double quotes. FIND's switches are listed in Table 5-4.

Table 5-4 The FIND Filter's Switches

Switch	Function
/C	Directs FIND to give only a numeric count of all lines containing matching text
/I	Ignores the case of the text to find (match either upper- or lowercase)
/N	Displays the relative line number in front of any matching text
/V	Shows only those lines without any matching text

6

Keyboard Control

There's no reason to struggle with a keyboard while using DOS. This involves more than just knowing how to type (though knowledge always helps). DOS is full of difficult-to-type words and convoluted steps required to complete ordinary tasks. Since the keyboard is a programmable part of the computer, many methods exist to modify its function and give you more control. This chapter discusses the most popular methods, all of which work under DOS without any extra software.

All about ASCII

To really understand how your PC's keyboard works, it helps to know a little about ASCII. Normally ASCII refers to a text file, one without any word processing formatting information or other garbage in it. But ASCII actually applies to anything that deals with characters in the PC. And the number one character-producing device is DOS's standard input — your keyboard.

ASCII is a standard means for representing characters. It stands for the American Standard Code for Information Interchange. The code assigns 128 values to numbers, letters (upper- and lowercase), special symbols, and control codes. These are all listed in Appendix A (but don't turn there just yet).

The idea behind ASCII is to create a common method of representing characters inside different computers. Internally, computers can store only values in bytes — they don't store characters at all. Because each byte can hold a value from 0 through 255, the first 128 values can be used as ASCII codes to represent characters. So when a computer stores an "A" in memory, it's really only placing the byte value 65 into memory. That value in ASCII represents the letter "A."

The benefit here is that all computers that support the ASCII standard can exchange ASCII files (text files). You can beam an ASCII file from your PC to a Macintosh and the text remains intact. Of course, this is rather limited. Modern software uses much more than ASCII codes to represent what's on the screen. So ASCII files are called "raw text," and require a lot of alteration after the "beaming" process. Still, the basic codes (as you'll soon see in Appendix A) are the same for all ASCII-compatible computers.

The Mysterious Control Characters

It's now safe to look at Appendix A, which lists all the ASCII codes and characters nice and even. You'll see the 128 characters listed in four columns of 32 characters. (Only the first part of the listing — the first 128 characters — are the ASCII characters; the remaining 128 are *extended* ASCII characters, which are covered later in this book.) Take a second to go stare at that listing now. *Grok* (sci-fi term for "think about") it, if you will.

The most obvious arrangement is between the upper- and lowercase characters. Their decimal values are unimpressive: Little s is code 115, while big S is 83. Yet, in hexadecimal (base 16), the numbers are similar: 73h for s and 53h for S. This shows up in the two columns as well: Uppercase letters are always 32 units away from their lowercase counterparts. (This is one of the reasons the 2UPPER filter from the last chapter was so easy to write.)

Note: In a way, the first column shows ASCII characters produced with the Ctrl key and the third column shows characters produced with the Shift key. The second column contains miscellaneous symbols, punctuation codes, and numbers.

The difference between "s" and "S" is 10h — ten hexadecimal or 16 decimal. That's how many characters are in each column in Appendix A. The math works out fine in hexadecimal, but don't let that boggle you right now. I'll be writing about hexadecimal in Chapter 7. (It's a sad fact that you need to know a little hex — but not much — to use DEBUG.)

Tips: Here are some interesting things you should note about the ASCII chart. This is stuff a tour guide would point out as the bus drives by the ASCII characters:

Ctrl-S is still used to pause the display. It works that way under DOS, although in the old teletype days, you had to press Ctrl-Q to get things going again. Now you can press any key — including Ctrl-S — again.

The character Ctrl-@ — the null — is difficult to produce on a DOS keyboard. When you press Ctrl-@ (actually Ctrl-2) you get a Ctrl-C, ^C, character under DOS. Most applications will ignore this keystroke as well, making it enigmatic.

Yes, it's true: The character ^^ is pronounced "control-control." (It's produced by pressing Ctrl-6 on your keyboard.)

ASCII code 127 is assigned to the character DEL or RUBOUT. This corresponds to the Ctrl-Backspace keystroke, although few programs recognize it. The symbol ^# or ^? is often assigned to code 127, though on a PC it appears as the Greek letter delta (Δ).

Even more similarities can be found if you look at the first column. This lists the control characters, the first 32 ASCII code values. These codes can be produced by pressing the Ctrl (key) plus a corresponding letter of the alphabet or symbol — the exact same symbols as are shown in the third column. Figure 6-1 elaborates on the control code listing.

> *Tip:* The relationship between the control codes and their uppercase letters is very apparent in DOS's EDLIN line editor. To enter a control character in EDLIN, type Ctrl-V followed by the letter for that control code. So to insert a Ctrl-C, type Ctrl-V then C. Escape is entered by typing Ctrl-V and a left bracket.

Practically speaking, control codes aren't really that important. They're basically leftovers from the old age of teletype communications. Most of the codes are ignored today, or are used for entirely different purposes. Some of them — Backspace, Tab, Enter and Esc — find themselves on computer keyboards. The rest have fallen by the wayside.

Modern keyboards sport the Backspace, Tab, Enter, and Esc, though they can all be produced by entering their Ctrl key combination as well: for example, Ctrl-I is the Tab key, Ctrl-H is the same as backspace, Ctrl-M is the same as pressing Enter, and so on.

Four additional control keys are also used by DOS: Ctrl-C is the cancel command, Ctrl-G will beep your speaker, Ctrl-S pauses the screen scroll, and Ctrl-Z marks the end of a text file. (Ctrl-P is the DOS printer echo toggle, but that's not a traditional teletype function for Ctrl-P.) Type this in:

```
C:\> ECHO ^G
```

That's the Ctrl-G key press, which displays as ^ and G. After pressing Enter, your speaker will beep. This always happens when you "display" a Ctrl-G, which makes it an excellent attention-getting routine in batch files (but annoying when overused).

Incidentally, the symbols shown in Figure 6-1 are for IBM only. Some programs allow you to display these characters as symbols. Other times, the characters are used instead of the ^-letter metaphor. Which method you use depends on the programs you're using.

Entering the Escape Character

The most crucial control key is Escape, Ctrl-[. This character is used to identify a special control sequence that follows, either when issuing a printer command or

ASCII Code	Control Char.	Keyboard Key	Symbol	Acronym; meaning
0	^@	–		NUL; Null character
1	^A	–	☺	SOH; Start of heading
2	^B	–	☻	STX; Start of text
3	^C	–	♥	ETX; End of text
4	^D	–	♦	EOT; End transmission
5	^E	–	♣	ENQ; Enquiry
6	^F	–	♠	ACK; Acknowledge
7	^G	–	•	BEL; Bell
8	^H	Backspace	◘	BS; Backspace
9	^I	Tab	○	HT; Horizontal tab
10	^J	–	◙	LF; Line feed
11	^K	–	♂	VT; Vertical tab
12	^L	–	♀	FF; Form feed
13	^M	Enter	♪	CR; Carriage return
14	^N	–	♫	SO; Shift out
15	^O	–	☼	SI; Shift in
16	^P	–	►	DLE; Data link escape
17	^Q	–	◄	DC1; Device control on (XON)
18	^R	–	↕	DC2; Device control two (AUXON)
19	^S	–	‼	DC3; Device control three (XOFF)
20	^T	–	¶	DC4; Device control four (AUXOFF)
21	^U	–	§	NAK; Negative acknowledgement
22	^V	–	▬	SYN; Synchronous file
23	^W	–	↨	ETB; End transmission block
24	^X	–	↑	CAN; Cancel
25	^Y	–	↓	EM; End of medium
26	^Z	–	→	SUB; Substitute
27	^[	Esc	←	ESC; Escape
28	^\	–	∟	FS; Form (or file) separator
29	^]	–	↔	GS; Group separator
30	^^	–	▲	RS; Record separator
31	^_	–	▼	US; Unit separator
127	^?	–	⌂	DEL; Delete or rubout

Figure 6-1 ASCII control codes and characters

an ANSI control code. The object is to insert the Escape character into the command without canceling anything (which is what pressing the Esc key normally does).

It's impossible to type an Escape character at the DOS prompt; pressing the Esc key erases the input line. The only way to manage it involves a convoluted method of using the PROMPT command to enter Escape text. This is done through the PROMPT command's meta-character, $e. (Refer to Table 4-1.) For example:

```
C:\> PROMPT $E[1;41;33m$P$G
```

Here, PROMPT issues the ANSI Set Graphic Mode command. The $E translates into the Escape character, which yields the following command:

```
←[1;41;33m
```

The "m" must be lowercase. This changes the screen color to bright yellow on a red background. The last part of the command, PG, sets the prompt.

Note: In this book, the character Escape is represented by the left pointing arrow (←), as seen in Figure 6-1.

I find this method of issuing ANSI commands most awkward. If anything, it screws up your system prompt. On the other hand, having the $E meta-command allows you to create really intricate prompts. There are just better ways to generate the Escape character.

Tip: If you change your screen to a different color, the command to get it back again is ←[m. In PROMPT-language, that's $e[m. More information on the different colors and various ANSI screen commands is found in Appendix C.

A better way to enter the Escape character is by using a text editor. Both EDLIN and EDIT support methods of entering control characters, such as Escape. EDIT uses the popular WordStar method for entering "literal" character: type Ctrl-P followed by the control character you want to insert into the document. For Escape, that's Ctrl-P, Esc. In EDIT that causes the ← character to appear in the text.

EDLIN uses the Ctrl-V prefix to enter control characters. Ctrl-V is followed by the capital letter or symbol associated with a particular control key combination. For example, for Escape, you type Ctrl-V, [(left bracket), which looks like this in the text:

```
^V[
```

When you list the file again, it looks like this:

```
^[
```

That's one character as far as EDLIN is concerned.

The same stunt can be pulled in various word processors. *WordPerfect* uses the Ctrl-V prefix to enter literal characters. Type Ctrl-V then Esc to insert the Escape character, which looks like this: ^[. You can insert the left arrow character by holding the Alt key down and pressing 2 then 7 on the numeric keypad. Release the Alt key and you'll see ← on the screen. Other word processors use this trick, which I've dubbed the "Alt-keypad trick." (It's covered in detail below.)

The Extended ASCII Character Set

ASCII defines only 128 character codes, from 0 through 127. Yet, 256 values fill one byte. The remaining 128 values aren't defined by the ASCII standard, so each computer (or printer) displays its own unique characters there. For example, the old TRS-80 computer displayed foreign characters, math symbols, and some Japanese Katakana characters; the Apple II showed the extra 128 characters using inverse text; your typical Epson printer displays a second ASCII character set — but all in italics for codes 128 through 255; and the IBM PC displayed what IBM dubbed the *Extended ASCII character set*.

The extended ASCII character set isn't as interesting as the basic ASCII characters. There is no correlation between the characters listed, though there are clusters of math symbols, foreign characters, and line drawing characters. Appendix A lists them all, and Appendix B contains special information about the box-drawing graphics characters.

All PCs since the first IBM model use the extended ASCII characters, and many printers support extended ASCII characters as a special font. But for interchange with non-PCs, don't expect things to work. Extended ASCII isn't a standard outside the DOS world. Even between PCs, you can use DOS's various code page commands to substitute other characters in place of the extended ASCII set. Windows doesn't even use them.

> *Tip:* The DOS armada of "code page" commands can be used to swap in various foreign language character sets in place of the standard, extended ASCII characters.

The Alt-Keypad Trick

All 128 ASCII characters are represented on your keyboard: upper- and lowercase, control characters, all of them. (Note that Ctrl-Backspace produces the DEL character, code 127. The Delete key on your keyboard does not have a corresponding ASCII value.) The only thing that's missing is direct access to the extended ASCII set. Regardless, you can get at these characters providing you know their code values and the *Alt-keypad trick*.

The Alt-keypad trick works like this:

1. Press and hold either Alt key.
2. Type the code value of a character on the numeric keypad. For example, ½ is code 171, so you'd type 1, 7, and 1 on the keypad.
3. Release the Alt key. The character matching the code you typed appears on the screen.

This trick works for all ASCII and extended ASCII character codes, from 0 through 255. (If you type a value greater than 255, its value is logically "anded" with 255.) Most word processors and a few text editors support this method of entering extended characters. But be careful! In some cases, the character produced is interpreted literally: Alt-2-7 makes the Escape character, which may produce the same effect as pressing Esc. (Refer to the previous section for hints on producing Escape.)

Using ANSI.SYS

The ANSI.SYS device driver is used to control your console, the screen, and keyboard. You can position the cursor on the display, change text colors, and reassign keys on the keyboard using ANSI commands available when ANSI.SYS is loaded into memory.

To take advantage of ANSI.SYS, it must be loaded in your CONFigureSYS file using the DEVICE or DEVICEHIGH configuration command:

```
DEVICE=C:\DOS\ANSI.SYS
```

This takes up about 4K of RAM, so it's not a huge sacrifice for the power it gives you. If you're making this change to your CONFigureSYS file now, save it back to disk and reset. (You must reset after editing CONFigureSYS for the changes to have effect.)

▶ *Tip:* You don't need to install the ANSI.SYS driver if you're using Windows. In that environment, using ANSI.SYS is a waste of memory. But if you want to run through these examples, you'll need to load it.

In *DESQview*, you can run the DVANSI.COM program in a DOS window. This saves the 4K of RAM ANSI.SYS uses, but I've found DVANSI to be extremely buggy and will not work with some of the examples in the following sections.

Alternative ANSI drivers exist. The best is the ZANSI.SYS driver, which contains a more accurate and complete rendering of the ANSI commands. It's also much faster than ANSI.SYS. This file can be picked up on national on-line forums such as CompuServe or GEnie, or it can be ordered from software warehouses such as the PC-SIG library (refer to the Introduction).

Once the ANSI driver is installed, you pass ANSI commands to the driver by sending them to the console. This can be done using the PROMPT command, by putting the commands in a BATCH file and displaying them with the ECHO command, or by putting them in a text file and TYPEing it on the screen. (The hangup here is the Escape character, which starts the ANSI command.)

All ANSI commands take on the following format:

```
←[code;code...command
```

The command starts with the Escape character, followed by a left bracket. That's followed by one or more code values or a string of text. If more than one code is used or a string is specified, they're separated by semicolons. Note that all values used in ANSI commands are plain text. For example, when a 31 is needed, you use the text characters 3 and 1 — not the value 31.

All ANSI commands end with the command letter — which is kind of backward. The letter tells the ANSI driver which command is being executed, and that command takes the appropriate action using the codes you've given it. If everything goes as planned, the command carries out its functions.

The ASCII command letters and their function formats are listed in Table 6-1. A full listing of all ANSI commands supported by DOS is provided in Appendix C. Note that case is important with the command letters! There is a difference between H and h.

Modifying the Keyboard

The ANSI command to modify the keyboard's function takes on this format:

←[*key;char*p

The command must end in a little p. It contains two items: The first is a key on the keyboard. If you can type the key, then you can specify it in double quotes.

Table 6-1 DOS-Supported ANSI Commands

Command	Format	Function
A	←[*n*A	Moves the cursor up *n* lines, or one line
B	←[*n*B	Moves the cursor down *n* lines, or one line
C	←[*n*C	Moves the cursor right *n* lines, or one line
D	←[*n*D	Moves the cursor left *n* lines, or one line
f	←[*row;col* f	Moves the cursor to the specified row and column, or home the cursor
h	←[=*n*h	Sets graphics mode, resolution
H	←[*row;col* H	Moves the cursor to the specified row and column, or home the cursor
J	←[2J	Erases the screen, home the cursor
K	←[K	Erases the line the cursor is on
l	←[=7l	Turns off character wrap
m	←[*n*m	Sets text color and attributes
n	←[*n*	Cursor status report; displays cursor position in row/col format
p	←[*key;char*p	Keyboard character/string replacement
s	←[s	Saves cursor position
u	←[u	Restores previously saved cursor position

If it's an unprintable key, such as a function key, then you must specify its *scan code*. ASCII codes work for some keys (Esc, Enter, ~), but special codes must be used for non-ASCII keys.

Following the key is a semicolon and then the text assigned to that key. The text can be another key's ASCII value or an entire string of text. If you enter a string, then it must be enclosed in double quotes.

To demonstrate how this works, create the following batch file:

```
@ECHO OFF
REM Keyboard modifying batch file
ECHO ←[126;"tilde"p
```

Code 126 is the ASCII code for the tilde character (~). The string assigned to that character is the text "tilde."

Save this batch file to disk as TILD-ON.BAT. (You must create this in a text editor where the Escape character can be entered. COPY-CON just won't cut it here.)

After running TILD-ON, press the ~ key. You'll see the text "tilde" displayed each time you press ~. Here's another way you can enter the command:

```
ECHO ←["~tilde"p
```

In this example, you're using the tilde itself instead of ASCII code 126. It's immediately followed by the replacement string — which is fine as far as ANSI.SYS is concerned; the end result is the same. In fact, if you were a real nerd, you could use the following format:

```
ECHO ←[126;116;105;108;100;101p
```

That's the code for the tilde plus the word "tilde" spelled out as ASCII code. It still works! Note how all the codes are separated with semicolons. Also, ANSI only replaces the key represented by the first value. (This is a key reassignment command, not string replacement.)

Reversing the Process

Using ANSI.SYS to modify your keyboard is reversible but only by using a second ANSI.SYS. In fact, it's always a good idea to have an un-ANSI batch file handy to remove your reassignments. The following batch file is TILD-OFF.BAT, which restores the tilde key to its original function:

```
@ECHO OFF
REM Keyboard modifying batch file
ECHO ←[126;126p
```

This reassigns the tilde back to itself; code 126 = code 126 and they all lived happily, etc. You can also use this format:

```
ECHO ←["~~"p
```

But beware of this! If you've already reassigned the tilde (or whatever other DOS character), then it's going to be hard to type it: If you press the tilde key you'll see "tilde" under DOS. Even if you use the Alt-keypad trick you'll still see "tilde." Therefore, it's a good idea to write *both* batch files first while you still have access to all your keys.

Note: Putting two keys together, as in ←["~~", is often listed as a "format" of the ANSI keyboard command. For example, you can reassign the P key to display a B with ←["PB"p. This really isn't a separate format of the ANSI keyboard command, just an inane way to swap two keys with each other which, I feel, lacks practical applications.

Be aware that ANSI only modifies DOS's input and output. Your ANSI modifications probably won't carry through into your applications. Only those programs that use DOS's standard input and output will be affected by the ANSI commands.

Tip: EDLIN, EDIT, and DEBUG all use DOS's standard input. Many of the batch files created in the following sections are designed to make life easier in those environments.

Using Keyboard Scan Codes

ANSI lets you use any key on the keyboard for key reassignment. The only keys you can't use are the modifiers and shift keys: Ctrl, Alt, Caps Lock, and so on. Everything else is fair game.

The way this works is to use a key's *scan code* value instead of its ASCII code. This is because some keys don't have ASCII characters assigned to them: the function keys, cursor keys, Home, End, and so on. To reassign these, you must know each key's scan code value and use it instead of an ASCII code. You can also use the scan code value instead of the ASCII code, for example, when using Alt-key combinations.

Note: Scan codes are produced by your keyboard and sent to the computer each time a key is pressed. Each key is given a unique scan code number. That number may change, depending on whether the key is pressed in combination with the Shift, Ctrl, or Alt keys. This is how programs can tell which keys you've been pressing on the keyboard.

All scan codes consist of two values, both separated by a semicolon. The ANSI driver can detect that you're using a scan code since all of them start with 0. For example: 0;68, which is the ANSI-approved scan code for the F10 key. Everything after the 68 (and a semicolon) is the text to be assigned to that key, F10.

Tables 6-2 and 6-3 list the scan codes for all the function key combinations as well as various Alt-key combinations. The full list of scan codes can be found in Appendix F. You can use these scan code values to put ANSI key reassignment to work, especially in programs such as DEBUG and the DOS Editor.

A question often asked is, why are the scan code values so weird? They aren't related to ASCII values. They just seem to follow that same horrid pattern that you find on all PC keyboards — which is exactly what IBM did when they created scan codes for their PC keyboard.

IBM started with the Escape key in the upper-left corner as scan code 1. The next key to the right at the time was the 1/! key, which has a scan code of 2. They continued across and down the typewriter part of the keyboard. This all makes sense if you look at how the Alt keys are numbered: Q is 16, W is 17, E is 18, and so on. Nonprinting keys even have scan code values, and the cursor keys and function keys were listed last.

In Table 6-2 you can see how the function keys increase in value, first when shifted and then when used with the Ctrl and Alt keys. When the Enhanced 101 keyboard came out in 1987, F11 and F12 were added. Notice how their scan codes sloppily fit into the picture in Table 6-2. The same holds true for the other, extra keys when you look at the scan code Big Picture.

This issue is anecdotal. It explains why the scan code values don't make much sense, but don't worry about it. Even the "real" programmers have to look up scan code values. I doubt if anyone has ever memorized these things.

Using ANSI Commands with the DOS Editor

Figure 6-2 contains a batch file to run the DOS Editor. It uses ANSI commands to create three keyboard shortcuts: Alt-O to open a file, Alt-X to quickly exit, and F2

Table 6-2 Alt-Key Scan Code Values

Alt-Key	Scan Code	Alt-Key	Scan Code
Alt-A	0;30	Alt-N	0;49
Alt-B	0;48	Alt-O	0;24
Alt-C	0;46	Alt-P	0;25
Alt-D	0;32	Alt-Q	0;16
Alt-E	0;18	Alt-R	0;19
Alt-F	0;33	Alt-S	0;31
Alt-G	0;34	Alt-T	0;20
Alt-H	0;35	Alt-U	0;22
Alt-I	0;23	Alt-V	0;47
Alt-J	0;36	Alt-W	0;17
Alt-K	0;37	Alt-X	0;45
Alt-L	0;38	Alt-Y	0;21
Alt-M	0;50	Alt-Z	0;44

Table 6-3 Function Key Scan Code Values

Key	Unshifted	Shift+	Ctrl+	Alt+
F1	0;59	0;84	0;94	0;104
F2	0;60	0;85	0;95	0;105
F3	0;61	0;86	0;96	0;106
F4	0;62	0;87	0;97	0;107
F5	0;63	0;88	0;98	0;108
F6	0;64	0;89	0;99	0;109
F7	0;65	0;90	0;100	0;110
F8	0;66	0;91	0;101	0;111
F9	0;67	0;92	0;102	0;112
F10	0;68	0;93	0;103	0;113
F11	0;133	0;135	0;137	0;139
F12	0;134	0;136	0;138	0;140

to search. These are all abbreviations for keystrokes you would otherwise have to issue in the Editor — what other applications commonly call *macros*.

If you like, create the batch file in Figure 6-2 using a text editor, save it to disk as EDIT.BAT, and use it to run the DOS Editor. (Make sure that line 9 reflects the actual location of EDIT.COM on your system.) Try out the new macros when you're in the editor: Alt-O, F2, and Alt-X.

```
 1: @ECHO OFF
 2: REM Reassign keys for the editor
 3: REM Alt-O to open..
 4: ECHO ←[0;24;0;33;"O"p
 5: REM Alt-X to quit...
 6: ECHO ←[0;45;0;33;"X"p
 7: REM F2 for Search/Find
 8: ECHO ←[0;60;0;31;"F"p
 9: C:\DOS\EDIT %1
10: REM Change everything back
11: ECHO ←[0;24;0;24p
12: ECHO ←[0;45;0;45p
13: ECHO ←[0;60;0;60p
```

Figure 6-2 The EDIT.BAT program runs the Editor and gives you three keyboard "macros"

▐▶ *Tip:* When you run the batch file, you'll see a few blank lines displayed on the screen. This is caused by ECHO sending the ANSI commands to the screen. Do not attempt to suppress the blank lines by redirecting output to the NUL device — a common batch file trick. For example:

ECHO ←[0;24;0;33;"O"p > NUL

This redirects the ANSI command to the NUL device instead of the console. Only by sending an ANSI command to the console does the command work, so, while not producing extra lines on the display, the above instruction will not send the ANSI command to the ANSI.SYS driver.

This batch file uses ANSI key reassignment six times: three to create and three to undo. Line 4 reassigns the Alt-O key combination to Alt-F, O. Those are the keystrokes required to open a file for editing. Note how both Alt-O and Alt-F are entered using their scan code formats (found in Table 6-2).

In line 6, Alt-X is reassigned to Alt-F, X. This will get you out of the Editor quickly when you're done working. If your file hasn't been saved, then you'll be prompted to save it before you leave. (This works just as if you selected Alt-F, X in the Editor.)

Line 8 reassigns the F2 key to the Search/Find command. Normally this is obtained by pressing Alt-S, F, which is shown in the ANSI command in line 8.

This is an important place to remind you why Alt-S wasn't reassigned as a "quick-save" macro. Alt-S (and Alt-F, Alt-E, and Alt-O) activates a pull-down menu in the editor. If you reassign that key, then there's no way to access the menu. This is why F2 was selected for the quick-find macro instead of Alt-F. Similarly, F3 could have been assigned to Alt-F, S for a quick-save macro instead of Alt-S.

▐▶ *Tip:* It's always a good idea to check for a program's valid keystrokes before reassignment. That way you won't back yourself into a corner.

Line 9 in the batch file runs the EDIT program, followed by the optional parameter %1 to edit a file (if specified). After EDIT runs, the keys reassigned are assigned back to their original values. This is done simply by repeating the scan codes in the ANSI key reassignment format. If you make any additional modifications to this file, creating your own keyboard macros, and so forth, always remember to undo them before your batch file quits.

Using ANSI Commands with DEBUG

Just as shortcut keys can be created for the DOS Editor, you can build them for DEBUG. You have more latitude with DEBUG than in the Editor. Unlike the Editor, DEBUG uses no Alt or function keys. This opens the door to creating any keyboard reassignments you want. Figure 6-3 contains the batch file program I use to run DEBUG. The keyboard shortcuts are documented in Table 6-4.

Use your text editor to enter the batch file shown in Figure 6-3. Remember to change line 12 to reflect the proper location for DEBUG on your system. Save the file to disk, then use it to run DEBUG.

It helps to know a little bit about DEBUG before explaining what the commands do. (See the second part of this book.) For now, notice how each of the key reassignments in the batch file has a 13 in it. That's the Enter key character, which is ASCII code 13. Putting in the code 13 simulates pressing the Enter key, which makes most of these Alt-keys fast replacements for DEBUG commands.

Line 5 is my personal favorite. It resets the microprocessor's instruction pointer (IP register) to 100h. Only true DEBUG diehards will appreciate this one. Basically, Alt-I saves you several required keystrokes, making it a true boon to productivity. The Alt-I macro looks like this on the screen:

```
-RIP
0127
:100
-
```

```
 1: @ECHO OFF
 2: REM Run DEBUG with ANSI keyboard macro enhancements
 3: ECHO ←[0;30;"A100";13p
 4: ECHO ←[0;32;"D";13p
 5: ECHO ←[0;23;"RIP";13;"100";13p
 6: ECHO ←[0;25;"P";13p
 7: ECHO ←[0;16;"Q";13p
 8: ECHO ←[0;19;"R";13p
 9: ECHO ←[0;20;"T";13p
10: ECHO ←[0;45;"Q";13p
11: REM Run DEBUG here
12: C:\DOS\DEBUG
13: REM Unassign macros
14: ECHO ←[0;30;0;30p
15: ECHO ←[0;32;0;32p
16: ECHO ←[0;23;0;23p
17: ECHO ←[0;25;0;25p
18: ECHO ←[0;16;0;16p
19: ECHO ←[0;19;0;19p
20: ECHO ←[0;20;0;20p
21: ECHO ←[0;45;0;45p
```

Figure 6-3 DEBUG.BAT is used to run DEBUG with keyboard macros

Table 6-4 Alt-Key Reassignments in DEBUG.BAT

Key	Command	What It Does
Alt-A	A100 <Enter>	Starts assembling a program at address 100h
Alt-D	D <Enter>	Dumps 80h bytes of memory
Alt-I	RIP <Enter> 100 <Enter>	Resets instruction pointer to address 100h
Alt-P	P <Enter>	Proceed command
Alt-Q	Q <Enter>	Quits DEBUG
Alt-R	R <Enter>	Register command
Alt-T	T <Enter>	Trace command
Alt-X	Q <Enter>	Quits DEBUG

Alt-I supplies the RIP and Enter. DEBUG comes back with a value (0127) and a colon prompt. Alt-I picks up with 100 and then Enter again. When you're testing programs in DEBUG, this resets everything back to the starting point (as well as saving you eight keystrokes).

An oddity in DEBUG.BAT is found in line 10. The keystroke Alt-X is assigned to DEBUG's quit command, Q. Alt-Q is already assigned in line 7. The reason Alt-X is assigned is that some programs quit via Alt-X. Line 7 helps make DEBUG people used to Alt-X to Exit. Of course, you can assign any key to exit if you like. If you're using Windows, you can even specify the Alt-F4 keystroke. Here's the command:

```
ECHO ←[0;107;"Q";13p
```

Alt-F4 has a scan code value of 0;107. The example assigns that value to the string Q followed by Enter (13). This could be stuck into DEBUG.BAT along with the other keys.

As usual, the DEBUG.BAT batch file ends by reassigning the keystrokes back to their original values. This is done in lines 14 through 21. As you learn more about DEBUG, you can edit and expand this batch file and its macros. If you do add or modify any macros in the future, remember to unassign them before the batch file quits. (For example, reassign Alt-F4 back to itself before DEBUG.BAT ends.)

Using ANSI Commands at the DOS Prompt

The traditional mode of thinking between ANSI key reassignment and DOS is that you can shorten your DOS commands and your typing time by cleverly reassigning common commands to the function keys. I've been guilty of writing this in several books. The problem is that function keys F1 through F6 are used in DOS for command line editing. If you add DOSKEY, F7 through F9 are used as well. So to avoid any conflicts with DOS, ANSI key reassignment is usually done only with Shift, Ctrl, and Alt function keys. This really isn't that efficient.

```
1:  @ECHO OFF
2:  REM Augment the DOS prompt with ANSI commands
3:  ECHO ←[0;72;"CD ..";13p
4:  ECHO ←[224;72;"CD ..";13p
5:  ECHO ←[0;46;"COPY "p
6:  ECHO ←[0;32;"DIR";13p
7:  ECHO ←[4;"DIR /W/L";13p
8:  ECHO ←[0;18;"EDIT";13p
9:  ECHO ←[0;44;"CLS";13p
```

Figure 6-4 The DOSCOM.BAT batch file makes using the DOS prompt easier

Handy Alt-key combinations for DOS — just like other programs — are missing. This was demonstrated in the previous section with DEBUG and the DOS Editor. Figure 6-4 shows the DOSCOM.BAT batch file, which attaches a few command shortcuts to some Alt-key combinations.

DOSCOM.BAT makes only six key reassignments, as described in the following paragraphs:

In line 3, the "CD .." command plus Enter is assigned to the up-arrow key on the keypad. Line 4 assigns the same command to the gray up-arrow key on Enhanced 101 keyboards. (The two keys have different scan codes.) This gives that key the "move *up* one directory" command (although the reassignment doesn't work when DOSKEY is loaded).

Line 5 assigns the COPY command to Alt-C. Only COPY plus a space is produced when Alt-C is pressed. Line 6 assigns Alt-D equal to DIR plus Enter.

Line 7 is interesting. It assigns a "quick" DIR command, with the /W and /L switches, to Ctrl-D. The ASCII code for Ctrl-D is 4, as seen in the ASCII table in Appendix A as well as in Figure 6-1. A scan code isn't necessary here, since the key you're reassigning has an ASCII value.

Line 8 assigns Alt-E to the EDIT command, then line 9 assigns Alt-Z to CLS.

More commands could be added to this list for the rest of the Alt keys, as well as the function keys. Not all of the reassignments need to be DOS commands; you can run your programs as well: Alt-W to run WordPerfect, Alt-M for a menu system, and so on. Or you can incorporate the Alt-key strokes into a menu system you create with batch files. Get as fancy as you want.

When DOSKEY isn't loaded, you can use the cursor keys for reassignment. (DOSKEY, covered later in this chapter, supersedes the ANSI key reassignments.) This was done in Figure 6-4 for the up-arrow key, which is logically remapped to equal "CD ..". Table 6-5 lists the scan code values for the eight cursor keys. On the Enhanced 101 keyboards, the gray cursor keys to the left of the keypad produce the same scan codes, but with 244 instead of 0 in the first digit. This allows you to assign those keys differently, or not to assign them at all.

Keyboard Control 119

Table 6-5 Cursor Key Scan Code Values

Key	Scan Code	Gray Key	Scan Code
↑	0;72	↑	224;72
↓	0;80	↓	224;80
→	0;77	→	224;77
←	0;75	←	224;75
Home	0;71	Home	224;71
End	0;79	End	224;79
PgUp	0;73	PgUp	224;73
PgDn	0;81	PgDn	224;81

As with any keyboard reassignment batch file, you should have a second batch file to unassign the keys. Figure 6-5 shows DOSOFF.BAT, which undoes the reassignments made in DOSCOM.BAT. If you expand DOSCOM to include your own commands, make similar commands in your own DOSOFF batch file.

As shown in the previous sections, DOSOFF.BAT merely repeats the keyboard scan code values in each of the ANSI commands. Note how the control key, Ctrl-D, is reassigned to itself in line 6. All the control key scan codes are listed in Table 6-6. The values are simply the letter's position in the alphabet.

As a fan of PC Tools, I created another batch file based on the control key reassignment in DOSCOM.BAT. This new batch file, QUICKDIR.BAT, is shown in Figure 6-6. It allows quick access to the disks in your system by assigning the disk-changing command for a drive to its corresponding control key. For example, Ctrl-A accesses drive A, Ctrl-C accesses drive C, and so on.

In Figure 6-6, lines 3 through 7, reassign Ctrl-A through Ctrl-E to various drive changing commands. This works even on Ctrl-C; press Ctrl-C and you're logged in to drive C with "C:" and then Enter. This nullifies Ctrl-C as DOS's cancel command, but Ctrl-Break is unaffected.

```
1: @ECHO OFF
2: REM Remove DOS prompt ANSI commands
3: ECHO ←[0;72;0;72p
4: ECHO ←[0;46;0;46p
5: ECHO ←[0;32;0;32p
6: ECHO ←[4;4p
7: ECHO ←[0;18;0;18p
8: ECHO ←[0;44;0;44p
```

Figure 6-5 The DOSOFF.BAT file to undo DOSCOM.BAT's key assignments

Table 6-6 Ctrl-Key Scan Code Values

Ctrl-Key	Scan Code	Ctrl-Key	Scan Code
Ctrl-A	1	Ctrl-N	14
Ctrl-B	2	Ctrl-O	15
Ctrl-C	3	Ctrl-P	16
Ctrl-D	4	Ctrl-Q	17
Ctrl-E	5	Ctrl-R	18
Ctrl-F	6	Ctrl-S	19
Ctrl-G	7	Ctrl-T	20
Ctrl-H	8	Ctrl-U	21
Ctrl-I	9	Ctrl-V	22
Ctrl-J	10	Ctrl-W	23
Ctrl-K	11	Ctrl-X	24
Ctrl-L	12	Ctrl-Y	25
Ctrl-M	13	Ctrl-Z	26

You can expand this batch file to access all your PC's drives, but watch out for the following:

- Don't use Ctrl-M to access drive M. Ctrl-M is the Enter key, and every time you press Enter, you would see "M:" on the screen.

- In DOSKEY, Ctrl-T will always be its command separator, producing a "¶" (paragraph symbol) on the display.

- It's a good idea not to translate Ctrl-Z, the end-of-file marker. While this can still be produced with the F6 key, it's best to leave it alone.

Figure 6-7 shows the QUICKOFF.BAT batch file, which undoes the reassignments made in QUICKDIR.BAT.

```
1: @ECHO OFF
2: REM Quick Directory Access batch files
3: ECHO ←[1;"A:";13p
4: ECHO ←[2;"B:";13p
5: ECHO ←[3;"C:";13p
6: ECHO ←[4;"D:";13p
7: ECHO ←[5;"E:";13p
8: REM Add more drive letters as needed
```

Figure 6-6 The QUICKDIR.BAT program simplifies disk access

```
1: @ECHO OFF
2: REM Undo QUICKDIR.BAT
3: ECHO ←[1;1p
4: ECHO ←[2;2p
5: ECHO ←[3;3p
6: ECHO ←[4;4p
7: ECHO ←[5;5p
8: :END
```

Figure 6-7 The QUICKOFF.BAT file undoes the control key reassignments

Command Line Editing

DOS allows you to edit the command line using the function keys F1 through F5. This is in addition to using the Backspace key for erasing and Escape to cancel the entire line. The editing is simple, "invisible," and awkward. It's also the same command line editing used whenever a program uses DOS's Buffered Input function (an internal DOS command). For example, EDLIN and DEBUG use the Buffered Input function and allow the same editing techniques (if you want to call them techniques).

Table 6-7 lists the function key commands used at the DOS prompt and with DOS's Buffered Input function. The editing takes place on a *template*, either the previous command (or input line in DEBUG or EDLIN) or a new template created with the F5 key.

The template is only visible before the cursor. You can see the rest of it one character at a time using F1 or the whole thing using F3. In fact, using F3 is the most common DOS function key; it repeats the previous command, allowing you to back up and edit if need be. The other function keys are more of a curiosity — especially now that DOSKEY is available for "real" command line editing.

Table 6-7 DOS's Command Line Editing Function Keys

Key	Function
F1	Displays the next character in the template (also → key)
F2 *char*	Followed by a character, *char*, displays all characters in the template up to that character
F3	Displays the template (previous command or input line)
F4 *char*	Followed by a character, *char*, deletes all characters in the template from the cursor's position to that character
F5	Accepts the current line as the template and allows you to start reediting on a new line

> **Tip:** DOSKEY expands upon DOS's function key editing commands, but DOSKEY only works at the DOS prompt; in EDLIN and DEBUG only the basic commands remain active. However, third-party command line editors, such as DOSEDIT, continue to be operational in EDLIN and DEBUG.

Using DOSKEY for Command Line Editing

Starting with DOS 5.0, the DOSKEY program has brought command line editing into the twentieth century. Loading DOSKEY is done by sticking it into AUTOEXEC.BAT. For example:

```
DOSKEY /INSERT
```

The above command loads DOSKEY into memory, creates a 512 byte history/macro buffer, and keeps DOSKEY in the insert mode. If you want a larger buffer, for example 1K, specify the following:

```
DOSKEY /BUFSIZE=1024 /INSERT
```

This should give you enough room to store several dozen DOS commands plus a hefty amount of macros. Stick that command into AUTOEXEC.BAT, reset, and DOSKEY will be a boon to your productivity at the DOS prompt.

> **Tip:** It's possible to load DOSKEY high using the LOADHIGH command. Just put LOADHIGH, or its LH abbreviation, before DOSKEY in AUTOEXEC.BAT. Refer to Chapter 2 for more information on memory management, or buy a best-selling book on the subject.

Editing with DOSKEY

With DOSKEY loaded into memory you have full, visible control over your command line editing. DOS's vanilla editing keys still work, but, in addition to them, you'll have word processor-like control over your DOS commands. For example, the left and right arrows move the cursor left and right one character; Home and End keys move to the start and end of the line; the Ctrl key works with the arrow keys to hop around a word at a time; and so on. Table 6-8 lists all the commands. Everything you work with appears right on the screen, with the cursor sliding under characters instead of erasing them.

The best way to edit a previous command in DOSKEY is to press the F3 key. This redisplays the command. From that point on, you can edit it just as you would any line in a text editor or word processor. When the command is perfect, press Enter. The cursor doesn't need to be at the end of the line for Enter to work.

The Command History

To recall a previous command in DOSKEY, press the up-arrow key. Keep pressing the up-arrow key until the command appears. This works because DOSKEY stores all your previous commands in the *command history* buffer — as many as will fit.

Table 6-8 DOSKEY's Editing Commands

Key	Command
→	Moves cursor right
←	Moves cursor left
Ctrl-→	Moves cursor right one word
Ctrl-←	Moves cursor left one word
Home	Moves to the start of the line
End	Moves to the end of the line
Ctrl-Home	Deletes to the start of the line
Ctrl-End	Deletes to the end of the line
Escape	Erases the line and starts over
Backspace	Deletes the character to the left of the cursor
Delete	Deletes the character the cursor is on
Insert	Switches between insert and overwrite modes

▶ *Tip:* The up-arrow key will be the most popular key you use with DOSKEY. The down-arrow key can also be used to recall the next command in the list, allowing you to scan up or down through your previous commands. The PgUp and PgDn keys show you the first and last commands in the buffer, respectively.

A shortcut to recalling a previous command is to type the first letter or first part of the command, then press the F8 key. F8 searches through the command history for a match. If the first match isn't what you want, keep pressing F8 until the proper one appears.

To see a list of previous commands, press the F7 key. F7 displays all the commands stored in the history buffer — and it numbers each command. (It even pauses the screen should the total number of commands exceed your screen size.)

▶ *Tip:* Checking the command history tells you what you've been doing with your computer. To get a hard copy, use this format:

```
DOSKEY /H > COMHIST
```

If you redirect output to a batch file name, then you've created a batch file transcript of your DOS session, ready for playback. (DOSKEY /H works like the F7 key does, but without the line numbers.)

If you don't like the idea of having everything you've typed at the DOS prompt available for display, then you can erase the command line history buffer with the Alt-F7 key.

You can use the line numbers with the F9 key. Pressing F9 causes a "Line number:" prompt to appear. Type in the line number of the command you want, then press Enter. The command appears, ready for editing.

DOSKEY also allows you to "stack" multiple commands at a single prompt. This is done using the Ctrl-T character, which acts to separate the commands. Pressing Ctrl-T displays a "¶" (paragraph) character on the screen:

```
C:\> CLS ¶ DIR
```

The CLS command is typed first, followed by DIR. No spaces are necessary on either side of the ¶ character. Also, when you press Enter, DOS will issue each command at its own prompt. Unlike a batch file, you'll see everything as it's displayed. Also, you cannot press Ctrl-C to cancel the whole command; Ctrl-C only cancels each command as it's executed.

Note: You can't use the ¶ separator in a batch file. This trick works only at the DOS prompt and only with DOSKEY in memory.

Abbreviating DOS Commands with DOSKEY

Most people will use DOSKEY for command line editing and its command history. DOSKEY also comes with a macro feature that works similarly to the ANSI key reassignment commands. The difference between the two is that ANSI uses single keystrokes and DOSKEY's macros can be individual words, some of which can replace DOS commands.

To create a DOSKEY macro, the following format is used:

```
DOSKEY macro=commands
```

Macro is the name of the macro. It can be anything, using any combination of characters, symbols, and even control characters, but no spaces or the equal sign. The name is followed by an equal sign and various DOS *commands*. Unlike the SET command, which has a similar format, you can put spaces on either side of the equal sign. For example:

```
C:\> DOSKEY MACRO = DOSKEY /M
```

Above, the word MACRO is assigned to the DOS command DOSKEY /M (which displays a list of DOSKEY's macros). If you type MACRO at the DOS prompt, you'll see something like the following:

```
C:\> MACRO
C:\> DOSKEY /M
MACRO=DOSKEY /M
```

Typing a DOSKEY macro causes DOSKEY to issue the command at the next DOS prompt. This is much more ugly than running a batch file, in my opinion. Also the command history stores the macro's name, not the command run.

✏️ *Note:* In the list of displayed macros you'll notice that the macro names are listed in uppercase, but the commands are all in the same case in which you entered them. Of course, DOS doesn't care about case; everything is capitalized internally by COMMAND.COM.

There are special macro characters you can use in DOSKEY's macro commands. These are all listed in Table 6-9, and they can be specified in upper- or lowercase. For example, if you want the pipe character as part of your macro, you would use $B instead of the pipe itself. (When you use the pipe, DOS will pipe the DOSKEY command through a filter.)

Here's a macro I use a lot when working with DOS's memory management:

```
C:\> DOSKEY M=MEM /C $B MORE
```

DOSKEY assigns M equal to the MEM /C command as piped through the MORE filter.

A distinct advantage with DOSKEY macros is that you can create macros with the same names as internal DOS commands. For example, to shield some users from the DEL command you can write the following:

```
C:\> DOSKEY DEL=DEL $1 /P
```

The $1 represents what was typed after DEL at the DOS prompt. The /P produces the following prompt as files are deleted:

```
filename, Delete (Y/N)?
```

Or, better still, the DOSKEY macro could run a batch file you've created to safely tuck "deleted" files into an invisible subdirectory for storage and later cleanup.

There are two oddities with DOSKEY's macros. First, they only work at the DOS prompt. You cannot use a macro in a batch file. Second, the macro only works when it's the first thing after the DOS prompt. If you put one or more spaces in front of the macro name, the macro won't be executed. (This is how you can get back at DOS commands if they have DOSKEY macro counterparts.)

Table 6-9 DOSKEY's Macro Command Characters

Macro Char.	Represents
$B	The pipe character, |
$G	The greater-than character, >
$L	The less-than character, <
$T	The DOSKEY command separator, ¶
$$	The dollar sign, $
$1 ... $9	Command line arguments, first through ninth
$*	All command line arguments

To remove a DOSKEY macro from memory, you use the same format as when removing an environment variable:

```
DOSKEY macro=
```

This removes the macro named *macro* from memory. To delete all the macros at once, press Alt-F10.

> ***Tip:*** If you've created and tested a bunch of macros you want to keep, use the following:
>
> ```
> DOSKEY /M > MAKEMAC.BAT
> ```
>
> This pumps the macro list to a batch file MAKEMAC.BAT. You'll need to edit MAKEMAC.BAT and put "DOSKEY" at the start of each line. Put the @ECHO OFF command at the top of the file and — ta da — your instant DOSKEY macro building batch file is ready.

Part II

Spelunking with DEBUG

DOS comes with the ideal tool for exploring your PC. It's called DEBUG and almost everyone who uses DOS avoids it, which I find sad. This part of the book concentrates heavily on using DEBUG and will remove the mystery and any anxieties you have about using it. DEBUG is a powerful tool, definitely the best way to explore some underground aspects of your PC. You'll be doing that in several entertaining and enjoyable chapters that:

- Describe the details of DEBUG, hexadecimal, and how the PC's memory works
- Peek and poke through memory using DEBUG
- Use DEBUG to manipulate files and work on disks
- Directly manipulate your computer's brain, the microprocessor

If you've never touched DEBUG before, or only have written DEBUG "scripts" found in magazines, then this will all be new and exciting territory for you. Don't let the "hexadecimal" stuff scare you away; there's no math here, no advanced science, or anything that will convert you into a Dorito chip-snarfing hacker. This is all useful information that will help expand your knowledge of the PC.

7

All about DEBUG

You've probably heard the tales: meek users who tried to wrestle with DEBUG and ended up destroying the data on their hard drives. Or maybe the innocent user typing away who suddenly writes "garbage" to his or her disk, requiring hours of tedious recovery using the Norton Utilities. Whether those stories are true or not is anyone's guess. It's a certain fact that DEBUG is a cryptic tool designed for use by programmers. That doesn't, however, mean "hands off" to the rest of us.

This chapter introduces you to the concepts and methods of DEBUG, perhaps the handiest tool that comes with DOS. There are so many things you can do with DEBUG, yet danger does lurk out there. This chapter is the kindly park ranger surveying the wilderness for you. Get familiar with the sights, but remember not to feed the bears.

What Is This Thing, This DEBUG?

Usually you're told that DEBUG is an obscure tool used only by the programming elite. "As a mere end user, you shouldn't meddle with the *dangerous* DEBUG," they'll sneer down their noses. But then you see DEBUG used in a magazine to create some handy little utility via a script file. So which is it, useful or dangerous?

Time for some facts and fictions about DEBUG: like most DOS commands, DEBUG can be deadly when used carelessly. And everything you've read is true: DEBUG is cryptic, powerful, and it's basically a programmer's utility. In fact, "debugging" is the process of removing bugs and quirks from software. But forget all that.

When you respect DEBUG for what it is, it becomes putty in your hands. You can use DEBUG to "peek" through memory, examine files and raw sectors on disk, meddle with the inner working of your PC's microprocessor, and write handy little programs and utilities. DEBUG covers a lot of ground in a PC, so sit up and pay attention. You don't want to miss a thing.

Why Is There DEBUG?

The reason why we have DEBUG is probably tradition. IBM and Microsoft based DOS on the earlier CP/M operating system. CP/M came with a programmer's tool called DDT, named after the infamous bug spray. Using DDT, a programmer could test-drive a program and inspect it for bugs.

CP/M users didn't need DDT just like DOS users don't really need DEBUG. So perhaps IBM couldn't figure out whether or not DDT's presence lent itself to CP/M's success. In any event, the first version of DOS came with a DDT-like debugger named DEBUG.

DEBUG was upgraded a bit for DOS 2.0 and reworked again for DOS 4.0 and 5.0. It's one of three programmer utilities included with DOS; the other two, EXE2BIN and LINK, have since vanished from the list of files included with DOS. Similar programs — and more powerful debuggers — are usually included with programming language packages.

Note: What more powerful debuggers are there? Both Microsoft and Borland, who made names for themselves writing programming languages, offer powerful debugging tools. Microsoft's is called *CodeView*, although a less-powerful version called SYMDEB (for Symbolic Debugger) is also used.

Over on planet Borland, the debugger is named *Turbo Debug* (TD). It's my personal favorite. TD displays "panels" of information, showing memory, the program you're debugging, variables, and all sorts of cool information required when exploring programs. Granted this is stuff that only excites a true DOS lunatic. However, I got my start programming a PC with a debugger called *Commander 80* on the old TRS-80. When you can visually see what assembly language does to your microprocessor and memory, it gives you a hint of the total control a programmer has over a personal computer.

What You Can Do with DEBUG

DEBUG does so much that it's hard to pin it down exactly. Right away, you should know that DEBUG is more of a program than a DOS command. When DEBUG runs you'll see the DEBUG prompt, the hyphen:

That's where you enter DEBUG's commands, which you'll be introduced to shortly. DEBUG has two dozen or so commands. Each command is a single letter, some of which are followed by optional information, memory values, and such.

The best way to tackle the subject of "what can be done with DEBUG" is to divide its commands into categories. There are four of them:

- Memory peeker/poker
- Disk transfer
- Microprocessor control
- Assembling/debugging (programming)

Peeking and poking are fancy terms for looking at and changing memory in your computer. This is a basic principle of how all computers operate: the microprocessor uses memory to store information. Everything you see on your screen — the stuff you work with and the programs you run — is stored in memory. Even when you use a disk utility, the software is loading information from disk into memory. Only in memory can information on disk be edited, and then it must be written back to the disk from memory.

Memory is where it happens and most DEBUG commands deal with memory. There are thousands upon thousands of bytes of memory in the PC, and using DEBUG, you can look at or change each of them individually or in chunks.

"Disk transfer" refers to reading and writing information from disk. The information is read into memory from disk, or written to disk from memory. Because DEBUG works primarily with memory, you can edit files and "raw" information on disk. Be aware that information on disk is changed only when you write memory to disk.

Although DEBUG can load any file into memory — and you can conceivably edit the file using DEBUG just as you would using a text editor — DEBUG's main purpose is to load program files for examination and test runs. This is where DEBUG gets its name; you can figuratively stomp out computer bugs by loading and running a COM or EXE program into DEBUG.

DEBUG also allows you to load in raw data from disk; you can select any number of sectors from any disk in your system, load them into memory, then manipulate everything using DEBUG's memory commands. The result can be written out to disk, if you like — although this is the dangerous part (which I'll get into later).

Aside from playing with disk and memory, you can use DEBUG to check out what's happening in the PC's microprocessor. The microprocessor is like a calculator, and it does basic calculatorlike things with values stored in memory or in the microprocessor's *registers*. Microprocessor instructions, called "machine language," manipulate values in memory as well as in the registers.

Sit back and take a deep breath. Memory, disk sectors, microprocessor registers, and machine language isn't the bubbling cauldron of pitch that it would seem to be. This is all such basic stuff most programmers (and book authors) gloss over it too quickly for everything to sink in. I'll carefully explain how it all works in later chapters.

Finally, DEBUG can be used both to build and take apart programs. The building part is called *assembling*, where you use a programming language called Assembly to create DOS programs. DEBUG comes with a "mini-assembler" you can use to create assembly language programs.

> ***Note:*** Assembly language is closely related to machine language, the microprocessor's "native tongue." The language consists of basic grunts and squawks — very unfriendly and extremely un-Englishlike.
>
> The advantage to using assembly language is that you're programming the computer on a subatomic level. This makes your programs small and tight and they'll run very fast. The disadvantage is that using assembly language for large projects is cumbersome — like building a car one molecule at a time.
>
> In this book, I'll show you an easy way to use assembly language with DEBUG. You'll be writing short, compact programs that are useful or interesting, but don't expect to be writing any Windows applications.

It's the programming part of DEBUG that you'll see most often in those script files appearing in magazines. This book also uses them: Figure 3-8 is an example of a script that uses assembly language, and Figure 5-4 "pokes" machine language instructions into memory to build a program. In just a few short chapters you'll understand how all of that works.

Taking programs apart is referred to as *disassembly*, which also describes what most four-year-old kids do to those cool little toys you buy for them. Disassembly is the basic idea behind DEBUG. A programmer will disassemble a program using DEBUG, taking it apart and displaying it in assembly language. (DEBUG cannot disassemble into any other language.) Once DEBUG's commands are in assembly language form, you can watch how the program works a step at a time. This will really show you how programs control your PC and how the microprocessor works with memory. And, when a program doesn't work, DEBUG gives you a clue as to what needs fixing.

There are commands for each of these areas in DEBUG (see Table 7-1). And while the primary purpose of all the commands is to remove bugs from programs, you can use the commands to see how your PC works and do all sorts of interesting things. "PC spelunking," I call it. How the commands are used, and what you can do constructively with them, is covered in detail over the next several chapters.

Running DEBUG

Start DEBUG by typing its name at the DOS prompt:

```
C:\> DEBUG
-
```

When you "run" DEBUG, it shows you the friendly DEBUG prompt, the hyphen character. At this prompt, you enter DEBUG's commands and tell it what to do.

Table 7-1 DEBUG's Commands by Category

Command	Function	Category
A	assemble	Programming
C	compare	Memory
D	dump	Memory
E	enter	Memory
F	fill	Memory
G	go	Programming
H	hex	Programming
I	input	Microprocessor
L	load	Disk
M	move	Memory
N	name	Programming/Disk
O	output	Microprocessor
P	proceed	Programming
Q	quit	None (Quits DEBUG)
R	register	Microprocessor
S	search	Memory
T	trace	Programming
U	unassemble	Programming
W	write	Disk
XA	Expanded memory	Memory
XD	Expanded memory	Memory
XM	Expanded memory	Memory
XS	Expanded memory	Memory

The commands are one character long except for the expanded memory commands which are two letters long. The command letter is optionally followed by values, all of which are in hexadecimal, base 16. In fact, everything in DEBUG is in hexadecimal, which is why the next chapter is about hexadecimal. (It's painless, don't worry.)

To see a list of DEBUG's commands, type ? (a question mark) at the prompt and press Enter. The ? command is available only with DOS versions 5.0 and later, so if you get an "Error," just take a look at Figure 7-1. There aren't that many DEBUG commands, and you will need only a few of them on a regular basis. Take a moment to scan the list carefully for the self-destruct command.

Surprise! There isn't any "self-destruct" command. DEBUG is really quite harmless when used properly. Any of the commands listed in Figure 7-1 can be

```
assemble                    A [address]
compare                     C range address
dump                        D [range]
enter                       E address [list]
fill                        F range list
go                          G [=address] [addresses]
hex                         H value1 value2
input                       I port
load                        L [address] [drive] [firstsector] [number]
move                        M range address
name                        N [pathname] [arglist]
output                      O port byte
proceed                     P [=address] [number]
quit                        Q
register                    R [register]
search                      S range list
trace                       T [=address] [value]
unassemble                  U [range]
write                       W [address] [drive] [firstsector] [number]
allocate expanded memory         XA [#pages]
deallocate expanded memory       XD [handle]
map expanded memory pages        XM [Lpage] [Ppage] [handle]
display expanded memory status XS
```

Figure 7-1 DEBUG's command list, displayed by the ? command

used to lock up or "hang" your computer — which happens to programmers all the time. They take it in stride, smile or curse, then reset the PC. (Having a reset button is handy when programming.) Table 7-1 shows DEBUG's commands according to the four categories discussed earlier in this chapter.

There will be no deliberate PC hang-ups here. (Trying to do it on purpose is like trying to fall off a horse.) However, one deadly command is W, which writes information to disk. Of all DEBUG's commands, W is the most dangerous. Be extremely careful when using it.

Using DEBUG

Nearly all of DEBUG's commands are followed by optional values, each of which must be expressed in hexadecimal. In most cases, these values represent memory locations because most DEBUG commands work with memory.

Assuming that DEBUG is waiting with its hyphen prompt on your screen, type the S command and press Enter:

```
-S
  ^ Error
-
```

S is the Search command. From Figure 7-1 and the DEBUG help menu, you can see that S has two parameters, *range* and *list*, both of which are required. (Optional parameters appear in square brackets — the standard DOS convention.) Since the required parameters weren't entered, DEBUG pops back with an "error" message.

DEBUG's error message is wholly undescriptive, yet eerily precise. It doesn't tell you what went wrong, but will tell you where the mistake was found. The carat (^) usually points to the spot in your command where DEBUG expected something but didn't find it. Try this command:

```
-A 12345
      ^ Error
-
```

The A command activates DEBUG's mini-assembler. The A command can optionally be followed by a memory location or address. In the example, a bogus address was specified. DEBUG identifies this by pointing the "error finger" at the last digit of the value. Had something else been required, DEBUG would have shown you this:

```
-A 12345
        ^ Error
-
```

When the error finger points beyond the value, then it means something else was required. This type of error reporting is limited since it doesn't tell you what was wrong, but it's better than the plain old question mark or "Huh?" that I've seen on other computers.

Of course, the major drawback to this type of error "handling" is that DEBUG will let you do disastrous and stupid things without any error warning whatsoever. For example, consider — but do not type in — this command from Chapter 1:

```
-G FFFF:0000
```

This is the command to reset your PC. DEBUG won't spit an error message at you here, nor will it do so if you misuse the W command and write a chunk of memory to a random place on disk. *Be careful!* As long as you follow the instructions in this book, you'll be fine.

Just to prove that I'm not nasty and won't teach you how to use DEBUG by tossing "Error" in your face, type in this command:

```
-E B800:A00 "EOROROOORO"
```

Double check your typing; watch your O's and zeros. Press Enter when perfect. (You'll read about what happened in Chapter 15.)

Tip: Didn't you see anything? If you didn't, then I'll bet you have a monochrome monitor. Type in this command instead:

```
-E B000:A00 "EOROROOORO"
```

Quitting DEBUG

The best DEBUG command to learn right away is the one you should also immediately memorize: Q, which means quit. Type Q and press Enter and you're back at the DOS prompt.

```
-Q
C:\>
```

As an interesting aside, you can also type *quit*, which does the same thing. In fact typing anything starting with Q quits DEBUG: *queen*, *quack*, *queasy*, etc. This laziness on DEBUG's behalf doesn't work with the other commands; only Q.

Learning More about DEBUG

The object of the next few chapters is to make you DEBUG-literate. In the process, you'll learn a bunch of stuff about your computer. Some would consider that this knowledge "empowers" you as a DOS guru. Whatever. It's all curious little tidbits that you need to know if you want to use DEBUG without getting a migraine. There are three basic subjects:

- The hexadecimal counting system
- How the PC uses memory
- Mundane microprocessor facts

Each of these is covered in the next few chapters; the rest of this book builds on that knowledge.

8

Removing the Hex from Hexadecimal

All values in DEBUG are *displayed* in hexadecimal, the base 16 counting system. That's okay, but you're also required to *enter* values in hexadecimal. That's the hard part — one of those painful, twisted things that you must contend with if you're going to explore your PC in any depth: computers don't count using ten fingers! Actually, they don't count in hexadecimal, either; PCs use the *binary* counting system, which is akin to counting the quills on a porcupine and nearly as painful. So be thankful hexadecimal is there to bail you out.

This chapter is about counting systems, primarily the hexadecimal or "hex" counting system used in DEBUG. Don't panic: you don't have to learn anything here. The main thrust of this discourse is to prevent you from thinking "10" means ten of something in DEBUG. It doesn't; "10" in DEBUG is equal to 16. But that won't puzzle you after reading this chapter.

Counting Systems

We use symbols to represent values the same way we use symbols to represent words. We do the same thing with numbers and values: Special characters are used to represent the values. The way these characters represent values is referred to as a *counting system.*

The ancient Egyptians used a hieroglyphic counting system that was quite clever. It used single symbols, say a lotus flower, to represent a large value, say 1,000. The problem was that expressing values in between the large numbers required multiple hieroglyphic symbols. For example, 27 symbols and slashes are required to represent 999. That took quite a while to chisel into the side of a tomb.

$$\boxed{\textbf{LXIV - XV = XLIX}}$$
$$64 \qquad 15 \qquad 49$$

Figure 8-1 "Simple" Roman numeral math

The most horrid of all counting systems was that used by the Romans. In fact, the worst job you could have in ancient Rome was that of an accountant. Why? Because the Roman numeral counting system lacked a symbol for the value zero! The Arabs had to invent zero several hundred years later. Also, working Roman math required a lot of brainwork; witness the simple math problem shown in Figure 8-1. And if that's easy, think about how you'd write the value 999 in Roman numerals. Be thankful computers don't use Roman numerals (although there's a rumor the IRS will be switching over to them for next year's tax form).

To represent values, most of us now use the Hindu-Arabic numbering system. We count things by tens, probably because we have ten fingers. In fact, our word *digit* has its root in the same word for finger. Counting by tens is referred to as a decimal counting system or "base ten."

No need to panic here: everyone knows the decimal counting system. In decimal there are ten digits: 0, 1, 2, 3, 4, 5, 6, 7, 8, 9. To represent larger values, the digits are grouped into columns, each column being ten times greater than the one before. "Empty" columns are held in place using the zero. Table 8-1 shows how all this works, which should be familiar to you.

Other counting systems exist as well. For example, some cultures use base five. In this system the value after 4 would be 10 — although 10 isn't "ten," it's five of something. Another ancient counting system is still in use today: Timekeeping is kept in base 60. After 59 seconds on the clock you get 1:00. (Maybe this is why some people program their microwave ovens for 1:50 when the instructions say a minute and a half.)

To get the most out of DEBUG, you need to be familiar with two other counting systems. The first is binary, base two. The second is hexadecimal, base 16. These

Table 8-1 Decimal Values

Base 10 Value	10^4 10000	10^3 1000	10^2 100	10^1 10	10^0 1
5					5
64				6	4
100			1	0	0
256			2	5	6
1,000		1	0	0	0

are merely different ways to represent values. Binary uses only ones and zeroes. Hexadecimal uses the numbers 0 through 9, plus letters of the alphabet, A through F, to represent values 10 through 15.

> **Note:** They might have invented symbols to represent values 10 through 15 for hexadecimal. I've seen upside-down letters A through F used, but it's not common, and all the other cool symbols, Greek and whatnot, are used in math for other purposes. Therefore, we're left with A through F for hexadecimal's high values.
>
> How can you keep this rational? Try thinking of a deck of cards. The jack is 11, queen is 12 and king is 13. If you're adept at card games, you may instantly see K + K = 26. The same thing holds true in hexadecimal; just remember that the symbols are used to represent values.

Don't go insane. Don't let those fears you developed in high school algebra bubble to the surface. Forget math! These are simply counting systems used to represent numbers.

The Binary Counting System

Here is a quick and painless introduction to the binary counting system:

    1
    0

There. You've seen it all.

As you can see by looking at them, computers don't have any fingers or toes. Base ten is definitely out. Instead, computers only have electricity and that only can be on or off. When the electricity is on, the computer reads 1; when the electricity is off, the computer reads zero.

In binary, like decimal, numbers are listed in columns. Each column in decimal is ten times greater than the column before it: 100 is ten times 10. In binary the same thing holds true, but each column is only two times greater than the previous column: You have the 2s column, 4s column, 8s column and so on, with each column being two times greater in binary.

Look at the top row in Table 8-2. Each column represents an increasing "power" of two — just like Table 8-1 showed with powers of ten. The second row shows the relative values; each is double the value of the previous column — again, the same as Table 8-1 showed with powers of ten. So far, so good.

Unlike decimal, however, binary only uses two values: 1 and 0. They represent anything: on/off, true/false, up/down, in/out, basically any two opposites, such as the electricity-on or electricity-off states that you find in a computer. Because of this, and the small jumps between the columns, many more binary digits — or *bits* — are required to represent numbers.

> **Note:** *Bit* is a contraction of binary digit.

Table 8-2 Binary Values

Base 2	2^{10}	2^9	2^8	2^7	2^6	2^5	2^4	2^3	2^2	2^1	2^0
Value	1024	512	256	128	64	32	16	8	4	2	1
5									1	0	1
64					1	0	0	0	0	0	0
100					1	1	0	0	1	0	0
256			1	0	0	0	0	0	0	0	0
1,000		1	1	1	1	1	0	1	0	0	0

Consider the value 5, which reads 101 in Table 8-2. If you look in the second row, you see that 101 is one 4, zero 2, and one 1; 4+0+1 equals 5.

The value one hundred in Table 8-2 is 1100100 binary. That translates as follows:

$1 \times 64 \quad = 64$

$1 \times 32 \quad = 32$

$0 \times 16 \quad = 0$

$0 \times 8 \quad = 0$

$1 \times 4 \quad = 4$

$0 \times 2 \quad = 0$

$0 \times 1 \quad = 0$

The end result is 64+32+4 = 100. You can do the same thing with the value 1,000, which is shown as 1111101000 in binary — an utterly huge number that you'll never have to deal with, but if you want to figure it out, feel free. (Don't waste your time figuring out other values here; this is a look-only lesson.)

The values 64 and 256 are "even" binary numbers since both are powers of two. Their binary numbers are 1000000 and 100000000, respectively, which you can see in Table 8-2.

See what I mean about counting quills on a porcupine? Binary numbers are cumbersome to deal with. Even programmers detest binary numbers. No one I know memorizes them, and no programmer can tell you right away whether 101100101 is 357 or not. They just don't bother.

Making Binary Easier to Read

To make huge decimal numbers more manageable, we divide them into groups of three (though some cultures use groups of four): 1064569 becomes the more readable 1,064,569. Even without the commas, you can squint at a number and mentally group it into threes (providing the number isn't too large).

Removing the Hex from Hexadecimal 141

Binary numbers can quickly get out of hand since they use only two digits. This rules out squinting altogether. Consider the following:

```
100000011111001111001
```

Above you have the value 1,064,569 displayed in its binary glory. (Don't worry about me, I used the computer to calculate the value; I'm not dumb.) To make this and all binary numbers more readable, programmers will divide them into groups of four:

```
1 0000 0011 1110 0111 1001
```

Since this value has a sole, leading 1, it should be prefixed with zeros to pad it out to the full four digits. In the end you get the following for 1,064,569 in binary:

```
0001 0000 0011 1110 0111 1001
```

Egads! The end result is still a terrible number that no one — not even Bill Gates or Peter Norton — would want to deal with. Although the groupings make the numbers more manageable, it's still hard to tell exactly what value is being expressed.

The solution lies in counting base 16, hexadecimal. Not that hexadecimal, or "hex," is any easier to understand. But it just so happens that hex makes for an excellent shorthand notation of the binary number shown above — something that humans can deal with.

The Hexadecimal Counting System

Hexadecimal is counting base 16. I don't know about you, but in the fourth grade, we only got up to our 12-times tables. Sixteens are interesting, particularly from the computer programmer's point of view because 16 is a nice, even multiple of two. This knits it close to binary, which is what your computer understands and uses internally.

Note: Programmers also once used counting base 8, called *octal.* You may still see this counting base referred to in programming literature and in scientific or programmer's calculators. However, today it's been totally supplanted by hexadecimal.

In binary there are two digits, decimal uses ten. In hex there are 16 digits. The first ten values are 0 through 9, just like decimal. To represent the values 10 through 15, the letters A through F are used. Table 8-3 shows how hex digits line up with their decimal values.

The letters A through F are pronounced as such, even though they represent values in a hexadecimal number. The number after F in hexadecimal is 10, which represents the value 16 (not ten!). Table 8-4 shows the same values illustrated in Tables 8-1 and 8-2, this time shown as hexadecimal numbers.

Five is still 5, thankfully. But the value 64 is shown in hexadecimal as 40. That's four times 16 plus zero. One hundred is 64 hex, which figures out as follows:

Table 8-3 Hexadecimal and Decimal Values

Hex.	Decimal	Hex.	Decimal
0	0	8	8
1	1	9	9
2	2	A	10
3	3	B	11
4	4	C	12
5	5	D	13
6	6	E	14
7	7	F	15

$6 \times 16 = 96$

$4 \times 1 = 4$

The total of 96 and 4 is 100. (But don't think for an instant you'll need to do these kind of calculations to work with DEBUG!)

The value 256 is shown as 100 hexadecimal, no problem. But 1,000 is equal to 3E8 hexadecimal. That would be pronounced as "three E eight hex." It figures as follows:

$3 \times 256 = 768$

$E \times 16 = 224$

$8 \times 1 = 8$

The letter E equals 14 (see Table 8-3), and 14 times 16 is 224. In the end you have a total of 768+224+8, which equals 1,000. Again, this isn't a calculation you'll ever have to make in this book; it just shows how the hexadecimal number pans out to its decimal equivalent. It also gets you used to the most unusual aspect of hexadecimal numbers: they contain letters.

Table 8-4 Hexadecimal Values

Base 16 Value	16^3 4096	16^2 256	16^1 16	16^0 1
5				5
64			4	0
100			6	4
256		1	0	0
1,000		3	E	8

Letters in hexadecimal numbers are one of the few clues you have that you're looking at a hex value and not a decimal number. In DOS, type the VOL command to display a disk's volume label and serial number. You'll see something like this:

```
Volume in drive C is SLUGGISH
Volume Serial Number is 2251-13F8
```

A disk's volume serial number is a hexadecimal number. In the example, it shows 13F8, a hexadecimal value. Some disks may show only decimal numbers, but you're still looking at a hex value. This poses the first dilemma when dealing with hexadecimal (and DEBUG): how do you know if you're dealing with a hex or decimal number?

Tip: Lying about your age? Forget it, use hexadecimal instead! You can claim you're 19 hex when you're 25 decimal. But who's 19 hex anymore? At the ripe "old" age of 41, you're really only a baby at 29 years in hex. Think of the money you'll save on candles!

Use the ASCII table in Appendix A to translate your age into hexadecimal. Unfortunately, during those five years where letters are used you'll still have to lie about your age. (I'm 1F hex as I sit here writing this, but next year I'll be 20 — again!)

To clear up the confusion, I'll refer to a hexadecimal value in this book as such-and-such hex. When writing down a hex number, programmers often suffix it with an H. For example, 100H is 100 hexadecimal — not the value 100. Your volume serial number should really be listed as 2251-13F8H, but since it's never needed in a mathematical computation, Microsoft can slide without specifying the H.

Note: A variation on the H is the $, dollar sign. This happens mostly on other, non-PC computers. In some environments, 100$ means 100 hexadecimal.

Just to make things sour, DEBUG uses hexadecimal but doesn't bother suffixing the values with an H. Yes, this even drives experienced programmers nuts. I often type in 100 in DEBUG thinking I want one hundred of something. In reality, 100 in DEBUG is equal to 256. (See Table 8-4 for verification.)

From Binary to Hex, and Finally to Decimal

You don't need to make decimal-to-hexadecimal calculations to survive in DEBUG. But you should understand that there's a reason behind this binary-decimal-hexadecimal madness: programmers use hexadecimal as a shorthand notation for binary. Take a look at Table 8-5, which lists the first 16 decimal values plus their hexadecimal and binary equivalents.

Consider how binary numbers are clumped into groups of four, as shown earlier in this chapter. Now, take another look at the table. If you maintain binary in groups of four, every possible combination of those four bits can easily be

Table 8-5 The Relationship Between Decimal, Hexadecimal, and Binary

Dec.	Hex.	Bin.	Dec.	Hex.	Bin.
0	0	0000	88	8	1000
1	1	0001	99	9	1001
2	2	0010	10	A	1010
3	3	0011	11	B	1011
4	4	0100	12	C	1100
5	5	0101	13	D	1101
6	6	0110	14	E	1110
7	7	0111	15	F	1111

represented by a single hexadecimal digit. For example, consider the obnoxious binary number shown earlier in this chapter:

```
0001 0000 0011 1110 0111 1001
```

Using Table 8-5, you can substitute each binary chunk with its proper hexadecimal equivalent:

```
0001 0000 0011 1110 0111 1001
  1    0    3    E    7    9
```

Without doing any complex math, the binary value has been painlessly translated into 103E79 hex. Now, of course, working that value back into decimal requires a bit of head-thought, but it's not necessary. This example simply shows you how quickly large binary values flow into smaller-sized hexadecimal numbers, which is why programmers use hexadecimal.

> *Note:* The octal counting base was used the same way as hex, as a shortcut for displaying the long binary values. The difference is that the binary values were hacked up into groups of three for octal representation.

Bits and Bytes

There are eight bits in one byte. Eight binary digits are grouped together to form one byte. Half a byte, or a "nybble," is four binary digits, which translates into one hexadecimal number. Therefore, two hexadecimal digits are required to represent one byte.

Chapter 6 told you that each byte was one character of information, and that a byte holds 256 values, from zero through 255. Binarily speaking, a byte holds from 0000 0000 through 1111 1111 values: That's eight bits, each of which can be 1 or

0, and there are 256 combinations. If you look back to Table 8-2, you'll see that 2^8 power is 256. Everything works.

Debug uses hexadecimal instead of binary. So byte values are shown in DEBUG as two-digit hex numbers. The hex number 00 is equal to 0000 0000 binary, which is zero. The value 255 is 1111 1111 binary, or FF hex. I figured out these values using the same information from Table 8-5: match up the binary pattern with its hex value and you have your number:

0100 1110 = 4E hex

1010 0101 = A5 hex

1111 0000 = F0 hex

0011 1011 = 3B hex

0110 0001 = 61 hex

From here you can figure out the decimal values if you like. The decimal values for the 1s column of a hexadecimal number are shown in Table 8-3. Table 8-6 shows the hexadecimal values for the next column, the 16s column.

Divide 256 by 16 and you get 16. If you know your 16-times tables then you know hexadecimal. Once more: the key here is to recognize a hex number for what it is, and not to confuse it with a decimal number. Generally speaking, hexadecimal values are much larger than their decimal look-alikes: 45 hex is equal to 69 decimal.

You can figure the math by yourself if you want to:

```
            4           E    hex
  =      4 × 16        14    decimal
  =        64    plus  14
  =        78
```

Table 8-6 Hexadecimal and Decimal Values for the Second Column

Hex.	Decimal	Hex.	Decimal
00	0	80	128
10	16	90	144
20	32	A0	160
30	48	B0	176
40	64	C0	192
50	80	D0	208
60	96	E0	224
70	112	F0	240

▶ *Tip:* The ASCII table in Appendix A is a great place to look up common hexadecimal numbers. It lists hex values from zero through 255 — one whole byte — along with binary, decimal, and character equivalents. Use it instead of doing any math.

Looking at Hexadecimal Numbers

I believe in such things as famous numbers: 1066, 1492, 1776, 1941, and so on. In computers, there are such things as "interesting" numbers. We have them in decimal: 5, 10, 20, 25, 50, 100. These are all interesting numbers, easy to add, divide, multiply, and so on — and they're also the denominations for our currency.

Those numbers aren't very interesting when you look at their hexadecimal equivalents:

    5   = 5 hex
    10   = A hex
    20   = 14 hex
    25   = 19 hex
    50   = 32 hex
    100   = 64 hex

Yeah, I could explain how some of these numbers can be exciting and point out something interesting. But the point is, decimal and hexadecimal have different sets of memorable numbers.

What it boils down to is this: using DEBUG requires you to be familiar with only a handful of memorable hexadecimal numbers. Of all the stuff covered so far in this chapter — all of it important for background purposes — you only really need to know the following, memorable hexadecimal numbers:

  8   one of the most revered of all computer numbers. There are 8 bits in a byte, and 8 is one half of 16 (like 5 is one half of 10). Look around any software package and you'll find 8 as a common value. In DEBUG, you'll see things grouped into eights all the time.

  10   pronounced 10 hex, equal to 16. DEBUG displays memory in a grid 16 bytes wide by 8 rows deep. The number 10 hex is also equal to one *paragraph* of memory in your PC. You'll see how this comes into play in the next chapter.

  40   40 hex is equal to 64, another holy computer number.

  80   80 hex is 128, halfway to 100 hex, 256. One less than 80 hex is 7F hex, which is 127 or the highest value given an ASCII character. Its binary representation is 0111 1111. The binary representation for 80 hex is 1000 0000. Anytime you have a change like that in a number, it's considered a big deal — just like how dad used to get excited when the car's odometer rolled over from 99,999 to 100,000.

FF	255, the highest value you can store in a byte. In a byte, if you were to add 1 to FF it would equal 0. The reason is that a byte can't hold more than 8 bits, so flipping that last switch simply toggles all the bits back to 0.
100	another revered number in computerdom: 100 hex is equal to 256. That's 16 × 16. The value 100 hex is one quarter of a kilobyte.
200	200 hex, 512 decimal, is important because information is stored on disk in 512-byte sectors. These are all equal to 200 hex bytes of information.
400	400 hex is equal to 1,024 — the magic number that defines a kilobyte of information. The reason 1,024 was chosen was because it's the closest power of 2 equal to 1,000. It has nothing to do with the value 400 hex.
1000	One thousand hex is equal to 4,096 decimal, 4K.
A000	It's pronounced "A-thousand hex." When you get letters in high hex numbers, you can pronounce them either way: "A, zero, zero, zero" or "A-thousand" are both accepted.
FFFF	Finally comes FFFF hex. This is the highest value that can be stored in a two-byte *word* of information. The value is 65535 or one byte shy of 64K which is 10000 hex). This is equal to one "bank" of memory in a PC. It's also the maximum value that can be stored in one of the microprocessor's *registers*, which you'll be reading about in Chapter 12.

Other hexadecimal numbers you'll commonly encounter include the values from 00 through FF — the ASCII character set, which you can view in Appendix A. You may also want to refer back to Chapter 6, where the differences between uppercase, lowercase, and control characters were discussed. Now that you understand a wee bit about binary and hexadecimal, these should all make sense.

Note: All numbers and values you see or enter in DEBUG are in hexadecimal. Unlike some official programming languages, however, you're not required to start a hexadecimal number with a leading zero.

In DEBUG, both FF hex and 0FF hex are recognized as the hexadecimal value FF, 255 decimal. In a "real" programming language, you *must* specify a leading zero when jotting down a hexadecimal number. If you don't, the interpreter or compiler may assume you're referencing a variable named FF, or DE, or C6, or you get the idea. In DEBUG, the leading zero is optional.

Diving into DEBUG

Start DEBUG at the command prompt. At DEBUG's hyphen prompt, type the D command:

```
-D
```

The D command displays a chunk of memory, exactly 128 bytes organized into 16 columns by 8 rows. Everything you see, all the values in those columns and rows, are hexadecimal values. What you see on your screen will vary, since the contents of memory changes as you use your PC.

The following chapter will explain how the "memory dump" works and what all the values you see represent. Just remember that everything there is shown in hexadecimal (save for the ASCII character display in the third, right-most column).

Using DEBUG's H Command

DEBUG has a command that lets you perform simple addition and subtraction of hexadecimal numbers. This is more of a curiosity than a handy tool; for really working with hexadecimal, binary, and decimal numbers, I recommend a good "programmer's" calculator. One of them comes with Borland's *SideKick* program; Windows' *Calculator* has a "scientific" mode that allows input of binary, hex, and decimal numbers; and there is a shareware program I'm fond of called *HEXCALC*, which can be found in the programmer's forum on *CompuServe* and on *GEnie*.

In DEBUG, you can use the H command to see the results of adding and subtracting two hexadecimal values. It's used in the following format:

```
H value1 value2
```

H must be followed by two values. It will add the first value to the second, then subtract them, displaying both results on the following line in this format:

```
added subtracted
```

Unfortunately, this command does not translate between hex and decimal. The following example shows how DEBUG will add and subtract 8 and 7 then 7 from 8:

```
-H 8 7
000F 0001
```

Eight plus seven equals F hex; the difference is one.

```
-H 8000 7FFF
FFFF 0001
```

In this example, H is followed by the hex values 8000 and 7FFF. The total of the two values is FFFF; the difference is one.

```
-H 9 10
0019 FFF9
```

In the above example, the total of 9 and 10 hex is 19 hex, or 25 decimal. The difference is FFF9. Sounds wrong, but it is not!

First of all, the difference between FFF9 and 10000 hex is 7, which is also the difference between 9 and 10 hex (16 − 9 = 7). Second, look at what's really happening with the command: You're subtracting 9 from 10 hex. Consider this variation:

```
-H 10 9
0019 0007
```

Here the values are clear: 19 hex is the total and 7 hex is the difference. What explains the FFF9 becomes apparent when you look at the binary values.

In binary numbers, you count from 0000 hex to 7FFF in the positive direction. The value 8000 is considered a "negative" binary number. In fact, it's negative 32,767. The hex value 8001 is −32,766; 8002 hex is −32,765, and so on. The values keep climbing until they approach zero. Negative one is FFFF. Figure 8-2 shows the hexadecimal number line.

As I've been promising all along, this is nothing to memorize. However, it's an accepted tradition in computers that the highest bit in a binary number is the "sign bit." When it's a one, then the value represented is considered to be a negative number. In the case of 8000 hex, you have the following binary number:

```
1000 0000 0000 0000
```

As the number increases, you approach zero until the following binary value, equivalent to negative one, is encountered:

```
1111 1111 1111 1111
```

The hexadecimal value FFFF is binary negative one. Is this worth memorizing? No. What's my point? The following tip should explain:

> **Tip:** To avoid confusion when using DEBUG's H command, always list the *largest* hexadecimal value first. Otherwise you'll be messing with negative binary numbers, which unlike counting the quills on a porcupine is more akin to playing catch with one.

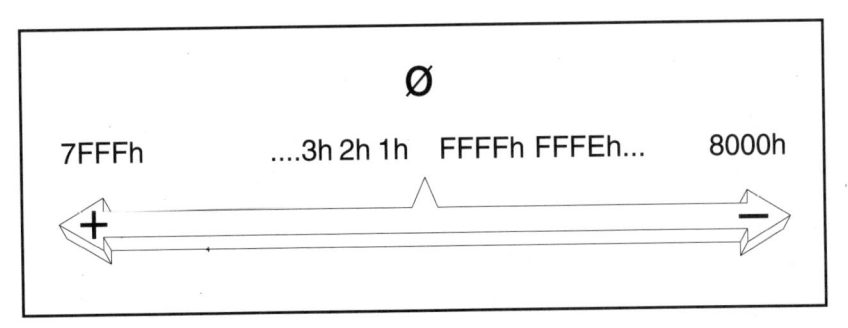

Figure 8-2 The hexadecimal number line, thanks to "negative" binary numbers.

9

The Ugly Truth about PC Memory

Don't you think PC memory is bizarre? Consider all the hoops you must jump through to do DOS memory management. Then look at all the oblique terms. Yuck! On a byte-by-byte basis, memory is easy to deal with. It's only when your programs want more and more memory that the web gets tangled.

This chapter tells you the truth about PC memory. It is bizarre! Here you'll read about the odd way a PC *addresses* or locates an individual byte in memory. Regrettably, that's something everyone must contend with when you use DEBUG. If it's something you'd rather not deal with, or feel you already know, then you can skim ahead to Chapter 10. I'd advise against it, however.

A Look at Memory

The byte is the basic unit of storage for PC memory. Memory in a computer is composed of thousands — sometimes millions — of bytes. Yet no matter how many you have, each byte is only eight bits big and can hold any value from zero through 255. Appendix A lists all the byte combination possibilities in decimal, binary, and hexadecimal, as well as the character displayed.

As far as DEBUG is concerned, all PCs use memory in the same way as the first IBM PC. Today's monster 386 and 486 computers work with memory differently, but for the sake of continuity and compatibility, for now assume you have an extremely fast 8088 PC. (After all, that's exactly what DOS does — which is a painful story I won't go into right now.)

The PC Memory Map

The first IBM PC used the 8088 microprocessor. That microprocessor could access or *address* one megabyte (1M) of memory. The 80286 that followed could address up to 16M of memory; and the '386 and '486 now address 4,096M or one gigabyte of memory (see Table 9-1). Still, with all that memory available, the first megabyte closely resembles the sole megabyte available to the 8088, especially when you run your PC under DOS. This means that no matter which microprocessor you have in your PC, DEBUG will show you memory in the same way.

Because of a weird design quirk you'll read about in a few pages, memory in a PC's first (or only) megabyte is arranged into 64K *banks*. When you divide 1,024K by 64K you get 16 banks in one megabyte. Each of these banks is numbered in hexadecimal, from zero through F, as shown in Figure 9-1.

> *Tip:* Always keep in mind that counting in a computer starts with zero, not one. Humans can start counting with their index finger as "one." Computers, lacking fingers, start counting with zero.

The PC memory map in Figure 9-1 starts at the bottom with bank zero and rises up in 64K slabs to bank F. Along the left side of the banks is the total memory listed in kilobytes — your basic "64K tables." You may notice the key value of 640K at the top of bank 9. Banks zero through 9 comprise the 640K of memory DOS uses; this is what's called *conventional memory*. Banks A through F, the letter banks, are what make *upper memory*. At the top of memory, at bank F, lies the 1,024K mark, one megabyte.

> *Note:* Early PCs on up to the IBM AT system had less than the full complement of 640K memory. For example, the first PC came with only 64K of memory — one slab. Later models had the popular 256K figure, only four banks of memory. Finally, the IBM PC/AT system came with 512K of memory, two banks short of the magic 640K number.
>
> When a computer has less than 640K, it doesn't decrease the total; the PC still has a potential of one megabyte, and the banks above the missing banks don't shuffle down like people waiting in line at the bank. Instead,

Table 9-1 Address Space in Common PC Microprocessors

Microprocessor	Address Space
8088/8086	1M
80286	16M
'386	4,096M
'486	4,096M

the missing banks are just "missing," and no information can be stored there.

By the way, the banks shown in Figure 9-1 aren't the same thing as a physical bank of memory in your computer. For example, that first 64K in the first IBM PC was composed of four banks of 16K RAM chips. Today's behemoth '386 and '486 systems usually come with one bank of 1Mb, "megabit" chips — a full megabyte of memory in a single bank. The banks shown in Figure 9-1 are for reference purposes only.

The memory banks can also be referenced using hexadecimal numbers. This is really cinchy: bank 1 is 1000 hex, bank 2 is 2000 hex, and so on. When you get to bank A, you have A000 hex, bank B is B000 hex, etc. (Peer ahead to Figure 9-6 to see how that works.) Some manuals may use this type of reference instead of

1024K	Bank F
960K	Bank E
896K	Bank D
832K	Bank C
768K	Bank B
704K	Bank A
640K	Bank 9
576K	Bank 8
512K	Bank 7
448K	Bank 6
384K	Bank 5
320K	Bank 4
256K	Bank 3
192K	Bank 2
128K	Bank 1
64K	Bank 0
0K	

Figure 9-1 The basic 1M of memory in all PCs is divided into sixteen 64K banks

bank numbers. For example, your PC's BIOS stays in bank F, which some manuals may reference as F000. Same thing.

Another place you may see these banks referenced is when performing DOS memory management. For example, if you're "excluding" a chunk of memory with the EMM386.EXE device driver, you may use the following:

```
DEVICE=C:\DOS\EMM386.EXE X=D800-DFFF NOEMS
```

In this example, the X command tells EMM386.EXE not to mess with memory locations between D800 and DFFF hexadecimal. These are memory locations in bank D, expressed in hexadecimal. (Much to the chagrin of everyone, memory management requires a knowledge of hexadecimal numbers.)

> **Tip:** Use the X command in EMM386.EXE, or a similar "exclude" command in any upper memory manager, to protect parts of upper memory that may be occupied with expansion cards, such as network drivers, video adapters, and so on. This ensures that the memory manager won't overwrite the card's memory with a device driver or TSR.

The first value from the above EMM386.EXE command is D800 hex. That address is in the middle of bank D: the value 800 hex is half of 1000 hex, which you can take to be the size of a bank of memory. (The value 1000 hex isn't really the size of a bank; 1000 hex = 4,096 decimal, but think of it as a "bank o' memory" for now.)

The second value, DFFF, is one notch below bank E. Therefore, the command *x=d800-dfff* protects half of bank D from misuse by EMM386.EXE. Figure 9-2 shows how this can work; substitute the little *x* in the hexadecimal values for bank D and you'll see that D800 up through DFFF is one half a bank of memory.

The values on the left in Figure 9-2 show how each bank of memory is divided into even parts. The values are in hexadecimal, but there's no need to translate them into decimal here. Instead, the values on the right side of the figure show you the size of each chunk of the bank of memory: a full bank of memory is 64K, half a bank is 32K, a quarter bank is 16K, and so on. File this information away in the back of your brain for future reference.

RAM and ROM

The entire memory map, all the memory locations from 0K up through 1,024K, is referred to as an *address space*. This is the maximum amount of memory a microprocessor can use. The old 8088 microprocessor had an address space of one million bytes. The newer microprocessors have larger address spaces, but are still consistent with the 8088 for the bottom, one megabyte of memory (see Table 9-1).

Your microprocessor can find any single byte — one in a million — in its address space. Each byte can be looked at and its value examined by the microprocessor. The byte's value can also be modified or replaced, depending on the type of memory, RAM or ROM.

The Ugly Truth about PC Memory 155

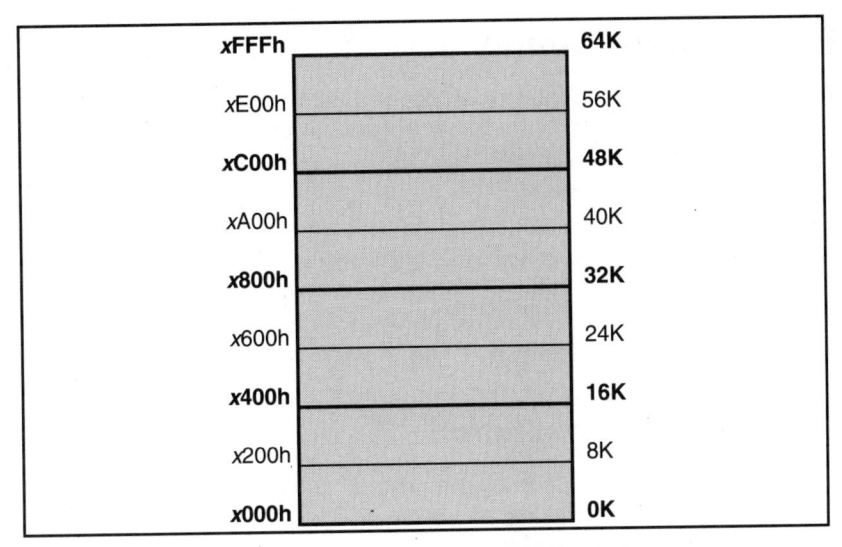

xFFFh	64K
xE00h	56K
xC00h	48K
xA00h	40K
x800h	32K
x600h	24K
x400h	16K
x200h	8K
x000h	0K

Figure 9-2 The hexadecimal portions of a bank of memory

RAM is Random Access Memory, the most common type of memory found in a computer. Bytes of RAM can have their values read, changed, manipulated, whatever. Most of your work on a computer, what you see on the screen and everything you create, is made in RAM. In Figure 9-1, banks zero through 9 make up the basic RAM in your computer.

To keep the contents of RAM alive, a constant flow of electricity is required. Without it, the contents of RAM disappear. This is why you save information to disk as a permanent copy. It's also why programs, files, and even DOS need to be loaded from disk into the RAM each time you turn it on.

The other type of memory is ROM, Read Only Memory. ROM fits into the microprocessor's address space just like RAM. And the microprocessor can read a byte of ROM just as it can RAM. But since the ROM is read-only, and its contents are permanently etched inside a chip, the microprocessor cannot change ROM.

ROM is used for important things inside a computer, such as the instructions that start your PC, the programs that control your video system and hard drive controller, and other information that doesn't change. You cannot modify ROM memory using DEBUG or any program.

In Figure 9-1, ROM can be found in banks A through F. Note that these banks aren't fully populated with ROM; there are some empty spaces and even some RAM up there. All of that area, however, is marked as "reserved" and generally not used for RAM memory storage.

▸ **Tip:** Parts of upper memory can be used as RAM memory storage. These areas are called upper memory blocks, or UMBs. They're used to store device drivers and memory resident programs (TSRs). Creating UMBs is done using memory management software; refer to Chapter 2 for a few words on the subject.

Finding a Byte in Memory

Before you can go byte hunting, you need to know how to locate a particular byte in memory. Bytes just aren't randomly thrown about inside your microprocessor's address space. There is order. Each of the million bytes in your PC has a specific location or *address* in memory.

This would make sense: Bytes in a computer have an *addressing scheme* just as you have a postal address where bill collectors can reach you. And take a second to revel in the logic of all this: a computer must have a terrifically sophisticated way of locating a single byte in memory, something much more coherent than, say, a ZIP code. Regrettably, it is not so.

The PC's 16-bit, 64K Limitation

You would think that with one million bytes in the first megabyte of a PC's memory that there would be one million addresses, one for each byte. Wrong! The original PC, although it could access every one of those million bytes, was limited by its *16-bit architecture*. This means that the PC was restricted to using only 64K of memory at a time. Here's how it all works (or doesn't work):

From your basic hexadecimal classes (in the previous chapter), you can figure out that 16 bits equals 64K. First, take a look at 16 bits, which I'll make all ones for you:

```
1111 1111 1111 1111 binary
```

Second, quickly translate this into hexadecimal. If you don't want to turn back to Table 8-5, know that 1111 equals F hex. So you have this:

```
FFFF hex
```

This is the maximum value that can be stored in 16-bits, FFFF hex. That equals 65,535 bytes, but since we start counting with zero, the total number of bytes is 65,536 or 64K. (Divide 65,536 by 1,204 bytes in a kilobyte and you get 64K.)

```
1111 1111 1111 1111 binary = FFFF hex = 64K bytes of memory
```

The ancient 8088, upon which the city of DOS computing is built, has only a 16-bit foundation. You'll see this in Chapter 12 when you're introduced to the microprocessor using DEBUG. For now, you need to know that the 16-bit, 64K limitation directly affects the way a PC accesses that one megabyte of memory. It introduces the twisted concept of *segmented architecture*.

That Awful Segmented Architecture

To directly address one million bytes of memory, you need a binary value that comes close to 1,000,000. The one settled upon as 1M is the value 1,048,576. Oddly, not exactly a million (although not bad if you're talking dollars). In any case, 1,048,576 just happens to be 1,024 x 1,024, or a kilobyte times a kilobyte, which is how you get a megabyte.

The Ugly Truth about PC Memory   157

The real reason the value 1,048,576 was selected is that, like 1,024, it's the "closest power of two." One kilobyte, 1,024 bytes, is 2^{10} — the closest you can get to 1,000 using powers of 2. The closest power of 2 to one million is 2^{20}, two to the twentieth power. That equals 1,048,576.

From a basic understanding of binary, the number 2^{20} is 20 digits long — four more than can be held in the 16-bit "word" that the PC uses. Drat! So the wizards at Intel devised a solution whereby 16-bit values can be used. You need two of them and they must overlap to cover all over memory. The first value is a *segment*, the second is called an *offset*. Using both values, you can pinpoint any byte in memory — but both values must overlap, which is what confuses everyone.

Together the 16 bits in the segment and 16 bits in the offset line up like this in binary:

```
Segment  =    0000 0000 0000 0000
Offset   =         0000 0000 0000 0000
Total    =    0000 0000 0000 0000 0000 (20 bits)
```

The segment and offset are 16 bits long, shown by the sixteen zeroes above. But the segment starts at bit 5. This is what gives you the extra four bits to equal 20 bits in the total. Those 20 bits, 2^{20}, equal 1,048,576 — one megabyte of addressable memory. Here's how it looks in hexadecimal, which is confusing, but it's what DEBUG uses:

```
Segment  = 0000
Offset   =  0000
Total    = 00000
```

In binary, the segment value doesn't start until bit 5. That's 2^4 or 16 (which you can verify using Table 8-2). The same holds true in the hexadecimal representation; the segment value doesn't start until the 16s column. This means that a segment starts every 16 bytes in memory. Let that sink in for a moment.

> *Note:* The segment describes one of 65,536 "paragraphs" in memory. A paragraph is 16 bytes (10 hex) long. Intel divided the 8088's address space into 65,636 paragraphs, making each of them start at an even, 16-byte location. This all works because 1,048,576 divided by 65,536 equals 16.

The first segment starts at the bottom of memory. It's numbered 0000. The second segment happens 16 bytes later — one paragraph — and is numbered 0001. The third is numbered 0003 on up through FFFF hex. Figure 9-3 shows how the segments sit in memory. The absolute memory locations indicate the offset of each segment every 16 bytes. This continues all the way up to the top of memory, segment FFFF hex.

You can't access all memory by skipping over 15 bytes at a time. Therefore, the second 16-bit value — the offset — is used to access individual bytes within the segments.

Like the segment value, the offset is 16-bits in size. It can hold a value from 0000 through FFFF hex, which lets the offset access 65,536 bytes or 64K of memory

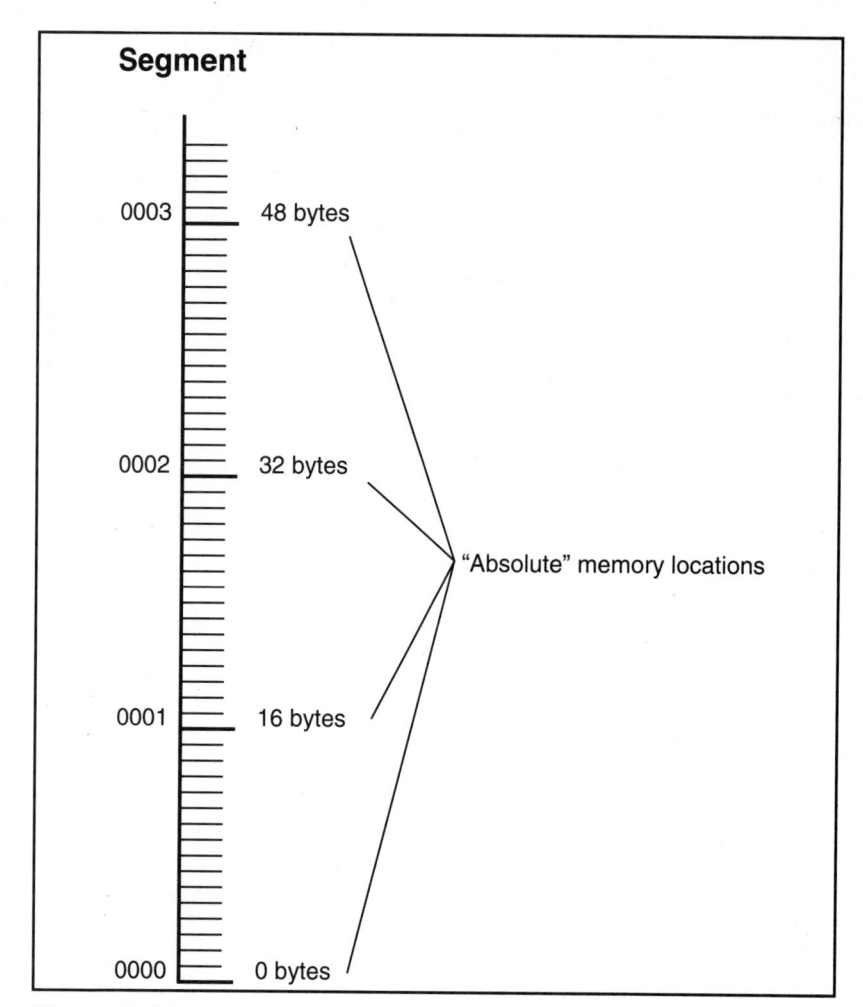

Figure 9-3 Segments in memory

directly. And since the offset value isn't "indented" like the segment, these are all individual bytes inside the PC's memory; there is no skipping here.

The offset makes sense. It's logical, and it's what you'll use to access individual bytes of memory. But that 16-bit limitation means the offset can only "see" 64K of a PC's one megabyte of address space at a time.

Welcome to why the PC's memory system is so eccentric. However, by working with both segment and offset values, you can access any individual memory location in a PC. Granted, this is weird. It's convoluted. It's what programmers call a *kluge*, but it works. Bear with me.

> ***Note:*** A kluge (klooj) is something thrown together. It's something that Earl would tinker with in his garage and barely get to work, but it still works so he's happy.

Locating a Byte in Memory

The previous section describes how and why segmented architecture came into being. However, the object of all this is to locate an individual byte in memory. The very first byte in memory is at segment 0000, with an offset of 0000. The second byte is also at segment 0000, but has an offset of 0001. Therefore, if you were to describe the first byte in memory, you would say:

```
Segment 0000, offset 0000
```

The accepted way to illustrate the segment and offset addressing scheme is to separate each value with a colon, as in *segment:offset*:

```
0000:0000
```

This example shows a memory address that DEBUG can understand and use. It describes the first byte in memory. Now suppose you want to access the 256th byte in memory. The value 256 is 100 hex; however, we started counting with zero, so the value would be FF hex:

```
0000:00FF
```

The 256th byte in memory can be located by starting at segment 0000 and setting an offset of 00FF, which points to the 256th byte in memory. Any location in the first bank of memory can be accessed this way. Want to find out what lies at byte 9000 hex? Use this address:

```
0000:9000
```

As long as your address is within bank 0 of memory, you can determine its location from segment zero using the properly sized offset.

Now consider a byte higher in memory. Say you want to peer halfway into bank C of memory. Bank C starts at segment C000. (In fact, all banks start at segment *x*000, where *x* is the bank number; see Figure 9-2.) Halfway between 0000 and FFFF is 8000 hex. So the address you want is:

```
C000:8000
```

Again, any location in bank C can be accessed using C000 as your segment, followed by the appropriate offset. Just consider the segment as a starting point and the offset as a 64K "window" looking at the memory that follows. Figure 9-4 illustrates the concept.

As long as you know in which bank your memory address is located, then it's really quite easy to find it. However, there are two things I need to point out before going on. The first is that segments do not always line up on bank boundaries. In fact, segments start at all sorts of oddball intervals: 1240 hex, 0004 hex, 8096 hex, and so on. (Remember, every 16 bytes you have a new segment in memory.)

The second thing to point out is that it's possible for one memory location to be described by several different addresses. In fact, some bytes in memory can be accessed using over 4,000 combinations of segment and offset values.

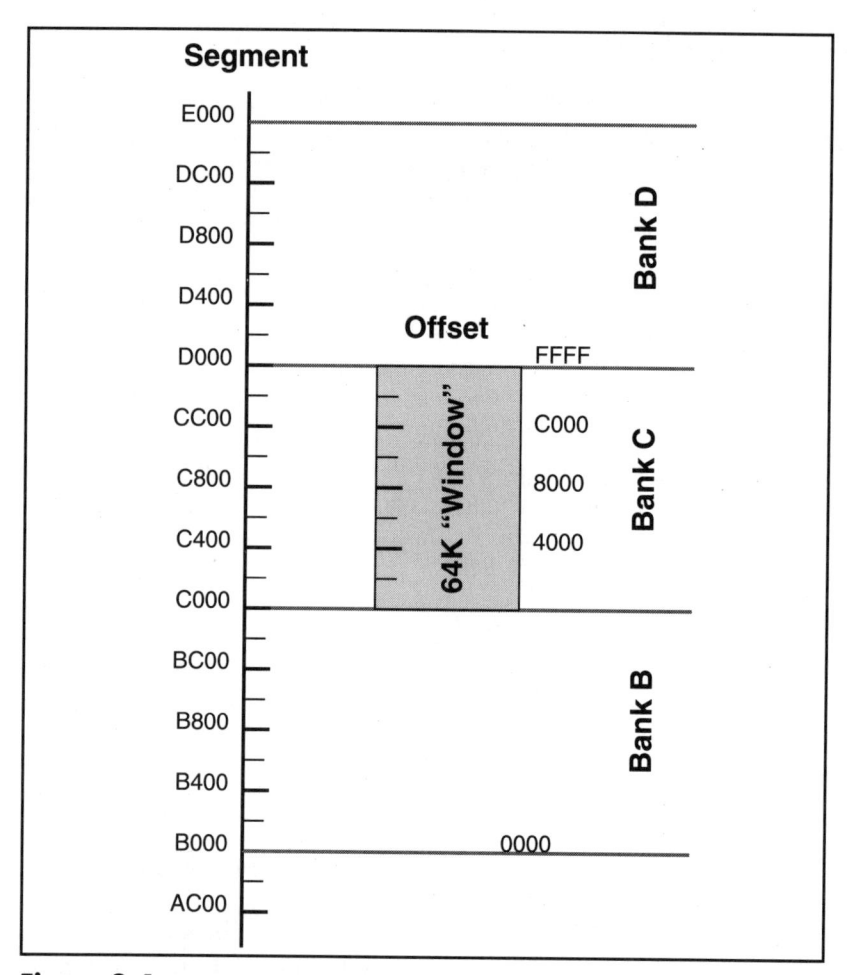

Figure 9-4 The segment sets the base and the offset allows you to "see" 64K of memory

One Byte, Many Addresses

There is more than one way to look at a single byte of memory. It all depends on where the byte is in memory, and how many segments are within 64K of it. But before filling your head with segment and offset combinations, consider the *absolute address*.

The absolute address is nirvana: it's how other non-PC computers access memory. If you want to look at byte 512,000, tell the microprocessor, "I want to look at byte 512,000" and it devotedly obeys your command. With a PC, you must bother yourself with segments and offsets.

Consider the byte at location 32 hex, way down low in memory. Since it's in bank zero, the byte's address is:

```
0000:0032
```

The Ugly Truth about PC Memory 161

Based on the above address, the byte will explain to us, "I am in segment zero, offset 32 hex." A perfect PC address. However, you can also access the byte from segment 1. In that case, the address for the same byte looks like this:

```
0001:0022
```

In this example, the byte can also be found in segment 1, but at offset 22 hex. This is the same location in memory, but a different address: segment 1 is 16 bytes long, 10 hex. Add 22 and 10 in hexadecimal and you get 32 hex, which is what the first address showed as the offset. But things get weirder:

```
0002:0012
0003:0002
```

Here are two additional addresses, both of which describe the same byte in memory. So far there are four addresses for one absolute memory location. These are each illustrated in Figure 9-5.

Each segment in memory forms a base. From that base you use the offset address to locate any byte within the next 64K of memory (the 64K "window" you see in Figure 9-4). Since segments start every 16 bytes, you have over 65,536 of them to choose from as a base for your offset.

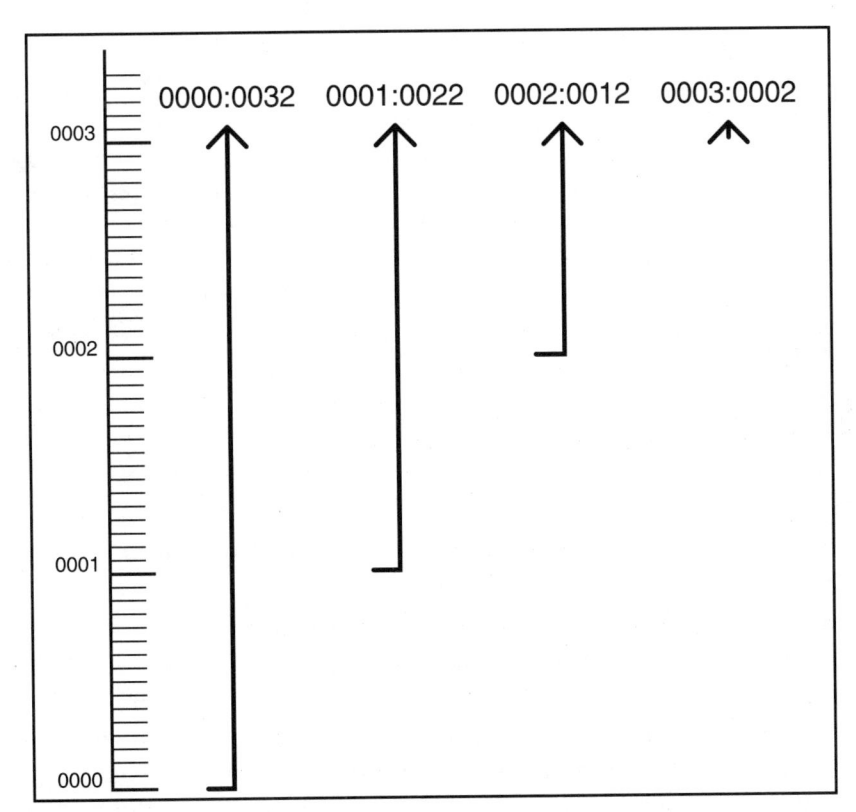

Figure 9-5 Different ways to address the same byte in memory

The memory location you're describing always remains the same, only its address changes. This can be proven by adding the segment and offset values:

```
Segment    = 0000
Offset     =  0032
Absolute   = 00032

Segment    = 0001
Offset     =  0022
Absolute   = 00032

Segment    = 0002
Offset     =  0012
Absolute   = 00032

Segment    = 0003
Offset     =  0002
Absolute   = 00032
```

In all the above cases, the absolute address is still 32 hex. This works no matter what address you have in your computer. Consider halfway through bank C, as used in an earlier example. That's written as C000:8000. Here is how it adds up:

```
Segment= C000
Offset= 8000
Absolute= C8000
```

This can also be written as C800:0000, C400:4000, C7FF:0010 and so on. You could conceivably create 4,096 different combinations to describe that sole byte in memory. (There are 4,096 — 1000 hex — segments in 64K of memory.)

The point here isn't to show off hexadecimal arithmetic. Instead, I'm trying to drive you mad because that's exactly what DEBUG will do. What is all boils down to is this: DEBUG will show you a memory address as a *segment:offset* value. What you do from there is up to you, but you now know the following things about that address and memory in general:

- DEBUG (and DOS) treat the first megabyte of memory in your PC like the memory found in the first IBM PC, which used an 8088 microprocessor. That computer was limited by its 16-bit architecture (which you'll soon learn to hate).

- The first megabyte of memory is divided into 16 banks, numbered 0 through F in hexadecimal. Each bank contains 64K of RAM.

- The total number of bytes in one megabyte is 1,048,576. That value is 2^{20} and requires a binary number 20 digits long to describe it. This is the root of the problem, since the first PC could only deal with 16-bit numbers.

- To address all of memory, the microprocessor uses segments and offsets. Both values are required to describe where bytes are located in memory.

- Both the segment and offset are 16-bit values, four hexadecimal digits long.

- The PC's one megabyte of memory is divided into 65,536 segments.
- Each segment starts every 16 bytes, one paragraph of memory.
- The offset describes a 64K block of memory starting at a specific segment.
- The format *segment:offset* is used to describe a byte's location in memory.
- Using a combination of segment and offset values, you can access any byte in memory.
- It's possible for some bytes to have thousands of addresses. The byte is still at the same absolute address, but it can be accessed using different combinations of segments and offsets.
- Whew!

Really Weird Stuff

This section contains some optional reading that you may want to skip over. This is not information required to deal with DEBUG. Since I'm writing about memory and I'm on a roll, I decided to wrap up this chapter with a few interesting tidbits. Feel free to skip to Chapter 10 if you'd like.

Refer back to Figure 9-4. Suppose you're using segment C000, as shown in the figure. From that base address, you can access the next 64K of memory using various offset values — all of bank C. But what happens when you try to reach beyond FFFF? Can you reach into bank D at all?

For example, consider the address C000:FFFF. This is one byte below bank D. If you add one to the offset value, however, the number "rolls over." It becomes 0000 and, once again, you're looking at the first byte in bank C, address C000:0000.

> **Tip:** In hexadecimal arithmetic, and in DEBUG, when you add one to the number FFFF hex, you get 0000 hex. You can prove this using DEBUG's H command:
>
> ```
> -H FFFF 1
> 0000   FFFE
> ```
>
> In this example, FFFF plus 1 equals 0000; FFFF minus 1 is FFFE. The reason for the rollover is the PC's old 16-bit limitation: FFFF hex is the highest value you can store in 16 bits. The next "highest" value is 0000.
>
> I know, I know: later PCs, such as the '386 and '486, have 32 bits. But both DEBUG and DOS stick with the ancient 8088 way of doing things.

Now consider that you're at segment F800. In this case, offset values from 0000 through 7FFF hex access memory at the top of the one megabyte address space. But where do offsets 8000 through FFFF point to? What lies beyond the top of memory? (Hum some eerie science fiction music here.)

Figure 9-6 illustrates what happens when you have 64K chunks of memory at offsets in bank F. The upper part of the memory bank *wraps around* back to

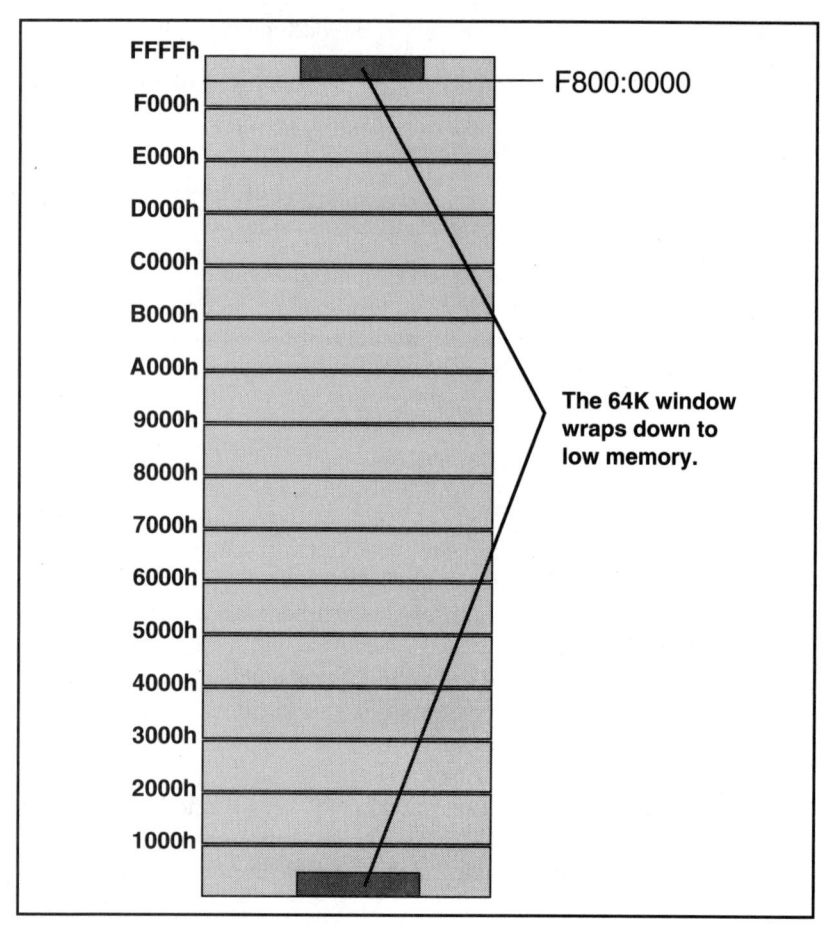

```
          FFFFh ┌─────────────┐
                │      ▓▓▓    │── F800:0000
          F000h ├─────────────┤
          E000h ├─────────────┤
          D000h ├─────────────┤
          C000h ├─────────────┤
          B000h ├─────────────┤
          A000h ├─────────────┤
          9000h ├─────────────┤  The 64K window
                │             │  wraps down to
          8000h ├─────────────┤  low memory.
          7000h ├─────────────┤
          6000h ├─────────────┤
          5000h ├─────────────┤
          4000h ├─────────────┤
          3000h ├─────────────┤
          2000h ├─────────────┤
          1000h ├─────────────┤
                │    ▓▓▓      │
                └─────────────┘
```

Figure 9-6 How a bank of memory "wraps"

memory location zero. So if you want to know what lies beyond the top of memory, it's the bottom of memory — a full circle.

> *Tip:* Remember the old Space Wars and Asteroids arcade games? When you flew your spaceship beyond the left part of the screen it reappeared on the right. If you flew your ship up off the top of the screen, it reappeared on the bottom. The same thing happens to your PC memory; it wraps around.

If you were scanning memory, the byte after address F800:7FFF would appear in DEBUG as F800:8000 but it would actually be absolute address 0000:0000. This works out mathematically:

```
Segment    = F800
Offset     = 8000
Absolute   = 00000
```

The absolute value above is really 100000 hex. But since there isn't a bit to hold that final one, the microprocessor lops off the value, truncating it to read 00000. Even though DEBUG may show you an address of F800:8000, you're really looking at the start of memory.

The example describes how the old 8088 handled addresses in upper memory. In that microprocessor, high memory locations wrapped around to low memory locations. The 80286, however, could access more than one megabyte of memory. Any memory above the 1,024K mark is *extended memory*. If that memory is present on an 80286, '386 or '486 computer, then the address F800:8000 may actually represent the first byte of extended memory — not absolute byte zero. It all depends on whether you have an A20 manager installed in your PC.

The "A20 line" in 80286 and later microprocessors determines whether memory locations above the one megabyte mark can be accessed as offsets, or whether memory will wrap, as shown in Figure 9-6. When you load a device driver such as HIMEM.SYS, it tells the microprocessor to go ahead and access memory above the 1M mark. This is done by accessing a 64K bank of memory starting at segment FFFF.

Segment FFFF is just 16 bytes below the top of memory. Yet, by using offset values from 0000 through FFFF, you can peer up into the first 64K chunk of extended memory and use that memory under DOS. That area of memory is referred to as the High Memory Area or HMA. It isn't really a full 64K chunk of memory; 16 bytes of that memory must maintain a small toehold at segment FFFF. Otherwise the HMA is accessible as extra memory in your PC.

The reason I bring this up is that you can see the HMA using DEBUG in your computer. This only works on systems where HIMEM.SYS or a compatible XMS (Extended Memory Specification) device driver has been installed. If you lack extended memory, or haven't loaded an XMS device driver, then memory will wrap in your PC, just as it does in the 8088.

10

Working with Memory

Time to get your hands dirty working in the depths of your PC. This is the stuff for which DEBUG was made. This chapter gives you a direct look at your PC's memory. I'm not going to bore you with long-winded explanations of EMS memory and how it differs from XMS memory or how both work. Instead, you'll see how you can use DEBUG to peer directly at the contents of memory and change that memory as you please.

Peeking at Memory

Ten of DEBUG's two dozen commands deal with memory. You can use them both to explore memory and optionally change its contents. Four of the commands are used to work with expanded memory, which isn't covered in this book (although you can dabble with them on your own if you like). The remaining six memory commands are listed in Table 10-1.

Only the D command is used to display the contents of memory. The other commands manipulate memory in one way or another, with the C command comparing memory and S searching through memory.

In the command formats listed in Table 10-1, the optional parameters *address*, *range*, and *bytes* are used. Here is what each means:

- *Address* represents a memory location. It can be an exact address, where you specify a segment and offset, or you can specify only an offset to work in the current segment. (If the words "segment" and "offset" cause your brow to furrow, then you should have read the previous chapter.) A space between the command letter and address is optional.

- *Range* defines a chunk of memory. It requires two values: a starting address and an ending address or in place of the ending address you can specify the size of the chunk using this format: L*value*.

- *Bytes* indicates individual byte values. You can specify a single byte, a list of byte values, or a string of text enclosed in quotes.

You'll see how each of these options is used as you work your way through the rest of this chapter.

> *Tip:* DEBUG allows for command line editing, just as DOS does. The most handy key to use is F3, which redisplays the previous DEBUG command. You can also use F1 through F5 if you like; refer to Table 6-7 to see what each function key does.
>
> Command line editors can also be used in DEBUG. The shareware utility DOSEDIT (or NDOSEDIT) works completely, including its command history function. DOS's DOSKEY command, however, does not work inside DEBUG.

DEBUG's Memory Display

Start DEBUG and at the hyphen prompt enter the D command. D shows you a chunk of memory in a three-column format. Figure 10-1 illustrates the DEBUG display on my computer. The individual values you see on your screen will be different. This is important to remember: each PC displays different values in RAM. Even the same PC will show you different values each time you look at it.

The first column of the memory display shows you memory addresses. The second column shows the values of the bytes found at that address. The final column shows the ASCII character representation of the byte values found. All the numbers you see in the first two columns are in hexadecimal.

Table 10-1 DEBUG's Memory Manipulation Commands

Command	Function
C range address	Compare one block of memory with another
D [address] D [range]	Display or "dump" a block of memory at a specific address, or display a block of memory
E address [bytes]	Enter bytes or a string of text at a specific address
F range bytes	Fill memory in the specified range with the bytes listed
M range address	Move (actually copy) bytes in the range to the specified address
S range bytes	Search a chunk of memory for the specified bytes

Working with Memory 169

```
-D
1F60:0100  01 74 C9 3D 50 01 74 AF-3D 51 01 74 CB EB DC 5E  .t.=P.t.=Q.t...^
1F60:0110  8B E5 5D C3 55 8B EC 83-EC 0A 8D 46 F8 50 8D 46  ..].U......F.P.F
1F60:0120  FC 50 E8 C1 75 83 C4 04-89 46 FE 3D 01 00 74 05  .P..u....F.=..t.
1F60:0130  3D 02 00 75 4E 8B 46 F8-8B 5E 04 2B 47 02 89 46  =..uN.F..^.+G..F
1F60:0140  FA 8B 47 08 89 46 F6 99-B9 03 00 F7 F9 3B 46 FA  ..G..F.......;F.
1F60:0150  7C 12 FF 36 EA 39 8B 47-1C 48 50 53 E8 4D 50 83  |..6.9.G.HPS.MP.
1F60:0160  C4 06 EB B6 8B 46 F6 D1-E0 99 B9 03 00 F7 F9 3B  .....F.........;
1F60:0170  46 FA 7F A6 FF 36 EA 39-8B 5E 04 8B 47 1C 03 46  F....6.9.^..G..F
```

Figure 10-1 DEBUG displays memory in a three-column format

Take a good look at the left column. You'll see a *segment:offset* address, pinpointing a location in memory. The first four-digit hex number is the segment. This will vary for each computer, depending on what you have loaded into memory and what you've been doing with your PC. On my system, and in Figure 10-1, I see segment 1F60, which I can guess is somewhere in bank 1. The specific memory location isn't important.

▥▶ *Tip:* If you want to calculate the exact memory location, you'll need to do some math. Warning! This is optional: start with the segment and add it to the offset value in the following format:

```
 1F60
 0100
1F700
```

Both numbers are hexadecimal and the total is 1F700 hex. To translate that into decimal, you can figure out the powers of 16, multiply them by the digit values, then add to get the totals. Or be like me and use a hexadecimal calculator to make the translation: the address 1F60:0100 on my computer is byte 128,768. This information is for trivial purposes only.

The offset value is 0100 hex, which will be the same on all computers when you first start DEBUG and type the D command. DEBUG always starts itself poised at offset 100 hex in a memory segment. You'll discover why when you read about how programs run under DOS later in this book.

You'll notice that all the memory values listed in the first column use the same segment. The offsets increase by 10 hex each row, going from 0100 up to 0170 hex. The reason for this is that each row shows you 10 hex (16) bytes of memory. Take a look at the middle column.

The middle column displays bytes in memory as two-digit hexadecimal values. The 16 bytes shown in each row are divided into two groups of eight with a hyphen separating them in the middle. Take a moment to spy the hyphen on your screen. It's important to locate the hyphen because it helps you determine the offset of individual bytes in the display.

Each of the bytes you see sits in memory at a specific address. The first byte is at offset 100, the second is at offset 101, the third at 102 and so on. The byte before the hyphen is at offset 107, after the hyphen is 108 on up to 10F at the right. Then the next row starts over with offset 110.

> **Tip:** You need to remember two things when locating a byte's address using DEBUG's D command. The first is that you must count in hexadecimal: the number after 9 is A — not 10. The second thing to remember is that you start counting with zero: 0, 1, 2, 3, 4, 5, 6, 7, the hyphen, 8, 9, A, B, C, D, E, F. That describes each byte's position relative to the segment and offset values in the first column.

As an example, in Figure 10-1, locate byte EC in the second row just the other side of the hyphen. The byte after the hyphen is always byte 8, so byte EC sits at offset 08. Add that to the address listed on the left of the screen, and you pinpoint the byte's location in memory: 1F60:0118.

The right column shows the same bytes in memory, but represented as ASCII characters. Non-ASCII characters and control codes are shown using a period. This allows you to locate text in memory, because most humans can't read hex and directly convert it into ASCII.

Using the D Command

DEBUG's D command stands for *dump*, an inelegant term used by computer people to describe the process of moving a large amount of information from one place to another. For example, a *screen dump* is a copy of the text on your screen sent to the printer. A memory dump is where DEBUG takes a swath of memory in your PC and displays it on the screen.

Without otherwise being told, the D command displays 128 bytes of memory at offset 100 hex in the current segment. The 128 bytes are displayed, along with their memory addresses, in a 16-column format eight rows deep. You should already see 128 bytes on your screen if you've followed the example in the previous section. If you enter the D command again, you'll see the next 128 bytes of memory, starting at offset 180 hex.

> **Tip:** Common hexadecimal numbers used in DEBUG:
>
> | Hex. | Decimal | Hex. | Decimal |
> | --- | --- | --- | --- |
> | F | 15 | 100 | 256 |
> | 10 | 16 | FFF | 4,095 |
> | 7F | 127 | 1000 | 4,096 |
> | 80 | 128 | FFFF | 65,535 |
> | FF | 255 | | |

If you're talking about an offset in memory, remember that numbering starts with zero. So the 256th byte in memory is reached using the value 255, FF. The first value is always zero.

Repeatedly pressing D without any options displays the next 128 bytes of memory. You can use one of the D command's optional parameters to display memory at a specific location in memory. For example:

```
-D 0
```

This command directs DEBUG to dump 128 bytes of memory at offset zero in the current segment. You'll see the same three-column memory format displayed, but the offset values will start at 0000 and rise to 0070.

To display more than 128 bytes of memory, you must specify a *range*. This can be done in two ways. First, suppose you want to display the first 256 bytes of memory in the current segment. You can use this command:

```
-D 0 FF
```

This command directs DEBUG to display memory from offset 0000 to offset 00FF, the first 256 bytes of the segment. The range specifies both starting and stopping addresses: 0 is the starting offset, FF hex is where the display stops.

The second way to display a range of memory is to use the L parameter. L specifies length:

```
-D 0 L100
```

This command displays the same block of memory, but uses a different syntax: the memory display starts at offset zero and goes on for a length of 100 hex (256) bytes. This format comes in handy when you want to display a definite chunk of memory but don't want to mess with hexadecimal math to find the ending offset. For example, suppose you want to see five bytes at offset E09. Don't fret with adding E09 and 5, type in this command:

```
-D E09 L5
```

> ✎ *Note:* The command *D E09 l5* translates into *D E09 E0D* using the other range format. That requires too much brain work for the average human to deal with.

So far you've only been looking at memory in the current segment. To see memory at any specific address in a PC, you need to use the *segment:offset* format. For example:

```
-D 0000:0000
```

The above command displays the first 128 bytes of memory. If you type the D command again — minus any options — you'll see the next 128 bytes of memory displayed. This works as it did when you first started DEBUG, but you've reset the segment and offset addresses to a new position in memory.

▶ *Tip:* As with any other counting base, you don't need to specify the leading zeros in hexadecimal. The command *D 0000:0000* can easily be written as *D 0:0*. In fact, the space is optional too: *D0:0*. The four hex digits are consistent with the way DEBUG displays addresses, but not necessary. DEBUG accepts input either way, so why do all that extra work typing zeros?

The following command displays values at the very tip-top of memory:

```
-D FFFF:0000 L10
```

The last segment in memory is FFFF. At offset zero you're looking at the highest 16 bytes in RAM ("L10" above). What you'll see there is a date, which happens to be the date of your PC's BIOS. Here is another address where you may find something interesting:

```
-D C800:0000
```

▶ *Tip:* The command *D FFFF:0000 L10* can be written *D FFFF:0 L10*.
And the command *D C800:0000* can be written *D C800:0*.

On many PCs, this is the address of your hard drive controller ROM BIOS. You may see a copyright notice or date on the screen. (If not, it's okay; you either have a unique hard drive controller or you're running memory management software that may hide the controller's ROM.)

```
-D C000:0
```

The above command displays copyright information for the VGA card controller in many PCs. If your VGA card is truly IBM compatible, look for the letters "IBM" in the ASCII part of the display. They can be found at offset 001E. This is how many software programs determine whether or not you have a VGA card.

✎ *Note:* The hex byte at offset 001E is 49 hex. From Appendix A, you can see that translates to an uppercase I, which is also seen in the right-most, ASCII column on the display. The letter B, 42 hex, is found at offset 001F, and the M, 4D hex, is found at offset 0020.
   The "IBM" text in all VGA-compatible graphic card ROMs is used by many software programs to confirm that you have a VGA card installed. What's funny is how they work the letters IBM into the ROM. Some systems will say "IBM compatible," others will go to great lengths to weasel in the letters IBM. Only by using DEBUG can you see what your VGA card says.

If you have an XMS device driver, such as HIMEM.SYS, installed into your PC, you can use the D command to peer into the High Memory Area (HMA). Try the following command:

```
-D FFFF:0
```

Working with Memory 173

The first line on your display will show the BIOS date, which you saw in a previous example. On systems with an XMS device driver installed, the next line will show the first 16 bytes of extended memory. There's no solid way to confirm this (at least, not by looking). On both my machines with RAM drive software installed, I can see the text "VDISK3.3" in the ASCII column. Your display may lack that clue, but as long as you have an XMS device driver, know that you're looking at the HMA.

The largest portion of memory you can view using the D command is 64K. For example, to scan all of bank 3 in memory, you can type the following command:

```
-D 3000:0 LFFFF
```

Or you can use this format:

```
-D 3000:0 FFFF
```

In both of these formats, only FFFF can be specified as the size of the memory block. In the first format, L is used to set the length of the block to FFFF. In the second format, the stopping address — which must be an offset — is set to FFFF.

▶ *Tip:* To pause the display, press Ctrl-S. Press Ctrl-S a second time to resume. To stop the display, press Ctrl-C.

Manipulating Memory

What's the good of finding something if you can't use it? The D command is used to look at memory, and you'll use it more than any other DEBUG command. Then, the other memory manipulation commands allow you to alter and manipulate the contents of memory.

DEBUG's E and F commands allow you to change the contents of memory. E lets you change or "poke" in individual byte values, and F allows you to instantly fill in a whole stretch of memory with one or more values.

The general manipulation commands are M, C, and S: the M command is used to copy a block of memory from one location to another. The C command compares one part of memory to another part of equal size. And the S command scans through memory for bytes or text.

Each of these five, remaining memory manipulation commands is covered in the following sections.

Changing Memory

The E command is used to change individual bytes of memory, one or several at a time. E stands for Enter, and by using it, you can enter new values into memory. This is done using the following format:

```
E address [bytes]
```

✎ **Note:** Changing the value of bytes in memory is often called *poking*. Looking at memory values without changing them is *peeking*. The BASIC programming language has two commands that do this, named PEEK and POKE.

DEBUG's E command must be followed by an address. If a segment isn't specified, then the address is assumed to be an offset in the current segment.

Quit DEBUG with the Q command, then restart it at the command prompt. At the hyphen prompt, type the *E 100* command:

```
-E 100
1F60:0100 00.
```

This command tells DEBUG that you want to start poking new bytes into memory at offset 100 in the current segment. After pressing Enter you'll see the *segment:offset* address displayed followed by the value of the byte at that address and a period, as shown above.

The E command is showing you the current value of the byte you want to replace. In the example, that value is 00 (which will probably be different on your PC). To type in a new value, enter a two-digit hex number. In this example, type 44. (Remember, all numbers you enter in DEBUG are hexadecimal; 64 hex is 100 decimal.)

After typing the number, press the Spacebar. This jumps you up to the next byte in memory, which you can also change. Type the hex value 45 and press the Spacebar again. Continue entering the following numbers, pressing the Spacebar after each:

```
42 4F 47
```

Altogether you will enter the following five bytes into memory: 44, 45, 42, 4F, and 47.

After you've entered the final byte value, press Enter. To see what five bytes you've entered into memory look like, type the following command:

```
-D 100 L5
```

The hex bytes 44, 45, 42, 4F, and 47 spell out one of the most frequently used words in this book — almost. It's not DEBOG, it's DEBUG. To change that O to a U, hex character 55, type the *E 100* command again:

```
-E 100
1F60:0100 44.    45.    42.    4F.55
-
```

This time, press the Spacebar after each byte until you encounter byte 4F. After that value, type 55 and press Enter. Type the *D 100 L5* command to display the results again.

▶ *Tip:* To skip over a byte, and leave its value unchanged, press the Spacebar.

After you reach eight bytes, the E command drops down to the next line on the screen:

```
1F60:0100  44.   45.   42.   55.   47.   00.   00.   00.
1F60:0108  00.   00.   00.
```

On the next line, the memory address is updated by eight bytes, as shown above. This keeps consistent with the memory addressing scheme; in the example you would be working on bytes starting at offset 108.

Pressing Enter cancels the E command and returns you to the hyphen prompt. Pressing Ctrl-C also cancels the E command.

Using the E command to change one byte at a time is slow, but accurate. If you don't know the exact offset of a byte value, then you can type E followed by a general offset value, then keep pressing the Spacebar until the offending byte appears. Type in a new value and press Enter. *No problem.*

A quicker way to use the E command is to follow it with an optional byte value. For example:

```
-E 110 24
```

The above command "pokes" the value 24 into the byte at offset 110. Type the *D 110 L1* command to view the byte (a dollar sign in ASCII). You can type in a group of bytes in the same manner:

```
-E 110 41 42 43 44 45 46 47 48 49 4A 4B 4C 4D 4E 4F 50
```

In this example, 16 bytes are poked into memory locations starting at offset 110. Each is separated by a space. To see them in memory, use the following command:

```
-D 110 L10
```

Entering bytes using the E command is a quick way to poke a program into memory. Back in Chapter 5, Figure 5-4 uses the E command to poke a rather sizable program into memory. The bytes poked are mostly machine language; they contain instructions that the microprocessor will read and obey. But if you notice from Figure 5-4 (and you don't have to look), the E command was also used to poke in strings. In that format, you surround the text to poke in double quotes:

```
-E 120 "QRSTUVWXYZ"
```

This command pokes the rest of the alphabet into memory. You can poke any string into memory you like. For example, poke in your name with the following command (use your name — not Abe's):

```
-E 130 "Abraham Lincoln"
```

The above command pokes in "your name" at offset 130. So far you should have three interesting things poked into memory:

- Offset 100 contains the word "DEBUG"

- Offset 110 contains the start of the alphabet, which continues at offset 120

- Offset 130 points to the start of your name.

To see everything in memory, type the following command:

```
-D 100
```

Keep that vision fresh because it's going to change in the next section.

Changing a Lotta Memory

If you need to poke the same value into a vast expanse of memory, the E command would be terribly inefficient. No need to expand on that bad idea. Instead, consider the F command, which is used to fill a range of memory with a specified byte value or pattern of bytes.

The F command has a similar format to the E command, although a range of bytes must be specified instead of a base address:

```
F range bytes
```

The *range* value is a starting address, either an offset or segment and offset, and an ending address (offset only). In place of the ending address you can specify L for length, followed by the size of the memory block, up to FFFF hex.

Bytes represents one or more bytes — or an optional string of characters enclosed in double quotes. Those bytes will be poked into the memory *range* specified. For example, type in the following command:

```
-F 100 L100 00
```

This command fills the bytes in a 100 hex-long block of memory starting at offset 100 with zeros. The first 100 shows the block's starting address, at offset 100 hex in the current segment. The L100 sets the length of the block to 100 hex bytes, 256 decimal. Finally, the bytes to stuff into that block are listed. Above, the bytes will have a value of zero.

▶ ***Tip:*** The command *F 100 1FF 00* would also fill the same 100 hex-long block of memory with zeros; it's just another way of expressing the same range.

I usually use this command to blank out 256 bytes of memory when I first work with DEBUG. Especially if you've had your PC on for a while, that area of memory will be littered with random bytes of information. The *F 100 LFF 00* command cleans everything away like the CLS command clears the screen. Mentally, it's just nicer to start work with a "blank slate" of RAM.

To see whether everything worked, type the following D command:

```
-D 100 LFF
```

All the bytes you see on your screen should be zero. And you'll notice that it took an amazingly short amount of time to fill that block of memory.

If you want to fill memory with two alternating bytes, specify them as follows:

```
-F 100 L10 55 AA
```

The command shown puts the byte value 55 into even memory locations starting at offset 100; the value AA will be poked into the odd bytes. Here's the D command to display your work:

```
-D 100 L10
```

The same can be done with three bytes:

```
-F 100 L30 55 AA FF
```

To see how those three bytes fill memory, use this D command:

```
-D 100 L30
```

The F command will fill the range of memory with the pattern until the final byte in the range. It will not try to squeeze in a byte; if the pattern doesn't fit, it's truncated.

You can also use the F command to fill memory with a text string. Use a format similar to the following command:

```
-F 100 180 "Help me!"
```

To view this urgent cry, use the following D command:

```
-D 100 L80
```

> **Tip:** The command *D 100 L80* can be abbreviated to *D 100*. The "L80" part is redundant; D always displays 80 hex (128) bytes of memory.

Like any DEBUG memory command that uses a *range* value, you're limited to working with only a 64K chunk of memory. The maximum *range* or offset address you can specify is always FFFF hex, 64K. Under most circumstances, however, you'll never need to fill a chunk of memory that large.

> **Note:** The handiest place for using the F command is in putting information on the screen. This is really cool, and you'll be reading about it in detail in Chapter 12.

Copying Blocks of Memory

DEBUG will let you copy memory from one location to another using the M command. In the manual — and probably in your brain as well — it's easy to think that M means *move*. It doesn't. M stands for Copy. While you do move bytes from one block to another, the originals are not erased. So it's a copy (I prefer to say Moo-copy). Here is the format:

```
M range address
```

The range sets the location and size of the block to be copied. You start with a base address or a *segment:offset* value, then a length or ending address. The block can only be 64K in size, FFFF hex.

The *address* is the location to which you're moving the bytes. It can only be an offset address, not another *segment:offset* location.

To demonstrate the Moo-copy command, first clear out a swath of memory using the F command:

```
-F 100 L80 0
```

This command zeroes out 128 bytes at offset 100. Now use the E command to poke in something interesting at offset 130:

```
-E 130 "The maid did it!"
```

Check your work with the D command:

```
-D 100
```

What you see on your screen should match what's shown in Figure 10-2. Your segment values will probably be different from what's seen on my computer, in Figure 10-2; the segment on my PC is 1F60. The text sits in memory at offset 130, which will be the same on all PCs. Above and below it will be bytes with zero values. So far so good.

From looking at Figure 10-2 or your screen, figure out how long the block of text is. This is an easy one: You should be able to tell just by looking. Figure out the text's starting address, offset only, then the ending address or length. Don't peek ahead to the next paragraph to find the answer. Fill in the blanks if it helps:

- The text starts at offset _____ hex
- The text ends at offset _____ hex
- The text is _____ hex bytes long

The "T" starts at offset 130. This is painfully obvious, since it's the same address you used with the E command above. The ending address is where the exclamation point is located in memory. That's 13F hex — not 140 hex. Remember that DEBUG displays bytes in 16 columns, numbered zero (not one!) through F hexadecimal. Finally, the text is 16 bytes long, which translates smoothly into 10 hex. You need

```
-F 100 L80 0
-E130 "The maid did it!"
-D100
1F60:0100   00 00 00 00 00 00 00 00-00 00 00 00 00 00 00 00   ................
1F60:0110   00 00 00 00 00 00 00 00-00 00 00 00 00 00 00 00   ................
1F60:0120   00 00 00 00 00 00 00 00-00 00 00 00 00 00 00 00   ................
1F60:0130   54 68 65 20 6D 61 69 64-20 64 69 64 20 69 74 21   The maid did it!
1F60:0140   00 00 00 00 00 00 00 00-00 00 00 00 00 00 00 00   ................
1F60:0150   00 00 00 00 00 00 00 00-00 00 00 00 00 00 00 00   ................
1F60:0160   00 00 00 00 00 00 00 00-00 00 00 00 00 00 00 00   ................
1F60:0170   00 00 00 00 00 00 00 00-00 00 00 00 00 00 00 00   ................
```

Figure 10-2 A block of text sits in memory, ready to be copied

to know these values to set the range and size of the memory block to copy with the Moo-copy command.

> **Tip:** How could figuring out "The maid did it!" be easy? Because it fills one row of bytes on the screen. Since each row is always 10 hex (16) bytes long, that means the block is that long as well.

To copy the block to offset 160, you can use one of two commands:

```
-M 130 L10 160
```

This command takes the block starting at offset 130 hex, with a length of 10 hex bytes, and moves it to offset 160. Or you can use this command:

```
-M 130 13F 160
```

In this format, the block starts at offset 130 hex and ends at offset 13F hex. The block is moved to offset 160 hex. Both commands do the same thing; pick one and enter it at DEBUG's hyphen prompt. To see how everything worked, type the following:

```
-D 100
```

You should now see the text in two places: At offset 130 and 160 hex. You can also move the block of memory to a location *below* its starting address. Type in the following Moo-copy command to copy the block, then the D command to see how it works:

```
-M 130 110 100
-D 100
```

You should note that the Moo-copy command will preserve your original block of memory when the destination overlaps it. For example, type the following two Moo-copy commands. Each of them copies a block of memory over the source block:

```
-M 130 L10 138
-M 160 L10 158
```

In the first command, the 10 hex-byte block at offset 130 is copied to offset 138. There is an overlap of eight bytes. The second command copies a 10 hex-byte block from offset 160 to offset 158. In both cases, the destination block overlaps the source. However, DEBUG is aware of this and will keep the contents of the source intact for the copy. Part of the original block will be overwritten, but the destination block will be identical to the source.

> **Note:** Normally, such an overlapping copy operation would alter bytes in the source block, corrupting the copy. DEBUG prevents this, and always copies a block of text identical to the source.

Comparing Memory

The C command is used to compare one part of memory with another. Here is its format:

```
C range address
```

The *range* and *address* values are similar to those used with the Moo-copy command: *range* sets the origin and size of the first bock, and *address* sets the location of the second block that will be compared with the first.

To see how the C command works, start off with a clean slate by typing in the following F command:

```
-F 100 LFF 0
```

The following E and M commands enter a string into memory, then copy it to another offset. The D command then displays your work, which can be seen in Figure 10-3. Take a second to compare your work with the figure. Then sit back and marvel at what feats you're working with memory. Who would have thought this type of thing could be done with DOS? This is direct control, raw-power stuff.

```
-E 100 "A rose is a rose"
-M 100 L10 140
-D 100
```

The two blocks of memory at offsets 100 and 140 are identical. You can verify this on your screen and in the figure. Use the C command to verify it in DEBUG using the following format:

```
-C 100 L10 140
```

In this example, the C command compares a block of bytes starting at offset 100, with a length of 10 hex-bytes, with the same sized block at offset 140. If you don't see anything after pressing Enter, then the blocks are identical. Cool. Now alter one of the blocks with the following E command:

```
-E 14C "weed"
```

```
-F100 LFF 0
-E100 "A rose is a rose"
-M100 L10 140
-D100
1F60:0100  41 20 72 6F 73 65 20 69-73 20 61 20 72 6F 73 65   A rose is a rose
1F60:0110  00 00 00 00 00 00 00 00-00 00 00 00 00 00 00 00   ................
1F60:0120  00 00 00 00 00 00 00 00-00 00 00 00 00 00 00 00   ................
1F60:0130  00 00 00 00 00 00 00 00-00 00 00 00 00 00 00 00   ................
1F60:0140  41 20 72 6F 73 65 20 69-73 20 61 20 72 6F 73 65   A rose is a rose
1F60:0150  00 00 00 00 00 00 00 00-00 00 00 00 00 00 00 00   ................
1F60:0160  00 00 00 00 00 00 00 00-00 00 00 00 00 00 00 00   ................
1F60:0170  00 00 00 00 00 00 00 00-00 00 00 00 00 00 00 00   ................
```

Figure 10-3 The final result of four DEBUG commands

Working with Memory 181

This command pokes the word "weed" into memory at offset 14C. You can use the *D 100* command to see how both blocks are now different.

▶ ***Tip:*** How did I know where to poke in the word "weed?" I looked at my screen, shown in Figure 10-3. The second "rose" at offset 140 is located at offset 14C, with the "r" starting in column C of the display. I didn't innately know that. Instead, I looked up the letter "r" in Appendix A and found it to be 72 hex. Then I counted bytes after the hyphen, which starts with 8, until I got to the byte 72 hex:

```
-73 20 61 20 72
 8  9  A  B  C
```

Adding C to 140, I came up with the address 14C to use with the E command. Since "weed" has the same number of letters as "rose," it poked in rather nicely.

Now type the same C command as you did above to compare the two blocks:

```
-C 100 110 140
```

Instead of seeing nothing, DEBUG will report to you the four bytes that are different, along with the *segment:offset* addresses of each:

```
1F60:010C  72  77  1F60:014C
1F60:010D  6F  65  1F60:014D
1F60:010E  73  65  1F60:014E
1F60:010F  65  64  1F60:014F
```

Keeping in mind that my segment values (above) are different than what you may see on your screen, note how the output is laid out: first comes the starting address, then the original byte, and then the destination byte and its address. In the display, four sequential bytes are different, starting at offsets 10C and 14C.

The C command reports the differences on a byte-by-byte basis, showing you each of the different bytes and their addresses. No attempt is made to correct the bytes; DEBUG's C command reports differences only. If you want to fix any differences, you can use the E command to poke in bytes on an individual basis, or simply use the M command to recopy the block. Or you may just want to see what's different, in which case the C command shows you.

There are two drawbacks to the C command. The first is that it doesn't show you any ASCII output. The second is that its output format can get long and tedious when more than a handful of bytes are different. Sadly, there's no way to correct these two disadvantages.

✎ ***Note:*** You also have no way of getting a hard copy of the C command's output, although this is a general drawback to DEBUG and not just the C command. You can always use the Print Screen key, but it's rather inelegant and can't adequately capture the long lists of bytes that the C command produces.

Searching Memory

The S command searches an area of memory for matching bytes or text. This is a powerful command, but it still has a 64K limitation on the range of memory it can search. Here is the S command's format:

```
S range bytes
```

The *range* works just like any other *range* value described so far in this chapter; it defines a block of memory in which DEBUG will scan for bytes or text. The *bytes* are a list of individual bytes to search for or a string of text enclosed in quotes, similar to what you would use after the E command.

The following three commands prepare memory for demonstrating the S command. First memory is cleared, then a text string is poked into memory, then that chunk of memory is displayed:

```
-F 100 L100 0
-E 100 "Does it hurt to be poked into memory?"
-D 100
```

The hexadecimal byte value of "d" is 64. To search for it in memory, use this command:

```
-S 100 L100 64
```

After typing in the above command, DEBUG will display the *segment:offset* address of the byte, providing it's found in the memory block specified. On my system, I saw "1F60:0117" displayed; you'll see the same offset, but probably a different segment value.

To search for more than one byte, separate each by a space:

```
-S 100 L100 75 72
```

▶ *Tip:* You can also use commas, as in *S 100 l100 75,72*.

It's assumed that the bytes you want to look for are sequential, so the address DEBUG displays shows you the start of the byte pair in memory. If more than one byte is found, you'll see multiple addresses displayed:

```
-S 100 L100 6F
1F60:0101
1F60:010E
1F60:0114
1F60:011C
1F60:0121
```

In the example, the byte value 6F hex equals the character "o." There are five "o"s in memory, their offsets are shown also.

If no match can be found, then S displays nothing:

```
-S 100 L100 FF
-
```

There is no byte FF in that part of memory, so all you'll see is another hyphen prompt; nothing was found.

To locate a string in memory, specify it in double quotes:

```
-S 100 1FF "poke"
```

Above, the S command scans for the word "poke" in memory, returning the address of the "p" in poke on the following line.

▶ *Tip:* The S command is case-sensitive; it would not find "POKE" in memory if you told it to look for "poke." The reason is that DEBUG internally translates text into byte values. The byte value of uppercase and lowercase letters is different (see Appendix A), so you need to be exact when searching for text.

Let's visit the outer limits of memory and scan for cool things. Type in the following command:

```
-S 9000:0 LFFFF "COPY"
```

This command scans bank 9 of memory — all of it, since the length value FFFF hex is specified. What you're looking for is the word "COPY." Bank 9 is at the top of conventional memory and is where COMMAND.COM stores its internal command list.

✎ *Note:* If you have less than the full 640K conventional memory, this command won't return anything. In that case, try scanning other banks for "COPY": use *S 8000:0, S 7000:0, S 6000:0* and so on in the above command until you find it.

On my PC, the S command returned three values:

```
9000:46CE
9000:CDAA
9000:ED2B
```

The offsets you see on your screen will probably be different; COMMAND.COM's "transient" portion loads into a different part of bank 9 depending on what you already have loaded into high memory. So follow these next instructions carefully.

Take the first address displayed by the S command and use it with the D command. In the example I saw the address 9000:46CE. I'll use that address on my PC with the following D command:

```
-D 9000:46CE
```

Type in the D command followed by the address you see on your screen — not the value above (unless it's identical to that on your screen). Press Enter and you'll see the COPY command in memory. Do the same with the other addresses. On my system, that would be the following two D commands:

```
-D 9000:CDAA
-D 9000:ED2B
```

If you see anything interesting in memory, use the D command to "scan" around that part of RAM. For example, when I peered at memory location CDAA, I saw the COPY command's help text. But CDAA is an odd offset. To see the entire message, I lopped off the final two hex digits and replaced them with zeros: CD00. To see the COPY command's full help text, I then used this command:

```
-D 9000:CD00
```

By continuing to type the D command (and press Enter), you can then scroll through the text messages in memory, which can be viewed on the right side of the screen. Remember: use the offset values you saw on your screen. Try the same trick if you like. Or just use the D command to peer into COMMAND.COM's transient portion loaded high in memory.

Do you have a mouse device driver installed in your PC? Verify it with the following S command:

```
-S 0:0 LFFFF "mouse"
```

This command scans the first bank of memory, bank zero. The base address is 0:0, the start of memory. The L value is FFFF, 64K. The text you're looking for is "mouse." If you didn't see anything, then it's probably because the S command is case-insensitive. Try the following command instead:

```
-S 0:0 LFFFF "MOUSE"
```

This time you may see an address pop up. Use that address with the D command to peer at your mouse driver in memory. Don't be disappointed; there probably won't be much to see.

11

Disks and DEBUG

DEBUG does everything in memory, which is why the previous chapter introduced you to all the memory commands. But truthfully, by itself RAM is boring. What's the point of creating something whiz-bang in memory when you can't immortalize it? DEBUG lacks a print command, so the only way to save your efforts is to take a chunk of memory and copy it to disk. And in the same vein, the only way to work on a part of disk using DEBUG is to copy it to memory.

This chapter covers DEBUG's disk commands. You'll read how to create and edit files on disk, as well as how to use DEBUG to scope out — and modify — "raw" sectors of disk information. Since DEBUG only works with memory, most of the manipulation taking place here is done using DEBUG's memory commands; the disk commands just save and load information to and from disk. If you're unfamiliar with DEBUG's memory commands, I strongly recommend reviewing the previous chapter.

Working with Files

DEBUG's main function is to get the bugs out of program files. As such, it's designed to work primarily with program files. An interesting side effect of this is that DEBUG can also work with text and data files. And since the programmers at Microsoft were probably rejoicing over their stock options that week, they decided to allow DEBUG to access raw information on disk as well. This makes DEBUG an ideal disk tool, although not as sophisticated as traditional hard disk utilities.

▶ *Tip:* If you really need to access raw information on disk and edit it in a painless and refined way, I recommend purchasing a professional, third-party disk utility. The top three are Symantec's *Norton Utilities*, Central Point Software's *PC Tools* and Fifth Generation System's *Mace Utilities*. The shareware program *Baker's Dozen* is also a handy collection of useful disk utilities. It can be ordered from PC SIG, the Software Labs, or a number of other shareware warehouses.

There are two main commands DEBUG uses with disks: L to load information from disk into memory and W to write memory to disk. Both commands have two formats, one that allows you to work with filenames and a second that allows you to read and write raw sectors. When working with filenames, another command, N, is used to name the file. All three commands are described in Table 11-1.

The deadliest part of working with disks and DEBUG is that it's entirely possible (although unlikely) to write random information to a vital part of your hard drive. To prevent this, I recommend that you create a sample floppy disk for your A drive. Use the highest capacity diskette for that drive and format it using the following command:

```
C:\> FORMAT A: /U
```

The /U switch is added in case you're using an old disk; it completely erases all files on the disk and reformats it on a low level. This ensures that everyone will start off with the same blank disk for the exercises in this chapter.

Label the disk "Sample Disk" on its sticky label. Use the LABEL command to give the disk the volume label TEST DISK.

Saving Memory to Disk

To take a chunk of memory and write it out to disk you need to supply DEBUG with three pieces of information:

- A filename
- The size of the memory block
- The starting address for the memory block

DEBUG's N command sets the filename. The size of the memory chunk is specified using the RCX command, which I'll be describing in a moment. And finally, the W command supplies the starting address and at the same time writes the block to disk. Because of this, the W command always comes last when you write memory to disk.

Rather than write any old random piece of memory to disk, you can use the memory manipulation commands from the previous chapter to put something interesting into memory. Start DEBUG (if you're not in it already), and clear out a swath of RAM:

```
-F 100 L80 0
```

Table 11-1 DEBUG's Disk and File Commands

Command	Function
L [address] L address drive sector number	Loads a file to a specific address, or loads several raw sectors of information into memory (depending on the format used).
N filename	Names a file to be loaded or written to disk with the L or W commands.
W [address] W address drive sector number	Writes memory to disk starting at a specific address and using the name specified by N; or writes memory directly to the disk and sectors specified. A deadly command.

Use the E command to poke a text string into memory. Enter the following DEBUG command:

```
-E 100 "This is a small text file" 0D 0A
```

The E command pokes a string of text into memory at offset address 100 hex. The text is followed by two byte values, 0D hex and 0A hex. These two characters represent the carriage return and line feed DOS sticks at the end of each line of text.

Tip: To end a line of text in DOS, the characters 0D hex and 0A hex are used. Character 0D hex is the carriage return, character 13, or Ctrl-M — the Enter key. Character 0A hex is the line feed, character 10, or Ctrl-J. This can be confirmed in Appendix A, however the best way to tell what they do is by displaying them on the screen: the carriage return will move the cursor to the left-most column, then the line feed will drop the cursor down a line. (A word processor or text editor interprets the Enter key as both a carriage return and line feed.) This works just like the typewriters of old: you whacked the carriage return to move the paper to the left margin, then slapped the line feed bar to advance the paper up a line.

To see your work so far, use the *D 100* command. You should see something similar to the display shown in Figure 11-1. Remember that the segment values in the Figure (what I see on my display) will probably be different than what you see on your screen.

So far, only one line of text sits in memory. To create the second line, you'll need to start poking bytes after the line feed character poked in using the previous E command. This is what prevents DEBUG from being a useful text editor: "real" text editor software will *know* where to start the next line in memory. In DEBUG, you must find the offset of the byte after 0A hex to know where to start poking. See if you can locate that offset on your screen.

```
-F100 L80 0
-E100 "This is a small text file" 0D 0A
-D100
1F60:0100  54 68 69 73 20 69 73 20-61 20 73 6D 61 6C 6C 20   This is a small
1F60:0110  74 65 78 74 20 66 69 6C-65 0D 0A 00 00 00 00 00   text file.......
1F60:0120  00 00 00 00 00 00 00 00-00 00 00 00 00 00 00 00   ................
1F60:0130  00 00 00 00 00 00 00 00-00 00 00 00 00 00 00 00   ................
1F60:0140  00 00 00 00 00 00 00 00-00 00 00 00 00 00 00 00   ................
1F60:0150  00 00 00 00 00 00 00 00-00 00 00 00 00 00 00 00   ................
1F60:0160  00 00 00 00 00 00 00 00-00 00 00 00 00 00 00 00   ................
1F60:0170  00 00 00 00 00 00 00 00-00 00 00 00 00 00 00 00   ................
```

Figure 11-1 A string of text is poked into memory

Tip: To find a byte offset, remember to start counting at zero with the first column of bytes.

The hyphen in the middle of the memory display separates bytes at columns 7 and 8.

After 9, comes offset A hex, then B hex, on up to F hex.

You calculate the offset address by adding the column number of the byte plus the offset address shown on the left of the memory display.

I located the byte 0A hex in column A hex on my screen. (How convenient!) Byte 65 hex is just after the hyphen, making it in column 8. Then the 0D hex byte is at column 9 and the 0A hex byte ends up at column A hex. Add that to the column offset and the byte sits at address offset 11A hex.

To poke in a second line of text, you must start poking in values at offset 11B hex, the byte *after* the line feed. Enter the following DEBUG command:

    -E 11B "I created using DEBUG." 1A

This command pokes a string of text into memory at offset 11B hex. You can use the *D 100* command to view both lines of text in memory:

    -D 100

Ensure that the second line of text falls into place right after the 0A hex byte, the line feed character. It should, as long as you've typed in all the commands correctly. If things don't line up, or you tried entering your own text strings, then rework the above commands until everything fits properly.

At the end of the final string of text, notice the sole byte 1A hex. This is character 26, Ctrl-Z. That character is used by DOS to mark the end of a text file. Your text editor will automatically tack on a Ctrl-Z to a file; and when you use DOS's COPY CON command, you must manually type Ctrl-Z to end the file. In DEBUG, you poked that byte into memory, which will soon be written to a file.

Now you have something interesting in memory. To write it out to a file on disk, you need a filename. Use the N command to specify the name SAMPLE1.TXT on drive A. Make sure your "Sample Disk" is in drive A and ready. Type the following:

    -N A:SAMPLE1.TXT

Disks and DEBUG 189

Nothing is written to disk after using the N command; it just "sets" a filename DEBUG will use in memory. (Only the W command writes information to disk.)

▐▶ ***Tip:*** The N command can be used again to change the name of the file. Until that happens, DEBUG will use the name you've specified to both load and write files using the L and W commands, respectively.

To reset the filename to nothing, use the N command by itself.

To see where DEBUG sticks the name in memory, use the *D80 L10* command. You'll see why this area of memory is chosen in Chapter 14.

The second step is to set the size of the memory block you want to write to disk. Use the *D 100* command again to see your block in memory. Then calculate the offset address of the last byte, 1A hex.

On my screen, I see byte 1A hex in the line that starts at offset 130. The byte is in the second column, which gives it an offset address of 131 hex. (It's not 132 hex because you start counting with zero — not one — in the first column.)

Don't rush to conclusions yet: The size of the block of memory you want to write isn't 131 hex. The block starts at offset 100 hex, so you must find the difference between the two values to hunt down the block's size:

End of the block   = 131 hex

Start of the block = 100 hex

Difference   = 31 hex

Now here comes the weird part: The calculation above inaccurately sets the size of the block to 31 hex bytes. However, since you start counting with zero at offset 100 hex, the true end of the block is at 32 hex bytes — not 31 hex. (The block *includes* the byte at offset 131; it doesn't end there.)

You can prove that the block is 32 hex bytes long by looking at your screen. Each row contains ten hex bytes. The block you want to write to disk is three rows down, hex plus 2 bytes over. That makes 3 x 10 hex plus 2, or 32 hex.

▐▶ ***Tip:*** When calculating the size of a chunk of memory to write to disk, subtract the starting offset from the ending offset and add one:

Block size = Block_End - Block_Start + 1

If you know the starting and ending offsets, you can use DEBUG's H command to make the calculation for you. Type H followed by the ending and starting offsets of your block:

```
-H 131 100
0231 0031
```

The first value is the sum, the second the difference. Add one to the second value and you get the block's size: 32 hex.

To tell DEBUG the size of memory block, you use the RCX command. This is actually a variation on the R, *register* command, which you'll be introduced to in the next chapter. For this chapter, consider RCX as the command that sets the size of a block of memory. Type the RCX command at the hyphen prompt and press Enter:

```
-RCX
CX 0000
:32
```

RCX starts by displaying CX and then a value (which might not be 0000 as shown in the example). That's followed by a colon prompt. At the prompt, enter the memory block's size, 32 hex, as shown above.

DEBUG now knows a filename and the size of the block of memory. You use the W command to write that block of memory to disk. W is followed by the block's starting address. Enter the following:

```
-W 100
```

The block starts at offset 100 hex, as shown above. After pressing Enter, you'll see your drive A light flicker and the block of memory will be written to disk. This is confirmed with the following message in DEBUG:

```
Writing 00032 bytes
```

▗▖ *Tip:* The W command will automatically assume that the block of memory starts at offset 100 hex unless you tell it otherwise. As long as a filename is selected, your block starts at offset 100 hex and the size is specified by the RCX command, *W* by itself will write the block to disk.

You can also specify any *segment:offset* address using the W command. For example, to write 32K of bank 9 to disk, you can use the following three commands in DEBUG:

```
N BANK9.DAT
RCX
 8000
W 9000:8000
```

Specify 8000 hex as the size of the block. Note that the file is named BANK9.DAT. It won't be a text file, just raw information from memory. (Use a utility like Vern Buerg's LIST to view the file.)

To view your efforts, quit DEBUG with the *Q* command, then use the TYPE command at the DOS prompt:

```
C:\> TYPE A:SAMPLE1.TXT
This is a small text file
I created using DEBUG.
```

If random characters are displayed, then you probably didn't hit the correct size of the file; delete it and try again. If everything looked perfect, use the DIR command to confirm the file's size: 32 hex equals 50 decimal. The file is 50 bytes long.

Now take a moment to sit back and reflect. You've written a chunk of memory to disk using DEBUG. That's pretty amazing. It's also a heck of a lot of work to create a puny, two-line text file. Even COPY CON — or EDLIN — is easier to use than that. This begs the question of "what's so useful about writing memory to disk?"

The practical aspects of writing memory to disk will become apparent when you create programs using DEBUG. And there are some interesting tricks you can pull writing "raw" memory to disk, which you'll read about later in this chapter. The purpose of the exercises in this chapter are to familiarize you with the way DEBUG's disk commands work.

Loading a File from Disk

There are two ways to load a file from disk into memory using DEBUG. The first is to specify the filename after DEBUG at the DOS prompt. Start DEBUG using the following command:

```
C:\> DEBUG C:\CONFIG.SYS
```

This command starts DEBUG and loads the file CONFIG.SYS into memory. Normally, the file loaded will be a program you would want to test run in DEBUG. However, DEBUG will load any file you specify into memory.

▶ *Tip:* DEBUG will load text, data, and program files into memory, which covers just about everything. Program files ending in EXE, however, are loaded using special formatting information in the EXE file. Unlike loading any other file on disk, DEBUG does not take bytes in an EXE file and plop them down in memory consecutively. Instead, the file is loaded in a special order. To avoid this, you can copy the EXE file, naming the duplicate *.BIN:

```
COPY SAMPLE.EXE *.BIN
```

The BIN file can then be loaded into memory just as any other file on disk.

Files are always loaded at offset 100 hex in the current segment. To view CONFIG.SYS in memory, use the *D 100* command:

```
-D 100
```

The output isn't formatted for text viewing, but you can see the contents of your CONFIG.SYS file in the third column, ASCII display. I chose CONFIG.SYS because it shows you recognizable text, it's a file that everybody has, and it can only be found in one place (the root directory on drive C).

It's possible to edit CONFIG.SYS in DEBUG — but painful! I suggest using a text editor instead. However, you can use DEBUG to insert interesting characters into a file. For example, you could use the S and E commands to search out all the asterisks (*) and change them to Escape characters. This would be useful when your editor doesn't allow you to enter the Escape character directly. In this case, if you want, you may quit DEBUG with the *Q* command, then restart it.

The second way to load a file into DEBUG is by using the N and L commands. N names the file, then L will load it at a specific address in memory. If an address isn't specified, offset 100 in the current segment is used.

At the hyphen prompt, type the F command to clear out an acre of memory:

```
-F 100 L80 0
```

Then type the N command to name a file on disk. In this case, use AUTOEXEC.BAT, which should be located in the root directory of drive C:

```
-N C:\AUTOEXEC.BAT
```

To load the file into memory, type the L command:

```
-L
```

There won't be any feedback; AUTOEXEC.BAT will be loaded into memory at offset 100 hex. View it with the *D 100* command to see the first few lines in the ASCII display column.

That covers the two ways a file can be loaded from disk into memory using DEBUG: typing a filename after DEBUG at the DOS prompt and using the N and L commands. Of the two, the second way is the most flexible; L can load a file anywhere in conventional memory.

Clear out another acre of memory at offset 800 hex using the following F command:

```
-F 800 L80 0
```

Confirm that this area is "naked" using the D command.

```
-D 800
```

Now load only AUTOEXEC.BAT into memory at offset 800 hex. The N command has already set the filename, so you only need to use the L command to load the file at offset 800:

```
-L 800
```

Use the *D 800* command and you'll see AUTOEXEC.BAT loaded into memory.

Saving and Restoring the Screen

In the grand scheme of things, the text you see on the screen is actually stored in memory. This is the way it is on all computers: Since the contents of the screen change, they're stored in memory. Specifically, it's *video memory* that's used to store the text you see on the screen.

I'll be mulling over all the interesting and fun things you can do with your screen in a later chapter. For now, think about your screen as a block of memory with a specific address and length. Here are the stats:

- Color video memory starts at address B800:0
- Monochrome video memory starts at address B000:0
- The size of video memory (in the text mode) is FA0 hex bytes.

Some comments on these figures are in order. First, there are two different addresses for monochrome and color video memory. This is because the PC will let you run with both a color and monochrome monitor at the same time. It's true; the original IBM PC could do it and so can your system. However, for locating your video memory, you need to use the proper address for whichever screen you have. For most of us, that's B800:0 since color text (VGA) is the most popular.

Second, monochrome video memory refers to a PC with a Hercules or compatible Monochrome Display Adapter (MDA). It does not refer to the "paper white" VGA graphics display. If you have VGA graphics at all, then you have "color" no matter what you see on the screen.

Third and last, the block of video memory is FA0 hex bytes long. That's 4,000 decimal. The value represents the total possible number of character positions on the screen. It's calculated by multiplying 80 columns by 25 rows to equal 2,000. The number must be doubled because of an invisible attribute byte that accompanies every character on the screen. (You'll read about these attribute bytes in Chapter 15.) The number 2,000 doubled is 4,000, and that equals FA0 hex. (I remember this value because of FAO Schwarz, my favorite toy store in San Francisco.)

Given the size and length of video memory, enter DEBUG and type the following commands:

```
-N A:\SCREEN.DAT
-RCX
CX 0000 — You see this on the screen; do not type it in.
:FA0
-W B800:0
```

Note: If you have a monochrome, Hercules or "monographics" video adapter installed in your PC, specify the value B000:0 as the start of video memory — not B800:0. Since the majority of PC owners use color video, I'll be specifying the value B800:0 in this book. If you have monochrome video, remember to substitute the value B000:0 instead. There are several places where this is required, so keep your monochrome eyeballs peeled.

The name of the file is A:\SCREEN.DAT. The length of the memory block, as set by the RCX command, is FA0 bytes. The W command specifies the base address of the memory block equal to the start of video memory. After pressing Enter, DEBUG will create a file on disk that contains screen memory and you'll see the following message displayed:

```
Writing 00FA0 bytes
```

The file containing screen memory is now on disk. Don't bother looking at it with anything; it's gross. Instead, quit DEBUG with the *Q* command and clear the screen using DOS's *CLS* command. Reenter DEBUG and type the following at the hyphen prompt:

```
-N A:\SCREEN.DAT
-L B800:0
```

The N command names the file A:\SCREEN.DAT, which contains video memory recently saved to disk. The L command attempts to load that file into memory at address B800:0, but it fails. You'll see the following message:

```
Insufficient memory
```

Don't worry, you didn't run out of RAM. This is just DEBUG's rude and inelegant way of telling you that it only works with *conventional memory*. The address B800:0 is in *upper memory*, which is off-limits to DEBUG. Yes, even though video RAM can be saved to disk and you even can use the E command there to poke around, DEBUG refuses to use the L command in upper memory. There is a solution, however. Start by loading the file into memory at offset 100, which can be done by using the L command alone:

```
-L
```

Without any options, L loads the named file, A:\SCREEN.DAT, into memory at offset 100. The size of the file is FA0 bytes and the final destination for it is at address B800:0. These values can be plugged into the Moo-copy command quite easily:

```
-M 100 LFA0 B800:0
```

After pressing Enter, your screen will suddenly change. The old contents of video memory, those bytes saved to disk in A:\SCREEN.DAT, will be rewritten to video memory, which has the effect of restoring the screen. This is interesting, but can it be made useful? Yes: with batch files.

This screen saving and restoring feat can be repeated at any time by using special DEBUG scripts in conjunction with custom batch files. You'll need to create four files on disk:

1. A text file with the DEBUG commands to save the screen, SAVE.SCR
2. A batch file to save the screen, SAVESCRN.BAT
3. A text file with the DEBUG command to restore the screen, RESTORE.SCR
4. A batch file to restore the screen, RESTSCRN.BAT

Each of these four files is shown in Figure 11-2. Create the files using your text editor and save them to disk using the names specified. Note that the batch files in the Figure assume that the *.SCR text files are in the C:\BATCH directory. Ensure that you specify the proper directory for their location on your hard drive. Double-check everything.

```
SAVE.SCR

N C:\SCREEN.DAT
RCX
FA0
W B800:0
Q

SAVESCRN.BAT

@ECHO OFF
DEBUG < C:\BATCH\SAVE.SCR > NUL

RESTORE.SCR

N C:\SCREEN.DAT
L
M 100 LFA0 B800:0
Q

RESTSCRN.BAT

@ECHO OFF
CLS
DEBUG < C:\BATCH\RESTORE.SCR > NUL
DEL C:\SCREEN.DAT
```

Figure 11-2 The screen saving and restoring batch files

The file SAVE.SCR is a DEBUG script file. It's used with I/O redirection in SAVESCRN.BAT to feed commands into DEBUG. The four commands are identical to those you typed in manually earlier in this chapter: the file is named C:\SCREEN.DAT, placed into the root directory of drive C for convenience; the RCX command is issued, then the following line specifies FA0 hex bytes; the W command writes out screen memory; and Q quits DEBUG. The output of all that is redirected to the NUL device so the screen doesn't fill with clutter (and overtly alter the captured image).

The screen is restored using the RESTORE.SCR script file. This script file issues the commands to DEBUG that name the file, load it into memory, and then move that memory up to screen memory. The script ends with the Q command to quit DEBUG.

▶ *Tip:* All DEBUG script files end with the Q command to quit DEBUG. Without it, DEBUG would sit there and continue to wait for input from the file on disk. When that happens, your computer is locked up and you'll be forced to reset.

196   Dan Gookin's Guide to Underground DOS 6.0

The RESTSCRN.BAT file starts by clearing the screen and then running DEBUG with the RESTORE.SCR script file. Output is redirected to the NUL device, preventing screen clutter. Finally, the C:\SCREEN.DAT file is deleted at the end of the RESTSCRN.BAT batch file.

These four files can be of use whenever you need to save and then restore the screen. The file SCREEN.DAT isn't really useful for anything (for example, you can't print or edit it), so it's deleted. The batch file shown in Figure 11-3 illustrates how the SAVE.SCR and RESTORE.SCR scripts can be used to temporarily blank the display and then restore it.

DEBUG is used in BLANK.BAT with the SAVE.SCR script to save the screen. Then the screen is cleared with a CLS command. The PAUSE command then waits for a key press, although the *Press any key to continue* message is redirected to the NUL device to keep the screen blank. After pressing a key, DEBUG is run with the RESTORE.SCR script to bring the screen back. The SCREEN.DAT file is deleted in the last line of the batch file program.

> ✎ **Note:** Specify the proper pathnames to the SAVE.SCR and RESTORE.SCR script files. I stick everything in my BATCH directory on drive C. Try to keep your PC consistently organized.

The only problem with the BLANK.BAT program is that the DOS prompt reappears at the top of the screen. It would be nice — and add a professional touch — if the cursor came back where it left. This can be accomplished using ANSI commands, but only if you've loaded the ANSI.SYS device driver in CONFIG.SYS. (Refer to Chapter 6 for information on ANSI.SYS; Appendix C lists DOS's ANSI command set.)

The two ANSI commands required are ←[s to save the cursor position and ←[u to restore it. Both the s and u must be lowercase. Figure 11-4 shows the resulting batch file, BLANK.BAT, which is merely an update of the original BLANK.BAT shown in Figure 11-3. To save and restore the cursor, two ECHO commands have been added with the proper ANSI command sequences.

You can use BLANK.BAT to zap out and then restore your screen. Unfortunately, it only works at the DOS prompt and it's not connected to a "hot key." However, what you've learned here are the basics for writing a simple, screen blanking type

```
@ECHO OFF
REM Blank the screen; restore on key press
DEBUG < C:\BATCH\SAVE.SCR > NUL
CLS
PAUSE > NUL
DEBUG < C:\BATCH\RESTORE.SCR > NUL
DEL C:\SCREEN.DAT
```

Figure 11-3   The BLANK.BAT screen blanking batch file

```
@ECHO OFF
REM Blank the screen; restore on key press
REM Requires ANSI.SYS for cursor position restore
DEBUG < C:\BATCH\SAVE.SCR > NUL
ECHO ←[s
CLS
PAUSE > NUL
DEBUG < C:\BATCH\RESTORE.SCR > NUL
ECHO ←[u
```

Figure 11-4 BLANK.BAT with ANSI commands to restore the cursor position

of program. The core knowledge is there: you know where screen memory is, how to write it to disk, then how to load it back into memory and redisplay it on the screen. This is a tremendous feat! Take a few moments to feel proud of your accomplishment.

Raw Disk Action

Here comes the scary part! The first part of this chapter dealt with DEBUG and filenames. Files are the traditional way information is stored on disk, and DEBUG works with them quite nicely using the W and L commands with the N command. Toss all that aside for now.

The W and L commands have longer, more detailed options beyond the first base address value used above. These options allow you to fetch out "raw" information from a disk and copy it into memory for examination or editing. You can then write the information back to disk if you like. This is all done by circumventing DOS's file system. Because of that, it's entirely possible that you can write random information to disk — but only if you're careless. As long as you follow the instructions offered in this chapter, you'll never goof up or lose any important data or files.

Reading Your Disk Directly

There is a rich computer jargon used to describe how information is stored on a disk. The disk itself is a *volume*. It has one, two, or several *sides* (several sides only in the case of a hard drive). On each side are *tracks* — concentric circles of information on which data is stored. And each track is divided into a number of *sectors*.

Most disks have 80 tracks, only the old 360K disks use 40 tracks. But on those tracks are a differing number of sectors (which is how each of the disk formats stores different amounts of information). Fortunately, all sectors store a consistent 512 bytes of data. This is true on all but the weirdest of storage media. And it's that 512-byte sector that DEBUG can access using the L and W commands.

> **Tip:** The value 512 is 200 hexadecimal. There are 200 hex bytes in a disk sector.

To read in raw information from disk, you need to know four things:

- The address in memory where you want the information loaded
- The drive from which information will be read
- The starting sector number
- The total number of sectors to read

The standard address used by the L command for loading information from disk is offset 100 hex — the same as is used for loading a named file. You can load the information anywhere in conventional memory, although 100 is perfect for "browsing."

To specify a drive, you use a number value instead of a letter. DEBUG considers drive A to be drive 0, drive B is drive 1, and drive C is always drive 2, and so on. This goes on up to drive Z, which is considered drive 1A by DEBUG. (Remember you're in DEBUG, land of hexadecimal!)

The starting sector number and number of sectors to read are up to you. Table 11-2 lists the total number of sectors and other information about various sized floppy disks available to DOS. The values in the table are all in decimal. The "Root directory sector number" value tells you in which sector the root directory starts for a given disk, relative to sector zero (the first sector on a disk).

Load the first two tracks of your Sample Disk into memory at offset 100 using DEBUG's L command. The general format will be as follows:

```
-L 100 0 0 n
```

The information will be loaded at offset 100 hex from the disk in drive zero (drive A), starting at sector zero with a total of *n* sectors loaded. I don't know what size your disk is, so you'll have to figure out how many sectors are in a track and double that value to calculate *n*.

Table 11-2 Disk Information

Disk Capacity/Size	Total Sectors	Sectors Per Track	Tracks Per Side	Root Directory Sector Number
360K/5¼-inch	720	9	40	5
720K/3½-inch	1,440	9	80	7
1.2M/5¼-inch	2,400	15	80	15
1.4M/3½-inch	2,880	18	80	19
2.8M/3½-inch	5,760	36	80	37

▶ *Tip:* You could look up the sectors per track hexadecimal value in Appendix A, but here is a handy conversion table:

Disk Capacity	The L Command you need is:
360K	L100 0 0 12
720K	L100 0 0 12
1.2M	L100 0 0 1E
1.4M	L100 0 0 24
2.8M	L100 0 0 48

My PC has a 1.2M, 5¼-inch floppy in drive A. To load the first two tracks into memory, I use the following command:

```
-L 100 0 0 1E
```

Be sure you type the proper command for your disk in drive A. After pressing Enter, the light on drive A will go on, the disk will spin, and the first track of information will be loaded into memory. To view the contents of the first sector on disk, use the following command:

```
-D 100 L200
```

Each sector is 512 bytes long, which translates into 200 hex. This command lists the first disk sector of drive A, which now sits in memory at offset 100 hex.

▶ *Tip:* There are many fabulous things concealed in a disk's first sector. By simply looking at that information, you can tell the disk's capacity, format, the operating system, or utility that formatted it and whether or not it's a boot disk. Lots of other information lurks in sector zero, which will be described in later chapters.

The following sectors, now in memory, can be viewed using the D command. Table 11-3 shows where you can find sector offsets when the first two tracks of a disk have been loaded into memory starting at offset 100 hex. The sectors will happen every 200-odd hex offsets, which are numbered 100, 300, 500, 700, 900, B00, D00, and F00. Only the key offsets are shown in the table.

One "exciting" thing you can do at this point is to find the root directory of your disk as it's stored in memory. From Table 11-2 look up the sector offset for the root directory according to the capacity of the disk in your A drive. Then use the corresponding value in Table 11-3 with the D command to display that memory. For my 1.2M diskette, I'll use the following D command:

```
-D 1F00
```

This command displays 128 bytes of the disk's root directory as it sits in memory. What I saw on my screen is shown in Figure 11-5. You should see something similar on your screen: The disk's volume label is TEST DISK, and the files SAMPLE1.TXT and SCREEN.DAT have been created on the disk. If you've added

Table 11-3 Sector Offsets in Memory

Relative Sector	Memory Offset	Relative Sector	Memory Offset
0	0100	8	1100
1	0300	9	1300
2	0500	14	1D00
3	0700	15	1F00
4	0900	18	2500
5	0B00	19	2700
6	0D00	36	4900
7	0F00	37	4B00

any additional files, they'll show up as well. Otherwise, the remainder of the "directory" will be filled with zeros.

You'll be reading about the directory details in a later chapter. But once you know them, as well as other information about a disk, you can use DEBUG's memory commands to modify the disk directly. This is perfectly safe, providing you know what you're doing and you properly write the information back to disk.

For example, type the following:

```
-F 100 L10 FF
```

This fills the first 16 bytes of memory at offset 100 hex with the value FF. That's fine, no damage is done; even though you've erased important bytes in the floppy disk's boot sector information, nothing has been written back to disk. As long as your alterations stay in memory, you can mess around as you please. The real power here, however, is knowing what to modify, how to modify it, and being able to write that back to disk. You'll be doing that in the next section.

Writing Raw Sectors to Disk

Writing information back to disk is done with the W command in the exact format as the L command is used to load data. You supply the W command with an address, drive number, starting sector, and sector count. DEBUG then writes the appropriately sized chunk of memory onto the disk.

The W command is the most deadly in all of DEBUG's arsenal. When the W command is used casually, you can write memory out to random parts of a disk and lose data immediately. Since the data is written directly to disk, DOS can't send it off to an unused part of disk and you may overwrite a file. And since DOS doesn't know about the information or its location, it may overwrite it later with a file properly saved on disk.

Don't get me wrong: The W command can be useful and highly beneficiary. Usually L and W are used in tandem: L loads a specific part of the disk, you use

DEBUG's memory commands to manipulate or fix that part of disk, and then a complementary W command writes the corrections back.

To see how "quick and dirty" this can be, make sure the Sample Disk is in drive A. You'll use the L command to load in the root directory sector from your disk, mend a filename, then write it right back out. Start by finding the proper root directory sector number for your disk type in Table 11-2. Then use the proper L command to load only that sector into memory in this format:

```
-L 100 0 root 1
```

Load from disk into memory at offset 100 hex, from drive A (disk zero), the *root* directory sector, one sector only. Remember that each sector is 200 hex bytes long, although you'll only be concerning yourself with the first few bytes for this exercise.

> **Tip:** Here are the root directory sectors and their hexadecimal equivalents. These are based on the data in Table 11-2; I'm helping you out here by doing the decimal-to-hexadecimal conversion (actually, the program HEXCALC is doing the mental stuff):

Diskette type	Root directory sector
360K/5¼-inch	5 hex
720K/3½-inch	7 hex
1.2M/5¼-inch	F hex
1.4M/3½-inch	13 hex
2.8M/3½-inch	25 hex

Use the proper value above for the *root* in your L command.

On my system, with its 1.2M floppy drive A, I've used the following L command:

```
-L 100 0 F 1
```

To see the first few entries in the root directory, type the *D 100* command. My screen shows something similar to Figure 11-5, although the offset addresses start with 0100 hex (since only the root directory's sector was loaded). The first directory entry I can see, the one at offset 100 hex, is the disk's volume label, TEST DISK.

```
1F60:1F00  54 45 53 54 20 44 49 53-4B 20 20 28 00 00 00 00   TEST DISK  (....
1F60:1F10  00 00 00 00 00 00 D6 5B-DC 18 00 00 00 00 00 00   .......[........
1F60:1F20  53 41 4D 50 4C 45 31 20-54 58 54 20 00 00 00 00   SAMPLE1 TXT ....
1F60:1F30  00 00 00 00 00 00 BC 7A-DE 18 02 00 32 00 00 00   .......z....2...
1F60:1F40  53 43 52 45 45 4E 20 20-44 41 54 20 00 00 00 00   SCREEN  DAT ....
1F60:1F50  00 00 00 00 00 00 BA 4E-E1 18 03 00 A0 0F 00 00   .......N........
1F60:1F60  00 00 00 00 00 00 00 00-00 00 00 00 00 00 00 00   ................
1F60:1F70  00 00 00 00 00 00 00 00-00 00 00 00 00 00 00 00   ................
```

Figure 11-5 The root directory from drive A in memory

The volume label is stored on disk like a filename, although it lacks any corresponding data elsewhere on the disk.

You can manually change the volume label here by poking in a string of text, up to 11 characters long, at offset 100 hex. And since we're in DEBUG, we can poke in interesting and forbidden characters into the filename. For example, type the following:

```
-E 100 "SUPER*DISK!"
```

This command pokes the 11 characters in "SUPER*DISK!" into memory, overwriting the current volume label. It contains the offending asterisk (*) character, which cannot be used in a volume label. You can poke in any combination of characters for a volume label on your own if you like. Note that lowercase letters will be converted to uppercase by DOS. Also, you must poke in exactly 11 characters; any extra characters you aren't using should be spaces:

```
-E 100 "<POWER>    "
```

In this example, the volume label ends with four spaces, which makes its total size 11 bytes.

➤ Tip: Here are the characters DOS forbids in a filename:

```
. " / \ [ ] : * | < > + = ; , ?
```

It's safe to poke in any of these for a volume label, since you'll never be typing in the name of the volume label directly. For a real file, however, changing its name using one of the above characters means you'll never be able to type it in at the DOS prompt again.

Once you've changed your volume label and have confirmed that it's only 11 characters long, write the sector back to disk. This is done by using the same command you used to load the sector, but with a W instead of an L. Use the proper root directory sector number for your floppy disk. With a 1.2M floppy, the proper command is:

```
-W 100 0 F 1
```

Write memory at offset 100 hex to disk zero (drive A), sector F hex for one sector only. Remember to replace the F hex above with the proper offset of the root directory for your disk.

The W command will not report back *Writing xxxx bytes* as it does when writing a file. Instead, you'll just see another hyphen prompt. Enter the *Q* command to quit, then pull a directory of drive A at the DOS prompt. Confirm that the volume label has been adequately changed:

```
C:\> DIR A:

Volume in drive A is SUPER*DISK!
Volume Serial Number is 3F44-12E2
Directory of A:\

SAMPLE1  TXT        50 06-30-92   3:21p
SCREEN   DAT      4000 07-01-92   9:53a
     2 file(s)      4050 bytes
                 1209344 bytes free
```

You can still change the volume label using the *LABEL A:* command. The funky label can be read no sweat and changed by DOS quite easily. But if you try to enter a label such as "SUPER*DISK!" using the LABEL command, it will report *Invalid characters in volume label.* Only when using DEBUG can you produce such a unique disk label.

If your attempts to change the volume label met with disaster, then one of two things happened: you didn't load in the root directory's starting sector, or you poked in too long a name. After the 11th character in a filename comes important information about a "file" that DOS stores on disk, even the volume label. Erasing that information will alter the disk, which is why this exercise is being performed on a floppy disk in the first place. If your disk is damaged, you can simply reformat it and continue.

Later chapters will explore the L and W commands in detail. Chapter 16 in particular will take you on a tour of your floppy disk, pointing out interesting things and performing more brain surgery on a disk.

12

Peeling the Lid off the Microprocessor Chip

Your PC is built around a unique chip called a *microprocessor*. It's the "micro" part of microprocessor from which we get *microcomputer*, although that term is sorely outdated given the power of today's personal computers. Others may call the microprocessor a *CPU* for Central Processing Unit, still others may call it "the processor." Whatever the term, the chip is the center around which your computer's universe spins. The microprocessor is the PC's brain.

So far you've dodged around the microprocessor. You've seen DEBUG manipulate memory and disk; however, the center of attention is always the microprocessor, which controls everything. This chapter shows you the PC's microprocessor and how DEBUG can manipulate it. This is the final step in preparation for the real exploring — and, yes, even programming — that takes place starting in the next chapter and Part III of this book.

Anatomy of a Microprocessor

A microprocessor is a little machine that manipulates numbers, like a calculator. It can compare, add, subtract, multiply, and divide various values. The microprocessor can also access memory for storing and retrieving information. And it communicates with the world via *inports* and *outports*, which are simple communication lines to various devices in the PC. This describes the microprocessor's role in life in a very simple manner.

✏️ ***Note:*** The key thing to remember about a microprocessor is that because it's very simple, it works only a little bit at a time. But it's also very fast, which is how things get done so quickly in a computer.

The microprocessor is also one of the most sophisticated devices made by humans. But don't for a minute think you need to know *everything* about it to make it work for you. The following sections will show you just about everything, while at the same time telling you what's important and what can be learned later (or not at all).

The Microprocessor's Registers

In DEBUG's eye, every PC uses the old Intel 8088/8086 microprocessor. That chip held information in 13 tiny storage places called *registers*, each of them 16-bits wide. To keep track of all these registers, and to identify their special purposes, each is given a two-letter name: AX, BX, SI, SP, DS, and so on. The 13 different registers of the 8088/8086 are illustrated in Figure 12-1.

	ODITSZAPC	**FLAGS**
AX	AH	AL
BX	BH	BL
CX	CH	CL
DX	DH	DL
SI		
DI		
BP		
SP		
IP		
DS		
ES		
SS		
CS		

Figure 12-1 The 8088/8086 microprocessor's registers

Think of a register as a storage place. They act like pockets for holding values. The size of the values a register can hold depends on the power of the microprocessor. Since DEBUG assumes you only have an 8088/8086 — a 16-bit microprocessor — that means each register can hold a value 16-bits "wide." From your vast knowledge of binary and hexadecimal (garnered in Chapter 8), you should know that values held in the register/pockets can range from 0000 through FFFF hex.

Note: The 8088/8086 is a 16-bit microprocessor. That 16-bit limitation applies to its internal registers for storage as well as how the chip deals with memory. Remember the 16-bit memory limitation from Chapter 9? All that weirdness with the *offset:segment* values is a direct result of the 8088/8086's 16-bits.

Modern microprocessors are the offspring of the original 8088/8086. Both the 80386 and '468 family microprocessors can store 32-bit values in their registers, which makes them powerful 32-bit microprocessors that can handle large values and lots of memory. However, the house of DOS is built upon the 16-bit 8088/8086, so DEBUG assumes everyone has that microprocessor. This all works out since the later chips are "upward compatible" with the 8088/8086. You just miss out on all the 32-bit madness.

Different Registers for Different Purposes

To keep track of the 13 registers, each is given a special name. Pay careful attention to the names! Although they're only two letters long, the names provide you with a clue to the register's function. There are three types of registers:

- Accumulator registers
- Index registers
- Segment registers.

The accumulator registers are named AX, BX, CX, and DX. The word *accumulator* means a storage place and the "A" in the AX register does actually stand for accumulator. The three other registers, BX through DX, are named after the next three letters of the English alphabet and have no cutsie acronyms, although they're all still accumulator registers. These registers hold values and are used to add, subtract, multiply and so on — general-purpose stuff.

The index registers are used to point at things, which is what the word *index* means ("to point"). These include the SI, DI, BP, SP, and IP registers. Actually, only the SI and DI registers are index registers. The "I" in their names stands for Index. The other registers, BP, SP and IP are all "pointers," but they're lumped into the same category in the Intel documentation. All of these registers point at something or mark a place in memory where something interesting did or will happen.

Finally, the segment registers are named DS, ES, SS, and CS. The S in the name means "segment." These registers play a role in how the microprocessor uses the

PC's memory. The value these registers hold is, in fact, a segment value from the PC's memory. (See Chapter 9 for more information on memory segments.)

> *Note:* The names and categories of the registers depend on which programmer you talk to. For this book, I'm sticking with the conventions used by DEBUG. For example, what Intel calls the "PC" or Program Counter register, DEBUG calls the "IP" or Instruction Pointer. It's the same thing with a different name.

Programmers and other PC people "in the know" refer to the registers by their two-letter names. They do have longer names that expand upon the two-letter abbreviations. These are shown in Table 12-1. The reasons behind these names will become apparent as you begin to explore the microprocessor, starting with the next section.

A Look at the Registers in DEBUG

Your microprocessor does not look like the illustration in Figure 12-1 (even if you have an old 8088). The microprocessor's registers are actually high-speed memory locations that appear as microscopic traces — little lines — etched in a "teensy" silicon wafer and encased in a ceramic chip. Oreo cookies are more interesting to look at (and eat). Yet, you need some kind of visual reference point when you think about how a microprocessor works. In DEBUG, the visual reference is provided by a "dump" of the microprocessor's register contents. That's done by using the R, Register command.

Table 12-1 Microprocessor Register Names

Register	Full Name
AX	Primary Accumulator/Accumulator
BX	Accumulator/Base register
CX	Accumulator/Counter
DX	Accumulator/I/O address
SI	Source Index
DI	Destination Index
BP	Base Pointer
SP	Stack Pointer
IP	Instruction Pointer (Program Counter)
DS	Data Segment
ES	Extra Segment
SS	Stack Segment
CS	Code Segment

Using the R Command

Enter DEBUG and type the R command:

```
-R
```

What you'll see on your screen is a visual representation of the registers in your microprocessor and their contents. DEBUG has magically peeled off the microprocessor's lid and peered inside to show you the values.

The R command can be used to both view and modify the contents of the microprocessor's registers. By itself, R displays all the 8088/8086 microprocessor registers and their contents, which you're currently viewing on your screen. The output on my screen is shown in Figure 12-2. Your screen will show a similar display, although the values may be different.

You need to concern yourself with only the first two lines of the R command's output. (The third line will be discussed in Chapter 13.) The 13 registers are shown in the following format:

```
rr=xxxx
```

The *rr* is the register's name, as seen in Figure 12-1 and Table 12-1. That's followed by an equal sign, then the contents of the register, *xxxx*. The value is shown as a four-digit hexadecimal number illustrating the 16-bits in each register. The value is always four digits long, padded with leading zeros if necessary.

In Figure 12-2, the AX, BX, CX, DX, BP, SI, and DI registers all have 0000 hex as their contents. The SP register has FFEE hex. The segment registers in the second row (DS, ES, SS, and CS) all have 2C94 hex and the IP register has 0100 hex. The values you see on your screen will probably be different for the segment registers. I can guess, however, that the AX, BX, CX, DX, BP, SI, DI, and IP registers will have values identical to those shown in Figure 12-2. (This is a safe guess since DEBUG always starts with the same values in those registers — unless you load a program for debugging.)

> **Tip:** The segment registers are all "pointing" at a segment in memory. It's the segment DEBUG is currently using for memory storage. If you type the D command, you'll notice that the segment address in the left column matches the values of the segment registers exactly. You'll read about why this is so in a few pages.

```
AX=0000  BX=0000  CX=0000  DX=0000  SP=FFEE  BP=0000  SI=0000  DI=0000
DS=2C94  ES=2C94  SS=2C94  CS=2C94  IP=0100   NV UP EI PL NZ NA PO NC
2C94:0100 0000            ADD     [BX+SI],AL                    DS:0000=CD
```

Figure 12-2 The output of DEBUG's R command

The Accumulator Registers

The four general-purpose registers are AX, BX, CX, and DX. They can each hold a 16-bit value, from 0000 through FFFF hex. The microprocessor can place the value there; poke a register's value into memory; read a value from memory; and stick it into a register and add, subtract, multiply, and divide the values. This is why they're general-purpose registers, like a good-sized pocket that can hold a variety of tools.

In DEBUG, you can change the value of a register by following the R command with the register name. DEBUG will show you the register's current contents and give you the opportunity to change them. For example, type the R command followed by AX to change the AX register pair (the space between the R and the AX is optional):

```
-R AX
AX 0000
:
```

DEBUG begins by reporting the current contents of the AX register, which is 0000 in the example. This report is followed by a colon where you can enter a new value. Type 1000 and press Enter. This moves the value 1000 hex into the AX register, and returns you to the hyphen prompt.

▐▶ *Tip:* If you don't enter a value at the colon prompt, the contents of the AX register aren't changed. This way the R*rr* command can be used to check the contents of a single register without altering it.

Putting a value into a register is called *moving* — just like putting a value into a memory location is called *poking*. The RAX command is used to *move* a value into the AX register. The value doesn't "move" from anywhere, the microprocessor simply sets the proper bits in the register.

The Assembly language instruction that puts values into registers is called MOV, for move. This is the most common assembly language command, one you'll be seeing a lot as you explore the rest of this book.

Other microprocessors *load* values into registers. For example, the Motorola 68030 found in the Macintosh computer uses the LOAD command. The old Z80 chip found in computers popular during the early '80s used the LD, "load," command as well. For Intel microprocessors, we *move* or MOV.

You can confirm the new value in the AX register with the R command; type *R* by itself and look up the AX register pair (first item, first row). It will have the value 1000 hex listed after the equal sign.

Working with Files and the CX Register

You can use the R*rr* command to change any register. If you worked through the examples in the previous chapter, then you've already used the RCX command to

Peeling the Lid off the Microprocessor Chip 211

change the value in the CX register. From Chapter 11, you used the following command before saving the SAMPLE1.TXT file to disk:

```
-RCX
CX 0000
:32
```

The CX register is used by DEBUG when saving a file to disk. The value stored in CX sets the size of the file — the amount of memory to write to disk. In addition to that, CX is also used when loading a disk file. Again, it contains the size of the file in bytes. To prove it, exit DEBUG, then restart it using the following command:

```
C:\> DEBUG C:\CONFIG.SYS
```

This command loads the file C:\CONFIG.SYS into DEBUG for editing. As it does so, DEBUG makes the following preparations:

- It loads the file at offset 100 hex in the current segment.
- It sets the IP register equal to 0100 hex.
- It sets the CX register equal to the size of the program loaded.

Check this out by typing the R command:

```
-R
```

You'll see a register display similar to Figure 12-2, but look at the CX register. On my screen it's equal to 282 hex, the size of my CONFIG.SYS file in hexadecimal. When DEBUG loads a file, either from the command line or using the N and L commands, the size of the file is stored in the CX register. The same holds true for saving a file to disk, which is why you were typing in the RCX command before saving a file in the previous chapter.

When a the file is larger than 65,536 bytes (FFFF hex), then both the BX and CX registers are used to hold the value. The BX register holds the upper 16 bits, CX holds the lower 16 bits. To prove this, you'll need to load a hefty file from your disk. One such file is the QBASIC.EXE program included with DOS. (If you don't have QBASIC.EXE, select another file of a similar girth.)

QBASIC.EXE is the QBasic interpreter and it weighs in heavy at 254,799 bytes. Load that file by quitting DEBUG then restarting it with the following command:

```
C:\> DEBUG C:\DOS\QBASIC.EXE
```

You'll need to specify the proper pathname for QBASIC.EXE. The example assumes the file is in the DOS directory on drive C. If it's elsewhere on your hard drive, specify the proper path. If you specify a file that doesn't exist, DEBUG will report a *File not found* error; you should quit and start over.

Once inside DEBUG, type the R command and look at the BX and CX registers.

```
BX=0003 CX=E14F
```

Both the BX and CX registers are required to hold the file's full size. On my system, I see 0003 hex in the BX register and E14F in CX. The full size of the file is 3E14F hex — more or less:

File size, upper sixteen bits	= BX
File size, lower sixteen bits	= CX
File size	= BX:CX
File size, upper sixteen bits	= 0003
File size, lower sixteen bits	= E14F
File size	= 0003E14F

Since QBASIC.EXE is an EXE file, it's not loaded the same as other files on disk. Therefore, the value 3E14F hex is not equal to 254,799 decimal. But this is a minor quibble. The purpose here is to show how the two registers are used to handle large file sizes. This applies when both saving and loading files to and from disk.

Tip: What you're actually seeing here, with the BX and CX registers used to hold the size of a file, is a limit of the DOS file system. Together, BX:CX (as it's written) makes up 32 bits. That's FFFFFFFF hex or 4,294,967,295 decimal, which is the maximum size of a file under DOS.

Program files ending in EXE are stored in a special format. They're loaded into memory in different chunks as opposed to one piece, which is how COM, text, and other files are loaded by DEBUG. Because of this, the size of an EXE file on disk, and as reported in DEBUG by the BX and CX registers, will be different.

A way to get around the file size difference, as well as to load an EXE file contiguously into memory, is to rename it before loading. Renaming an EXE file to a BIN extension works, however, it's also possible to rename it with a COM extension. If you do rename the file with a BIN extension, remember to rename it back to EXE if you want to run the program again.

More information about the COM and EXE program file formats is presented in Chapter 17.

Specific Accumulator Register Tasks

Each of the accumulator registers does serve a special function. Although they all can be used to hold values and for basic math, AX, BX, CX, and DX do play individual roles when telling the microprocessor what to do next:

- AX is the most commonly used register, the primary accumulator. If a register is a hand for holding values, AX is your right hand.

- BX is often used as a "base" register. For example, if you have a bunch of names neatly stored in memory, BX will help you point to a given name.

- CX is the counter register. If you're moving a block of memory, CX is often used to give the size — just as it reports the size of a file loaded from disk, or specifies the size of a memory block written to disk. CX may also be used when programming a "loop," or a repeated set of steps. The CX register usually holds the number of times the loop will repeat.

- The DX register is used when the microprocessor talks to the rest of the computer using its input/output lines. DX will hold the number of a specific input or output line, which is how the microprocessor controls the disk drives, serial ports, printer ports, and so on.

There's no need to commit these individual functions to memory; you'll learn how they're used as you learn how the microprocessor operates. All of these registers can be changed using the proper R*rr* command; however, when you program the computer, you're directing the microprocessor itself to fill them with a specific value.

Split Personalities

The accumulator registers each have a split personality. This is something that's peculiar only to registers AX, BX, CX, and DX. These registers are actually pairs of registers. (See Figure 12-1.) Register AX is actually the "register pair," AH and AL. Register BX has two halves as well: BH and BL. The same holds true for the CX and DX registers.

There are two reasons for this duality: first, the ancestors of the 8088/8086 came with only 8-bit registers. The 8088/8086's registers are all 16-bit, so they were split in half to be compatible (more or less). The second, and more logical reason, is that the 8-bit "half" registers allow you to more easily manipulate byte values. So while you have four 16-bit registers, you also have eight 8-bit registers.

The way that the split works is that the lower 8-bits of each register can be referred to as *r*L, where *r* is the register name. The higher 8-bits are referred to as *r*H. You can direct the microprocessor to put a value of FF hex into AL and you're only working with half of AX register. The other half, AH, remains unaffected by what's done to the AL register.

Note: Technical types use the term "Most Significant Byte" or "MSB" to refer to the higher 8-bits of a register, the *r*H. They use the term "Least Significant Byte" or "LSB" to refer to the lower register, *r*L.

Sadly, in DEBUG you cannot reference the higher and lower registers individually; the R command only works with full, 16-bit registers. (If you try to *RAH* you get a "br" error — bad register.) The way to deal with the problem is to use simple hexadecimal math. For example, if a program says to put the value 55 hex into the AH register, you would use the following R command:

```
-RAX
AX 0000
:5500
```

In this example, the value 55 hex is put into the AH register — but at the same time, 00 is put into AL. Don't fret over this on your own; I'll flag any places in the text where you need to load half registers in DEBUG.

Which register is which? It depends on what you need. When you're working with byte values, you'll be using the *r*H and *r*L registers. Obviously, 16-bit values will require the full *r*X register. For now, remember that AH is the upper half of the AX register, and AL is the lower half. The same holds true for all the other accumulators.

Special Purpose Registers

The accumulator registers serve a general purpose. Even though they have specific names and can serve different functions, you can do just about anything with them. The nine remaining registers, however, serve very specific functions. These include the index and segment registers, as well as the unique flags register.

The Index Registers

The index registers are named SP, BP, SI, and DI. (The IP register is the instruction pointer, and is covered in detail in Chapter 13.) What these registers do is to point at things. For example, say you wanted to copy a block of memory from one location to another, just as you copied screen memory around using the M (Moo-copy) command in the previous chapter. If so, then you need an index register.

The SI and DI registers are the Source Index and Destination Index registers. SI points at the start of a block of memory and DI points at the start of another block. By using the proper instructions, you can tell the microprocessor to copy the block of memory from SI's location to DI's, to compare the blocks or to swap the blocks. To see how this works, clear out a patch of memory using the F command:

```
-F 100 L80 0
```

Now enter the following two R commands to change the contents of the SI and DI registers:

```
-RSI
SI 0000
:110
-RDI
DI 0000
:120
-
```

First you move the value 110 hex into SI, then the value 120 hex is moved into the DI register. SI points at the start of a block of memory, DI points at the start of another block. The size of the block is specified using the CX register. Enter the following:

```
-RCX
CX 0000
:10
```

This command moves 10 hex into the CX register pair. Now you have a starting location in SI, a destination in DI, and a length in CX. Put something interesting into memory at 110 hex (the block "pointed to" by the SI register). Poke in the following:

```
-E 110 "I've been moved!"
```

The above command pokes a string into memory at offset 100 hex. Now you have a block of "interesting" memory, a size, and a destination. All that's required is an instruction telling the microprocessor what to do. That instruction is REPZ MOVSB, which doesn't make sense in anything but assembly language, but means "copy a block of memory from the offset address stored in register SI to the address in DI with a length stored in register CX."

Note: REPZ means "repeat the next instruction." The Z tells the microprocessor that it will repeat the instruction until the value in the CX register is *decremented* to zero. (To decrement is to subtract one from something.) So, if the CX register contains 10 hex, the next instruction will be repeated 16 times.

The MOVSB instruction tells the microprocessor to copy a byte value from the memory offset specified in the SI register to the offset specified in the DI register. After the byte is copied, both the SI and DI registers will be incremented. (To increment means to add one to something.)

The complete instruction, REPZ MOVSB, moves a block of memory CX bytes long from the offset in SI to the offset in DI.

The microprocessor itself understands REPZ MOVSB less than you and I do. Instead of reading those words or "mnemonics," it reads bytes of machine language. Type the following command:

```
-E 100 F3 A4
```

The two bytes F3 and A4 hex are actually machine language instructions the microprocessor will eat. The instructions direct the CPU to copy a block of memory, as described above. (Don't concern yourself with what commands do what; just look at the values in the registers for now.)

Use the R command to view your microprocessor setup. You'll see something similar to that shown in Figure 12-3. Check to see that the CX register contains 10 hex, the SI register contains 110 hex, DI contains 120 hex. This is what you've set up so far using the R command. The E command poked machine language into memory — REPZ MOVSB — which you can also see in the R command's display.

You should also confirm that the IP register equals 100 hex: IP=0100. If it doesn't, then use the *RIP* command to reset that register to 100 hex. This is important, so double-check your screen to make sure.

```
AX=0000  BX=0000  CX=0010  DX=0000  SP=FFEE  BP=0000  SI=0110  DI=0120
DS=2617  ES=2617  SS=2617  CS=2617  IP=0100   NV UP EI PL NZ NA PO NC
2617:0100 F3              REPZ
2617:0101 A4              MOVSB
```

Figure 12-3 The microprocessor has been set up to copy a block of memory

To make everything happen, and move a block of memory, enter the *P* command — proceed. You'll see another register (R command) display. Before examining the register display, use the *D 100* command to view memory and confirm that the block was copied. Your screen should look something like Figure 12-4. The 10 hex block has been copied from offset 110 hex to offset 120 hex.

The REPZ MOVSB command uses three registers:

- SI points to the start of the source block
- DI points to the start of the target block
- CX sets the length of the block.

When the microprocessor sees the REPZ MOVSB command (actually bytes F3 and A4 hex), it copies a byte from the offset address listed in SI to the offset listed in DI. It then increments (adds one to) SI and DI and decrements the value in register CX. It continues to do this until CX contains zero. From Figure 12-4, you can see that CX contains zero and both SI and DI have had 10 hex added to their values. And, of course, the direct result of all this is that a block of memory has been copied from one place to another.

What you've done here is to write a small program of sorts. This program does the same thing that DEBUG's M command does: It copies a block of memory. You specify a start, length, and destination. The only difference here is that you've done so by *programming* the microprocessor. If this were a "real" program, you would have told the microprocessor to move 10 hex into CX, 110 into SI, and 120 into DI. In DEBUG you used the R command. Figure 12-5 shows how everything is set up using microprocessor and memory maps.

```
AX=0000  BX=0000  CX=0000  DX=0000  SP=FFEE  BP=0000  SI=0120  DI=0130
DS=2617  ES=2617  SS=2617  CS=2617  IP=0102   NV UP EI PL NZ NA PO NC
2617:0102 0000            ADD     [BX+SI],AL                       DS:0120=49
-D100
2617:0100  F3 A4 00 00 00 00 00 00-00 00 00 00 00 00 00 00   ................
2617:0110  49 27 76 65 20 62 65 65-6E 20 6D 6F 76 65 64 21   I've been moved!
2617:0120  49 27 76 65 20 62 65 65-6E 20 6D 6F 76 65 64 21   I've been moved!
2617:0130  00 00 00 00 00 00 00 00-00 00 00 00 00 00 00 00   ................
2617:0140  00 00 00 00 00 00 00 00-00 00 00 00 00 00 00 00   ................
2617:0150  00 00 00 00 00 00 00 00-00 00 00 00 00 00 00 00   ................
2617:0160  00 00 00 00 00 00 00 00-00 00 00 00 00 00 00 00   ................
2617:0170  00 00 00 00 00 00 00 00-00 00 00 00 00 00 00 00   ................
-
```

Figure 12-4 Here is what you see after copying the block

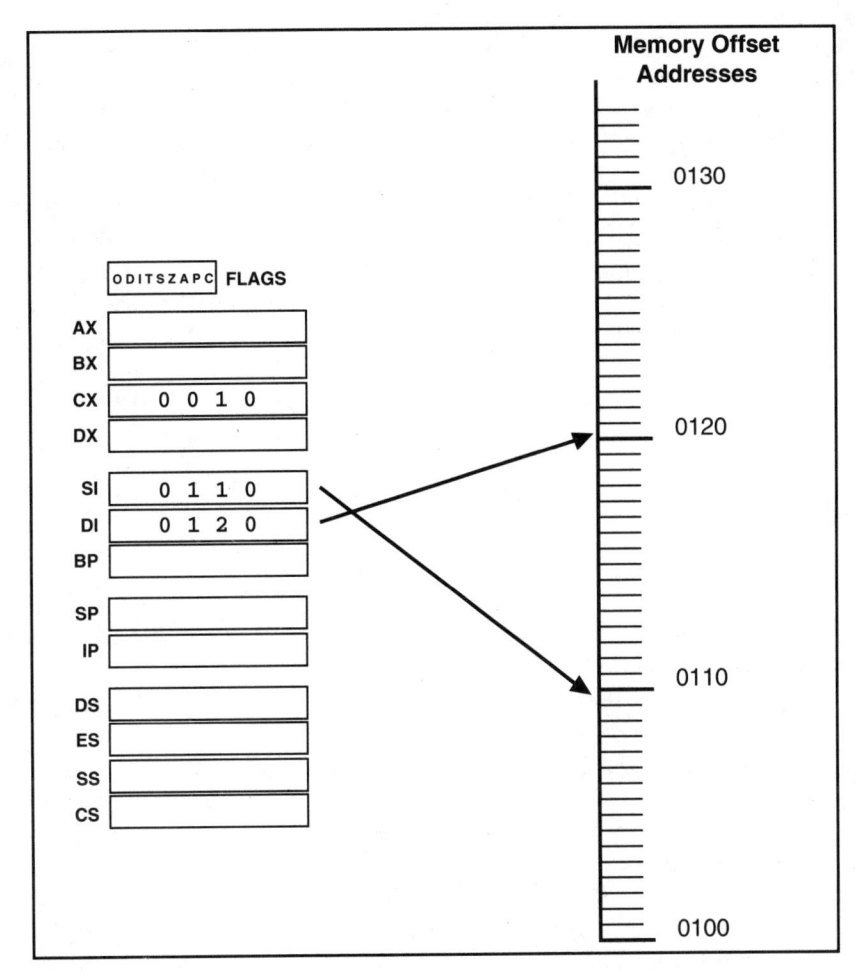

Figure 12-5 How the microprocessor's registers manipulate memory

The purpose of this section wasn't to teach you programming. Instead, you saw how the index registers are used to point to memory locations. True, SI and DI held values. However, those values were read by the microprocessor as memory locations — not numbers. The value 10 hex in the CX register is read as a value, however, since CX is an accumulator register.

Note: The other index registers, BP, SP, and IP also point to memory locations. However, only the SI and DI registers are used when copying, comparing, or otherwise manipulating blocks of memory.

The Segment Registers

The microprocessor's segment registers are similar to the index or pointer registers in that they indicate a place in memory. The values these registers hold, however, are segment values, not offsets. It's the segment registers, DS, ES, SS, and CS, that help the microprocessor locate where things are in memory.

If a register display is visible on your screen, look at the four segment register values on the second line. (If you don't see a register display, enter the *R* command.) Unless you've changed any of the segment registers, they should all indicate the same segment address, which is also the segment used by the D command to display memory — the "current segment" or DEBUG's segment.

The DS and ES segments tell the microprocessor where to find data. DS is the data segment. Offset addresses used in the index and other registers are relative to the segment specified by the DS register. For example, if the DS register equals 2617 hex and the SI register equals 0110, the absolute memory address being referenced is:

```
DS:SI
```

or,

```
2617:0110
```

For the "program" you ran in the previous section, the microprocessor used the address shown in this example — both DS and SI's values — to find out where the block of memory started.

The ES, extra segment, register works the same way as the DS register; it keeps track of data in a specific segment of memory. By having two data segment registers, the microprocessor is able to manipulate blocks of memory across the PC's entire address space. For example, suppose you wanted to copy a block of memory from the current segment into video memory. To make it happen, the DS register would indicate the current segment and you would set the ES register equal to the video memory segment (B800 hex for color or B000 for monochrome). You'll see how this works in a later chapter.

The SS register keeps track of a special storage place called the *stack*. The stack is a collection of information pointed at by the Stacker Pointer (SP), index register. Chapter 13 shows how this works.

Finally, the CS segment is the Code Segment register. This tells the microprocessor where to find the program it's currently running. (The individual byte of machine language code is pointed at by the IP register.)

The segment registers aren't really something you want to mess with. For most simple programs constructed in DEBUG, all four registers will point to the same memory segment. And while you can use the R command to change a segment's value, it's not necessary most of the time.

▶ *Tip:* DEBUG uses the segment registers to specify a work place in memory. If you want to work in another area of memory, you can use the *RDS* command to specify a new segment. For example:

```
-RDS
DS=xxxx
:B800
```

In this example, the DS register is changed to segment B800 hex, the start of color screen memory. In DEBUG, the D command can now be used to specify offset addresses in that segment. The E command can be used to poke in new bytes in that segment as well. This is because DEBUG's commands work with memory offsets relative to the segment specified by the DS register.

The Flags Register

At the end of the second row of the R command's output, you'll see eight pairs of letters, looking like they've wandered out of the Periodic Table of Elements. These are *flags*, status bits that can be either "on" or "off." The flags are actually stored in a special microprocessor register called the *flags register*. You can see it depicted in Figure 12-1. (There are actually nine flags, although DEBUG only reports on eight.)

The flags come in handy to tell you the result of certain operations. The two most common flags are the *carry flag* and the *zero flag*. The zero flag zips up to the top of the flagpole when a mathematical operation results in zero. For example, if you were comparing two values in two registers and they were both equal, the zero flag would fly high. If the values were different, the zero flag pole would be "clear."

The carry flag gets raised under a variety of circumstances. It's used in DOS programs to test for the success of an operation. When the carry flag isn't flying (or reset), the operation is successful; when the carry flag is flapping in the breeze (or set) the operation failed. Based on those results, the program tries again, tries another way, or displays an error message.

Figure 12-6 lists the flags' full names and their set and reset positions. Normally, DEBUG starts with all the flags clear, or reset, save for the interrupt flag, which is

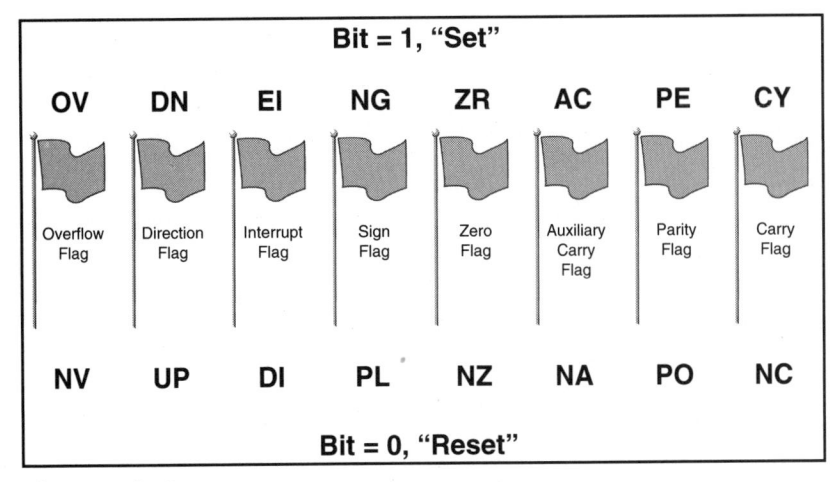

Bit = 1, "Set"							
OV	DN	EI	NG	ZR	AC	PE	CY
Overflow Flag	Direction Flag	Interrupt Flag	Sign Flag	Zero Flag	Auxiliary Carry Flag	Parity Flag	Carry Flag
NV	UP	DI	PL	NZ	NA	PO	NC
Bit = 0, "Reset"							

Figure 12-6 Flag registers in the 8088/8086

set to EI (Enable Interrupts). You can change the flags using the R command as follows:

```
-RF
NV UP EI NG NZ NA PO NC -
```

DEBUG responds to the RF command by displaying the current flag settings. To change a flag, type the new, two-letter setting at the hyphen. (Refer to Figure 12-6 for the settings.) For example, to change NZ to ZR, type *ZR* at the hyphen prompt. You can enter more than one combination to change multiple flags, or you can just press Enter alone to leave the flags as they are. If you want to change multiple flags, put a space between each of the letter combinations.

Changing flags isn't something you'll normally do in DEBUG. Flags are used in programs to test the outcome of certain operations, mostly comparisons. You'll see how this works in Part III of this book where you create several interesting little programs.

13

How the Microprocessor Works

A microprocessor contains registers that hold values, and you can change the values using DEBUG all day long and have a modicum of fun. But that's not what it's all about. In the big picture, putting values into registers is done to meet some end, to carry out a task, to make the computer do something. That's the microprocessor's role in life. Your job is to tell it what to do. This is called programming.

This chapter concludes your introduction to DEBUG by showing you how the microprocessor works. You'll read about controlling the microprocessor using assembly language and DEBUG's mini-assembler. This chapter even offers an introduction to DOS programming, which gives you a feeling for what those script files in the magazines do.

The Art of Programming

Programming is the art of writing computer software. Software consists of instructions that tell the computer what to do. Take a moment to swallow these two concepts one at a time.

First, programming is an art — not a science. The best programmers are musicians, not mathematicians. In fact, most people who hire programmers at major software developers shove the math and engineering majors to the bottom of the stack. Assembling a program requires insight and creativity beyond the ability to add and subtract binary numbers. Think of the difference between a handmade

Swiss clock from the 18th century and a common digital watch. Which would you rather have crushed under a steamroller?

Second, software tells the hardware what to do. This is done according to a plan that you can make up yourself. So programming puts you in charge of a fast little device, the microprocessor, and everything it's wired into. As long as you know what it is you want to do, the only job that remains is to express that desire properly to the microprocessor. That's where the programming language part comes in.

Seven Paragraphs on Programming Languages

The microprocessor must be told what to do next. It doesn't second guess you. A CPU never assumes or supposes. Instead, it understands and obeys only one type of command: The *machine language* instructions it is designed to read.

Machine language is the "grunt and point" of programming languages. It consists of byte values that the microprocessor reads into memory: B7, E8, 39, E8, etc. No human memorizes these bytes! Instead, humans who want to program a microprocessor directly use a programming language called *assembly language*.

Assembly language directly corresponds to machine language. Instead of bytes, however, assembly language uses clipped words and acronyms to represent the machine language instructions. These words are referred to as *mnemonics*. You saw two of them earlier in this chapter: REPZ MOVSB. These two assembly language mnemonics represent the machine language bytes F3 and A4. The four hex bytes in the previous section translate into assembly language MOV and CMP mnemonics: MOV is "move" and CMP means "compare." That's much easier than memorizing B7 E8 and 39 E8, but it is still cryptic.

I'll be the first to confess that assembly language is an awkward way to program a computer; only the most insane use it. Still, there are many advantages to assembly language. For example, since you're programming the computer in its (almost) native tongue, the programs will run faster than anything. Also, assembly language programs are very small. On the downside, they take forever to construct — like building a scale model of the Eiffel tower using toothpicks. To solve this problem, and speed program development, "high-level" languages were developed.

High-level languages include BASIC, Pascal, Logo, and others that use recognizable words and sentences to program a computer. Those words are converted into machine language by use of a special program called a *compiler*. However, while the compiler does the job and saves time, it isn't as efficient as programming the microprocessor directly using assembly language.

Note: The C programming language is considered a mid-level language. It's not as Englishlike as BASIC or Pascal, but not as crude as assembly language. Nearly all the software sold for PCs today is written in C with some assembly language tossed in to speed up the slower parts.

In the end, to program a computer you have a trade-off: the convenience of a high-level language versus the quick compactness of assembly language. For small projects, nothing beats assembly language. You'd be a fool to write a Windows program in it. (But if you did, it would certainly be fast.)

As a DEBUG user, you're stuck with programming the microprocessor a byte at a time. Yet, you're also blessed with DEBUG's internal assembly language program, the "mini-assembler." You can use it to create swift little programs in no time. And all this is accomplished by knowing how the microprocessor and DOS works, how your computer works, and having a purpose in mind. The last part of this book will show you the ropes. Presently, we have more studying to do.

Telling the Microprocessor What to Do

The microprocessor works by reading machine language instructions stored in memory. The instructions are collectively referred to as computer programs or software. Without the instructions, the microprocessor would just sit there. With the instructions, the microprocessor can do just about anything.

To read the instructions, the microprocessor uses two registers: CS and IP. The CS register identifies the code segment, the segment address in memory where the program is located. The IP register points at the offset in that segment where the next machine language instruction is located.

When DEBUG starts, it sets a segment in memory for its use and puts that segment value into all the segment registers: DS, ES, SS, and CS. It points the IP register at offset 100 in that segment, which is where you will always start writing programs in DEBUG.

Start DEBUG (if you're not currently in it), and type the following commands. Make sure the three E commands are all followed by the proper values. Double check your work:

```
-F 100 L80 0
-E 100 B8 23 01 BB
-E 104 67 45 B9 AB
-E 108 89 BA EF CD
```

These commands clear out a chunk of memory, then poke in a brief set of machine language instructions. (It's not really a program, just a demonstration.)

Type the R command to view the register contents:

```
-R
```

> *Tip:* Now is a good time to use the DEBUG keyboard macros created in Chapter 6. If you haven't used them, refer to Table 6-4, which lists a few of my favorites. Feel free to add your favorites according to which DEBUG commands you use most frequently.

The first two lines describe the microprocessor's 13 registers, their contents, and the flags register. This should all look familiar to you. The last line tells you which instruction the microprocessor will run next. That line on your screen should appear something like this:

```
2617:0100 B82301        MOV     AX,0123
```

The first value, the segment address, will probably be different on your PC. My system shows a segment address of 2617 hex, but everything else on that line should be identical to what you see above. (If it's not, then you didn't type in the proper E command; reenter the F and E commands described above.)

What you're looking at on that last line are three things. First, is the address of the next machine language instruction in memory. Second, are the machine language instructions shown as byte values (without spaces between them). Third are the assembly language mnemonics. The line is illustrated in Figure 13-1.

The first item, the address, is a combination of two register values. The CS register sets the segment; the IP register holds the offset. The machine language bytes at that location are shown next to the address: B8, 23, and 01. You can confirm this by using the following D command:

```
-D 100 L3
```

The instruction is three bytes long, but the microprocessor doesn't know that (yet). It's actually DEBUG that looks up the instruction internally, sees what it is, knows that it's three bytes long, then displays the three bytes plus the corresponding assembly language mnemonic. The microprocessor only sees the B8 hex-byte at offset 100 hex in the CS register's segment. It's poised for action.

The third column shows the machine language instruction translated into assembly language mnemonics: MOV AX,0123. This means the value 123 hex will be moved into the AX register. The syntax is reversed, so it helps to think of the command as being "move into register AX the value 123 hex."

Note: The microprocessor only sees the machine language instruction B8 hex. That instruction directs it to move a value into the AX register. The value to move is contained in the next two bytes, 23 and 01. Yes, those two bytes are reversed. That's the way the Intel microprocessor works: First it loads 23 hex into AL then 01 into AH. The result is the value 123 loaded into register AX.

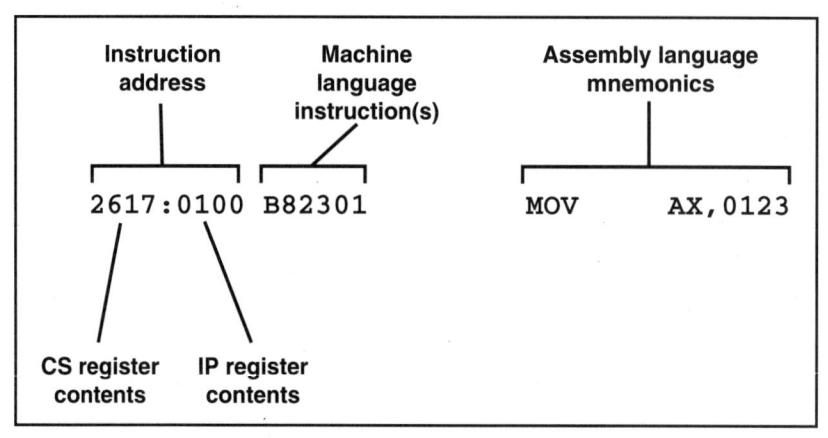

Figure 13-1 The bottom line of DEBUG's R command display

To engage the microprocessor's engine, use DEBUG's P command to proceed. Type *P* and press Enter. The output on your screen will look similar to Figure 13-2.

Here is what has happened, according to what you see on your screen: The MOV AX,0123 instruction has been executed. You see the value 0123 hex in the AX register. Great, everything worked.

Check out the IP register. It's now pointing at memory offset 103 hex. This is the location of the next machine language instruction in memory. You can see that instruction at the bottom of the register display; the BX register will be loaded with the value 4567 hex. Enter P to make it happen:

```
-P
```

In the register display that appears, confirm that the BX register is loaded with the value 4567 hex. You'll see that the IP register is now pointing at the next instruction in memory, at offset 106. That instruction is shown at the bottom of the screen:

```
2597:0106 B9AB89      MOV     CX,89AB
```

The MOV command directs the microprocessor to fill the CX register with the value 89AB hex. Type *P* and Enter to make it so. Then you'll see the final instruction in memory, MOV DX,CDEF. Press *P* again to move CDEF hex into the DX register.

In the final register display, confirm that all four accumulator registers are filled with hexadecimal values:

```
AX=0123
BX=4567
CX=89AB
DX=CDEF
```

To see a summary of the instructions that made that possible, use the following command:

```
-U100
```

The U command *unassembles* a program in memory. In this example, U100 directs DEBUG to unassemble the machine language instructions starting at offset 100 hex. DEBUG takes that chunk of memory and translates the bytes stored there into assembly language mnemonics. What you'll see on your screen are several MOV instructions, followed by a bunch of ADD commands. Ignore the ADD commands (they're simply the translation of the byte 00 hex into assembly language).

```
-P
AX=0123  BX=0000  CX=0000  DX=0000  SP=FFEE  BP=0000  SI=0000  DI=0000
DS=2617  ES=2617  SS=2617  CS=2617  IP=0103   NV UP EI PL NZ NA PO NC
2617:0103 BB6745          MOV     BX,4567
```

Figure 13-2 The microprocessor has processed a machine language instruction

The MOV command is used to move a value into a register. In this exercise, you've moved values into the four accumulator registers, AX through DX. You could have done this with the R command. Instead, you've taken the first step toward programming the microprocessor directly. There's only one problem: The bytes were poked enigmatically into memory. A better way is to use DEBUG's mini-assembler.

The Mini-Assembler

There are two ways to program in DEBUG: poke in machine language bytes or create the program using assembly language. Since no human memorizes machine language bytes, just about everyone uses DEBUG's mini-assembler to write in assembly language. This poses the question, why did I use the E command to poke in machine language bytes in the previous section?

The answer is that, as usual, I cheated. I first used the mini-assembler to create the program. Then I used the D command to see what the byte values were, and then I plugged the values into the E commands. This method of programming is common in DEBUG scripts and preferred when you don't want to overwhelm someone. Besides, the corresponding assembly language instructions would be more involved and take longer to type.

Back to the subject: To create a program in assembly language, you activate DEBUG's mini-assembler. This is done with the A command. The A command can optionally be followed by an address showing where the program is to be placed in memory. Most of the time, you'll start a program at offset 100 hex.

> *Tip:* If the A command isn't followed by an address, then 100 hex is used. If you've been using the A command for a while, then typing A by itself will "pick up" at the last-used memory address. This works like the BASIC language's AUTO command that automatically inserts line numbers into programs.

Building the Program

Type *A100* at DEBUG's hyphen prompt to begin assembling a program. You'll see the following on your screen:

```
-A 100
2597:0100
```

DEBUG shows you the *segment:offset* address where you'll be writing the program in memory. Presently, DEBUG is waiting for you to enter assembly language instructions. It will take those instructions — the mnemonics — and translate them into machine language bytes that it immediately pokes into memory. This happens until you press Enter on a line by itself or press Ctrl-C. Type the following and press Enter:

```
PUT FEDC HEX INTO REGISTER AX
```

Gong! You didn't really expect it to work (but hopes were doubtlessly high!). DEBUG comes back with an "^ Error" message, telling you it didn't like what it saw after the P command. You can only type proper assembly language instructions when you're using the mini-assembler.

A list of assembly language instructions can be found in any microprocessor programming book. Anything that covers the 8088/8086, 80286, '386 or later CPUs will work, although DEBUG only accepts 8088/8086 instructions. If you want to go out and buy a programming book, great! Otherwise, this book will tell you everything you need to type. Try the following:

```
MOV AX,FEDC
```

This instruction directs the microprocessor to move into register AX the value FEDC hex: MOVe into register AX the value FEDC hex.

> **Tip:** There's no need to put a "hex" or H after the value; DEBUG believes all numbers to be hexadecimal. This is how DEBUG's mini-assembler differs from "real" assembly language compilers. With most of them, you must put an "H" after a hexadecimal number or the compiler will assume it's in decimal.

After double-checking the command, press Enter. You'll see the following:

```
2597:0103
```

Of course, the segment address on your screen will probably be different. But the offset will be the same, 103 hex. The reason is that DEBUG just translated MOV AX,FEDC into machine language bytes and poked them into memory. It's now waiting for you to enter the next instruction, which will be poked into memory at offset 103 hex. Continue by entering the following three lines:

```
MOV BX,BA98
MOV CX,7654
MOV DX,3210
```

The general format of the MOV command is to follow it with a register name and a value. The value will be placed into the register when the program runs. So far you have an interesting, but not very useful program assembled in memory.

> **Tip:** Moving a value into a register actually *copies* the value there. For example:
>
> ```
> MOV AX,BX
> ```
>
> In this example, the value in register BX is copied to register AX. Both AX and BX will hold the same value after the above instruction. The value does not vacate BX and move into AX. Think "copy."

To make a real program, you need to tell DOS when the program is done running. This is done by typing in the following instruction at offset 10C hex:

        INT 20

The INT 20 command tells the microprocessor to execute "interrupt 20 hex." That interrupt is one of DOS's hotlines — like the old hotline that used to connect Washington and Moscow. When you "call" interrupt 20 hex, DOS picks up the phone and orders the program in memory to stop running. Therefore, the INT 20 instruction marks the end of a DOS program. (It's DOS that runs the programs; the microprocessor simply carries out the orders.)

> *Tip:* The INT 20 hex instruction is similar to the STOP or END command in a BASIC program. Forget about what the microprocessor does when it sees "INT 20". Just know that everything will stop and DOS will take over at that point. In DEBUG, the program being run stops and control returns to DEBUG.

On the last line, at offset 10E hex, press Enter. This exits the mini-assembler and returns you to DEBUG's hyphen prompt.

Check your work. Use the U, unassemble command, to verify that you've entered the program properly. Type the *U 100* command and you should see something like the following:

```
xxxx:0100 B8DCFE     MOV     AX,FEDC
xxxx:0103 BB98BA     MOV     BX,BA98
xxxx:0106 B95476     MOV     CX,7654
xxxx:0109 BA1032     MOV     DX,3210
xxxx:010C CD20       INT     20
```

I've substituted *x*s above for the segment values. Also, what you see below offset 10C doesn't matter; the INT 20 acts like a brick wall, stopping the program and returning control to DEBUG. (If anything is amiss, or the program doesn't look right, start over with the *A100* command above.)

If everything goes as planned, the program will run, the microprocessor will move the proper values into the accumulator registers, and the INT 20 will grind everything to a halt. This will really be something to celebrate.

Now you have two choices: run your program a step at a time with the P command, or run the whole thing at once with the G command. Try both, each in the following two sections.

Running the Program a Step at a Time

The P command steps through a program one instruction at a time. Typing P tells the microprocessor to inch forward, stopping after each machine language instruction to display the register's contents. This is the ideal way to view how a program controls the microprocessor.

Start by making sure that the instruction pointer register is pointing at the start of the program, at offset 100 hex. Confirm this by typing the *R* command and checking the value by the IP register. If it's not equal to 100 hex, then use the RIP command to reset it.

At the hyphen prompt, type the P command. You'll note that the value FEDC hex is moved into the AX register and the next instruction is poised to put BA98 hex into the BX register.

The next three instructions are MOV commands. To see them executed one after another, type the following:

```
-P3
```

This tells DEBUG to repeat the P command three times. You'll see three register displays on your screen, each showing the result of the previous assembly language instruction. Observe that all four accumulator registers are filled with the proper values; the last instruction should now be INT 20.

Type P one final time to execute the INT 20 instruction, call DOS, and quit the program.

```
Program terminated normally
-
```

The catchy phrase "Program terminated normally" means that the program in DEBUG has run its course. Had the program been run at the DOS prompt, you'd see another DOS prompt. In DEBUG, things are terminated.

Note: The process of watching the microprocessor work a step at a time is called *debugging*. This is DEBUG's true purpose. With the above examples, you've used DEBUG to observe how the microprocessor works. There were no errors to catch, but if some did exist, they could be fixed in DEBUG.

Go for It with the G Command

The G command is the way you run an entire program in DEBUG. G means "go." Reset the instruction pointer register to offset 100 hex with the following command:

```
-RIP
IP 010C
:100
```

Tip: If you're using the DEBUG keyboard macros created in Chapter 6, press Alt-I to reset the instruction pointer to offset 100 hex.

Confirm that IP=0100 by typing the *R* command. You should always do this before using the G command. Truly, if there were a single command that could send your computer out wandering in the garden, G is it. (It doesn't crash anything, but will force you to reset if you type G without knowing what the IP register is pointing at.)

With the instruction pointer set, type G, and press Enter:

```
-G

Program terminated normally
-
```

Since the program contains no instructions for displaying information, you get no visual feedback. The program did "terminate" normally, however. Type the *R* command to confirm that it did what it was supposed to do to the accumulator registers.

> ***Tip:*** The old Western Digital hard drive controllers came with a formatting program in ROM. That program started at memory location C800:0005. To activate it and low-level format a hard drive, the manual told you to dive into DEBUG and type the following command (don't type this in!):
>
> ```
> -G=C800:5
> ```
>
> This tells the microprocessor to "go" to address C800:0005 and run the program there. (The equal sign is optional.)
>
> Some hard drive controllers used different addresses. The old Adaptecs used G=C800:CCC. Modern hard drives come with formatting programs or hide their formatting program in ROM so that you can't find it. After all, disaster will strike if you low-level format a hard drive on a whim.

Choosing whether you use G or P to run a program in DEBUG is up to you. I use P often to run through parts of a program that are causing trouble. The G command can be used after spotting the trouble to run the rest of the program — like releasing the break once you hit smooth pavement.

The G command can optionally be followed by an address:

```
-G=100
```

This command will rerun the program at offset 100 hex. There is no need to reset the instruction pointer with an RIP command in this case.

> ***Note:*** An interesting question that pops up around this point is, "How come we can manipulate the microprocessor at the same time DEBUG is running?" After all, isn't it the same microprocessor that's running DEBUG?
>
> The answer is rather flip: You can manipulate the microprocessor at the same time DEBUG is running because, well, that's what DEBUG lets you do. DEBUG is a mysterious program that does some highly undocumented thing with DOS in order to run. All debuggers do. The simplified explanation is that DEBUG maintains a separate "area" for the programs you run inside DEBUG and the things you do to manipulate the microprocessor.

Saving Your Program to Disk

How about saving something meaningful to disk? The program you just wrote can be saved to disk and given a filename, just like the chunk of memory you wrote to disk back in Chapter 11. You need to know the size of the program, its starting address, and a name.

To figure out the program's size, use the U command:

```
-U 100
```

Look at the unassembled program on your screen. The last instruction is INT 20 at offset 10C hex. Look at the next line. It starts at offset 10E hex. If you subtract 100 hex from that value, you get the size of your program, E hex bytes. Put that value into the CX register with the *RCX* command:

```
-RCX
CX=xxxx
:E
```

▶ ***Tip:*** To determine the size of a program in memory, use the U command to unassemble it. Then find the instruction after the INT 20 command. That instruction's address is equal to the size of your program, minus 100 hex.

This tip is a general rule of thumb for determining a program's size. Not all assembly language programs will end in INT 20. Some may have text strings stored in memory after the INT 20 instruction. For them, you need to use the memory-block size formula presented in Chapter 11.

Name the program using the N command. The programs you create in DEBUG are COM programs, so name it with a COM extension:

```
-N TEST.COM
```

All program files start at offset 100 hex in DEBUG. Just type the W command to write your file to disk:

```
-W
Writing 0000E bytes
-
```

Now you can quit DEBUG and run your program at the DOS prompt. Since TEST.COM just loads registers, no visual feedback is provided. However, you can reload your program back into memory using DEBUG, modify it, and save it again. You can edit programs in DEBUG just as you edit documents in a word processor. It's an amazing program.

Jumping, Looping, Interrupting

Few programs are run from top to bottom, like TEST.COM written earlier in this chapter. Most programs make decisions and branch off to other routines stored in memory — just as a batch file or BASIC program will use GOTO to branch to some new instructions. The microprocessor works in the same way.

The following sections complete your introduction to the microprocessor. The subject is *flow control*, or the ability to change how a program runs and let the microprocessor make decisions. I'll also pick up the last few pieces of how the microprocessor works, including a discussion of the baffling "stack."

Loading the Instruction Pointer

The instruction pointer inches its way along in memory, eating one machine language instruction after the other, pointing at the next byte in memory as it completes each task. But it doesn't always have to be that way.

You can load a value into the instruction pointer to make it execute instructions at a different place in memory. The assembly language mnemonic is quite simple: JMP, which means *jump*. You can direct the microprocessor to jump to another location and start executing the instructions there. This is directly similar to the GOTO command in a batch file or the BASIC programming language.

Clear an acre of memory using the following F command:

```
-F 100 L80 0
```

Now, poke in the following machine instruction at memory offset 100 hex:

```
-E 100 EB 0E
```

And, finally, reset the instruction pointer register equal to address 100 hex:

```
-RIP
IP xxxx
:100
```

Use the *R* command to see how everything looks. What you see on your screen should look similar to Figure 13-3. The assembly language mnemonic is JMP 110, which tells the microprocessor to "jump" to offset 110 and continue executing instructions found there.

Type *P* to process the command. The only register that will change is the IP register; it will show IP=0110. The next instruction at that location will be ADD something or other. That's just the way DEBUG interprets all those zeros you poked into memory.

Jumping around using the JMP instruction isn't something you do haphazardly. Usually a JMP command appears right after a CMP, compare, command — just as a GOTO will typically follow an IF command in a batch file. The CMP command compares the values in two registers, the value of a register with a value stored in

```
AX=0000  BX=0000  CX=0000  DX=0000  SP=FFEE  BP=0000  SI=0000  DI=0000
DS=2597  ES=2597  SS=2597  CS=2597  IP=0100   NV UP EI PL NZ NA PO NC
2597:0100 EB0E           JMP      0110
```

Figure 13-3 The instruction pointer is poised to jump at address 110 hex

memory, or the value of a register with a constant value. To see how this works, use the *A100* command to assemble the following:

```
-A 100
xxxx:0100 CMP AX,8000
xxxx:0103 JL 110
xxxx:0105 JG 120
xxxx:0107 JE 130
xxxx:0109 JMP 100
xxxx:010B
```

The first instruction compares the value in register AX with 8000 hex. The next four lines are actually jump instructions. They will be executed depending on the result of the CMP comparison. Here's how to read them:

JL 110   Jump if less than to address 110

JG 120   Jump if greater than to address 120

JE 130   Jump if equal to address 130

JMP 100   Jump no matter what to offset address 100 hex

The CMP instruction will compare the value in the AX register with 8000 hex. When it does so, certain flags will be set in the flags register. The jump instructions are triggered by those flags, and the microprocessor can then tell if the values compared were less than, greater than, or equal to each other.

▶ *Tip:* Keep in mind that assembly language instructions are backward:

```
MOV AX,FFFF
```

This reads, "move into register AX the value FFFF hex." The same holds true with a CMP comparison:

```
CMP AX,8000
```

This reads, "compare with register AX the value 8000 hex" or, "compare 8000 hex to the value stored in AX." The results, greater than, less than, or equal to, are based on the comparison in that order.

Set the IP register to 100 hex using the *RIP* command. Using the *RAX* command, put the value FFFF hex into the AX register. That value is greater than 8000 hex. Type the *R* command to preview the registers, making sure IP=0100 and AX=FFFF. Type *P* to proceed.

You'll notice that the PL flag in the flags display changes to NG. This is how the microprocessor knows that 8000 hex is less than the value in AX. Because of this, the next instruction is JL — jump if less than — should be executed. Type and the microprocessor jumps to address 110.

✎ **Note:** It's actually both the sign flag and the overflow flag that trigger the JL operation; both must be equal for the JL instruction to execute. So not only is the sign flag NG, the overflow flag is OV. This is a minor aside. What's more important is remembering the "JL" means Jump if Less than.

Reset the IP register equal to 100 hex. This time, put the value 0 into register AX. Type the *R* command to confirm that IP=0100 and AX=0000. Type the *P* command and keep an eye on the flags.

Note how both the PE and CY flags shoot up. With this comparison, where 8000 hex is greater than the value in AX, the JL instruction will be skipped. Type *P*. The next instruction, JG, will send the microprocessor to offset address 120 hex since the value is greater.

For the final test, reset the IP register to offset 100 hex, and this time fill the AX register with 8000 hex. Type the *R* command to confirm the values, then type *P*.

The flag that's set immediately is the ZR flag, zero. The zero flag only flies when a comparison is made and the difference is zero. The microprocessor won't jump to address 110 (JL) because the value isn't less, and it won't jump to address 120 (JG) because the value isn't greater. Instead, it jumps to offset 130 because the values are equal.

▶ **Tip:** You probably didn't see the JE 130 command at offset 107. This is because the instruction JE, jump if equal, is equivalent to the instruction JZ, jump if zero. JE equals JZ. Refer to Table 13-1 if this confuses you. Many of the jump instructions have equivalent mnemonics.

Jumping around is necessary in a program to handle unpredictable situations or to weed out the possibilities. When you see the guts of the ASK.COM program in Chapter 18, you'll be looking at an ideal purpose for the JG and JL jump commands.

Incidentally, the 8088/8086 has several ways to jump. Table 13-1 lists the various jump commands and the conditions that make them go. Please don't memorize any of these. This book will always tell you what's going on. However, you should note that they're all pretty easy to figure out once you get the "if not greater than or equal to" patter down.

Labels in Assembly Language

Although DEBUG does have a mini-assembler, it's not like a real assembly language compiler. When you use one, you'll be writing assembly language with specific format. Take a look at Figure 13-4. It shows a portion of an assembly language program written for Borland's *Turbo Assembler*.

Assembly language programs are written using a text editor, like DOS's Edit or *QEdit*. What's created is called *source code*. That text file is then fed into the *compiler* or assembler, which builds a machine language program.

The format used in Figure 13-4 is typical of most assembly language source code. The first column contains a label — not a memory location. It's up to the compiler to give labels memory locations. This allows you the luxury of assigning descriptive

Table 13-1 The 8088/8086 Assembly Language Jump Commands

Jump Mnemonic	Definition
JE	Jump if equal
JZ	Jump if zero
JG	Jump if greater than
JNLE	Jump if not less than or equal
JGE	Jump if greater than or equal
JNL	Jump if not less than
JL	Jump if less than
JNGE	Jump if not greater than or equal
JLE	Jump if less than or equal
JNG	Jump if not greater than
JMP	Jump no matter what
JNE	Jump if not equal
JNZ	Jump if not zero

labels to parts of your program, as well as forgetting about memory offsets and locations.

The second column contains assembly language mnemonics. These are generally the same as they appear in DEBUG. One exception is how memory offsets are referenced; you must use the word *offset* in front of the label. This is moot since DEBUG doesn't require it.

Finally, the third column contains (cryptic) comments. The comments and labels are two luxuries you don't have in DEBUG.

> **Tip:** You can enter comments in DEBUG's mini-assembler; DEBUG will ignore everything after the semicolon:
>
> ```
> MOV AX,1234;PUT A VALUE INTO AX
> MOV BX,5678;PUT A VALUE INTO BX
> ```

These two commands can be entered into the mini-assembler, no sweat. However, when you list the program using the U command, the comments are gone. And they aren't saved to disk when you create your program.

Comments are necessary sometimes to tell you what you're doing. Especially in a language as cryptic as assembly, you need little notes telling you which register is doing what and where the various routines are. You don't need to comment on every line, but a few notes help.

```
Start:                          ;
    mov dx,offset good          ;message in memory
    mov ah,9                    ;DOS function 9, display string
    int 21h                     ;DOS function call
    mov ah,2ch                  ;get time
    int 21h                     ;DOS function call
    cmp ch,12                   ;Test hour value for before noon
    jge cknoon                  ;Jump to afternoon
    mov dx,offset morn          ;It's morning!
    jmp done                    ;Jump to DONE routine
                                ;
Check_Noon:                     ;
    cmp ch,17                   ;Test for after 5 p.m.
    jge ckeven                  ;If so, it's evening
    mov dx,offset aft           ;afternoon message
    jmp done                    ;Jump to DONE routine
Check_Evening                   ;
    mov dx,offset eve           ;It's evening
done:                           ;
```

Figure 13-4 A section of an assembly language source code listing

While DEBUG can "sort of" deal with comments (see the TIP box), forget about using labels. Labels mark the locations of routines in an assembly language program's source code. In Figure 13-4, the label DONE marks the end of the program (which isn't shown in the Figure). When you want to tell the microprocessor to jump to the DONE instructions, you use a JMP DONE command. In DEBUG, you need to know the memory offset address.

I bring this up because using the JMP command (or any of its cousins) in DEBUG can be frustrating unless you know what it is you're jumping to. So allow me to let you in on a secret: the pros actually create a program using an assembler, then load it into DEBUG and use the U command to see what's going on. That's how they make DEBUG script files. You can always create the program manually in DEBUG, but it is a pain — even more so for long programs (more than 30 bytes).

✎ *Note:* My advice is, if you want to learn assembly language, buy an assembler, and select a good book or tutorial that will show you the ropes. The purpose of this material is to familiarize you with the microprocessor and some cute little programs to be introduced in the next part of this book.

How the Stack Pointer Works

One of the most confusing parts about a computer is the *stack*. CONFIG.SYS has a STACKS configuration command. And sometimes you may have seen a "Stack overflow" error message, typically before your computer hangs. All that dreadfulness surrounds a thing called the *stack*. What could it be: Smokestack? Stack of pancakes? Stacked deck?

The answer is that the stack is merely a storage place in memory used by the microprocessor. The two registers that deal with the stack are the SP, Stack Pointer,

How the Microprocessor Works 237

and the SS, Stack Segment register. (Refer to Figure 12-1 if you need a mental image.)

The Stack Segment register points to a segment of memory in which the microprocessor will keep its stack storage area. For most of the programs you write in DEBUG, that's the same segment as everything else. If you type the R command in DEBUG, you'll see that the SS register and all the other three segment registers are pointed at the same 64K block of memory.

The SP register is called "the stack pointer." It's a pointer, like the SI and DI index registers. What it points to is the *bottom* of the stack. The microprocessor stores new or added values on the bottom of the stack and decrements the value in the stack pointer. Don't let that phase you — don't even think about it. Instead, use DEBUG's mini-assembler to create the following program:

```
-A 100
xxxx:0100 MOV AX,1111
xxxx:0103 PUSH AX
xxxx:0104 MOV BX,2222
xxxx:0107 PUSH BX
xxxx:0108 MOV AX,3333
xxxx:010B MOV BX,4444
xxxx:010E POP BX
xxxx:010F POP AX
```

Press Enter on the last line to return to the hyphen prompt. Reset the IP register equal to 100 with the *RIP* command. Then type *R* to look at the registers. Confirm that IP=0100, then type the *P* command.

The program you've written will show you how the stack works. The stack is primarily a storage place. Since you only have four accumulator registers, you can use the stack temporarily to save a register's value. The value can be restored later from the stack. The command to save a register's value on the stack is PUSH, followed by the register's name. To get a register back, you POP. PUSH-POP. Think of your own cute metaphor.

⏩ ***Tip:*** To put a register's value on the stack, you PUSH.
To remove a value from the stack into a register, you POP.

Type the *P* command and see how 1111 hex is moved into the AX register. Now type *P* again. You'll see that the stack pointer register has had 2 subtracted from its value. On my system, it went from FFEE hex down to FFEC hex. The value in the AX register, 1111 hex, was saved on the stack. (Actually it was copied since AX still holds that value.)

✏️ ***Note:*** Remember that the stack pointer's value is a memory address. It's an index register, like the SI and DI registers. Also, your PC's stack pointer may not indicate address FFEE hex. If so, it only means you don't have a '386 family microprocessor or are using a different version of DEBUG. No problem, the stack works the same regardless.

Type *P* two more times. The first moves 2222 hex into the BX register, the second *pushes* the value in the BX register onto the stack. You'll see the stack register decrement by another two memory addresses. Now the values in the AX and BX registers are "saved" on the stack. Figure 13-5 shows how this looks in memory. The values in the AX and BX registers were poked into memory locations pointed at by the stack. After putting the values on the stack, the stack pointer moved down two bytes (a word) in memory. Note that the registers weren't put on the stack, only their values.

Type the *P* command two more times. This fills the AX register with 3333 hex and moves 4444 hex into the BX register. The registers' original values are now "gone." However, they were saved on the stack. If a real program were running, you could tinker with the registers any way you saw fit, but their old values are saved nice and warm on the stack.

To get values back from the stack, use the POP command, followed by a register name. Type *P* in DEBUG to pop the value 2222 hex from the stack and into the BX register. You'll see 2222 hex return from the stack and into the BX register. You'll also see the stack pointer increment up to memory offset FFEC.

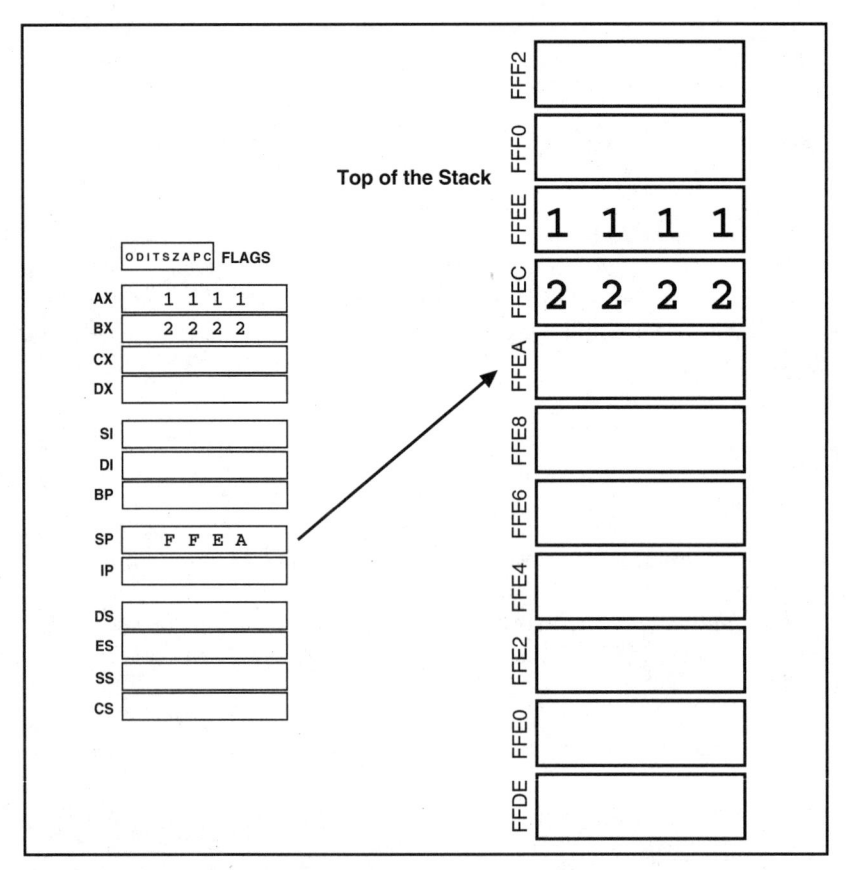

Figure 13-5 How the stack pointer works

To retrieve the original value of the AX register, type P again. This removes 1111 hex from the stack and moves the stack pointer back to its original value.

"Real" programs will mess around a lot with the stack. Values are pushed and popped all the time. And it's when the stack runs down too low in memory that you see a "Stack overflow" error message.

For our purposes, you can use the stack to save values in registers. After all, with only four general-purpose accumulators, there is little room to do any serious number juggling. Pushing register values on the stack is a quick solution to that problem. (You only need to remember to pop them back off the stack in the *opposite* order they were pushed on — but that's really an assembly language issue and not anything to concern yourself with right now.)

Two Stack Examples

Here are some cool tricks you can pull with the stack. The first uses the stack to swap the values between the AX and BX registers. Type in the following assembly language program in DEBUG's mini-assembler:

```
-A 100
xxxx:0100 PUSH AX
xxxx:0101 PUSH BX
xxxx:0102 POP AX
xxxx:0103 POP BX
```

Now use the *RAX* command to put 1111 hex into register AX, then use *RBX* to put 2222 hex into register BX. Use the *RIP* command to reset the instruction pointer to offset 100 hex. Type the *R* command to review how everything stands, then type the following:

```
-P2
```

This command runs the two PUSH commands, putting the value in AX and then BX on the stack. Normally, to return the values to the same registers, you would first pop BX and then AX; you always pop registers in the opposite order they were pushed. However, the next two instructions tell the microprocessor to pop AX and then BX. Type the following:

```
-P2
```

After being POPped in the reverse order, AX now contains 2222 hex and BX contains 1111 hex. The registers have changed values.

Okay, so the first example was rather esoteric. This second example offers a practical solution to a program in DEBUG: you cannot move a value directly into a segment register:

```
MOV ES,B800
```

This instruction doesn't work in DEBUG. You cannot move a value into a segment register. To change a segment register's value, you have two options:

1. Move the value into an accumulator register and then move it into the segment registers:

```
MOV AX,B800
MOV ES,AX
```

2. You can also put the segment value into an accumulator register, push it on the stack, and then pop it back into the segment register. This is kind of sly, but it works and is a few milliseconds faster than the code used in the example:

```
MOV AX,B800
PUSH AX
POP ES
```

In this example, the value B800 hex is moved into register AX. That value is the segment address of color video memory (monochrome video's memory is at segment B000 hex). To move it into the ES segment register, you first push it on the stack, then pop it into AX. That works.

You can use the above trick to access video memory and move something interesting there. This involves two tricks from previous chapters: poking information directly into video memory and demonstrating the Move command using the SI and DI registers.

Enter the mini-assembler, and type in the following program:

```
-A 100
xxxx:0100 MOV AX,B800
xxxx:0103 PUSH AX
xxxx:0104 POP ES
xxxx:0105 MOV SI,120
xxxx:0108 MOV DI,A46
xxxx:010B MOV CX,A
xxxx:010E REPZ MOVSB
xxxx:0110 INT 20
```

Press Enter on the last line to exit the mini-assembler and return to the hyphen prompt. Here is what each part of the program does:

```
MOV AX,B800
PUSH AX
POP ES
```

The first three instructions are used to put the video memory segment, B800 hex, into the ES register. If you have monochrome, change the first line to read MOV AX,B000. (Nothing else in the program is affected if you have monochrome video.)

```
MOV SI,120
```

The fourth line points the SI register at offset 120 hex. This is the start of a block of memory. To put something interesting there, use the following E command:

```
-E 110 "DEBUG"
```

Unfortunately, you can't poke characters like that directly into video memory. For reasons you'll read about in the next part of this book, video memory only displays every other character. Bytes in the even memory addresses are displayed as text, odd memory locations contain *attributes*. To poke the text string DEBUG into video memory, you have to skip every other byte. Use the character "O" to separate each:

```
-E 110 "DOEOBOUOGO"
```

Okay, it's weird. But it will look great on the screen. (Sounds like something David Lynch often promises to studio executives.)

```
MOV DI,A46
```

The fifth line points register DI at what will be an offset in video memory. The DI and ES registers are linked like this: ES:DI. Bytes moved from SI (actually DS:SI) will be transferred into the middle of the screen since ES points to screen memory and DS is poised at an address that will show near the middle of the screen.

```
MOV CX,A
```

The sixth line moves the value A hex (10) into the CX register. That's the size of the block of memory to move, the word "DEBUG" plus its five-character byte attributes (the letter "O" interspersed).

```
REPZ MOVSB
```

The seventh line is the REPZ MOVSB instruction to move a block of memory starting at SI, to offset DI — actually offset ES:DI this time. The block's size is held in the CX register pair. (Review the section "The Index Registers" in Chapter 12 to bone up on how this works.)

```
INT 20
```

The final line is our old friend, INT 20, which tells DOS the program is done. To make magic happen, use the G command as follows:

```
-G=100
```

This means "Go at offset address 100 hex!" Two clues will point to this program's successful conclusion: The word "DEBUG" will magically appear in the middle of the screen, and the catchy phrase, *Program terminated normally*. Now there's a program with *feeling*.

What has been done? You've simply copied a block of memory from one location to another. Unlike the SI-DI register example in the previous chapter, here you've copied a block of memory from one bank into another. The destination bank is located in "video memory," which means the text you poked there appears on the screen.

This isn't the traditional way information is written to the screen, although it is the fastest. It also demonstrates how the stack can be used to store a value, then put it back into a segment register.

▶ *Tip:* If you'd like to save this program, put the value 2A hex into the CX register. (Also, you should put zero into the BX register; if it still contains 1111 hex you'll be writing a 273-plus megabyte file to disk!) Use the N command to give the file a name that ends in COM. (Do not name it DEBUG.COM!) Then use W to write your work to disk.

Call and Return Instructions

The microprocessor's GOTO instruction is a JMP. It jumps around to instructions here and there. An additional way to control the flow of a program is to use the CALL and RET (return) commands. These allow the microprocessor to access *subroutines*, or mini-programs, within a larger program.

CALL is similar to the CALL command in batch file programming. In a batch file, CALL is followed by the name of a second batch file. When that batch file runs, the first is put on hold. When the second batch file ends, control returns to the first batch file, just where it left off. For example:

```
CALL STARTNET.BAT
```

This command used, say in AUTOEXEC.BAT, causes DOS to go out and run the batch file STARTNET. After STARTNET is done, control returns right back to AUTOEXEC.BAT. In a way, STARTNET.BAT is a subroutine accessed from the main batch file.

The microprocessor's CALL command is actually more similar to the BASIC language's GOSUB and RETURN commands. The BASIC program shown in Figure 13-6 shows a BASIC program with a subroutine at line 100. The subroutine ends at line 120 with a RETURN statement. Note how it's "called" in lines 30 and 40 using the GOSUB commands. The output for the program is shown at the bottom of the figure.

In assembly, you use the CALL command to access a subroutine, following it with the routine's address. (In a "real" assembly language program, you would use a label.) The instructions at that routine are read just as the subroutine is executed by GOSUB in BASIC. With the microprocessor, control returns to the main program with the RET, return, command. This works exactly like BASIC's RETURN command.

I'm not going to show you this magic at this point in the book, primarily because a program that needs a CALL command is a bit complex for DEBUG. But there is an important thing to remember that fits into context: When the microprocessor encounters a CALL command, it saves the value in the instruction pointer *on the stack*. The RET command at the end of the subroutine actually pops a value off the stack and puts it into the IP register. This demonstrates another, important use of the stack and the stack pointer register.

```
10 REM Gosub Example
20 PRINT "Here we are, running along"
30 GOSUB 100
40 PRINT "And now we're back in the main program."
50 GOSUB 100
60 PRINT "And now we're done!"
70 END
100 REM Subroutine
110 PRINT "** In the subroutine now!"
120 RETURN

Program Output:

Here we are, running along
** In the subroutine now!
And now we're back in the main program.
** In the subroutine now!
And now we're done!
```

Figure 13-6 A BASIC program showing a subroutine

Calling DOS

The microprocessor doesn't do everything. Software actually controls what's going on in your computer. On your PC, that software is both the BIOS and DOS. Those programs sit in memory and keep track of what's going on. DOS is in charge, but it uses the functions and routines etched in the BIOS all the time.

To take advantage of the routines stored in the BIOS and DOS, you must "call DOS." However, instead of using the CALL command, you use a special instruction called an *interrupt*, INT. This is like a phone call to DOS or the BIOS, depending on which *interrupt number* you use.

You've already seen a good example of an interrupt in action. The few programs you've entered so far that "quit" have used Interrupt 20 hex, INT 20. The INT 20 instruction tells DOS that a program wants to quit. DOS handles that operation, releasing the memory used by the program, and returning control to itself or DEBUG.

There are quite a few interrupts available for use by the PC's microprocessor. Of the bunch, only a handful receive common attention:

- Interrupt 10 hex, INT 10, handles the screen.

- Interrupt 13 hex, INT 13, deals directly with the disk drives.

- Interrupt 16 hex, INT 16, handles the keyboard.

- Interrupt 20 hex, INT 20, tells DOS a program is quitting.

- Interrupt 21 hex, INT 21, handles the rest of DOS.

Note: All the interrupt numbers above are in hexadecimal.

244   Dan Gookin's Guide to Underground DOS 6.0

Each one of these interrupts accesses an internal program that controls part of the computer. Interrupts 10, 13, and 16 are all linked into your PC's BIOS. Interrupts 20 and 21 allow your program to talk with DOS. So while the microprocessor can work with registers and memory, these interrupts are how you program the rest of the computer.

The interrupt you've used so far, INT 20, is a straightforward call — a hotline. The other interrupts have several functions associated with them. For example, you use INT 10 to display a character on the screen, set the background color, set the cursor size and position, and so on. DOS interrupt 21 has dozens of functions associated with it: opening and closing files, creating files, and accessing network functions, date and time functions, and on and on.

> *Note:* I've listed many of the popular interrupts and their functions in Appendix F. The complete list can be obtained in any reference book.

The functions assigned to each interrupt are given various numbers. So when you want a specific keyboard function, you specify that function number before using the keyboard interrupt. This is done by loading the AH register with the function number.

As an example, here's a description function zero from Interrupt 16 hex, which controls the keyboard:

Interrupt:	16 hex
Function:	0 hex
Name:	Read character
Call:	AH=00 hex
Return:	AH=keyboard scan code
	AL=ASCII character code
Description:	This function reads a character from the keyboard. It will wait until a key is pressed. Shift keys and some odd key combinations are not readable by this function.

Function zero for Interrupt 16 hex is named "Read character." To call this function, you load the registers as specified in the "Call" section; move zero into register AH. When the function returns, or immediately after the INT 16 command is run, the AH register will contain the keyboard characters scan code and AL will contain the ASCII code.

To demonstrate this function, enter the following program in DEBUG:

```
-A 100
xxxx:0100 MOV AH,0
xxxx:0102 INT 16
```

Press Enter alone on the last line to return to the hyphen prompt. At the hyphen, type the *RIP* command and reset the instruction pointer equal to 100 hex. Press the *P* command once to put zero into the AH register. Then type P again. This will process the INT 16 command, which is the hotline to the keyboard control program in your PC's BIOS. The computer will sit and wait for you to press a key. Type A.

After pressing the key, control returns to DEBUG. Check out the AX register on your screen. The output on my screen is shown in Figure 13-7. The register AX contains 1E41 hex. The value in register AH is 1E hex, which according to the above information is the scan code for the A key (30 decimal; confirm this with Appendix F). The value in register AL is 41 hex. You can confirm that 41 hex is the ASCII value for the letter A in Appendix A if you wish.

Interrupts are how you make everything work in a PC using assembly language. Other functions, including some DOS interrupt functions, will be presented to you throughout Part III. Most of it is just "observe and recognize" material. There's no sense in training yourself to program a PC using DEBUG, so don't commit anything to memory. But you should know what's going on when you see the famous INT 21 instruction in a program listing.

```
-RIP
IP 0100
:100
-R
AX=0000  BX=0000  CX=0000  DX=0000  SP=FFEE  BP=0000  SI=0000  DI=0000
DS=2597  ES=2597  SS=2597  CS=2597  IP=0100   NV UP EI PL NZ NA PO NC
2597:0100 B400           MOV     AH,00
-P


AX=0000  BX=0000  CX=0000  DX=0000  SP=FFEE  BP=0000  SI=0000  DI=0000
DS=2597  ES=2597  SS=2597  CS=2597  IP=0102   NV UP EI PL NZ NA PO NC
2597:0102 CD16           INT     16
-P


AX=1E41  BX=0000  CX=0000  DX=0000  SP=FFEE  BP=0000  SI=0000  DI=0000
DS=2597  ES=2597  SS=2597  CS=2597  IP=0104   NV UP EI PL NZ NA PO NC
2597:0104 0000           ADD     [BX+SI],AL                    DS:0000=CD
-
```

Figure 13-7 Processing the INT 16 hotline to the keyboard control center in your PC's BIOS

Part III

The Interesting, Curious, and Exotic

Now that you're fairly well versed with DEBUG, you can don your miner's helmet and flick on the lamp. It's time to go underground. Only by knowing how DEBUG works with memory and disk can you continue to explore your PC and what makes it tick. And the knowledge you've gained about the microprocessor will help you write some truly nifty programs coming up. In the next several, exciting chapters, we will cover the following topics:

- Discovering the mysteries and magic lurking in the PC's memory banks
- Figuring out how a floppy disk works and how information is stored there
- Digging in the trenches and writing some interesting and useful programs using DEBUG.

These chapters assume that you have an intimate knowledge of DEBUG. I won't rip through anything without explaining it, but you are expected to understand how the commands work and what to type in. The previous parts of the book showed you all the ropes; now comes the time to put the DEBUG exploration tool to work.

14

Ugly Memory Stuff

Carved in marble on the ancient Greek temple at Delphi were the words "Know thyself." The same concept is laced throughout your PC's RAM. One thing a computer is very good at is knowing itself. All the information about your computer, what it's connected to and what it does, is held inside RAM at various locations. Now that you know how DEBUG works, a complete exploration of your PC's memory is possible.

This chapter uses DEBUG's memory tools to explore several interesting areas of your computer's memory. These include the useful Program Segment Prefix and the BIOS Data Area. Both of these places contain a lot of interesting and descriptive information about your PC. As you'll soon discover, the computer does indeed know a lot about itself.

The Program Segment Prefix

A chunk of memory that will be near and dear to your heart is the Program Segment Prefix, the PSP. DOS creates the PSP every time you run a program. Into that 256-byte chunk of memory, DOS sticks all sorts of interesting information that your program can examine and use.

Before you unlock the PSP's mysteries, it helps to know the differences between COM and EXE programs under DOS. DOS uses those extensions (along with BAT) to separate program files from data and text files. And while DOS will run a COM program the same as an EXE program, beneath the surface there's quite a bit of difference between the two.

How Programs Run under DOS

When you type something at the DOS prompt and press Enter, DOS attempts to decipher your utterings in three steps:

1. DOS looks to its internal command table to see if you've typed the name of an internal command; COPY, DEL, CLS, etc. If you have, then the command is executed from the copy of COMMAND.COM stored high in conventional memory — the transient portion (see Chapter 3, "All about COMMAND.COM"). If the command isn't found, DOS moves on to Step 2.

2. DOS looks for a COM, EXE, or BAT file in the current directory matching the command name you typed — the first item after the DOS prompt. It will match files in that order, COM, EXE, then BAT. So if you have three files, HELLO.COM, HELLO.EXE, and HELLO.BAT, DOS will only run HELLO.COM. This holds true even if you type in a full filename at the prompt. If the command isn't a program name in the current directory, DOS moves on to Step 3.

3. DOS searches the directories listed in the PATH environment variable. It stops off at each one, in order, and looks for a matching COM, EXE, or BAT file to match the command name you typed. This is repeated for each and every directory on the path. If a command isn't found, and DOS has exhausted all the possibilities, you'll finally see a *Bad command or file name* error message.

When DOS does find a program to run, it loads it from disk into memory. The way the program is loaded depends on its extension: COM files are loaded directly into memory; EXE files are loaded according to a specific format; and BAT files are opened, read, and then closed for each line in the batch file. DOS then executes each batch file command one at a time. Batch files aren't real programs and don't contain machine language instructions for the microprocessor. They also lack a PSP, so this discussion concentrates on the COM and EXE files.

> *Tip:* DOS accesses batch files twice for each line in the batch file. This is why batch files run so much faster from a RAM drive; thanks to the speed of the RAM drive, all the disk overhead is barely noticeable.

Whether a program file ends in COM or EXE makes no difference to DOS. In fact, you can rename COM files to an EXE extension and vice versa. This is a great trick to pull when two files have the same name but different extensions and you want to run one instead of the other. Internally, there are great differences between a COM and EXE file.

The COM File Format

A COM file is a *binary image* file. DOS takes a program you write in memory and saves it to disk as one continuous chunk. Likewise, COM files are loaded into memory all in one piece. There is no fancy footwork, no shuffling of memory blocks, and no sophistication.

COM files are actually quite primitive. Their design limits them to being less than 64K in size. Check your hard drive to prove this. No COM file will be larger than 64K or 65,024 bytes. This is a drawback to be sure, especially since the PC can load files many times that size into conventional memory. But that's just the way COM files work. Larger, more sophisticated programs are kept in the EXE program file format.

Note: Okay, if you rename an EXE file to a COM extension, it will be larger than 64K. Internally, the file is really an EXE file. COM files are all limited to 64K in size and DOS will not load anything larger.

When a COM file is loaded, DOS first allocates a 64K bank of memory for it. If the file is too big, or 64K isn't available, you'll see an *Insufficient memory* error, and the program won't be loaded. If there is memory available, DOS creates the 256-byte PSP at offset zero, then points the SP (stack pointer) register at the top of the 64K block of memory, creating the stack. The program is sandwiched between them in the 65,000-odd bytes that remain. DOS then allocates the rest of memory to the program. Yes, the rest of memory, hundreds of thousands of bytes, even though the COM file itself has to be less than 64K.

Before the program starts, DOS points the IP, instruction pointer, register at offset 100 hex. It then jumps to that location. Therefore, all COM programs must have their first instruction at offset 100 hex. You've seen this demonstrated when creating and loading programs from the last part of this book.

Note: All memory locations in a COM program are relative to offset 100 hex. This only plays a role in writing COM programs in an assembler, not in DEBUG. In the assembler, you must use the "offset" command when referencing memory. For example, in DEBUG you would use the following:

```
MOV SI,120
```

This "points" the SI register at memory address 120 hex. In an assembler, not only would you use a label to reference whatever is at 120 hex, you would need to use the word "offset":

```
MOV SI,OFFSET LABEL
```

The "offset" indicates that the "label" is relative to the start of the program at 100 hex.

The EXE File Format

The EXE program file differs from the COM file format in two ways. First, EXE files can be embarrassingly huge. The file EXCEL.EXE, *Microsoft Excel for Windows*, is 2,740,736 bytes long. (Don't bother me with letters asking how a program that big can load into memory — I haven't the foggiest!) Second, EXE files start with a special "header," a small area of memory that tells DOS how to load the program.

So whether it's named COM or EXE, DOS will always spot the EXE file thanks to its header.

The EXE file header is a block of information that tells DOS how to load the file. The size of the block varies, but it will always start with the two bytes 5A hex and 4D hex. These are the hexadecimal ASCII codes for the letters "MZ," which is the file signature DOS uses to identify the EXE file. It's also how you can internally spot an EXE file when you're using a "disk peeker" program.

There's no need to go into detail about the contents of the EXE file header. It contains information about the size of the program, the initial contents of the segment, stack and instruction pointer registers, and where to load, move, and juggle the various parts of the program.

After DOS reads the EXE file header, it loads the various parts of the file in memory. If there isn't enough room for anything, an *Insufficient memory* error appears. If there is enough memory, DOS creates the PSP and then starts the program according to information in the EXE file header. Unlike COM files, the EXE program will have sections located at different segments and offsets.

> ***Note:*** A typical EXE program will have a "code" segment that contains machine language instructions; a "data" segment that contains strings, tables, and other information; and a "stack" segment that's used for the stack pointer and storage. Other EXE files may have additional segments, they're all identified and loaded into different parts of memory according to information in the EXE file header.
>
> Microsoft Windows programs have a special "extended" EXE file header. When run under DOS, the extended header displays the message *This program requires Microsoft Windows*, and then quits to DOS. In Windows, the extended header is used to load the file according to Windows' needs. This is why all Windows applications end in EXE (not to mention their usually huge size).

To see how all this works, you'll need a sample EXE file. My choice is DOS's SORT filter, SORT.EXE. Copy this file to a RAM drive for inspection. Or if you don't have a RAM drive, copy it to a temporary directory, preferably one that's not on the path.

Once SORT.EXE has been copied, create a duplicate named SORT.COM and a second duplicate, SORT.BIN:

```
G:\> COPY SORT.EXE SORT.COM
    1 file(s) copied

G:\> COPY SORT.EXE SORT.BIN
    1 file(s) copied
```

In this example, drive G is my RAM drive, where I'm keeping the SORT program files for experimentation. You should also have three identical files to work with: SORT.EXE, SORT.COM, and SORT.BIN. Each of these has the same content, but different names.

Start DEBUG with the following command:

```
G:\> DEBUG SORT.BIN
```

DEBUG will load the SORT.BIN file, which it assumes to be a binary image file. Type the *D 100* command and look at the first two bytes, at offsets 100 and 101 hex. They'll be MZ, denoting the start of an EXE file's header. Other information is held in the header as well, although it's of trivial importance now.

You can continue to use the D command to peer into SORT's workings. You'll see a copyright notice, some error messages, and the help information. Nothing new. But only by loading SORT.EXE renamed as SORT.BIN will you see an exact image of the way the file sits on disk. If you load the EXE file, DEBUG will obey the instructions there and place the file into memory in a relocatable fashion.

Quit DEBUG, and restart it with the following command:

```
G:\> DEBUG SORT.EXE
```

DEBUG, like DOS, will now load the SORT program using information in the EXE file header. Type the *R* command to review the register contents. What I see on my screen is shown in Figure 14-1. You may not see the exact numbers (depending on the version of DOS you're using and the segment DEBUG is in), but there will be some interesting similarities.

For starters, note that the CX register still contains the size of the file in hex, which is normal for DEBUG. (DOS doesn't do that, by the way; CX usually equals zero when you start a program.) Everything else — the contents of the segment, stack, and IP registers — will be in accordance with information in the EXE file header. You'll note that unlike a COM file, the IP register does not point to offset 100 hex. And the segment registers have different values. This is what the programmer wants, and is the essence of an EXE file.

Earlier I mentioned that you can rename a COM file to EXE and vice versa. This works, but doesn't fool DOS. The reason is that DOS can still spot the EXE file header and load the program properly. Quit DEBUG again and restart it using the following command:

```
G:\> DEBUG SORT.COM
```

Type the *R* command, and look at the registers. They should appear identical to the display you saw when you loaded SORT.EXE. The reason is that DOS isn't

```
AX=0000  BX=0000  CX=191A  DX=0000  SP=024A  BP=0000  SI=0000  DI=0000
DS=25B7  ES=25B7  SS=2734  CS=25C7  IP=0B49  NV UP EI PL NZ NA PO NC
25C7:0B49 E8BBF9          CALL     0507
```

Figure 14-1 SORT's EXE file header has configured the microprocessor's registers

fooled by the COM extension. It always looks for and recognizes the EXE file header and loads the file appropriately.

> **Tip:** If you need to edit the image of an EXE file, copy it to *.BIN. Use DEBUG to edit the BIN file, then save it to disk when you're done. Rename the file to EXE to test it.

DEBUG only makes COM files, since it can only write a binary image to disk. Third-party compilers all generally make EXE files. However, some EXE files can be converted into COM files using the EXE2BIN utility. I've summarized the basic differences between COM and EXE files in Table 14-1. (For an EXE file to be converted into a COM file it must be smaller than 64K, start at offset 100 hex, and the Code, Data and Stack segments must all be equal.)

> **Note:** The EXE2BIN program used to be included with DOS, along with another programming tool called LINK. Both of these have since vanished from DOS's repertoire of files. Instead, you can obtain similar utilities with third-party programming languages. Some languages will give you the option of creating a COM or EXE file, however the restrictions in Table 14-1 still apply: a COM file can be only so big.

Quit DEBUG and then delete the copies you made of the SORT.EXE file. Be careful that you don't delete the original (which should still be in your DOS subdirectory).

The PSP Up Close and in Person

Regardless of their format differences, both COM and EXE programs have the same Program Segment Prefix, the PSP. It's a 256-byte block of memory chock full of interesting nuggets. These nuggets are available to any program that runs under DOS. The information includes all options typed after the program name at the

Table 14-1 COM and EXE Program File Differences

	COM Program	EXE Program
Type	Binary image	Relocatable image
File Header?	No	Yes
Maximum Size	64K or 65,024 bytes	Unlimited
Memory Allocated	All of it	As needed
Segment Registers	All point to the same 64K segment	Kept in header
Program start (IP=)	Offset 100 hex	Kept in header

Ugly Memory Stuff **255**

DOS prompt, vital information on memory and DOS, and any filenames you may have typed after the program name at the DOS prompt.

The PSP is always found at offset zero in the segment identified by the DS register. For a COM program, that's always offset zero. For an EXE program, you can still use the *D0* command to display the PSP, but note that its segment may be different from the CS and SS segments.

> **Tip:** The fact that the PSP is always at offset zero and it's a 256-byte block of memory explains why COM files start at offset 100 hex. It also explains why that offset is so frequently used by DEBUG and its commands. (Now you know.)

To view the PSP, enter DEBUG and type the following D command:

```
-D 0 L100
```

This command displays memory at offset zero for 100 hex bytes. You'll see the complete PSP displayed on your screen. You may not notice anything interesting right away, although you may see some previous DOS commands (or parts of them) at offset 80 hex. That's the *command tail*, which DOS stores in the PSP for examination by your software. The complete list of goodies in the PSP is shown in Table 14-2.

Table 14-2 Interesting Stuff in the PSP

Offset	Length	Description
00 hex	2	INT 20 instruction
02 hex	2	Segment address of next paragraph of memory
04 hex	1	Reserved
05 hex	5	MS-DOS Dispatcher
0A hex	4	Termination address
0E hex	4	Ctrl-C "handler"
12 hex	4	Critical error "handler"
16 hex	22	Reserved
2C hex	2	Environment Segment address
2E hex	46	Reserved
5C hex	16	File Control Block 1
6C hex	16	File Control Block 2
7C hex	4	Reserved
80 hex	128	Command tail

The 256 bytes of the PSP hold 14 pieces of information, as seen in Table 14-1. A description of each is listed below and you can use the "map" in Figure 14-2 to help locate each of them on your screen.

1. At the start of the PSP is the machine language INT 20 instruction. This is a holdover from older versions of DOS, when it was considered Okay to end a program by calling offset zero (CALL 0).

2. Offset 2 in the PSP contains two bytes that are actually a segment address. This identifies the "next paragraph" of free memory following the program. A program would use this value to determine if it was given enough memory.

Tip: Segment addresses, and all 16-bit values, are stored in memory in reverse order. For example, in Figure 14-2, the next paragraph segment reads EF 9F. The actual segment address is really 9FEF hex. This must be done to all 16-bit values stored in memory. (When you load a register with a value in memory, there is no need to swap the values. It must only be done by using the D command to peek through memory.)

3. The fifth byte of the PSP is marked "reserved." It's not used for anything other than properly aligning the next instruction, which is an odd number of bytes long.

4. The MS-DOS dispatcher is a 5-byte "long call" to DOS. It's provided for compatibility with earlier versions of DOS and isn't used today.

The next three chunks of the PSP are 4-byte long addresses. They're stored in memory in the *segment:offset* format, although each part of the address is stored in reverse order. For example, the "Termination Address" in Figure 14-2 consists of four bytes: 4F 03 FB 1F. This is magically transmuted into the

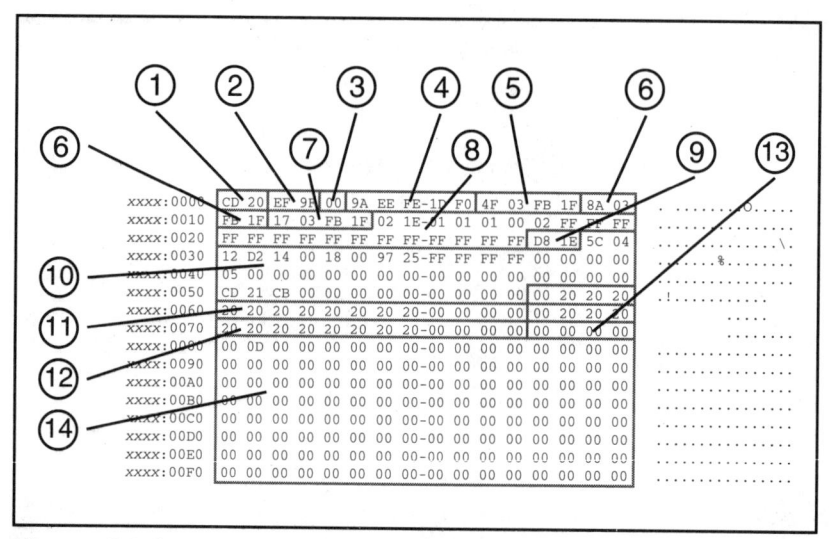

Figure 14-2 The various items in the PSP

address: 034F:1FFB. The three addresses stored in memory in that format are as follows:

5. This is the address for the INT 22 command, used when a program quits.
6. This is the address for the INT 23 command, used to trap the Ctrl-C key press.
7. This is the address of the INT 24 command, the "critical error" handler. A critical error is one that causes DOS to display the "Abort, Retry, Ignore?" message.

    Each of the above addresses is used by DOS. If a program wishes to access their functions (and that's rare), the corresponding INT command will be given.

8. The 22 bytes at offset 16 hex are marked as "reserved." They contain undocumented information saved by DOS, memory locations, and other stuff that excites only hard-core programmers.
9. The two bytes at offset 2C hex set the location for DOS's environment in memory. The bytes are stored in reverse order; in Figure 14-2 the bytes are D8 1E, which translate into the segment address 1ED8. That's where this program keeps a copy of DOS's environment. (You'll see how this works later.)
10. The 46 bytes at offset 2E hex are marked as "reserved." Again, this is internal information used by DOS, memory locations, pointers, and so on.
11. Offset 5C contains the first File Control Block, FCB. This is where DEBUG will store the name of a file you type at the DOS prompt, or where the filename specified by DEBUG's N command will be stored. To see how this works, type the following in DEBUG:

    ```
    -N SAMPLE.BIN
    ```

    This specifies the filename SAMPLE.BIN for DEBUG to use with the L and W commands. The filename will be stored in the first FCB in the PSP. To prove it, use the D command:

    ```
    -D 0 L100
    ```

    As a bonus, you'll see the filename also specified at offset 80 hex — but don't get ahead of yourself. The N command sticks a filename in the first FCB, which DOS will use when loading or writing a file to disk. A filename is also stuck there when you specify a file when starting DEBUG.

12. This area of the PSP is a second FCB used for specifying a second file. To see it filled, quit DEBUG, then restart it with the following command:

    ```
    C:\> DEBUG C:\CONFIG.SYS ONE.DAT TWO.DAT
    ```

    This command is tricky: DEBUG believes that you want to load a "program file" named CONFIG.SYS. Further, the first two parameters after the program filename are files you want to work with. DEBUG will load CONFIG.SYS into memory, assuming it's a program file. Then DEBUG will put ONE.DAT and TWO.DAT into the two FCB storage areas just as DOS would when you run a program. Confirm this with the following:

```
-D 0 L100
```

You'll see ONE.DAT and TWO.DAT stuffed into the FCB fields. Keep in mind that this is something DOS does, not DEBUG. When you run a program, DOS sticks the first two parameters into the two FCB fields — providing that they're named like files. This is done to provide you with quick access to those files should your program wish to use them. (I've used CONFIG.SYS as an example since it's a file everyone has.)

There is a format for the FCB field, but one you really don't need to get into unless you plan on doing a lot of DOS programming. Even then, FCBs are the older way of accessing files, dating from the prehard-disk days of DOS.

> *Note:* Here is a brief rundown of the contents of an FCB:
>
> The first byte of an FCB is the drive id. A value of zero means the current drive. Otherwise the drives are given numbers, A = 1, B = 2, and so on.
>
> The next 11 bytes specify the filename and extension. Spaces (character 20 hex) are used to pad filenames with fewer than eight characters, and extensions with fewer than three characters.
>
> The next few bytes indicate the size of the file, the file's date and time, and information used by DOS when reading and writing to the file.

13. The four bytes at offset 7C hex are marked as "reserved."

14. Finally, the last 80 hex (128) bytes of the PSP are used for the "command tail." This is an ASCII string of text, equal to everything you typed after a program name at the DOS prompt.

    The byte at offset 80 hex is a count byte. It indicates the length of any optional parameters you typed. Offset 81 hex is the start of the parameter list, essentially everything you typed after your program's name, in the same format and case. The string ends with the character 0D hex, the carriage return.

    Of everything in the PSP, the command tail is the most popular and useful. No program run under DOS would be able to intercept any optional parameters or filenames without it. The next section details the use of the command tail in a sample program, SAY.COM.

The SAY Program

The program SAY.COM is used to display a string of text, similar to the ECHO command. The format of the command is:

```
SAY string
```

Ugly Memory Stuff   259

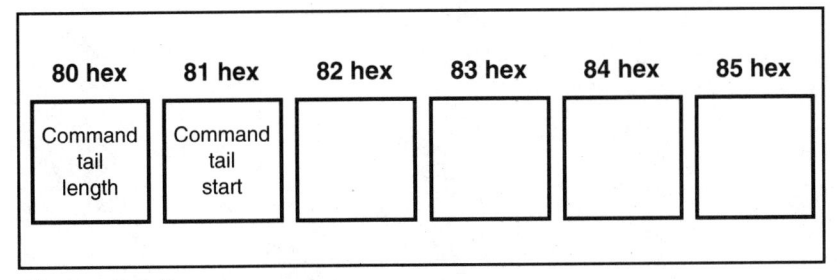

```
  80 hex    81 hex    82 hex    83 hex    84 hex    85 hex

 Command  Command
   tail      tail
  length    start
```

Figure 14-3 The command tail's format

The *string* is any text that follows SAY at the DOS prompt. That text is copied by DOS into the PSP's command tail, at offset 80 hex. Once you know that, it's a matter of finding the bytes in memory and displaying them on the screen.

Figure 14-3 shows how the command tail stores strings. Offset 80 hex holds the length of the string. If nothing was entered, that byte will contain 00 hex.

If there is a string, offset 81 hex will contain the first byte, which is always 20 hex, the space character. In fact, if you've typed more than one space after the command at the DOS prompt, they'll all be stuffed into the command tail. Normally, people only type one space.

The real start of the string is usually at offset 82 hex. It will continue in memory for the length specified in the byte at memory offset 80 hex. After that location you'll see byte 0D hex, the carriage return.

To see how this works, use DEBUG to load the "program" CONFIG.SYS as follows:

```
C:\> DEBUG C:\CONFIG.SYS HELLO!
```

DEBUG loads CONFIG.SYS as a program, then sticks everything else into the PSP's command tail at offset 80 hex. Use the D command as follows to see how "HELLO!" is stored in memory:

```
-D80 L10
```

Take a look at the first few bytes on that line. You should see something like that shown in Figure 14-4. Offset 80 hex holds the value 7, the length of the string. The next byte is 20 hex, a space. Then comes the ASCII hexadecimal codes for "Hello!" This ends at offset 88 hex with the character 0D hex, the Enter key.

The way to write a SAY.COM program that can display that string is to look up each byte in memory, one at a time, and display that byte on the screen. Use DEBUG's mini-assembler to type in the following program:

```
xxxx:0080  07 20 48 45 4C 4C 4F 21-0D 00 00 00 00 00 00 00    . HELLO!........
```

Figure 14-4 Here is how the string "HELLO!" is stored in the command tail

```
-A 100
xxxx:0100 MOV BX,80
xxxx:0103 MOV CL,[BX]
xxxx:0105 MOV CH,0
xxxx:0107 CMP CX,00
xxxx:010A JZ 116
xxxx:010C INC BX
xxxx:010D INC BX
xxxx:010E MOV DL,[BX]
xxxx:0110 MOV AH,2
xxxx:0112 INT 21
xxxx:0114 LOOP 10D
xxxx:0116 INT 20
```

On the last line, at offset 118 hex, press Enter. Save this program to disk as SAY.COM. Since the last line was 118 hex, that makes its size 18 hex. Use the *RCX* command to set that size, name it SAY.COM with the *N* command, then type *W* to write it to disk:

```
-RCX
CX xxxx
:18
-N SAY.COM
-W
Writing 00018 bytes
-
```

Quit DEBUG and try out the program at the DOS prompt. SAY works like the ECHO command in that it displays whatever you type after it. Unlike the ECHO command, SAY followed by nothing doesn't display "Echo is on" or "Echo is off." You can also follow SAY with the words "on" or "off" to display them, which the ECHO command can't do. (Alright, SAY.COM won't win an award, but it's useful.)

To view the guts of this program in action, reload it back into DEBUG with the following command:

```
C:\> DEBUG SAY.COM Hello!
```

Type the *R* command to display the initial register setup. You'll see the first instruction at the bottom of the display, MOV BX,0080.

To trace through this program, you'll use the T command. T works just like the P command, but will allow you to step through loops and calls — which you'll see in a moment. Type *T* to move the value 80 hex into the BX register.

The BX register is going to store memory locations, like a pointer register. Putting 80 hex in the BX register allows us to examine what byte may exist at that location. That's done with the following instruction:

```
MOV CL,[BX]
```

The square brackets tell the microprocessor that BX holds a memory location, not a value. The contents of that memory location are seen at the far right of the screen:

```
DS:0080=07
```

The BX register contains 80 hex. Memory location 80 hex (in the segment specified by register DS) contains the byte value 7 hex. The instruction MOV CL,[BX] will put that value, 7 hex, into the CL register. Type *T*.

```
MOV CH,0
```

With 7 hex in the CL register, the instruction in the example puts 0 into CH. This way, the entire CX register will contain the length of the string. (CX is used with the LOOP command later in the program.) Type *T*.

```
CMP CX,00
```

This is a test to see whether or not a string was entered. If the value at offset 80 hex is zero, a string wasn't entered. Otherwise the value is the length of the string (which we already know to be 7 hex). Type *T*.

```
JZ 116
```

This jump instruction tests the result of the CMP command. Offset 116 is the INT 20 instruction that ends the program, so if there is zero stored at offset 80 hex, the program will end right away. In our text, the ZR flag isn't raised, so the program continues. Type *T*.

```
INC BX
```

This command increments the BX register one value. Type *T* and BX will increase from 80 hex to 81 hex.

```
INC BX
```

Register BX is incremented a second time here. Type *T* to increment BX from 81 hex to 82 hex. The reason for this is to skip the initial space that is usually stuck at offset 81 hex (refer back to Figure 14-4).

```
MOV DL,[BX]
```

This instruction transfers the byte value at the memory location specified by BX to the DL register. The value is previewed on the far right of the screen: DS:0082=48. The ASCII code 48 hex, the letter H, will be put into the DL register. Type *T*.

```
MOV AH,2
```

To display a character on DOS's standard output device, Interrupt 21 function 2 hex is called. The character to display is in the DL register, as has already been set up. (Refer to Appendix E for more information.) Type *T* to put 2 hex into the AH register, which specifies function 2.

```
INT 21
```

This instruction calls DOS and displays a character. Instead of typing T here, type *P*. (If you type T, you'll go traipsing through DOS's internals; P processes the command immediately.) You should see the letter "H" displayed, meaning DOS did its thing.

> ***Tip:*** By using Interrupt 21 function 2 hex, the character is output to DOS's standard output device. This means the SAY command's output can be redirected using I/O redirection. The same program could have been written using the BIOS display character routine, Interrupt 10 function E hex. However, you cannot perform I/O redirection when output is made through that function.

```
LOOP 10D
```

This is a LOOP command. The microprocessor will jump back to offset 10D hex and repeat the instructions there, decrementing the CX register once each time until CX equals zero. Looking on your screen now, you can see that register CX equals 7 hex, the length of the string. This LOOP command goes back to the INC BX command at offset 10D. This points at the next character in the command tail, and the subsequent instructions will display that character.

If you want to, continue typing the *T* command to trace through the program. Remember to type *P* when you see the INT 21 instruction. You'll see every character in the command tail displayed one at a time.

> ***Tip:*** To hurry the operation up, type *P* when you see the LOOP command.

```
INT 20
```

The final instruction is INT 20, which "terminates" the program. Type *P* to process this command.

Just about every program that has you type optional parameters will scan the command tail for information. The programs offer much more sophisticated ways of scanning than SAY.COM, but you have the basic idea down now.

Know Thyself by Reading Thy ROM

Lurking in your PC's memory are special places where a rich amount of information is stored. Low in memory is "information central," called the *BIOS Data Area*. Hidden within the bytes at that location are descriptions of your PC's hardware, memory, keyboard status, display information, and so on.

Additional locations where you can scope out information are dotting the upper memory area, from banks C through F. The information found there isn't as descriptive as the BIOS Data Area, but it is interesting to look at. The following two sections explore each of these fascinating memory regions.

The BIOS Data Area

The BIOS Data Area is a 256-byte expanse of memory that contains descriptive information about your PC. The masters of DOS have put the BIOS Data Area at segment 40 hex in low memory. To view it, use the following command in DEBUG:

```
-D 40:0 L100
```

You will find little of interest in the ASCII display, but there is still an abundance of information on your screen. The best way to view it all is to take a byte-by-byte tour in DEBUG.

Note: The BIOS Data Area is a look-only item. Don't mess with it using the E command. Only the most nimble of DOS programmers will tread on this part of memory.

The following D commands will display the interesting bits and pieces of the BIOS Data Area. Type in each and observe what's on your screen, starting with:

```
-D 40:10 L2
```

The two bytes, or "word," at offset 10 hex in the BIOS Data Area describe the hardware you have in your PC. This information is gathered from the Power-On Self Test (POST) that your PC performs when it starts. It's also held in a bit pattern, which means you have to decipher each byte to figure out what it's telling you.

The first step in deciphering is to swap the bytes you see on your screen. The value stored in memory is a word, or 16-bit value. For some twisted reason, it's stored in memory backward. For example, if you see 27 44 hex, the value is really 4427 hex. Swap those two values on your screen! After doing so, look up each byte's binary bit patterns in Appendix A. For example, for 4427 hex, the pattern would be:

```
0100 0100 0010 0111
```

Plug the bit patterns into the tables in Table 14-3. The bits are numbered F through 0, left to right. Fill in the blanks in the tables with a "1" or "0" corresponding to the number you have. Work each column and only fill in the blanks in the table. (The other values are either "reserved" or apply to the original IBM PC only.)

To show how this works, my PC shot back with the byte values 27 and 44 hex, which translated into 4427 hex and the corresponding bit pattern shown above. Fitting that into Table 14-3, I find the following bits:

- Printer(s) installed = 01, one printer installed.
- Game Adapter (yes/no) = 0, no joystick on my PC.
- Serial port(s) installed = 010, two serial ports. (This is binary stuff: 001 = 1, 010 = 2, 011 = 3, 100 = 4, and so on.)
- Number of disk drives = 00, which means "one drive." A value of 01 means two drives; 10 means three drives; and 11 means you have four floppy drives. Hard drives and other drives aren't included here.

- Initial Video Mode = 10, corresponding to color text, 80 columns — probably what everyone will get. A value of 01 means color text, 40 columns; 11 means 80 columns, monochrome text; and 00 means "none of the above." (Double zero often appears in older PCs with EGA or VGA video.)

- Math coprocessor = 1, since I have a '486 with a built-in math coprocessor. If you see 0, you don't have a math coprocessor installed.

- Disk drive present = 1, which means you have a floppy drive. A program will examine this value, then look to bits 7 and 6 to see how many floppy drives are present.

This information is by no means detailed. In fact, modern PCs have this information stored in their CMOS, or battery-backed up RAM. Older PCs, however, relied on the POST to tell them what was installed. In fact, if you didn't notice, everything on the list was particular to the old IBM PC. There are no switches for a hard drive, extended memory, or anything else we've come to expect in a modern computer.

Tip: The information in the two bytes at offset 10 hex in the BIOS Data Area is referred to as the "Equipment List." You can also get this list by calling Interrupt 11 hex in DEBUG. The 16-bit value will be returned — unadulterated — in register AX. If you want to try this, type the following in DEBUG:

```
-A 100
xxxx:0100 INT 11
```

Press Enter on the next line. Confirm that IP=0100, then type the P command. In the register display that follows, you'll see the equipment list bit pattern in the AX register.

```
-D 40:17 L1
```

Table 14-3 Bit Patterns in the Equipment List Bytes

Bit Pattern:	F	E	D	C	B	A	9	8
Printer(s) installed				-	-	-	-	-
Game Adapter (yes/no)	-	-	-			-	-	-
Serial port(s) installed	-	-	-					-

Bit Pattern:	7	6	5	4	3	2	1	0
Number of disk drives	-	-						
Initial Video Mode			-	-				
Math coprocessor						-		
Disk drive present	-	-	-	-	-	-		

Like the equipment list at offset 10 hex, this byte contains bit values. The values represent the status of special keys on your keyboard. This can be fun, especially if you have a 100 key "enhanced" keyboard. Type in the following E command and watch the lights on your keyboard (it's okay, just this once):

```
-E 40:17 70
```

The above command toggles on the Num Lock, Caps Lock, and Scroll Lock keys and their corresponding lights on an enhanced keyboard. On older keyboards it will merely toggle on the "state" of each key, affecting the keyboard's function but not the lights. Table 14-4 lists the bit patterns associated with this byte. The value 70 hex, poked in above, corresponds to the bits for the Num Lock, Caps Lock, and Scroll Lock keys being toggled "on."

Note: If the keyboard lights do not change, then you may be running some sort of control program that overrides poking values into the BIOS Data Area. Quarterdeck's *DESQview* may do this, as may some keyboard enhancement programs.

A practical use of this information is a program designed to switch off the Num Lock key when you first start your PC. Such a program, NUMOFF.COM, was created back in Chapter 6.

```
-D 40:1E L20
```

This is an interesting area of memory called the "keyboard buffer." It holds the last 16 keystrokes, a combination of the ASCII character codes plus the scan code values, that you've typed. ASCII codes come first, followed by the scan code value.

If you look carefully at the ASCII listing, you may see the following text: "D 4.0.:'1.E. 9L&'2.0." Look at every other character. It's the same D command as shown above: D40:1E L20. The even characters are the ASCII keystroke values, odd

Table 14-4 Bit Patterns in Keyboard Status Byte at Offset 17 Hex

Bit Pattern:	F	E	D	C	B	A	9	8
Insert "state"	*							
Caps Lock		*						
Num Lock			*					
Scroll Lock				*				
Alt key down					*			
Ctrl key down						*		
Left Shift key down							*	
Right Shift key down								*

* 1 = pressed or active; 0 = not pressed.

characters are scan codes. Your screen may not show this — especially if you needed to use the Backspace key to erase. Look for the backspace key code, 08 0E, in the listing.

✎ *Note:* The 32-byte keyboard buffer allows you to type up to 16 characters ahead. Some programs may extend this buffer, such as keyboard macro enhancers and command line editing utilities. If so, you may not see the characters you type listed in the buffer.

```
-D 40:49 L1
```

This byte describes the current video mode. For most color systems, this will be video mode 3, color with 80 × 25 rows of text. Other video modes are listed in Table 14-5. Note that VGA video adapters support all EGA and CGA modes, as well as some of the monochrome modes.

You can change the video mode using BIOS Interrupt 10 hex, function zero. To do so, place the new mode value in the AL register and zero in the AH register. For example, to switch your display into mode 1, 40 column color text, do the following in DEBUG:

```
-A 100
xxxx:0100 INT 10
```

Table 14-5 PC Video Modes

Mode	Resolution (H × V)	Description	Adapter
0 hex	40 × 25	16-color text	CGA composite
1 hex	40 × 25	16-color text	CGA
2 hex	80 × 25	16-color text	CGA composite
3 hex	80 × 25	16-color text	CGA
4 hex	320 × 200	4-color graphics	CGA
5 hex	320 × 200	4-color graphics	CGA composite
6 hex	640 × 200	2-color graphics	CGA
7 hex	80 × 25	Monochrome text	MDA/Hercules
D hex	320 × 200	16-color graphics	EGA
E hex	640 × 200	16-color graphics	EGA
F hex	640 × 350	2-color graphics	EGA
10 hex	640 × 350	16-color graphics	EGA
11 hex	640 × 480	2-color graphics	MCGA/VGA
12 hex	640 × 480	16-color graphics	VGA

Press Enter on the next line. Then use the *RAX* and *RIP* commands to change the AX and IP registers:

```
-RAX
AX=xxxx
:1
-RIP
IP=xxxx
:100
```

The first command puts 00 in AH and 01 in AL — essentially 0001 in register AX. This sets up the INT 10 call. The second command confirms that the IP register equals 100. Type the *P* command to proceed and your display will change to 40 columns. You can confirm this new mode by reusing the *D40:49 L1* command. The byte will reflect the new video mode.

⏭ ***Tip:*** Do not use the E command to poke in a new video mode value at address 40:49. That's not the way the BIOS Data Area works. The video BIOS high in memory is what changes the screen resolution. That program then updates the BIOS Data Area with the proper byte.

Older microcomputers — notably the Apple II, TRS-80, and Commodore 64 — had special "poke" areas that would change the screen and make the computer do other, arresting tricks. The PC isn't built exactly that way.

To see what video mode 6 looks like, use the *RAX* command to put 6 hex into the AX register. Then put 100 hex back into the IP register with the *RIP* command. Type the *P* command again to see video mode 6. Although it's a graphic screen, mode 6 displays 80-column text. You can even quit DEBUG and continue to DOS in that graphics screen, — although the display will behave slowly.

To restore your screen to normal, use the previously mentioned commands but set the AX register equal to 3 hex. Or, if you're in DOS, use the MODE 80 command.

```
-D40:4A L2
```

These two bytes represent a word, or 16-bit value, in memory. Therefore, you have to reverse them to see what they represent. Most likely, you'll see the bytes 50 and 00 hex. Rearrange them to 0050 hex. This value indicates the number of columns on the screen, 80 decimal.

Some video adapters are capable of displaying a great number of columns in the text mode. Some Super VGA cards support a teensy text mode where 132 columns can show up on a screen. I've seen this mode — *WordPerfect* even supports it — but the little As and little Es look alike. The word at offset 4A hex in the BIOS Data Area segment is where your programs learn about the width of your screen. They can tell the number of rows by examining the byte at offset 84 hex (covered below).

```
-D40:4C L2
```

Again, the two bytes displayed are a word value; reverse them to see the 16-bit value stored in memory. The value represents the total number of bytes used to store one screen of text. If you have an 80 x 25 display, that value will be 1000 hex.

I know, I know: In a previous chapter the value FA0 hex was used. That's the actual sum of 80 x 25 x 2, which is the number of characters — plus attributes — that can be displayed on a single screen. DOS adds an extra 48 bytes to "screen memory" to round it out to an even 1000 hex.

```
-D40:50 L2
```

These two bytes give the cursor's current location. The first byte tells the cursor's column position (zero since you just typed Enter) and the second byte gives the row.

> *Tip:* Programmers will use BIOS Interrupt 10 hex, function 3 to get the cursor's location. Unlike DEBUG, that function will not alter the cursor's current position.

```
-D40:6C L4
```

This four-byte memory location stores a single value, your PC's "master clock count." DOS reads this value when you ask for the time and it's used to time-stamp program saved to disk. Of course, it's translated from bits to hours and minutes instantly by DOS.

The master clock count value is updated 18.5 times a second. Type *F3* and Enter in DEBUG and you'll see a new value stored there — the new clock count. The value starts at midnight with zero, then keeps ticking until 24 hours have passed, when it's reset to zero again.

```
-D40:72 L2
```

These four bytes are set to 34 12 — actually the word value 1234 hex — to produce a "warm boot" when Ctrl-Alt-Delete is pressed. The warm boot skips over the memory test.

You've already seen these bytes in action from Chapter 1 in the batch file REBOOT.BAT. In that DEBUG script, the value 1234 hex is poked into memory location 40:72 to prevent the time-consuming memory check after a reset. (See Figure 1-3.)

```
-D40:84 L1
```

The single byte held at offset 84 hex describes how many lines of text are displayed on the screen — minus one. For a 80 x 25 screen, the value will be 18 hex, 24. As with offset 4A hex, this byte is used by programs to determine how big a screen they have to display information.

```
-D40:F0 L10
```

At the top of the BIOS Data Area are 16 bytes that make up the Intra-Application Communication Area, ICA. IBM designated this area as "available" for programs to share data. (Yeah, this makes about as much sense as when your mother told you to share that ten-cent bag of peanuts with your brother; there just isn't enough to go around. Sixteen bytes ain't much to store anything.)

The only program I know of that uses the ICA is Norton's Time Mark. That program will store up to four time values in the ICA for its "stopwatch" function. Other than that, applications use other methods of communication.

This section has touched upon only a few of the more interesting places in the BIOS Data Area. Most of the bytes, words, and longer values store detailed information that is painfully boring to observe. But there are many treasures hidden in low memory. This is why I always raise an eyebrow when a diagnostic program claims to be so clairvoyant. It also causes anguish: Now that you know the information is in there, why can't some "INSTALL" programs look there as well? It baffles and frustrates me to no end.

The Various BIOSs Found in Upper Memory

Upper memory, or "reserved" memory as it was formerly called, is the domain of video memory and ROM. Most of upper memory, however, is reserved for future expansion. I've created an upper memory map in Figure 14-5 that shows you approximately where things are.

Video memory is traditionally located in two places: For color systems it starts at segment B800 hex. That chunk of video memory is 16K to 32K in size and is the traditional video text and graphics memory for CGA systems. Monochrome video memory is only 4K in size and starts at segment B000 hex. Hercules graphics memory is 32K or 64K in size, and also starts at segment B000 hex.

EGA and VGA systems have more powerful graphics than CGA. While they use the same 32K chunk of memory at segment B800 hex, they also use all of bank A for graphics memory. Note that bank A starts at segment A000 hex — the 640K "barrier."

Video memory acts like any other RAM in your PC with the exception that its information is displayed on your screen. Therefore, any characters you poke into video memory appear on the screen. This is covered in a later chapter as well as the interesting way attributes are assigned to characters.

Note: Some VGA adapters can have up to 1M or more video memory installed. That memory is kept on the card and accessed through the VGA hardware. It is not memory that fits into the PCs memory map.

The old CGA graphics are controlled by the PC's BIOS. EGA and VGA graphics require their own BIOS, which is located on a ROM chip mapped into upper memory. Typically, the Video BIOS will start at segment C000 hex and is anywhere from 16K to 32K in size. I have seen video BIOSs in bank E on occasion, so this is not a standard or fixed spot in upper memory.

270   Dan Gookin's Guide to Underground DOS 6.0

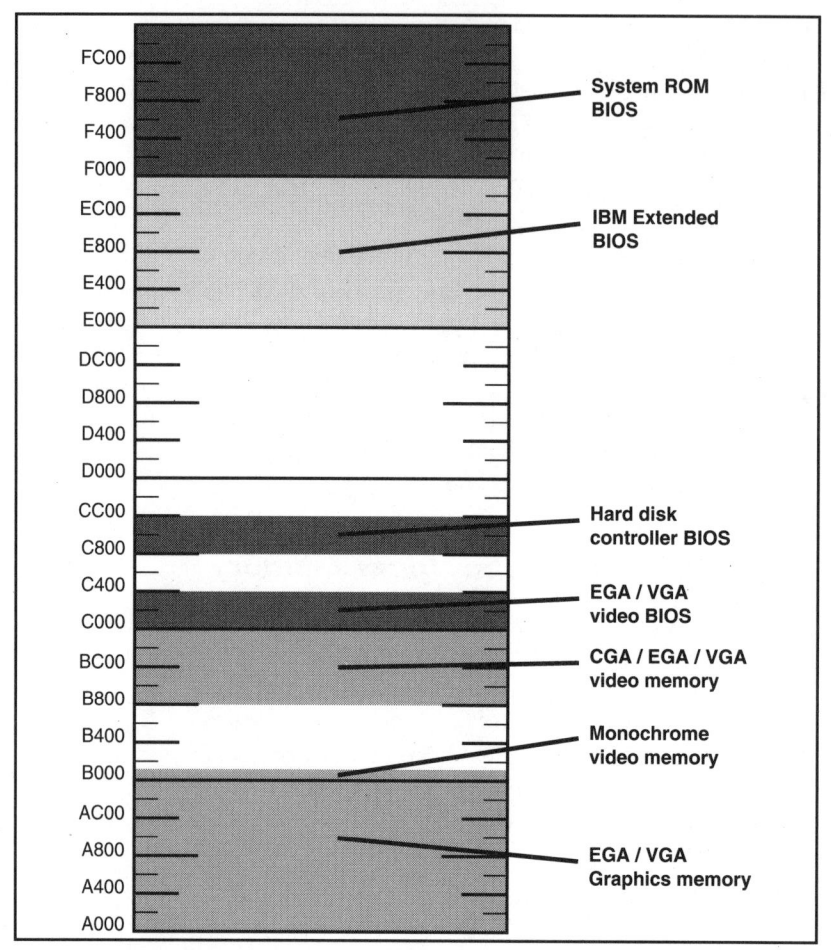

```
FC00  ┐
F800  │  System ROM
F400  │  BIOS
F000  ┘
EC00  ┐
E800  │  IBM Extended
E400  │  BIOS
E000  ┘
DC00
D800
D400
D000
CC00  ┐  Hard disk
C800  ┘  controller BIOS
C400  ┐  EGA / VGA
C000  ┘  video BIOS
BC00  ┐  CGA / EGA / VGA
B800  ┘  video memory
B400  ┐  Monochrome
B000  ┘  video memory
AC00
A800     EGA / VGA
A400     Graphics memory
A000
```

Figure 14-5   The upper memory map

Some video adapters may have a copyright message held in ROM, smack dab at segment C000 offset zero. In fact, all VGA adapters will have the letters IBM at offset 1E hex, as you may have seen in a previous chapter. To view your video ROM copyright, use the following command:

```
-D C000:0
```

✎ *Note:*   If you don't see a copyright message, your video ROM may be located elsewhere. Or, the ROM may have been "mapped out" by a '386 memory manager.

The hard disk controller BIOS is typically located in the middle of bank C, at segment address C800 hex. It's anywhere from 8K to 16K in size. As with the video BIOS, this ROM chip may or may not be located at segment C800 hex. That was the location used by the original IBM PC/XT's hard disk ROM, so everyone else followed suit. See your hard drive's BIOS with the following:

    -D C800:0

If you can't see anything, don't despair. Your hard drive controller BIOS may be located elsewhere, or a '386 memory manager may have moved it, stealthed it, or mapped over it. No problem, as long as the hard drive works. (It just makes this tour a little dull.)

Your PC's BIOS — the big enchilada — is kept in memory bank F. It's full of machine language instructions that control the rudiments of your PC. It also contains many interesting messages and other information.

> *Note:* Some systems have an "extended BIOS" in bank E. The early PCs stored the BASIC programming language in ROM there. Late model PS/2s store extra BIOS and startup code in bank E.

    -D F000:0

This command will display your BIOS's copyright notice. On the fancier systems, you may see a company name and copyright. Some "generic" systems may display the Original Equipment Manufacturer's (OEM) label. On some Phoenix Technologies BIOSs you'll see every letter listed twice. Weird.

There are actually many ROMs that make up your PC's BIOS in bank F. Some of them are packed in pretty tight, others have spaces between them. Feel free to scan this bank on your own for some interesting messages. Or you can jump to what should be a common point of interest to everyone. Type the following:

    -D FFFF:0 L10

This command displays the last paragraph, or 16 bytes, of information in the PC's basic one megabyte address space. There are three interesting items here. The first is the jump-start instruction at offset zero:

    -U FFFF:0 L5

This unassemble command shows you the JMP instruction that restarts your PC. It's the same instruction used by the RESET.BAT and REBOOT.BAT programs from Chapter 1. The JMP instruction there points at a reset routine in low memory, which will vary from system to system.

    -D FFFF:5 L8

This command displays the BIOS date.

    -D FFFF:E L2

This command displays your machine "model number" ID number byte, followed by a submodel number. The IBM PC/AT used a model ID byte of FC hex. Most '386-family PCs are considered to be AT "clones," so they share the AT's model number ID. The submodel number of zero hex is often used on these machines as well.

15

More Ugly Memory Stuff

Memory is so full of interesting things it just can't all be contained in a single chapter. This chapter continues the discussion of the PC's memory. The concentration here is on DOS's memory blocks and how programs store things in memory, plus a big section on video memory — how it works and what you can do with it.

DOS and Memory Blocks

Believe it or not, DOS does have some method of memory management. It's not sophisticated, most programmers ignore it, and there isn't really much "management" involved; DOS has routines that request and allocate memory blocks — that's it. There are no hard rules, no enforcement, and no penalty for doing things your own way. In a way, memory management under DOS operates under the same rules as taxicab drivers in New York.

Most programmers ignore DOS's memory allocation scheme. The normal way a DOS program works is like this:

- Call DOS Interrupt 21, function 48 hex, and request 640K of RAM — all of memory. The program is demanding: "I want *all* of RAM!"

- Function 48 hex will return with an error message, politely telling the program exactly how much memory is left. DOS says, "Whoa, boy! I only have *xxx*K of memory free. Sorry." The total amount of memory available is returned by Interrupt 21, function 28 hex in the BX register.

- The program will turn around and call function 48 hex again, grabbing the full "memory available" amount returned in the BX register. It says, "Okay, so you don't have 640K, I'll just take the *xxx*K free instead. Heh, heh."

DOS programs are greedy. Each one assumes it's the only program in memory and it has control over everything in the machine. Windows attempts to change this and does a good job. DOS programs remain, however, ignorant of the rules.

How DOS Allocates Memory

DOS divvies out memory in 16-byte chunks or "paragraphs." This is because each block of memory in DOS must start at a given segment, which always happens every 16 bytes. You've seen this all over already: The PSP starts at a given segment, offset zero, COM programs start at offset zero, everything starts at offset zero, which means everything has a specific segment address in memory.

> *Note:* The total amount of memory in a PC is 1,048,576 bytes. Divide that by 16 bytes in a paragraph and you get 65,536 — the total number of segments possible in a one-megabyte address space. Refer back to Chapter 9 if you need additional boning up on memory.

To see how a block of memory is allocated, and what a DOS memory block looks like, hop into DEBUG, and enter the following code using the mini-assembler:

```
-A 100
xxxx:0100 MOV AH,48
xxxx:0102 MOV BX,1
xxxx:0105 INT 21
```

Press Enter after the line with INT 21 to exit the mini-assembler mode. What this code will do is direct DOS to allocate a one-paragraph block of memory. That's done with Interrupt 21, function 48 hex. The value 1 moved into the BX register tells DOS you want one paragraph — 16 bytes — of memory. (Refer to Appendix E to see details on how function 48 works.)

Reset the instruction pointer to 100 hex, or confirm that it's already equal to 100 hex with the RIP command:

```
-RIP
IP xxxx
:100
```

Type the *P3* command to process these three instructions. You'll see three register displays. First 48 hex is moved into register AH (actually, register AX will contain 4800 hex); then 1 is moved into register BX; and finally the INT 21 instruction is processed.

Check the flags register display. If the CY (Carry) flag is up, then memory couldn't be allocated. (If so, then just keep reading as if there was enough memory available.) Otherwise, the AX register will contain the segment address of your 16-byte block of memory.

To see your block of memory, take the value in the AX register and use it as a segment address with the D command. For example, if the AX register contains 34BC hex, use the following D command:

```
-D34BC:0 L10
```

This command displays the block of memory allocated on my computer. Use the value you see on your screen by "AX=" with the D command as shown above. This displays your recently allocated block in memory.

Chances are the block may be empty. Still, you may see some memory "garbage" located there. Whatever its contents, DOS has given the block to you for your program to use. Take a moment to appreciate your block in memory, but don't leave DEBUG.

The Memory Block "Arena Header"

DOS's feeble attempts at memory management mean that it keeps track of all the various allocated blocks in memory. To do so, each block starts with a special paragraph of information that tells DOS about the block's "owner," the block's size, and whether or not it's the last block of memory. The special paragraph is located just below the memory block, and it's called the *arena header*.

The block of memory you created in the previous section has an arena header. Even though the block is as tiny as they come — 16 bytes — DOS still keeps track of everything. In this case, the arena is as big as the memory block.

To see the arena header, refer again to your block's segment address, as found in the AX register and used in the previous section. Subtract one from that segment address. If you want to, use DEBUG's H command in this format:

```
-H segment 1
```

Of the two values returned, the second is the one you want. That's the next lowest segment in memory. To view both it and your memory block, use the D command with the second value (returned as shown in the sample) as shown below:

```
-D 34BB:0 L20
```

I used this command on my machine. My memory block is located at segment 34BC hex. Subtract one from that and I get 34BB hex. The L20 lets you view both the arena header and your memory block. The output from my screen is shown in Figure 15-1.

The arena header contains five items, one of which is immediately noticeable: the byte 4D hex at offset zero (big "M" in the ASCII column). That byte identifies

```
-D34BB:0 L20
34BB:0000   4D 96 36 01 00 00 00 00-00 00 00 00 00 00 00 00   M.6.............
34BB:0010   00 00 10 08 F2 A9 83 72-95 12 01 E0 1B 54 E6 D0   .......r.....T..
```

Figure 15-1 The allocated block and its arena header

a block of memory allocated by DOS. An M indicates a plain old block, a Z (5A hex) indicates the last allocated block in memory. Table 15-1 shows the other values in the arena header.

Look for the various items in the arena header on your screen:

- The first byte will be an M block, which you can see on your screen. You have a normal block.

- The next two bytes are the segment address of the block's "owner." Since a 16-bit value is being displayed, you need to reverse the bytes to get the actual segment address. (You'll be doing this in a moment.)

- The two bytes that follow, at offset 3, indicate the size of the block in paragraphs. The bytes you see will be 01 and 00. The size of your block is 0001 paragraphs long — as you requested. (Since the bytes represent a 16-bit value, they're switched in memory.)

- Skip over the three "reserved" bytes, up to the hyphen.

- After the hyphen is the block's "owner" name. Since your memory block was allocated by a program running in DEBUG, it's owner name is unknown. On your screen, the owner area will either be blank or contain junk. If you were running a program from disk, its name would be kept in that field, ending with a zero hex byte if it's less than eight characters long.

Note: Memory blocks allocated by DOS may be given the name SC or SD, indicating a system data area. This is how the MEM /D or MEM /P command identifies those blocks when it gives you a rundown of what's in memory.

Here's a secret: The actual, real owner of your memory block is DEBUG. You can prove this by backtracking through memory to find "DEBUG" as the owner of the block that owns your memory block. (Yes, it's true, you're subletting a block from another subletter. That may be illegal in your state, so keep it mum.)

To locate your block's owner's owner, then, you must look at the arena header of your memory block's "Parent Block." Look at offset 1 hex on your screen. The

Table 15-1 Contents of the Arena Header

Offset	Length	Description
0	0	Signature byte; "M" (4D hex) = valid block of memory; "Z" (4A hex) = last block in memory
1	2	Parent Block, the segment address of this block's "owner"
3	2	Size of the block in paragraphs
5	3	Unused
8	8	Owner filename

two bytes shown there indicate the segment address of the block's owner. Take those bytes, reverse them, and use them as a segment value in the D command.

For example, on my screen (and in Figure 15-1), I see the values 96 hex and 36 hex. Reversing them makes 3696 hex, the segment address of the owner block. Do the same on your system, and use the segment address you end up with in the following D command:

```
-D3696:0 L100
```

What you're looking at is the memory block DOS allocated for the parent program, which in this case is DEBUG itself. The block you see on your screen is actually DEBUG's PSP — if you can believe it. The earmark "CD 20" hex bytes at the start of the block are a dead giveaway for a PSP. (Refer to Chapter 14 for more information on the PSP.) You may even see the command tail — the options at the DOS prompt you typed when you first started DEBUG.

No matter what goodies are revealed in the PSP, it's only the start of a block of memory. What's more interesting to us now is the block's arena header, located just one paragraph below the PSP. To view it, subtract one from the segment value — just as you did for your own memory block earlier in this chapter. (Use the H command if you need to.) Plug the resulting segment address with the following D command:

```
-D3695:0 L20
```

In this example, I've used the address 3695 hex on my computer, one less than segment 3696 hex. Do the same on your system, and display the 20 hex bytes at that location shown in the example. What I see on my screen is shown in Figure 15-2.

In Figure 15-2, and on your screen, note the block's signature is M, a normal block. That's followed by DEBUG's owner's segment address and the size of DEBUG's block of memory, both as 16-bit values. At offset 8 (after the hyphen) you'll see "DEBUG" listed. That's the owner filename of the block. Since it's less than eight characters, it ends with a zero hex byte.

Finding Blocks with the MEM Command

It's the filename owner field in the arena header that the MEM command uses when it displays the programs in memory. MEM also uses the block size value from the various arena headers to tell you how much memory is taken by various things in memory. This can be proven quite easily by using the MEM command at the DOS prompt.

Quit DEBUG, and type the following command at the DOS prompt:

```
-D3695:0 L20
3695:0000  5A 96 36 69 69 00 00 00-44 45 42 55 47 00 00 00   Z.6ii...DEBUG..
3695:0010  CD 20 FF 9F 00 9A F0 FE-1D F0 DC 01 DF 35 4B 01   . ...........5K.
```

Figure 15-2 DEBUG's block and its arena header in memory

```
C:\> MEM /D | MORE
```

The MEM command's /D switch displays more detailed information than the /C switch you may have used with DOS's memory management. Piping the output through the MORE filter pauses each screenful of information. Or you can use the Mem command's /P switch.

At the top of the screen you'll see the four columns of output from the MEM command: Address, Name, Size and Type. The Address is a six-digit hexadecimal number showing the absolute address of a block in memory. All the numbers end in zero, since all memory blocks must start at a segment address.

At address 000400 you see the "ROM Communication Area." That's really the BIOS Data Area at segment 40 hex that was explored in the previous chapter. You can see in the Size column that it's 100 hex bytes long.

Press Enter to view the next screen, and you'll see other things in memory. The address by each shows the start of their block in memory — including the arena header. Look for COMMAND.COM on the list, shown as "COMMAND" in the column. Take the address in the first column, and make a note of it. Next time you're in DEBUG, use that address to look up COMMAND.COM's block in memory.

> **Tip:** To translate a MEM command address to a DEBUG address, sandwich a colon between the final zero and the rest of the number. For example, if the MEM command shows you the address 0367B0, the D command to display that address in DEBUG would be: *D 367B:0.*

If you're using the DOS=UMB command in CONFIG.SYS and loading device drivers and TSRs high, then you can see their blocks in upper memory. Any address that starts with a value greater than 0A0000 hex in the MEM /P command's output qualifies. You can view that block in upper memory just like a block in conventional memory. Use the information from the TIP box to display the upper memory block in DEBUG.

Before moving on, I need to remind you that memory blocks are a look-only thing. If you ever alter a memory block or an arena header, you will corrupt the DOS "memory chain." Since all the blocks are linked, corrupting the chain is equivalent to removing the key Ace of Spades in a house of cards; DOS will come tumbling down and immediately screech to a halt. Remember, memory blocks are "look-only" things.

The Environment Memory Block

One interesting memory block worth looking at is your PC's environment. DOS displays the environment's contents with the SET command. You can also use SET to create and remove environment variables. This is all stored in a memory block called the "Master Environment," which is owned by the first copy of COMMAND.COM low in memory. You can use the following DOS command to find the Master Environment's exact location:

```
C:\> MEM /D | FIND /I "ENVIRONMENT"
```

DOS will locate the string "Environment" in the MEM /P command's output. However, instead of finding one environment, you'll see at least two. On my system, I saw the following:

```
00575           272      (OK)    COMMAND        Environment
009A7           160      (OK)    MEM            Environment
```

If you're running Windows, you may see as many as six different environments in memory. No matter what, the first block you see, the first one owned by COMMAND.COM, is the Master Environment. Everything else is a copy — a cheap imitation!

Whenever DOS runs a program, it allocates two blocks of memory, one for the program and a second for a copy of the Master Environment. Only the contents of the environment are copied, not any empty space. So if you have a 2K environment but only 384 bytes is used, only the 384 bytes are copied to the cloned environment.

A program can use its local environment to examine the variables listed there. But nothing can be changed in a local environment. Changes to the environment can only be made in the Master Environment. Changes made to your program's environment are lost when the program quits, since DOS will deallocate that memory block. In any case, it doesn't hurt to look.

To use the environment you need to be able to find it in memory. You can find any program's local environment by looking in the PSP. At offset 2C hex you'll find the segment address of the local environment block. View that 16-bit value with the D command as follows:

`-D2C L2`

The two bytes displayed represent a 16-bit value, so reverse them to create the proper segment address. For example, on my screen I saw the bytes D8 1E hex. Reversing them to equal 1ED8 hex gives me a segment address, which can be plugged into the D command:

`-D1ED8:0`

Use the proper D command for the bytes you see on your screen. The resulting memory display shows you a copy of the environment in memory. You should see the COMSPEC= variable, PATH, PROMPT, and whatever else is stored into the environment. Each string is shown with the variable name in all caps, followed by the equal sign and the string's contents. A single zero hex byte separates each string. The entire environment ends with a double-zero byte.

▏▶ *Tip:* Locate the Master Environment in memory using the MEM command as described earlier in this section. Plug the address given into DEBUG's D command and look through the Master Environment.

Some intrepid programmers have written utilities to modify and manipulate the Master Environment. These utilities allow batch files to insert strings into the environment "on the fly." Since they're not major league programs, I can't mention anything in particular or where you could find it. However, I recommend scanning the popular batch file utility disks offered by the big-name shareware and public domain software sources.

If you continue to explore the memory block by pressing the *D* command, you'll eventually stumble upon the original block of memory and your program's PSP. And if you're really adventurous, you can examine the arena header of the various memory blocks and trace back all the blocks allocated since your PC started. But keep in mind the MEM command does this for you automatically, and its output is a bit less ugly.

Video Memory

Perhaps the most interesting and exciting chunk of memory in any computer is video memory. It's exciting because you get immediate visual feedback from the bytes you alter in video memory. After all, the purpose of video memory is to hold the characters you see on the screen.

The PC has many text and graphics modes. For this exercise, you'll be working exclusively with text, either color text or monochrome. If you have a color system, which includes VGA gray scale monitors, then video memory is located at segment address B800 hex. Monochrome video memory, which includes Hercules and all "monographics" systems, starts at segment B000 hex. (Refer to Figure 14-5 in the upper memory map to see where video memory is located.)

This book assumes that you have a color system. Therefore, the address B800 hex is the start of video memory. If you have a monochrome PC, substitute the value B000 hex for B800 hex below. Otherwise, you'll never see the fruits of your labors.

Peeking and Poking through Video Memory

The characters you see on your screen, no matter which way the program puts them there, are held in video memory. If you see an "A" on the screen, that means a byte in video memory is holding the value 41 hex, ASCII for A. You can see this by using the E command in DEBUG. First, before using that command, reset the DS segment register equal to your PC's video segment:

```
-RDS
DS=xxxx
:B800
```

In this example, the DS register is set equal to the color video segment, B800 hex. Now all D and E commands will be local offsets to that segment. (Remember to use B000 hex if you have a monochrome screen.)

If you poke the value 41 hex into the byte at offset zero you'll see an "A" displayed on the screen. However, DEBUG will also scroll the screen and you probably won't see the A displayed. Therefore, the following E command will poke an A into the third row:

```
-E A0 41
```

Look for the "A" in the first column toward the top of your screen. It may be hard to spot, so press F3 and Enter to reissue the command. Now look for the two A's above each other near the top of your screen.

If you want to poke an entire string into video memory, feel free. Address 7D0 hex is just about smack dab in the middle of the screen. Use it with the E command to do something wonderful:

```
-E 7D0 "See me?"
```

Alas, the results are a little disappointing. The reason is that video memory is composed of two bytes for each character displayed. The even-numbered byte offset holds the character displayed. The bytes at odd-numbered offset hold special attribute values.

> **Note:** The typical PC screen has 80 columns by 25 rows for displaying text. That means you have a potential of 2,000 character positions on the screen. But video memory is actually 4,000 bytes long, due to all the attribute bytes. This is why the value FA0 hex — 4,000 decimal — was used in a previous chapter to indicate the entire block of video memory.
>
> If you want to find a specific byte on the screen, you need to factor in the "hidden" attribute bytes. For example, a character at the second column in the fifth row can be located using this formula:
>
> $(row - 1) \times 80 \times 2 + (column - 1) \times 2 = $ offset
>
> The formula assumes the row and column offsets are relative to position 0, 0 at the upper-left corner of the screen. There are 80 characters in a row. The extra "× 2s" takes into account all the attribute bytes. The second column at the fifth row is calculated as:
>
> $(5 - 1) \times 80 \times 2 + (2 - 1) \times 2 = $ offset
>
> $(4) \times 160 + (1) \times 2 = $ offset
>
> $640 + 2 = $ offset
>
> $642 = $ offset
>
> The offset is at 642 decimal, which translates into 282 hex. (Use a decimal-hexadecimal calculator to find the offset in hex; this example has too much brainwork in it already!)

The attribute values describe the foreground and background colors of each character displayed, its intensity, and whether or not it's blinking. On a monochrome screen, the attribute also controls whether or not the character is underlined. This information is discussed in full detail in the next section. The lesson here is that every other byte of video memory is an attribute.

To see the attribute bytes in action, use the D command:

```
-D 0 LA0
```

Here, the D command displays the first A0 hex (160) bytes of video memory. You may recognize some of the information on the screen in the ASCII column, but notice the "picket fence" pattern. That's due to all those attribute bytes, which should show up in the middle column as the value 07 hex at every odd byte offset. (If you're using a screen-coloring program or have changed the screen color using ANSI.SYS, a value other than 07 hex may appear; but it will be the same in all the attribute bytes regardless).

The attribute bytes can offer the same visual feedback as the character bytes. For example, try the following E command:

```
-E A1 70
```

In this example, the value 71 hex is poked into the attribute byte at offset A1 hex, the second row on the screen. Note that it's an odd-numbered offset. The attribute value poked in will "inverse" the character displayed at that position; you'll see a black character on a white background.

> *Tip:* Odd hexadecimal digits: 1, 3, 5, 7, 9, B, D, F.

Attributes and characters can be poked in individually without affecting each other. To prove this, enter the following program in DEBUG:

```
-A100
xxxx:0100 MOV CX,7D0
xxxx:0103 MOV BX,1
xxxx:0106 MOV AL,70
xxxx:0108 MOV [BX],AL
xxxx:010A ADD BX,2
xxxx:010D LOOP 108
xxxx:010F INT 20
```

Press Enter after the last line to exit the mini-assembler. Use the *R* command to confirm that the IP register is set equal to 100 hex, and confirm that DS equals B800 hex, your video segment. (Use the *RIP* or *RDS* command if either register isn't properly set.) Type *G* to change all the attributes on your screen.

What this program does is poke the value 70 hex into all the attribute bytes in video memory. An attribute of 70 hex is black text on a white background, as you've seen from the E command above. Here is what the program does line by line:

```
MOV CX,7D0
```

This command puts the value 7D0 hex into the CX register. That value is 2,000 decimal, the total number of attributes bytes on the screen. (Remember that CX is the count byte used with the LOOP instruction at offset 10D hex.)

```
MOV BX,1
```

The BX register is set to point at offset 1, the first attribute byte in video memory.

```
MOV AL,70
```

The AL register is filled with the value 70 hex, which will be poked into all the attribute bytes in video memory. This value is the key; if it's changed to something else, then that attribute will be poked throughout video memory.

```
MOV [BX],AL
```

This command moves the value in the AL register into the memory address pointed at by the BX register, poking the value 70 hex into an attribute byte in video memory.

```
ADD BX,2
```

This command adds 2 to the value in BX. Since all the attributes are at odd memory offsets, this instruction continues to point BX at each successive attribute byte on the screen.

```
LOOP 108
```

The LOOP instruction directs the microprocessor to repeat the commands between it and offset 108 hex (MOV [BX],AL). The loop will repeat the number specified in the CX register. This means that BX will eventually point at and fill every attribute byte in video memory.

```
INT 20
```

The INT 20 command ends the program.

You'll notice that the attribute bytes are unaffected by the values in the character bytes, and vice versa. Even as you scroll the screen, it stays inversed. In fact, you can run the program again to try out a new attribute. Simply change the value moved into the AL register, which can be done with the following E command:

```
-E CS:107 1E
```

The "CS:" is used in the E command because the program is located at the CS register's segment, not in video memory. The E command is now referencing locations in video memory thanks to the new value of the DS register. Type *G* and see yellow text on a blue background.

> ***Tip:*** The E and D command work with memory offsets specified by the DS segment register. The A command builds a program in the segment specified by the CS segment register. To use the E or D command in the program segment, you must prefix the offset with "CS:". Of course, you could use the

segment value in hex, but CS works just as well and works the same for everybody in any situation.

Poke around if you like. It's like stumbling in the dark, however, since you don't yet know what the attribute bytes represent. That's covered in the section below. For the present, you can return the screen to normal by specifying an attribute byte of 07 hex:

```
-ECS:107 7
```

Type *G* to save your eyeballs.

Note: Each attribute byte can be different, just as each character byte can be different. This program filled all the attribute bytes with a single value. Most programs will use different attribute bytes in different areas of the screen to organize information clearly. For example, *WordPerfect* uses different color text to show underline, bold, italic, and so on.

All about Attribute Bytes

Character bytes are simple: Poke in a value from zero through 255 and the corresponding character appears on the screen. People can trust that. Attribute bytes are weird, which stems from the fact that attribute bytes are controlled by their bit settings. This can drive you nuts, but if you follow closely, it can make immediate sense.

Unlike kindergarten, the three primary colors on your video monitor are Red, Green, and Blue. I remember this because of the old RGB monitors: Red, Green, Blue. Those are the only three colors you have to deal with, from them all other colors of the rainbow are made.

Tip: The colors you painted with in your finger painting days were red, yellow, and blue. These are *subtractive* colors. When you deal with light, you use *additive* colors, red, green, and blue.

Inside your monitor are three electron guns that paint the image on your screen. There is a red gun, a green gun, and a blue gun. Color is created on the screen by firing one or a combination of the guns at a single spot. In the text mode, that spot is defined as the character on the screen and a rectangular space around it. The character itself can have a color, as can the background that surrounds it.

Using various combinations of red, green, and blue light, the PC is able to create eight different colors for text, as shown in Table 15-2. When all three guns are "off," the color black is produced. The red, green, and blue guns individually produce their own colors — green and blue make cyan, or light blue; red and blue make purple or violet; red and green make yellow or brown; and all three colors together make white.

The astute reader will immediately notice the on-off patterns in Table 15-2. These correspond to various bit patterns that can be translated from binary into decimal.

Table 15-2 The Red, Green, and Blue Color Values

Red	Green	Blue	Color
0	0	0	Black
0	0	1	Blue
0	1	0	Green
0	1	1	Cyan
1	0	0	Red
1	0	1	Purple
1	1	0	Yellow
1	1	1	White

Yes, it's true, the bit patterns in the Table are values representing eight color attributes for text in the foreground:

Color	Number
Black	0
Blue	1
Green	2
Cyan	3
Red	4
Purple	5
Yellow	6
White	7

Note: If you've ever dabbled in the BASIC programming language, then you recognize the color number values as the same ones used with BASIC's COLOR command.

Tip: Monochrome users don't have three electron guns working in their monitors. There's only one. The "colors" available on a monochrome screen are 0 for black and 7 for white. Color 1, however, shows text on the screen as underlined. This is something unique to the monochrome monitor, and it also explains why some programs use blue text to represent something underlined.

For example, red is color number four. If you want red text, you use attribute 4, which is 0100 in binary. Try the following in DEBUG:

```
-E A0 41 4
```

This command pokes 41 hex — the letter A — into the character byte at offset A0 hex. The value 4 hex is poked into the attribute byte, rendering the "A" in red. You can poke in the first eight letters of the alphabet in the eight colors shown in Table 15-2 with the following command:

```
-E A0 41 0 42 1 43 2 44 3 45 4 46 5 47 6 48 7
```

The letters A through H are represented by byte values 41 through 48 hex. After each is the attribute byte values of zero through 7 hex. See how they correspond to the color values in Table 15-2? The black character doesn't show up at all, and every other character is the proper color (although there is a raging debate over whether "yellow" should be called "brown"; it varies from monitor to monitor).

Of course, there are eight bits in the attribute byte. The first three, bits 0 through 2, correspond to the color values from Table 15-2. The rest describe additional color and display attributes for the corresponding character. The whole attribute byte at once is organized into two groups: The first four bits describe the foreground text color, the second four describe the background. This is illustrated in Figure 15-3.

Bit 3, from Figure 15-3, controls the intensity of the colors listed in Table 15-2. So in actuality, there are 16 possible foreground colors. The new batch of eight is created by adding the word "bright" to the colors listed in Table 15-2.

The background colors are controlled by bits 4, 5, and 6, as shown in Figure 15-3. They correspond exactly to the bit values in Table 15-2, except they control the background color and they're in the second hex digit. This is handy: 10 is a blue background, 1 is a blue foreground; 40 is a red background, 4 is a red foreground. Type in the following E command:

```
-E A0 41 00 42 10 43 20 44 30 45 40 46 50 47 60 48 70
```

This is similar to the E command you typed earlier; the letters A through H are poked into video memory. But this time, only their background attribute bytes are set; the foreground attribute is set to zero, or black. You can continue to set their

	Background				Foreground		
7	6	5	4	3	2	1	0
Blink	Red	Green	Blue	Bright	Red	Green	Blue

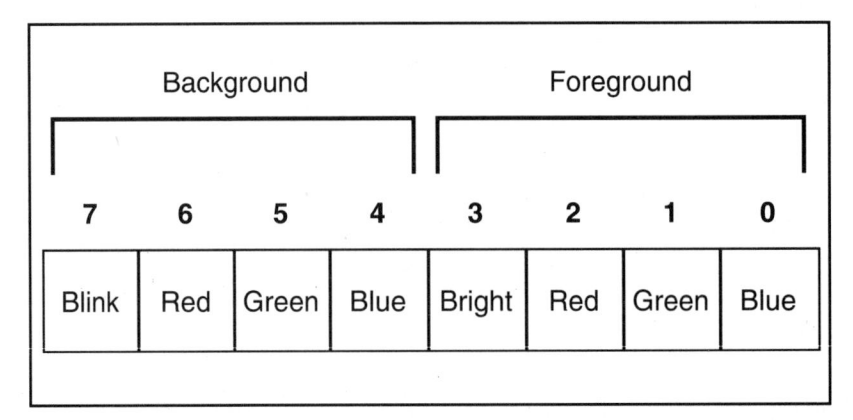

Figure 15-3 Bit values in the attribute byte

foreground attributes if you like, but note that if you set the foreground color equal to the background (00, for example), the character will be "invisible."

With the foreground color, there can be a "bright" value, activated by setting bit 4. For example:

```
-EA0 57 0F 4F 0F 57 0F 21 0F
```

Here, "WOW!" is displayed on the screen in bright white letters. (This also works on monochrome screens.) The bit pattern is 0000 1111. That means you get all three colors — red, green, and blue — plus the bright bit. If you just wanted bright green, you'd only set bits 3 and 1: 0000 1010 translates into 0A hex:

```
-EA0 57 0A 4F 0A 57 0A 21 0A
```

There is no "bright" background bit. Instead, bit 7 in the attribute byte controls whether or not the character is blinking. This can be very annoying:

```
-EA0 48 84 45 84 4C 84 50 84 21 84
```

The bytes 48, 45, 4C, 50, and 21 hex poke "HELP!" into character bytes. The byte 84 hex is poked into the attribute bytes. That translates into binary 1000 0100. If you plug that into Figure 15-3 it equals "Blink on, Red foreground on."

▶ *Tip:* If you didn't see blinking text, you probably saw a "fuzzy" gray background instead. This comes up in certain screen modes and when some special video accelerators are running. There is an option in ROM that switches between the dim display and blinking text.

Monochrome users will also see blinking text. However, just like the foreground colors, the only background colors available are black and white.

Table 15-3 lists all the foreground and background text attributes in existence. To create a specific color text, just combine a foreground and background attribute. For example, bright yellow text on a red background are attributes 0E hex and 40 hex. Combine them and you get 4E hex. Now try this command:

```
-F0 LFA0 21 4E
```

This command fills the screen with yellow-on-red exclamation points. The exclamation point is character 21 hex. Attribute 4E hex is bright yellow on a red background.

From Appendix A you should recognize that some interesting attribute bytes also appear as handy character codes. For example, lowercase "p" is ASCII 70 hex. That code corresponds to the attribute of black text on a white background:

```
-E140 "Hpeplplpop!p"
```

This command pokes the string "Hello!" into the character bytes at offset 140, and it pokes in "p" — attribute 70 hex — into the attribute bytes.

If the screen is really bugging you, good! You've been experimenting with how the video display works. To give yourself a break, quit DEBUG, and type the CLS

Table 15-3 Foreground and Background Attribute Byte Values

Foreground Colors:

Color	Value (Hex)	Color	Value (Hex)
Black	00	Bright Black	08
Blue	01	Bright Blue	09
Green	02	Bright Green	0A
Cyan	03	Bright Cyan	0B
Red	04	Bright Red	0C
Purple	05	Bright Purple	0D
Yellow	06	Bright Yellow	0E
White	07	Bright White	0F

Background Colors:

Color	Value (Hex)	Color	Value (Hex)
Black	00	Blinking Black	80
Blue	10	Blinking Blue	90
Green	20	Blinking Green	A0
Cyan	30	Blinking Cyan	B0
Red	40	Blinking Red	C0
Purple	50	Blinking Purple	D0
Yellow	60	Blinking Yellow	E0
White	70	Blinking White	F0

command at the DOS prompt. CLS restores the video screen to "normal." If that doesn't work, then the MODE 80 command does the job.

CGA Video Pages

One unfortunately neglected aspect of color text concerns the various "video pages" that can be used. The CGA video system, and all its descendants, have four or more different video screens or *pages* that can be used to display text. Normally, all programs use page zero, the one you're looking at on your monitor right now. You can, however, activate and use the three other pages.

> ***Tip:*** You'll often see the "video page" number specified in one of the Interrupt 10 hex function calls. It's usually specified in the BX, BL, or BH register. Most of the time, page zero is used by all DOS programs, which is why this book always recommends you put zero in the register when calling the various BIOS video functions.

If you're in the 80-column color text mode, then there are four video pages available. In the 40-column mode, you have eight pages available. Set up DEBUG to switch a page by activating the mini-assembler:

```
-A 100
xxxx:0100 MOV AH,5
xxxx:0102 MOV AL,1
xxxx:0104 INT 10
xxxx:0106 JMP 100
```

Press Enter after the last instruction a second time to exit the mini-assembler. This program calls Interrupt 10 hex, function 5. The value 5 is put into the AH register, then the new video page is put into register AL at offset 102 hex. Interrupt 10 hex is called in the next line. Finally, the last line loops back to offset 100 hex, allowing you to restart the program.

> ***Note:*** This program constitutes an "endless loop." If you were to type the G command, the microprocessor would continuously execute the instructions between offsets 100 hex and the jump instruction at offset 106 hex. The only way to get out of such a loop is to reset your PC. So don't type the G command!

Reset the instruction pointer to offset 100 hex, if necessary. Then type *P3* to process the first three instructions. The screen will seemingly clear, and you'll see the final register display.

Did the screen clear? No, you're now using video page 1. Video page 0 is still intact. To see it again, you'll need to run the same program over, but move the value zero into the AL register. You can modify the program with the following E command:

```
-E103 0
```

Press Enter, then type *P4* to execute the JMP instruction and run the rest of the program again. Ta-da! You're now back at page 0. Return to page 1 with the following two commands:

```
-E103 1
-P4
```

Now test video page 3:

```
-E103 3
-P4
```

Again, the screen clears, but not really; you're actually on video page 3.

Incidentally, these pages are all at different locations in video memory. Try the following command:

```
-E B800:A00 "EOROROOORO"
```

According to all you know, this command should have poked a string into video memory. Yet, you didn't see anything. The reason is that the string was poked into page 0's video memory. Return there to view it with the following command:

```
-E103 0
-P4
```

You'll see the red and white "ERROR" message where it should be, once you've returned to page 0.

Note: I once wrote a program that took advantage of the multiple video pages. One page held a help screen, another an input screen, and so on. Switching between the screens proved to be a rapid method of displaying information back in the old days of the 8088 PC. I abandoned that approach, since the monochrome screen didn't support this page switching. At the time, most PCs were monochrome.

The video page switching ability of your color graphics system is more of a curiosity than anything used in a "real" program. But there may be one exception: As long as no other program uses the video pages, they'll remain blank. Therefore, it would be a snap to write a screen blanking program that works by switching to an empty video page. The screen can be "restored" by switching back to page 0.

To create the simple screen blanking program, enter the mini-assembler and type in the program shown below:

```
-A 100
xxxx:0100 MOV AH,5
xxxx:0102 MOV AL,1
xxxx:0104 INT 10
xxxx:0106 MOV AH,0
xxxx:0108 INT 16
xxxx:010A MOV AH,5
xxxx:010C MOV AL,0
xxxx:010E INT 10
xxxx:0110 INT 20
```

Take a note of the address after the INT 20 instruction. Press Enter alone on that line to exit the mini-assembler. Then use that offset, 112 hex, to set the size of the program — 12 hex bytes. Tell DEBUG that's the amount of memory you want to write to disk with the RCX command:

```
-RCX
CX=xxxx
:12
```

Name the program BLANK.COM, and save it to disk:

```
-N BLANK.COM
-W
Writing 00012 bytes
```

When you run BLANK, it will switch the screen from video page 0 to page 1 and wait for a key to be pressed. After a key is pressed, the screen is switched back to page 0. As long as page 1 is blank, your screen will clear and then be restored after you press a key. (Page 1 probably isn't blank now, since you've been working there in DEBUG; you may have to reset to clear it.) As long as no other program messes with video page 1, this is a short and nifty program to use.

BLANK.COM is composed of three parts, each a call to your PC's BIOS. First comes the call to the video interrupt, 10 hex, to switch to page 1:

```
MOV AH,5
MOV AL,1
INT 10
```

Register AH identifies function 5 and register AL holds the new page number. INT 10 makes the phone call that switches the page. The next instruction calls the BIOS keyboard interrupt, 16 hex, and waits for a key to be pressed:

```
MOV AH,0
INT 16
```

Function zero is loaded into register AH, then the call is made to INT 16. The BIOS will wait for a key to be pressed. We really don't care which key was pressed, because that's the signal to end the program, done by switching the video page back to zero:

```
MOV AH,5
MOV AL,0
INT 10
```

These are the same instructions used above to switch to page 1, except zero is put in the AL register. The program ends with the standard INT 20 instruction:

```
INT 20
```

It would be really neat to have this program activated by a "hot key." It would be super if you could make it into a TSR, having it pop up and clear the screen after a given period of inactivity. Trust me, that's a major project. Also, switching the video pages is a sneaky way to save the screen and it may not always work. But it is an interesting application.

▬▶ *Tip:* It's not always necessary to load individual registers in a program. While the instructions may say "AH=this" and "BL=that," you can load both upper and lower registers at the same time. Witness this version of the program:

```
MOV AX,501
INT 10
MOV AH,0
```

```
INT 16
MOV AX,500
INT 10
INT 20
```

With both the Interrupt 10 hex calls, the values in the AL and AH registers are simultaneously loaded into the AX register. This would also be how you load the registers in DEBUG using the RAX command. The end result is a smaller, faster program, but one that also requires a wee bit more brain work to see what's going on.

Video Character Sets

Enter the following program in DEBUG to switch your PC over to mode 6, the 640 x 200 graphics mode. (This mode is unavailable on monochrome systems.)

```
-A100
xxxx:0100 MOV AH,0
xxxx:0102 MOV AL,6
xxxx:0104 INT 10
```

Press Enter at offset address 106 hex to end the mini-assembler mode. The above commands call Interrupt 10 hex, function zero. That resets the video mode to the value in register AL. In the example, mode 6 is selected.

Confirm that the IP register is set equal to 100 hex, then type the *P3* command to switch into video mode 6.

Video mode 6 is a graphics mode, not a text mode. It's available on all color video systems, CGA, EGA, and VGA. Yet, if it's a graphics mode, why do you see text? The answer is that the text characters are stored in your PC's BIOS as graphic bitmaps. That way you can use text in your PC's various graphic modes.

The CGA character set you're looking at now is stored in ROM in bank F. Specifically, offset FA6E hex in bank F, address F000:FA6E hex:

```
-D F000:FA6E
```

What you see on your screen is just another chunk of ROM in memory. Indeed, if you deliberately scanned your ROM BIOS in bank F from a previous chapter, you probably glossed over this area without a second thought. Yet, this location stores character bitmaps for text displayed in video mode 6.

The characters are stored in eight-byte chunks. Each chunk represents a grid of 8 bits by 8 bits, the grid forming the character on the screen. The first character is blank — all zeros:

```
-DF000:FA6E L8
```

The second character is the map for Control-A, the happy face:

```
-DF000:FA76 L8
```

You'll see these bytes displayed on the screen:

```
3C 42 A5 81 BD 42 3C 00
```

The bit values of these numbers can be plugged into an 8 × 8 grid, as shown in Figure 15-4. This is how the character is created. Each of the 128 characters in the ASCII character set are stored in your PC's ROM in this manner.

> **Tip:** Only the first 128 characters are defined in ROM. The extended ASCII characters are located in a table in low memory. Normally, this table doesn't exist. It can, however, be loaded into memory using DOS's GRAFTABL command.

Unlike the CGA graphics system, EGA and VGA graphics support multiple character "fonts" that can be used in several graphics modes. You may have seen some of the fancier fonts used in programs like *Norton Utilities* and *Norton Desktop for DOS*, *PC Tools* and a few other graphical interfaces. There's nothing graphical about them; the programmer's have written a new character font and are using it instead of the standard font.

Writing your own font can be fun, and there are many public domain and third-party utilities that let you do so. Your graphics adapter may have even come with font generating software. This can be a blessing, since a character grid 16 bits high by 9 bits wide times 256 possible characters means a lot of bit-maddening programming.

Interrupt 10 hex, function 11 hex is the video BIOS Character Generator Interface. This function has a dozen or so *subservices* that are used to implement various character sets for EGA and VGA systems. I haven't bothered to document this function in Appendix F, since it can be very complex. You can, however, use subservice 30 hex to gather information about your PC's current video mode. Set up that function call by entering the following program in DEBUG:

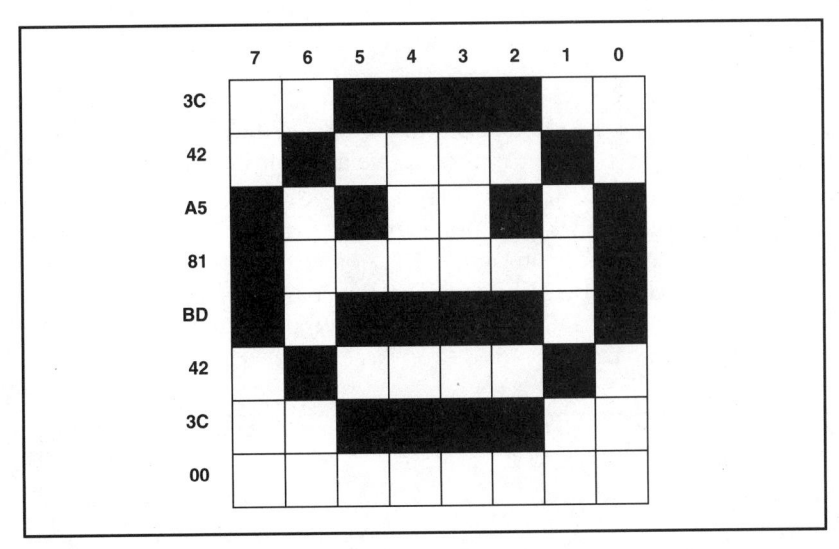

Figure 15-4 How bitmaps translate into characters

```
-A 100
xxxx:0100 MOV AH,11
xxxx:0102 MOV AL,30
xxxx:0104 MOV BH,6
xxxx:0106 INT 10
```

Press Enter after the last line to exit the mini-assembler and return to DEBUG's hyphen prompt. Reset the IP register equal to 100 hex with the *RIP* command, then type *P4* to process the four instructions.

Interrupt 10 hex, function 11 hex, subservice 30 hex with optional parameter 6 in the BH register tells you a few things about your video system's character set. In the final register display on your screen, you should note the following:

- The CX register holds the height of the grid used to create characters.

- The DL register holds the number of rows on the screen (it indicates which row is at the bottom, assuming row zero is at the top).

- The ES:BP register pair points to the character set stored in ROM.

On my screen, the final register display is shown in Figure 15-5.

The CX register holds the value 10 hex, meaning the character on my VGA display are 16 bits high. The bottom row on the screen is 18 hex, as seen in the DL register. The value 18 hex is 24 decimal, meaning my screen is currently displaying 25 rows (by 80 columns).

The ES:BP registers point to the location of the character set in ROM. From Figure 15-5, I can calculate this address as FC01:221B. Your system may show a different address. (For example, my test system shows C000:3960.) Display that address using the D command:

```
-DFC01:221B
```

Remember to plug in the values you see on your screen, from the ES and BP registers. The size of the characters is in the CX register, which for most of us will be 10 hex, or 16 bytes. You can then create a character grid of 16 bytes by 8 bits in a byte, a 16 × 8 grid used by the EGA/VGA adapters to display text on the screen. I've filled such a grid using the byte values found in ROM to create character 1, the happy face, in Figure 15-6. Contrast this to the CGA graphics image in Figure 15-4 and you'll see how much more resolution is possible in VGA graphics — and why it doesn't strain your eyes. (Also, the little guy looks happier to be shown in VGA resolution.)

```
AX=1130  BX=0600  CX=0010  DX=0018  SP=FFEE  BP=221B  SI=0000  DI=0000
DS=2494  ES=FC01  SS=2494  CS=2494  IP=0108   NV UP EI PL NZ NA PO NC
2494:0108 CD16           INT     16
```

Figure 15-5 This register display gives you clues about your EGA/VGA character set

More Ugly Memory Stuff 295

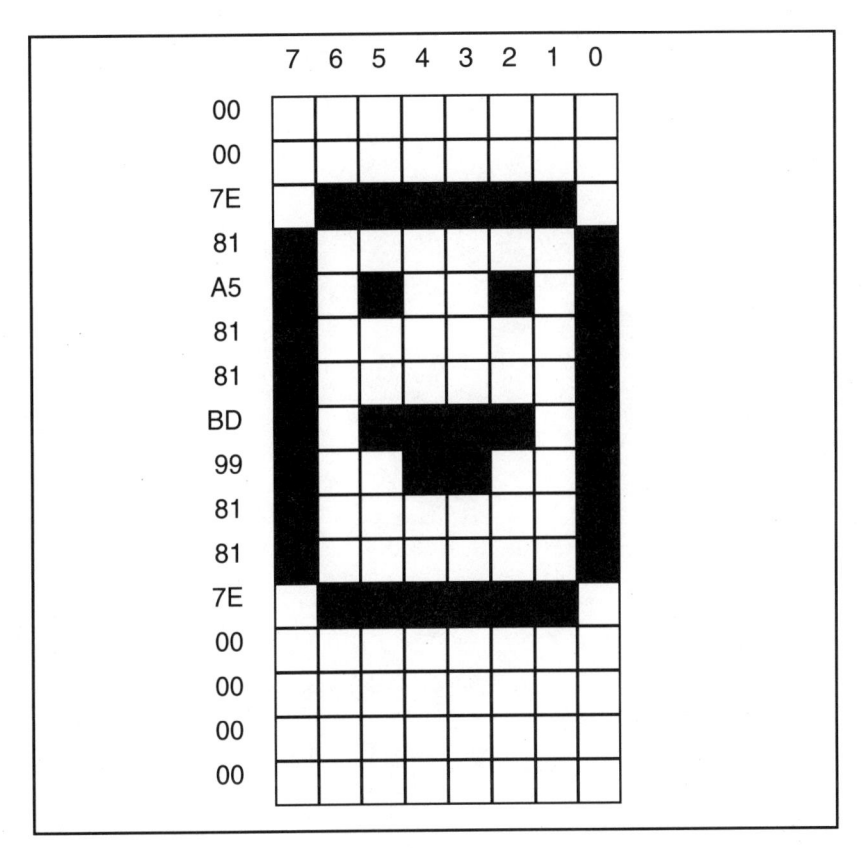

```
     7 6 5 4 3 2 1 0
00
00
7E
81
A5
81
81
BD
99
81
81
7E
00
00
00
00
```

Figure 15-6 A 16-by-8 character bitmap

Loading in a new graphics image is possible using the various functions of Interrupt 10 hex. *WordPerfect*, for example, uses these commands to create an underlined and italicized character set for use in that program. Other software also takes advantage of the flexibility of the EGA/VGA character sets.

▶ *Tip:* If you're interested in exploring your video system in more depth, I recommend the book *PC & PS/2 Video Systems* (Microsoft Press) by Richard Wilton. It's a bit technical, but I regard it as the definitive source for information about your video system.

16

Disks, Files, and Stuff

Just as memory is chock full of interesting things to look at, the typical disk is permeated with curiosity quenching goodies. First you have the all-important boot sector, the key that unlocks your PC and allows DOS to walk right in. Next comes the FAT, the disk space map that tells DOS where to find files on disk. Last is the disk directory itself. Trust me, the DIR command only tells you half the story.

Using DEBUG with disks was first uncovered back in Chapter 11. The current chapter expands upon those skills by using DEBUG to load interesting parts of your disk into memory for examination and possible editing. If you need any brushing up on DEBUG and disks, I recommend skimming through Chapter 11 again.

Nothing you're going to do in this chapter is deadly. Remember, working on disk means loading a part of disk into memory and working on it in memory. It's only by carelessly using the W command that you can mess up a disk. Even so, you should dust off that Sample floppy disk created in Chapter 11 and use it for the exercises demonstrated here.

The Wondrous Boot Sector

As your PC boots, it takes an inventory of itself, runs a few diagnostic tests, then sits down and straightens its tie. At last, in a final, uncivilized attempt to grasp for control, it desperately looks to a disk drive for an operating system. First drive A is touched, then the hard drive C. The PC hopes to find a disk and, if so, it will load the first part of that disk into memory. If no disk is found, an *Insert DOS diskette and press any key* message is displayed, and the PC waits and hopes.

The first part of the disk the PC's BIOS tries to load is called the *boot sector*. It's the first 512 bytes of every DOS disk that contains all sorts of wondrous information about the disk, plus a small program. If the disk is a bootable DOS disk, the small program starts to load DOS. If the disk is a plain old "data disk," the small program displays a message explaining that it's not a boot disk. This you may already know from experience.

If you don't have the disk you created previously, then create a new one. Format a diskette for your PC's A drive. Select a disk that matches drive A's maximum size and capacity. For example, if you have a 1.4M 3½-inch drive, get one of those high-density "drink coasters" and stick it in the drive. Format the disk with the following DOS command:

```
C:\> FORMAT A: /U
```

Enter "Test Disk" as the volume label. Then, after formatting is complete, press *N* to return to the DOS prompt. On a sticky label, name the disk "Sample Disk." You're ready now for action.

Looking at the Boot Sector

Load the boot sector from the Sample Disk in drive A using the following DEBUG command:

```
-L 0 0 0 1
```

The L command format is L*address drive start count*. *Address* is where the chunk of disk memory will be loaded; *drive* is the drive number, starting with zero as drive A; *start* is the starting sector number; and *count* is the total number of sectors to load. The command in the example loads only the boot sector — the first 512 bytes — into memory at offset 0 hex. Yes, this overwrites the PSP. That's okay for this exercise, since we're only looking at memory. Also, it makes the offsets on your screen match up with the true offsets of items stored in the boot sector.

Display all of your boot sector at once with the following command:

```
-D 0 L200
```

The D command displays 512 bytes of memory at offset 0 hex. The first few lines will have scrolled off the top of the screen, but the majority of the boot sector is visible. You may instantly recognize the text string at offset 2A0 hex. This is one of several interesting tidbits stored in the boot sector. The entire list is shown in Table 16-1. I've mapped out the locations of these items in Figure 16-1.

Most of the interesting stuff is kept in the first 128 bytes of the boot sector, although I will show you everything. To see those bytes, type in the following D command:

```
-D0
```

This command will display the 128 bytes at offset 0 hex. The following will describe which bytes describe what; use Figure 16-1 to help you locate stuff as well. (I'm sorry I couldn't put the little numbers in the figure, but I ran out of room.)

Table 16-1 Interesting Stuff in Boot Sector

Offset	Length	Description
000 hex	3	Jump instruction, jump to bootstrap routine
003 hex	8	DOS name and version
00B hex	2	Bytes per sector
00D hex	1	Sectors per cluster
00E hex	2	Reserved sectors
010 hex	1	Total number of FATs
011 hex	2	Maximum root directory entries
013 hex	2	Total sectors on this disk
015 hex	1	Media descriptor byte, indicates disk type
016 hex	2	Sectors per FAT
018 hex	2	Sectors per track
01A hex	2	Total number of read/write heads
01C hex	4	Total number of hidden sectors
020 hex	4	"Huge" sector field (hard drives 32M)
024 hex	1	Drive number
025 hex	1	Reserved
026 hex	1	Extended boot signature
027 hex	4	Volume serial number
02B hex	11	Volume label
036 hex	8	File system type
03E hex	423	Bootstrap program (typical location)
1A0 hex	69	"Nonsystem disk" error message
1E6 hex	11	IO.SYS boot filename
1F1 hex	11	MSDOS.SYS boot filename
2FE hex	2	Boot sector signature

1. The first three bytes in the boot sector contain a JMP instruction. This jumps over all the information bytes right to the start of the "bootstrap loader," or the small program that loads the rest of DOS. (See number 21.)

2. At offset 3 you'll find the name and version number of the operating system that formatted the disk. Under MS-DOS 5, that's "MSDOS5.0" as seen in the figure. Other versions of DOS will reflect their ownership in this 8-byte space as well. The old PC-DOS 3.3 shows "IBM 3.3" in the same bytes.

3. The juicy information starts at offset B hex. The word (16-bit) value there tells you the number of bytes per sector on the disk. This is usually 512 shown

300   Dan Gookin's Guide to Underground DOS 6.0

```
 0  EB 3C 90 4D 53 44 4F 53-35 2E 30 00 02 01 01 00    .<.MSDOS5.0.....
10  02 E0 00 40 0B F0 09 00-12 00 02 00 00 00 00 00    ...@............
20  00 00 00 00 00 00 29 EA-17 30 22 54 45 53 54 20    ......)..0"TEST
30  44 49 53 4B 20 20 46 41-54 31 32 20 20 20 FA 33    DISK  FAT12   .3
40  C0 8E D0 BC 00 7C 16 07-BB 78 00 36 C5 37 1E 56    .....|...x.6.7.V
50  16 53 BF 3E 7C B9 0B 00-FC F3 A4 06 1F C6 45 FE    .S.>|.........E.
60  0F 8B 0E 18 7C 88 4D F9-89 47 02 C7 07 3E 7C FB    ....|.M..G...>|.
70  CD 13 72 79 33 C0 39 06-13 7C 74 08 8B 0E 13 7C    ..ry3.9..|t....|
80  89 0E 20 7C A0 10 7C F7-26 16 7C 03 06 1C 7C 13    .. |..|.&.|...|.
90  16 1E 7C 03 06 0E 7C 83-D2 00 A3 50 7C 89 16 52    ..|...|....P|..R
A0  7C A3 49 7C 89 16 4B 7C-B8 20 00 F7 26 11 7C 8B    |.I|..K|. ..&.|.
B0  1E 0B 7C 03 C3 48 F7 F3-01 06 49 7C 83 16 4B 7C    ..|..H....I|..K|
C0  00 BB 00 05 8B 16 52 7C-A1 50 7C E8 92 00 72 1D    ......R|.P|...r.
D0  B0 01 E8 AC 00 72 16 8B-FB B9 0B 00 BE E6 7D F3    .....r........}.
E0  A6 75 0A 8D 7F 20 B9 0B-00 F3 A6 74 18 BE 9E 7D    .u... .....t...}
F0  E8 5F 00 33 C0 CD 16 5E-1F 8F 04 8F 44 02 CD 19    ._.3...^....D...
100 58 58 58 EB E8 8B 47 1A-48 48 8A 1E 0D 7C 32 FF    XXX...G.HH...|2.
110 F7 E3 03 06 49 7C 13 16-4B 7C BB 00 07 B9 03 00    ....I|..K|......
120 50 52 51 E8 3A 00 72 D8-B0 01 E8 54 00 59 5A 58    PRQ.:.r....T.YZX
130 72 BB 05 01 00 83 D2 00-03 1E 0B 7C E2 E2 8A 2E    r..........|....
140 15 7C 8A 16 24 7C 8B 1E-49 7C A1 4B 7C EA 00 00    .|..$|..I|.K|...
150 70 00 AC 0A C0 74 29 B4-0E BB 07 00 CD 10 EB F2    p....t).........
160 3B 16 18 7C 73 19 F7 36-18 7C FE C2 88 16 4F 7C    ;..|s..6.|....O|
170 33 D2 F7 36 1A 7C 88 16-25 7C A3 4D 7C F8 C3 F9    3..6.|..%|.M|...
180 C3 B4 02 8B 16 4D 7C B1-06 D2 E6 0A 36 4F 7C 8B    .....M|.....6O|.
190 CA 86 E9 8A 16 24 7C 8A-36 25 7C CD 13 C3 0D 0A    .....$|.6%|.....
1A0 4E 6F 6E 2D 53 79 73 74-65 6D 20 64 69 73 6B 20    Non-System disk
1B0 6F 72 20 64 69 73 6B 20-65 72 72 6F 72 0D 0A 52    or disk error..R
1C0 65 70 6C 61 63 65 20 61-6E 64 20 70 72 65 73 73    eplace and press
1D0 20 61 6E 79 20 6B 65 79-20 77 68 65 6E 20 72 65     any key when re
1E0 61 64 79 0D 0A 00 49 4F-20 20 20 20 20 20 53 59    ady...IO      SY
1F0 53 4D 53 44 4F 53 20 20-20 20 53 59 53 00 00 55 AA    SMSDOS    SYS..U.
```

Figure 16-1 The boot sector

as 0200 hex. Since it's a word value stored in memory, it's reversed; the bytes you see on your screen will be 00 02 (unless you're examining a drive with a different number of bytes per sector).

4. Offset D hex's one byte value tells you how many sectors per cluster are used in the drive. For floppy disks that's either 1 or 2. The larger capacity diskettes use one sector per cluster; lower capacity diskettes use 2 sectors per cluster.

5. The word value at offset E hex tells you how many reserved sectors exist on the disk. Most drives may have only one reserved sector, the boot sector you're now looking at. Since this is a word value, the bytes need to be reversed: 01 00 is actually 0001 hex.

▶ Tip: I won't be repeating the instructions for deciphering a word value in memory from now on. You should know that the microprocessor, for reasons unknown and bewildering, stores a word or two-byte value in memory backward: 1234 hex is stored in memory as the bytes 34 and 12 hex. Whenever you see a "word value" mentioned in the text, know that you must reverse the bytes on your screen to obtain the true value.

6. Offset 10 hex reveals the total number of File Allocation Tables (FATs) on the disk. This byte value is usually 2 for all DOS disks; DOS maintains two copies of the FAT.

7. The word value at offset 11 hex tells you how many files can be kept in the root directory. For a floppy disk this value indicates the number of sectors allocated to the root directory with 16 files in each sector. For hard drives the value is the number of files in the root directory. Personally, I dislike this value representing two different things.

   For example, in Figure 16-1, the word value is 000E, or 14. On a 1.4M diskette that means there are 14 sectors reserved for the root directory. (Obviously, the disk can hold more than 14 files.) DOS puts 16 files in a sector, which means the disk can hold 224 files in its root directory.

   If the disk in Figure 16-1 were a hard drive, then the word value would represent the true number of files that can be stored in the root directory. For most hard drives, that's 200 hex or 512 files. So as not to confuse you further, Table 16-2 lists the total number of files available on all types of diskettes.

8. The word at offset 13 hex tells you the total number of sectors on the disk. For example, in Figure 16-1 the word value is 0B40 hex, which translates into 2,880 sectors. This is what you'd expect on a 1.4M diskette; the number of sectors will always be double the capacity of the diskette in kilobytes since a sector is one-half a kilobyte.

Tip: If the word value at offset 13 hex is blank, then you're dealing with a disk that has a capacity greater than 32 megabytes. The number of sectors for those disks is kept in the "Huge Sectors" field, covered in number 14.

9. The Media Descriptor Byte is stuck at offset 15 hex. This single byte is used to tell DOS which disk this boot sector is attached to. I've listed the "valid" media descriptor bytes in Table 16-3.

   Note that descriptor bytes F0 hex and F9 hex just happen to describe different types of disks. The way a program tells the difference is by looking

Table 16-2 Disks and Root Directory Size and Information

Disk Type	Root Directory Size (Sectors)	Maximum Entries
5¼, 360K	7	112
3½, 720K	7	112
5¼, 1.2M	14	224
3½, 1.4M	14	224
3½, 2.8M	14	224
Hard drive	32	512

Table 16-3 Media Descriptor Bytes for DOS Disks

Descriptor Byte Value	Disk Type(s)
F0 hex	5¼, 1.2M
	3½, 1.4M
	3½, 2.8M
F8 hex	All hard drives
F9 hex	3½, 720K
	5¼, 1.2M
FA hex	5¼, 320K "single sided"
FB hex	3½, 640K
FC hex	5¼, 180K
FD hex	5¼, 360K
	Various 8-inch floppies
FE hex	5¼, 160K
	Various 8-inch floppies
FF hex	5¼, 320K "double sided"

at the number of sectors per track on the disk, which is found at offset 18 hex (number 11):

- A 720K diskette has 9 sectors per track
- A 1.2M diskette has 15 sectors per track
- A 1.4M diskette has 18 sectors per track
- A 2.8M diskette has 36 sectors per track.

10. The word at offset 16 hex tells you how many sectors there are in one of the disk's FATs. This depends on the capacity of the disk, where larger capacity disks will have more sectors per FAT. I have a very large hard drive that shows a word value of 00C8 hex, or 200 sectors for a single FAT!

11. At offset 18 hex is a word that describes how many sectors per track are on the disk. This is a function of the disk's capacity. Common sector-per-track values are listed in Table 16-4. For a hard drive, the number of sectors per track varies. The standard PC/AT hard drive typically had 17 sectors per track. Modern hard drives may have 32 or more sectors per track.

Tip: Information about a disk is gathered from many sources in the boot table. The quickest source is the Media Descriptor Byte at offset 15 hex. Given that all DOS disks are formatted using a standard number of tracks, sectors,

Table 16-4 Common Disk Capacities and Their Sector-Per-Track Values

Disk Type	Sectors/Track
5¼, 360K	9
3½, 720K	9
5¼, 1.2M	15
3½, 1.4M	18
3½, 2.8M	36
Hard drive	(varies)

and clusters, once you know a disk's media descriptor byte you know it all. However, for some disks, the descriptor must be cross-checked against the number of sectors per track to differentiate between 720K, 1.2M, 1.4M, and 2.8M diskettes.

A program can manually calculate the number of bytes available on any disk by multiplying the bytes per sector value at offset B hex by the total sectors on the disk value at offset 13 hex. (If offset 13 hex reads 0000 hex, then the sectors per disk value must be read from offset 20 hex — the "huge" sector offset used by large hard drives.)

Dividing the sectors per track value at offset 18 hex by the total number of sectors at offset 13 hex yields the number of tracks on the disk. Divide that by the number of "heads" at offset 1A hex and you get the number of cylinders on the disk.

12. The word at offset 1A hex gives the total number of read/write heads used in the drive. For floppy disks, this value will always be 0002 hex; there are only two sides to a floppy disk. Hard drives can have multiple "platters," so this value will be greater. My hard drive shows a value of 0004 hex, for four heads. This means there are two platters on that hard drive.

13. Offset 1C hex contains a four-byte "double word" value indicating the total number of hidden sectors on the disk. Most floppy disks lack hidden sectors. Hard drives may have one or two lurking around. In fact, your hard drive will probably have a whole track full of hidden sectors — the *Partition Table*. (The hidden sectors value will equal the sectors per track value at offset 18 hex.) More information about the partition table is covered later in this chapter.

▶ ***Tip:*** If you think a word value is stored in memory backward, wait until you decipher a double word value! The double word (dd) value is four bytes long. The microprocessor stores that number completely backward: the hexadecimal number 12345678 is stored in memory as the four bytes 78 56 34 12.

Double word values are stored in memory differently from *segment:offset* addresses. Those values are stored as two word, or 16-bit, numbers. Therefore, the address 1234:5678 is stored in four bytes 34 12 78 56.

I've already promised that I won't keep reminding you how word values are stored in memory. Double word and *segment:offset* address values still deserve a small note to the side.

14. Offset 20 hex is used by hard drives greater than 32M in size. This is the "Huge" sector field, and it's a double word value indicating the total number of sectors on a hard drive. For example, the four bytes I see on my hard drive are:

    `E0 3F 06 00`

    That translates into the double word value 0063FE0. In decimal that indicates 409,568 sectors. At 512 bytes per sector, that's a 200M hard drive, give or take a few kilobytes.

    The huge sector field is only used if the total sectors on disk field at offset 13 hex reads double zero. Also, this field is unused on versions of DOS prior to 4.0.

Note: Memory locations from offset 20 hex onward are specific to DOS versions 5.0 and later, although many of them also apply to DOS 4.*x*. If your disk was formatted by a previous version of DOS, skim up to item number 21.

15. The single byte at offset 24 hex is what the manual calls the "drive number." Actually, this byte is zero unless the disk is the first hard drive in the system. If so, a value of 80 hex will appear.

Tip: Sometimes you may see your boot drive, hard drive C, referenced as drive 80 hex or 80h. The byte at offset 24 hex is where the hard drive gets that value.

16. The byte at offset 25 hex is marked reserved.

17. At offset 26 hex is a byte called the "extended boot signature." The byte value 29 hex at this location is what identifies a disk formatted by DOS 4.0 or later. Other disk formats will lack the specific information that follows, so programs will check for a value of 29 hex at offset 26 hex before peeking further.

18. The four bytes at offset 27 hex represent a double word value, your disk's "Volume serial number." For example, if you see the bytes EA 17 30 22 your disk's serial number appears as 2230-17EA. You can confirm this later, outside of DEBUG, using the VOL command.

Disks, Files, and Stuff 305

19. The 11 bytes marching along at offset 2B hex represent your volume label. This is probably one of those items you first recognized in the ASCII column. For the Sample Disk, you'll see "TEST DISK" displayed. This field will be padded with space characters (20 hex) if the volume label is shorter than 11 characters.

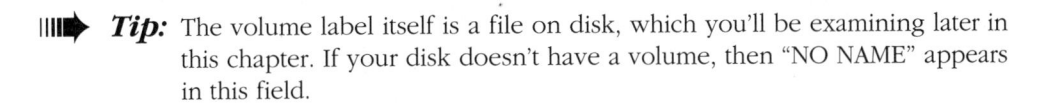

▶ *Tip:* The volume label itself is a file on disk, which you'll be examining later in this chapter. If your disk doesn't have a volume, then "NO NAME" appears in this field.

20. An eight-byte character string at offset 3C hex describes the "file system type," or the way that DOS stores the files on disk. DOS presently uses the FAT, File Allocation Table, system. There are two versions of the FAT, the 12-bit FAT and the 16-bit FAT. These will be identified in the file system type field as "FAT12" or "FAT16," followed by three spaces to pad out the rest of the field. If another file system is used, it will appear in this field. (How the FAT file system works is described later in this chapter.)

21. Finally, at offset 3E hex is the bootstrap program. This is the target for the JMP instruction at offset zero. Actually, offset 3E hex is specific to MS-DOS 5.0; other versions of DOS may specify other offsets for their bootstrap routine.

    The bootstrap routine is what the BIOS loads into memory in an attempt to start the rest of the operating system. The program is the same, whether you have a bootable or nonbootable DOS disk: it attempts to load the files IO.SYS and MSDOS.SYS into memory. The two files can be seen near the end of the boot sector, at offsets 1E6 hex and 1F1 hex.

▶ *Tip:* If you're using PC-DOS or some versions of Compaq DOS, the boot filenames will be IBMBIO.COM and IBMDOS.COM. They may also appear at different offsets than their MS-DOS counterparts.

If the boot files are found, they're loaded and control is transferred to them in memory. If the files aren't found, the bootstrap routine displays the message you see at offset 1A0 hex, which may be at a different location depending on your DOS version.

✎ *Note:* DOS 3.3's bootstrap program was at offset 36 hex. Other versions of DOS will have different locations as well. To find out the specific address for this exercise, type in the following command in DEBUG:

```
U0 L2
```

This command disassembles the JMP instruction at offset zero in the boot sector. (It also assumes you loaded the boot sector at offset zero, otherwise you'll get an INT 20 instruction — and I'll give a nickel to the first person who figures out why that is so.)

22. The final, designated item in the boot sector can be found at offset 1FE hex, the last two bytes of the sector. This is the boot sector "signature," which identifies the sector as the boot sector. The word value will be AA55 hex on all disks.

That wraps it up for the boot sector, a rather interesting and information-filled place on disk. If you'd like to examine your hard drive's boot sector, type the following command in DEBUG:

```
-L0 2 0 1
```

The above L command loads the first sector from the hard drive C to offset zero hex in memory. Use the D command and repeat the above step-by-step journey to explore the specifics of your hard drive if you're so inclined. Just don't change anything; if you do, don't use the W command to write those changes back to your hard drive!

Note: The hard drive's boot sector is actually part of the "logical" hard drive. The true boot sector is the partition table's sector, which will be discussed later in this chapter.

You should also note that some hard drive controllers simulate the hard disk's boot sector for the benefit of programs that snoop there. The actual disk information is usually hidden and inaccessible on these drives. For this chapter, however, you can still peek through the simulated boot sector. (Only the truly sophisticated disk utilities ferret out the true disk information from that simulated in the boot sector.)

Changing the Boot Message

You should never alter the information held in a disk's boot sector. If you do, you'll risk losing all the information on the disk. However, you can alter the boot sector's "Nonsystem disk" error message. This is a fun thing to do with very little risk — especially on a floppy disk.

Reload your floppy disk's boot sector into memory with the following command:

```
-L100 0 0 1
```

Offset 100 hex is being used this time instead of offset zero. Type the following D command to locate the "Nonsystem disk" error message, which will always be located in the second half of the boot sector:

```
-D200 L100
```

If the disk was formatted under DOS 5.0, as the one in Figure 16-1, the message will be at offset 2A0 hex. Other versions of DOS will have the message at different locations, which you should determine on your screen. For example, PC-DOS 3.3 disks have the message at offset 27D hex.

▶ *Tip:* PC-DOS 3.3 also had an additional message in the boot sector: "*Disk Boot failure,*" which appeared at offset 2C0 hex. If you see it, you can change it as well. Try something like, "Oh, shoot!" or an equivalent expletive. Remember to end the string with a zero byte.

What you can do is use the E command to poke in a new message. Then use the W command to write that message out to disk. The new message must be the same length or shorter than the current message. (Under MS-DOS 5.0, the message is 69 bytes long.) Also, the message must end with a zero byte, 00 hex, which you can see at offset 2E5 hex in memory.

If you can think of your own cute message, and keep it within the parameters discussed in the previous program, go for it. Otherwise, you can try the following two E commands to poke in a new boot message:

```
-E 2A0 "You cannot boot this diskette." 0D 0A
-E 2C0 "Replace it and press any key:" 00
```

When you've poked in your new message, confirm that it fits using the following D command:

```
-D 2A0 L60
```

Ensure that your string ends with the byte 00 hex. Also, check to see that it didn't overwrite the first part of IO.SYS at offset 1E6 hex. What I saw on my screen is shown in Figure 16-2. Yours should match if you've been following these instructions to the letter.

If you goofed, reload the boot sector and try again; no damage is done as long as you don't write anything to disk. If everything is okay, write the boot sector back to disk by carefully typing the following command:

```
-W100 0 0 1
```

This command is the exact opposite of the L command you used to load the boot sector. It sticks the boot sector in memory right back to the same spot on disk. Just make sure that second value above is zero and no other number; you don't want to accidentally write a floppy disk's boot sector to a hard drive. (If you do, DOS's MIRROR command can recover from it.)

To test the new boot message, quit DEBUG. Keep the diskette in drive A, and reset your PC. You'll see the error message you poked into memory displayed on

```
2494:02A0  59 6F 75 20 63 61 6E 6E-6F 74 20 62 6F 6F 74 20   You cannot boot
2494:02B0  74 68 69 73 20 64 69 73-6B 65 74 74 65 2E 0D 0A   this diskette...
2494:02C0  52 65 70 6C 61 63 65 20-69 74 20 61 6E 64 20 70   Replace it and p
2494:02D0  72 65 73 73 20 61 6E 79-20 6B 65 79 3A 00 72 65   ress any key:.re
2494:02E0  61 64 79 0D 0A 00 49 4F-20 20 20 20 20 53 59   ady...IO     SY
2494:02F0  53 4D 53 44 4F 53 20 20-20 53 59 53 00 00 55 AA   SMSDOS   SYS..U.
```

Figure 16-2 The modified boot sector message in memory

the screen. Pat yourself on the back, then remove the disk, and continue to boot the computer.

> **Tip:** Some third-party disk formatting programs insert their own boot messages on the boot track. They do this because copying the same boot information as a DOS disk would violate DOS's copyright.
>
> For example, a diskette formatted by the *Norton Format* command has a DOS name and version of "IBM PNCI." The PNCI means Peter Norton Computing, Incorporated. Other information stored in the disk's boot sector is nonstandard, including a hefty error message. Don't freak out if you encounter such a disk; just marvel at the many different ways of doing things in a PC.

The Hard Disk Partition Table

When you boot from a hard drive, you aren't booting directly from your hard disk's boot sector. That disk is actually a *logical* disk sitting on the *physical* hard drive. What's loaded when you first boot a hard drive is the first part of the physical drive. That first sector is actually the hard drive's *partition table*. This is true whether you've partitioned your hard drive or not.

The partition table serves two purposes. First, it describes how the rest of the hard drive is divvied up into logical drives. It contains information about where the various partitions (or logical drives) start, under which operating system they're formatted, and whether or not the partition can be booted. Second, the partition table contains a bootstrap program that will seek out and load the boot sector from the designated boot partition/logical drive.

Obviously, the partition table is a highly sensitive place on a hard drive. If anything happens to it, all the information on your hard drive would be instantly lost. This is why the MIRROR program is used under DOS to help protect your partition table. (If you haven't yet used the MIRROR /PARTN command, do so now; follow the directions on your screen.)

You may have already observed that the partition table was not loaded when you directed DEBUG to load the "boot sector" from your hard drive. What DEBUG did was to load the boot sector from the DOS partition designated as logical drive C. You may have also noticed in that boot sector that one whole track's worth of sectors was marked as "hidden." That's the real boot sector, the partition table.

To load the partition table for examination into DEBUG, you need to use the PC's BIOS Interrupt 13 hex. I do not recommend doing this, however. In fact, doing so under Windows will cause the PC to lose "system integrity." And many antivirus utilities will prevent you from using Interrupt 13 hex. On the bright side, if you're really curious about the boot sector, use *Norton Utilities* or another good disk utility program to examine it.

Norton Utilities will display the information in that sector in a number of formats, including a partition table editing format that's perfect for disk recovery. Figure 16-3 shows the partition table editor from an old version of *Norton Utilities*.

Under DOS, the partition table is read and interpreted using the FDISK program. FDISK's option 4 displays information about your disk's partition. If you elect to use FDISK, do not alter or delete any existing partitions on your hard drive.

> *Tip:* Some of the most nefarious viruses will infect your PC by replacing the partition table with their own programming. These programs will then load the real partition table, which has been moved elsewhere in the hard drive's track 0, after the virus has embedded itself in memory.
>
> To see if you have such a viral infection, use a disk utility to scan all the sectors on your hard drive's track zero. Only the first sector should contain any information. If you see anything other than empty spaces elsewhere, you may have an infection. Use an antivirus utility to remove it.

The File Allocation Table

Just after the boot sector comes the first of two File Allocation Tables on a DOS disk. The size of the table varies depending on the disk's capacity. You can determine the size for any disk by checking offset 16 hex in the boot sector. That word-sized value indicates the number of sectors per FAT for the disk. To keep this presentation in as painless a manner possible, Table 16-5 lists the FAT table sizes for the common disk formats.

> *Note:* No one knows exactly why there are two copies of the FAT. DOS updates both and, consequently, will write errors to both at the same time. Therefore, no real reason exists for having two copies of the same FAT.

```
┌─ Side 0, Cylinder 0, Sector 1 ══════════════════ Partition Table format ─┐
│                                                                          │
│                           Partition Table Editor                         │
│                                                                          │
│         ┌──────┬─────────────────────┬─────────────────────┬──────────┬──────────┐
│         │      │  Starting location  │   Ending location   │ Relative │ Number of│
│  System │ Boot │ Side Cylinder Sector│ Side Cylinder Sector│ Sectors  │ Sectors  │
│         │      │                     │                     │          │          │
│  BIGDOS │ Yes  │   1      0       1  │  63    199      32  │     32   │  409568  │
│  EXTEND │ No   │   0    200       1  │  63    635      32  │  409600  │  892928  │
│    ?    │ No   │   0      0       0  │   0      0       0  │      0   │       0  │
│    ?    │ No   │   0      0       0  │   0      0       0  │      0   │       0  │
│                                                                          │
│                          Press Enter to continue                         │
│  1Help   2Hex     3Text    4Dir    5FAT    6Partn    7    8Choose 9Undo  10QuitNU│
└──────────────────────────────────────────────────────────────────────────┘
```

Figure 16-3 *Norton Utilities* are used to examine a hard drive's partition table

Table 16-5 FAT Sizes for DOS Disk Formats

Disk Type	Sectors/FAT
5¼, 360K	2
3½, 720K	3
5¼, 1.2M	7
3½, 1.4M	9
3½, 2.8M	18
Hard drive	(varies)

What the FAT contains is a map of disk space. The FAT lists all available clusters on a drive, a cluster being one or more contiguous sector. (The number of sectors per cluster can be found at offset D hex in the boot sector.) This is why the size of the FAT varies with disk capacity; a larger capacity disk needs a larger map to show all the available storage.

Whenever DOS writes a file to disk, it checks the FAT for available space. DOS uses information available in the FAT to place the file on disk, searching for an available cluster. When the file is put on disk, its starting cluster number is recorded in its directory entry. That cluster is then marked in the FAT. Any additional clusters are also marked in the FAT. The FAT will map out all the clusters belonging to a file, linking them together. This is how DOS will eventually locate that file and load it into memory.

To summarize, here are the steps DOS takes when it writes a file to disk:

1. Looks for available space in the FAT.

2. Locates a starting cluster for the file, copies the file to that part of the disk.

3. Looks in the FAT for additional clusters, if needed. Writes the next part of the file to that cluster, then updates the FAT, marking each cluster used by the file.

4. Saves the file's name, date, time, size, and starting cluster in a directory entry. (You'll be reading about the directory entry later in this chapter.)

    When DOS needs to access the file again, it loads the directory entry and finds the first cluster using the FAT. Any additional clusters on disk are also located using the information in the FAT.

This method of storing files on disk is by no means efficient. For example, some hard drives have clusters that are 8K in size. It's a waste of disk space to put a 26-byte batch file into an 8K cluster. This makes you wonder why DOS doesn't allocate disk space with one sector equaling one cluster. The reason is overhead: It would take DOS an eternity to scan for and locate the hundreds of thousands of clusters possible on a large hard drive.

Disks, Files, and Stuff 311

The FAT file system allows larger files to be split up into noncontiguous clusters. The FAT keeps track of the pieces, and DOS assembles them just fine. But such fragmented files take longer to load and save, slowing disk access.

✎ ***Note:*** There are several file systems other than the FAT. OS/2 uses a more efficient system called the High Performance File System or HPFS. Windows NT, as well as a yet unnamed future version of DOS, will use the NTFS. These file systems will be more efficient than the FAT, faster, allow for longer filenames, and contain other blessings DOS users have long yearned for. At present, however, we must contend with the FAT.

The important thing is that DOS manages the FAT with few errors and little hassle on our behalf. The next two sections describe how the FAT works as well as how you can find and repair errors in the FAT.

Walking the FAT

Load the boot sector from the floppy disk in drive A using the following command:

```
-L100 0 0 1
```

From the boot sector you need two tidbits of information. First, you need to know which type of FAT the disk is using, the 12-bit or 16-bit FAT. Gather that information with the following command:

```
-D136 L8
```

You'll see either "FAT12" or possibly "FAT16." Most floppy disks use the 12-bit FAT; hard drives use the 16-bit version. It depends on the size of the disk. Commit that information to your short-term memory.

The second piece of information you need is the size of the FAT on your floppy disk:

```
-D116 L2
```

The value you see on your screen is a word value. That probably doesn't matter because the first byte is usually enough to hold the number of sectors the FAT occupies. Use that value with the L command to load your disk's FAT at offset 100 hex. For example:

```
-L100 0 1 9
```

This command is for a 1.4M diskette, although it will successfully load most of the FAT for any other disk as well. The FAT starts at sector 1, and it's 9 sectors long on a 1.4M diskette. Use a command on your system that's compatible with your disk; the first, *L100 0 1* part will be identical to the command shown, but the number of sectors might be different.

Now sitting at offset 100 hex in memory is the first copy of the FAT from your floppy disk. View it with the following command:

```
-D100
```

Don't expect anything to jump out at you. The structure of the FAT is weird and differs from disk to disk, since different things are stored on the disk. The fewer files your disk has, the less "junk" you'll see on the screen. I've loaded up my Sample Disk with several files since the last time it was used. The FAT I see on my screen is extremely busy (see Figure 16-4). Other FATs may contain only a few bytes, then lots of zeros.

The first byte in the FAT is identical to the Media Descriptor Byte ID on your disk, from the boot sector, offset 15 hex. You can also look up this value in Table 16-3. The next two or three bytes will be FF hex. In Figure 16-4, the first byte is F0 hex, indicating a 1.4M diskette (or a 2.8M or 1.2M diskette).

The first two entries of the FAT are always FF hex. If your disk is using the 12-bit FAT, the two bytes FF hex will be seen. If you have a 16-bit FAT, three bytes of FF hex will be seen. This leads into the 12-bit versus 16-bit FAT argument: Why did they choose such a weird number like 12-bits?

The bit size depends on the total capacity of the disk, the total number of clusters available for storing files. The FAT is a map of clusters. In 12 bits of information, you can store 2^{12} or 4,096 different items. This means a disk can have up to 4,096 clusters, all of which are mappable in the FAT. Since only 12 bits are used, the overall size of the FAT on disk is ¼ smaller than it would be if the full 16 bits were used.

On larger capacity disks, a 16-bit FAT is used. This allows for over 65,000 possible clusters. And on the larger disk, a FAT that's 16 bits won't be such a space hog as it would be on a floppy disk.

Those are the arguments. What we're left with are 12-bit FATs used primarily on floppy disks and 16-bit FATs for hard drives. How do you figure a 12-bit FAT? Twelve bits are represented by three hexadecimal digits. Sixteen bits are represented by four. In Figure 16-4, and possibly on your screen, you see a 12-bit FAT. Figure 16-5 shows how to translate that into 12-bit values.

If you thought dealing with word values was strange, welcome to the 12-bit world. Figure 16-5 shows how to translate the 12-bit values into cluster numbers. For the even bytes, you take the first byte plus the lower "nybble" (four bits) of the second byte. With odd bytes, you take the upper "nybble" of the first byte and then the second byte. Reverse the "nybble"/byte values and you have your 12-bit value. Thankfully, this book won't force you to do any 12-bit binary math!

Each of the FAT entries represents a cluster on disk, starting with cluster 2. (Cluster 1 is marked reserved.) Each FAT entry points to the next cluster occupied by a file.

```
2494:0100  F0 FF FF 03 40 00 05 60-00 FF 8F 00 09 A0 00 0B   ....@..'........
2494:0110  C0 00 0D E0 00 0F 00 01-11 20 01 13 40 01 15 60   ......... ..@..'
2494:0120  01 17 80 01 19 A0 01 1B-C0 01 1D E0 01 1F 00 02   ................
2494:0130  21 20 02 23 40 02 25 60-02 27 80 02 29 A0 02 2B   ! .#@.%`.'..)..+
2494:0140  C0 02 2D E0 02 2F 00 03-31 20 03 33 40 03 35 60   ..-../..1 .3@.5`
2494:0150  03 37 80 03 39 A0 03 3B-C0 03 3D E0 03 3F 00 04   .7..9..;..=..?..
2494:0160  41 20 04 43 40 04 45 60-04 47 80 04 49 A0 04 4B   A .C@.E`.G..I..K
2494:0170  C0 04 4D E0 04 4F 00 05-51 20 05 53 40 05 55 60   ..M..O..Q .S@.U`
```

Figure 16-4 The first 128 bytes of a disk's FAT

Disks, Files, and Stuff 313

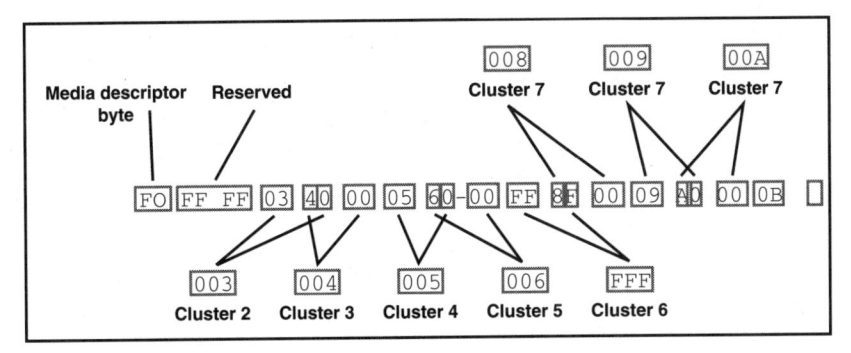

Figure 16-5 How to convert from an 8-bit, byte format to a 12-bit FAT format

The cluster value FFF hex marks the last cluster used by the file. If you look at Figure 16-5, you'll see that the first file on disk sits in clusters 2, 3, 4, 5, and ends in cluster 6. Note how each cluster points to the next one. Confirm this on your screen, where the first file should lay contiguously over the first several clusters.

The clusters marked in the FAT all point to each other, which is how DOS locates and loads files on disk. It's like links in a chain: Cluster 2 points to cluster 3, which points to cluster 4, which finally contains FFF hex marking the end of the file. All the possible values for the cluster entries in the FAT are shown in Table 16-6.

Dealing with a 16-bit FAT is a bit easier, since the values are stored as words. Word values need only have their bytes reversed for you to get the cluster numbers. Twelve-bit values can make you shudder. Fortunately, what we're dealing with is a computer; a program can be written to quickly extract values from the FAT, "walking through the chain" of linked clusters to see where a file sits on disk.

Incidentally, files deleted from disk have all their corresponding clusters in the FAT marked with zero. After all, that space is now available for other files. To prove this, quit DEBUG and delete a file from your Sample Disk. Try to delete one of the first files you put on the disk, since that will show up early in the FAT.

After deleting the file, return to DEBUG. Load the first FAT into memory with the proper L command (described above), then view it with the *D100* command. You should see a parade of zeros where the file once stood.

Table 16-6 Possible Cluster Values in the FAT

12-Bit Value	16-Bit Value	Meaning
000 hex	0000 hex	Available cluster
002 – FEF hex	0002 – FFEF hex	Cluster used by a file; value indicates next cluster in the chain
FF0 – FF6 hex	FFF0 – FFF6 hex	Reserved
FF7 hex	FFF7 hex	Bad sector in the cluster, marked as such during formatting
FF8 – FFF hex	FFF8 – FFFF hex	Last cluster in file

✏️ *Note:* "Undelete" programs work because a file's directory entry isn't completely removed from disk. Using the starting cluster information in the directory entry, plus the file size, an undelete program tries to reconstruct the FAT and recover the file. As long as no new files were written to disk, and given that the disk isn't too badly fragmented, full recovery is almost always possible.

Using the CHKDSK Command

There's no need to traipse mentally through a disk's FAT. After a while your eyeballs would bulge from your head and you would start to be rude to your family. Instead, DOS comes with a handy tool for checking the integrity of a disk's FAT. It's call CHKDSK, the Check Disk command.

What CHKDSK does is to "walk the FAT." It compares clusters marked in the FAT with all the files in all the directories on disk. CHKDSK ensures that each file has clusters assigned to it and that all clusters are assigned to files. If any "rogue" clusters exist, they're flagged as "lost allocation units" or "noncontiguous blocks" or "missing chains." At your command, CHKDSK will convert the lost clusters to files, which you can examine but will probably delete.

How do the lost chains happen? Primarily, it's through sloppy software. If a program only partially writes a file to disk, or you improperly shut down without quitting a program, "half a file" may be on disk. I used to CHKDSK a drive in my old office constantly, bewildered by how it could have so many "lost chains." Then I found out the staff was quitting *WordStar* by whacking the reset switch. "That's the way you're supposed to do it," they bemoaned. Wrong! Always properly quit a program or an environment like Windows before you quit.

I won't bother to go into the details on CHKDSK. You should know, however, that CHKDSK only looks two places when it's run: the boot sector and the FAT. It uses basic information from the boot sector as part of its summary display. The FAT is "walked" to check for lost clusters. CHKDSK does not do a surface scan of the disk; any bad sectors it reports are discovered in the FAT.

▌▶ *Tip:* If you want a real disk-scanning program, check the major third-party utilities. All the biggies offer them, although one of the best is *Disk Technician Advanced*. It's available from Disk Technician Corporation at (619) 274-5000.

The Truth about the Directory

DOS's DIR command is the link between you and the files stored on disk. Internally, DOS knows where files are by looking at the FAT. Externally, you know where files are by identifying their name in a particular subdirectory. The name is what provides the link between the physical file on disk and you as a human.

When you type the DIR command, you're asking DOS to display information about files in the current directory. DIR tells you three things up front:

Disks, Files, and Stuff   315

- The file's name and extension
- The file's size or whether or not the file is a subdirectory
- The date and time the file was saved or last updated (changed).

Additional information is tossed in: the drive's volume name, serial number, and the subdirectory in which you're viewing files. Bonus information includes the total number of bytes used by the files and remaining space on the disk. This is how you locate files, and it proves quite handy and informative.

As usual, DOS is really only giving you part of the picture. It's not exactly holding back information, but there are certain pieces of information stored about a file that aren't displayed in a directory listing. To find that information, you need to look at how DOS stores a directory on disk.

What a Directory Listing Really Looks Like

All directories are files. Specifically, a directory is a database file that contains information about other files stored on disk. When you create a subdirectory, you're actually creating a special type of file — a DOS directory.

All disks come with one main directory. That file is of a given size and sits at a specific location on disk, depending on the disk's capacity. To see how everything works, stick your Sample Disk into drive A if it's not there already. Then enter DEBUG, and type the following command:

```
-L100 0 0 1
```

This command, used so often in this chapter, loads the boot sector from the disk in drive A into memory at offset 100 hex. There are two bits of information needed to help you locate the root directory file and its size: the size of the FATs that come before the root on disk, and the number of entries in the root directory. Start with the following D command:

```
-D 116 L2
```

This D command displays a word of information indicating the size of the FAT in sectors. Two FATs come before the root directory on disk. So to figure out the root directory's starting sector, double the word value you see on your screen and add one to it — one for the boot sector. For example, on a 1.4M diskette, I see the word value 0009 hex. Double that value and you get 12 hex, 18 decimal. Add one and I get 13 hex, the root directory's starting sector:

Root directory starting sector = FAT sector size * 2 + 1
Starting sector = 0009 hex * 2 + 1
Starting sector = 12 hex + 1
Starting sector = 13 hex

Do the same math with the value you see on your screen, then jot down that number.

To obtain the size of the root directory, you need to locate the total number "entries" in the root directory. That's obtained by looking at offset 16 hex in the boot sector. Use this D command:

```
-D111 L2
```

Here, DOS cuts you a break. For floppy disks, the value listed is actually the number of sectors in the root directory. (Good! No math.) However, for a hard drive, the value listed is actually the number of entries in the root directory. (Refer to the Tip box to see how to compute the root directory's size in that case.)

> *Tip:* I don't know why, but it seems only floppy drives give a sector size instead of the root directory entry count that the manual says it provides. Anyway, each directory entry is 32 bytes long. There are 16 entries per sector. Therefore, you take the total number of entries, divide it by 16, and you get the sector size of the root directory.
>
> For example, on my hard drive, there are 0200 hex (512) root directory entries possible. That translates into 20 hex sectors:
>
> Sectors = Entries / 16
>
> Sectors = 512 / 16
>
> Sectors = 32 decimal, 20 hex.

On my system, a 1.4M floppy shows 000E hex sectors in the root directory. That value can be combined with the starting sector of the root directory and used with DEBUG's L command to load the root directory file into disk. If you're having trouble with the math, Table 16-7 will tell you all the information you need to load your floppy disk's root directory. (Now he tells us. . . .)

Select the proper L command from Table 16-7, and type it at DEBUG's hyphen prompt. That will load the root directory file into memory at offset 100 hex. You can then view the file using the D command:

```
-D100
```

Table 16-7 The Root Directory's Starting Sector

Disk Capacity/Size	Root Directory Sector Number	Root Directory Size (Sectors)	L Command
360K/5¼-inch	5 hex	7 hex	L100 0 5 7
720K/3½-inch	7 hex	7 hex	L100 0 7 7
1.2M/5¼-inch	F hex	E hex	L100 0 F E
1.4M/3½-inch	13 hex	E hex	L100 0 13 E
2.8M/3½-inch	25 hex	1C hex	L100 0 25 1C

Disks, Files, and Stuff   317

Table 16-8 Directory Entry Contents, Sizes, and Offset Values

Offset	Length	Description
00 hex	8	Filename, left-justified
08 hex	3	Filename extension, left-justified
0B hex	1	Attribute byte
0C hex	10	Reserved (not used)
16 hex	2	Time field
18 hex	2	Date field
1A hex	2	Starting cluster number
1C hex	4	File size

This command will display the first four entries in the root directory on drive A. Each entry is stored in 32 bits, which translates into two rows on the screen. What you're seeing is all the information DOS saves to disk each time it saves a file. This information is also used by DOS when loading the file into memory. Altogether, there are eight fields of information in a directory entry. Table 16-8 lists them all; Figure 16-6 maps them out on the screen.

1. The first field, the one most immediately identifiable, is the filename field. The filename will be left-justified and padded with space characters (20 hex) if it's less than 8 characters long. Note that the file is converted to uppercase by DOS.

   The first character in a file is significant as far as DOS is concerned:

   - Normally, filenames will start with an ASCII character code value from 21 hex on up to FF hex. This excludes the following, forbidden characters:

     . " / \ [ ] : * | < > + = ; , ?

   You also cannot have a space character or control code in a filename.

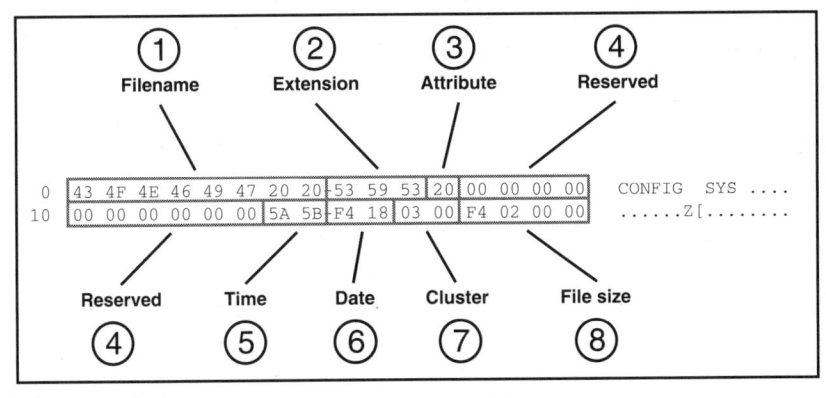

```
      ①            ②           ③           ④
   Filename     Extension   Attribute   Reserved
        \           \          /           /
 0  |43 4F 4E 46 49 47 20 20|53 59 53|20|00 00 00 00|   CONFIG SYS ....
10  |00 00 00 00 00 00|5A 5B|F4 18|03 00|F4 02 00 00|   ......Z[........
       /           /        |         \          \
   Reserved     Time       Date     Cluster    File size
      ④          ⑤          ⑥         ⑦          ⑧
```

Figure 16-6 Directory entry map

- A filename starting with byte 00 hex is "unused," a clean directory entry. (All the other bytes will be zero as well.)

- Filenames starting with byte E5 hex have been deleted. If you see any, note that DOS doesn't remove all of the file's entry; it merely replaces the first character with byte E5 hex — the "tombstone" byte, marking deleted files.

- Since you can start a "live" file with character E5 hex ("σ" the sigma), that character is denoted by the byte value 05 hex. This avoids confusing a filename starting with character E5 hex with a file that's been deleted.

- A filename starting with character 2E hex — the period — is a directory entry. A single 2E hex in the entry earmarks the current directory. A double 2E hex entry marks the parent directory. These are identical to the dot and dot-dot directory entries you see in all DOS subdirectories.

Note: Another exception to the file-naming rule is a volume label — which you'll probably see as the first entry on your Sample Disk. Volume labels do not fit into the file-naming scheme exactly.

2. At offset 8 hex, after the hyphen in DEBUG, you'll see the filename's extension. Up to three characters can be specified. If less than three appear, they'll be left-justified and space characters (20 hex) will fill the remaining bytes.

3. The byte at offset B hex is the file's attribute byte. This byte tells DOS a bit about the file: whether it's a hidden or system file, whether the file identifies a subdirectory or volume label, whether the file is read-only, and whether the file has been modified since the last backup. The bits in the attribute divulge this information to DOS, according to Table 16-9.

Most files will have an attribute of 20 hex, meaning the file has been created or modified since the last backup. If not, the file will have an attribute of 00

Table 16-9 Bits in the Attribute Byte

Bit Pattern:	7	6	5	4	3	2	1	0
Unused	*							
Unused		*						
Archive/File modified			*					
Subdirectory				*				
Volume label					*			
System file						*		
Hidden file							*	
Read-only file								*

hex. Other attributes have to be figured at the bit level. That's easy: Take the hexadecimal value in the byte at offset B hex and look it up in Appendix A. Refer to the bit pattern, then plug in the values in Table 16-9.

For example, my volume label has an attribute byte of 28 hex. That translates into the following bit pattern:

```
0010 1000
```

From Table 16-9, you can tell that the file hasn't been backed up and that it's a volume label.

Starting with DOS 5.0, you have a little bit more control over a file's attribute byte: Both the ATTRIB and DIR commands allow you to examine and change a file's attribute with ease. Prior to DOS 5.0, that could only be done using special utilities. (This process is well documented in the DOS programming manual.)

> ***Tip:*** To display only archive files, use DIR /AA.
> To display only read-only files, use DIR /AR.
> To display only hidden files, use DIR /AH.
> To display only system files, use DIR /AS.
> To display only directories, use DIR /AD.
> To change the read-only attribute of a file, use ATTRIB ±R *filename*.
> To change the archive attribute of a file, use ATTRIB ±A *filename*.
> To change the system attribute of a file, use ATTRIB ±S *filename*.
> To change the hidden attribute of a file, use ATTRIB ±H *filename*.
> To view all files and their attributes, use ATTRIB *.*.

4. The 10 bytes at offset C hex are marked "reserved." They serve no function under DOS.

5. The word value at offset 16 hex is the file's time field. This is where DOS stores the time the file was last saved to disk. As you may have feared, this number uses a bit pattern to store the hours, minutes, and seconds. Table 16-10 shows how the bits fit, although you shouldn't ever worry about deciphering these bytes; the DIR command does a fine job of it.

6. The word value at offset 18 hex holds the file's date field. Like the time field, this value is stored in a bit pattern that no one in their right mind could figure out by squinting at it. The secrets the bits hold are listed in Table 16-10, along with the time field bit patterns.

> ***Note:*** The time word stores seconds as two-second intervals. You will never see a file saved to disk at an odd number of seconds after the hour!
> The date field's year bit pattern is relative to 1980. Year 0=1980, and Year 13=1993. Incidentally, the 7 bits available for the year can hold a value as big as 127. That means DOS is good until the year 2107. (I'd hate to be the user who tries to boot his PC on New Year's Day, 2108!)

Table 16-10 Time and Date Field Bit Patterns

Bit Pattern:	F	E	D	C	B	A	9	8	7	6	5	4	3	2	1	0
Seconds												X	X	X	X	X
Minutes						X	X	X	X	X	X					
Hours	X	X	X	X	X											

Bit Pattern:	F	E	D	C	B	A	9	8	7	6	5	4	3	2	1	0
Day												X	X	X	X	X
Month								X	X	X	X					
Year	X	X	X	X	X	X	X									

7. The word value at offset 1A hex indicates the staring cluster number for the file. This is the link between the bytes stored on disk and the filename you see in the DIR command. In a way, the starting cluster number is the file's "address" on disk. In Figure 16-6, the starting cluster for CONFIG.SYS is 3. This is how DOS locates the file on disk. It would also look into the FAT to see if there are any additional clusters that make up the file.

8. The final piece of information in the directory entry can be found at offset 1C hex. It's a four-byte, double word value that indicates the file size. These bytes are listed in the directory entry 100-percent backward (although the microprocessor and compilers read them out well). In DEBUG, you have to do some reassembling to put things together. For example, in Figure 16-6, the size of CONFIG.SYS is shown using the following bytes:

```
F4 02 00 00
```

This translates into the double word value:

```
0000 02F4
```

In decimal, the file is 756 bytes long. As usual, I used a hexadecimal-decimal calculator to figure that out. Of course, it's much easier just to use the DIR command under DOS. But now you know how that information is stored on the disk.

Tip: The double word value means that a file under DOS can be up to 4,294,967,295 bytes long. Call it "four megabytes." That's truly a Department of Defense–sized number.

Finding a Subdirectory

Quit DEBUG, and log on to drive A. You're going to create a subdirectory on drive A, then return to DEBUG and hunt that subdirectory down on disk using the

Disks, Files, and Stuff 321

contents of the directory entry. This isn't as painful as it sounds, and it will show you how the directory entry and FAT work together to store information on disk.

At the DOS prompt on drive A, create a subdirectory. Name it SUBDIR:

`A:\> MD SUBDIR`

Copy a few files to this new subdirectory, just one or two. You'll need some files to see in the directory listing when you peer at this part of disk using DEBUG. When you're done, log on to another disk.

Start DEBUG again, and load the root directory into memory. Use the same command you used in the previous section, or refer to Table 16-7. Type the *D 100* command, and search for the SUBDIR entry. You may have to type *D* a few more times to find it.

Once you find SUBDIR, take a minute to look it over. Figure 16-7 shows how that entry looks on my screen. The attribute byte at offset B hex (1CB hex in the figure) is 10 hex, identifying the file as a directory. Also, the file's size is shown as 00 00 00 00. But the key value to look for is at offset 1A hex from the entry's start; that's the starting cluster number for the subdirectory.

▶ *Tip:* You'll notice in Figure 16-7, and on your screen, that a directory's size on disk is zero — four 00 hex bytes. That's not entirely true. DOS allocates one or two clusters for each subdirectory you create. They aren't counted as bytes used by files, although they are clusters used on disk.

Subdirectories do take up space — you've seen it firsthand. This is verified by using the CHKDSK command. The *xxx bytes in yy directories* summary tells you how many directories are on the disk, not including the root directory.

You can't really divide *xxx* by *yy* to get the number of clusters per directory, since DOS extends a subdirectory should it get full. This is yet another miracle of subdirectories: In addition to helping you organize your files, when a subdirectory gets too full, DOS will allocate more clusters to it, just as it would to a file you made larger.

Take a moment to look for the starting cluster number on your screen. In Figure 16-7, it's 000D hex. It will probably be different on your screen. Whatever, the object here is to locate that sector on disk and load it into memory for observation. This can be tricky.

When you know a cluster number and want a sector number, you need to do a wee bit of math. First, you need to know two things:

1. There isn't a 1:1 relationship between sectors and clusters, even if the cluster size is one sector.

2. The first cluster used to store a file is cluster 2, not cluster 1 or cluster 0.

```
25A4:01C0   53 55 42 44 49 52 20 20-20 20 20 10 00 00 00 00   SUBDIR     .....
25A4:01D0   00 00 00 00 00 00 7C 7D-F4 18 0D 00 00 00 00 00   ......|}........
```

Figure 16-7 The SUBDIR directory file, "raw" on disk

To find out how many sectors there are per cluster on a disk, you need to look at offset D hex in the boot sector. Then you need to know where the first cluster (cluster number 2) starts on disk. To figure that out, you need to know the size of the FATs and the root directory. Basically, you need to know a lot of stuff. I've conveniently summarized this information in Table 16-11.

If you have 1.4M floppy, then the first cluster starts at sector 21 hex. It's cluster number 2, and there are 1 sectors per cluster on the disk. To figure out where a specific cluster is located, you need to plug this information into the following formula:

Sector = Starting Cluster Sector# + ((Cluster − 2) * Sectors/Cluster)

The SUBDIR entry in Figure 16-7 is in cluster 000D hex. Using that information, plus the goodies from Table 16-11, I can work the formula as follows:

Sector = Starting Cluster Sector# + ((Cluster − 2) * Sectors/Cluster)
Sector = 21 hex + ((000D hex − 2) * 1)
Sector = 21 hex + (B hex) * 1
Sector = 21 hex + B hex
Sector = 2C hex

The "file" SUBDIR can be found at sector 2C hex on the disk. To load that sector, I'll use the following L command:

```
-L100 0 2C 1
```

That command loads sector 2C hex into memory at offset 100 hex.

You need to repeat these steps for the cluster used by SUBDIR on your screen. Plug the proper values into the formula from Table 16-11. Then use the resulting sector number with the L command; load in only one sector.

When the sector is in memory, display it with the *D100* command. What you see should look similar to Figure 16-8. If not, then you miscalculated the sector number in the formula. Try again if you like, or just continue reading (but tell everyone you did it just to impress them).

Table 16-11 Starting Cluster Locations for Various Disk Capacities

Disk Capacity/Size	Starting Cluster Sector Number	Sectors/Cluster
360K/5¼-inch	C hex	2
720K/3½-inch	E hex	2
1.2M/5¼-inch	1D hex	1
1.4M/3½-inch	21 hex	1
2.8M/3½-inch	65 hex	1

```
-D100
25A4:0100  2E 20 20 20 20 20 20 20-20 20 20 10 00 00 00 00   .               .....
25A4:0110  00 00 00 00 00 00 7C 7D-F4 18 0D 00 00 00 00 00   ......|}........
25A4:0120  2E 2E 20 20 20 20 20 20-20 20 20 10 00 00 00 00   ..              .....
25A4:0130  00 00 00 00 00 00 7C 7D-F4 18 00 00 00 00 00 00   ......|}........
25A4:0140  53 54 41 52 54 53 59 53-20 20 20 00 00 00 00 00   STARTSYS   ....
25A4:0150  00 00 00 00 00 00 81 5B-F4 18 0F 00 11 00 00 00   .......[........
25A4:0160  43 4F 4E 46 49 47 20 20-53 59 53 20 00 00 00 00   CONFIG  SYS ....
25A4:0170  00 00 00 00 00 00 5A 5B-F4 18 10 00 F4 02 00 00   ......Z[........
```

Figure 16-8 The subdirectory's sector in memory

Note: For extra help, here is how you can load a specific cluster on a 720K diskette, where there are 2 sectors per cluster. Assume the root directory says the SUBDIR is located at sector 21E hex:

Sector = Starting Cluster Sector# + ((Cluster − 2) * Sectors/Cluster)

Sector = E hex + ((21E hex − 2) * 2)

Sector = E hex + (21C hex * 2)

Sector = E hex + 438 hex

Sector = 446 hex

The SUBDIR directory is found at sector 446 hex. It would be loaded with the following command:

```
-L100 0 446 1
```

On your screen, and in Figure 16-8, you see the subdirectory file on disk. The first two entries are dot and dot-dot — both directories, which can be seen from their 10 hex attribute. Other files are listed in the subdirectory just as in the root directory.

What you've done is exactly what DOS does when it goes out to disk to load a file. It checks the directory entry, gets the cluster number, calculates the absolute sector number, then loads in the file. DOS also checks the FAT, taking note of all the clusters used by the file and loading each into memory from disk. Thanks to the microprocessor and DOS's internal programming, this happens as fast as the hardware can make it happen. You've just done it manually, which is a feat in itself.

Granted, there's not much you can really do by hunting down sectors and clusters. However, getting your hands dirty in a disk like this can help in complex file recovery. For example, suppose the UNDELETE command claims that the "first cluster of the file isn't available." You can use DEBUG to load that directory into memory, then look up the file's first cluster for yourself. You can even step through the FAT to look for pieces of the file which may still be on disk. If you find a scattered sector or cluster, load it into memory with DEBUG, then use the N and W commands to write it out to a file on disk.

Sometimes DEBUG isn't the best vehicle for repairing disks at the byte level. *Norton Utilities* or Mace's *Muse* facilitate reading and writing disks. Often you can work with clusters as the basic unit instead of sectors, which makes file hunting easier. And if the disk utility lets you easily walk through the FAT, all the better. (Since these utilities are constantly being changed and updated, I can't recommend anything outright.)

17

File Editing in DEBUG

Chomping through a disk byte by byte is only half the fun you can have with disks in DEBUG. The other half involves what I call "hard-core file editing." This is where you take advantage of DEBUG as a byte editor. Just as a word processor edits words, you can use DEBUG to manipulate bytes in a file — sometimes with humorous results. This chapter discusses how you can do that with DEBUG, as well as how DEBUG can be used to resuscitate files lost in memory.

Hard-Core File Editing

Taking a file and modifying it a byte at a time is technically referred to as *patching*. Many operating systems, including IBM's OS/2, have a PATCH command. That command reads a script, similar to a DEBUG script, and uses the information to alter or update a program file on disk.

Normally an operating system must be patching-compatible. My old TRS-80 had lots of software that had rows and rows of "PATCH" text hidden in each program file. That allowed the programmer to create new routines, update programs, and fix bugs after the product was released. DOS lacks this facility, but you can still effectively patch programs using DEBUG.

Patching is very dangerous. In all cases, I recommend patching a backup version of a program and testing it before using it every day. And since DOS programs aren't built around the patching idea, you've got to be extremely careful with what you alter. If there was ever a possibility that anything could run amok, patching a program increases that possibility.

Editing a Program File

You can use DEBUG to load and edit a COM file on disk. The same can be done with an EXE file, but you need to rename it to BIN so that you can properly edit the file's disk image. Either way, editing should take place on a copy of the file and only after it's been tested should you replace the original with the edited copy.

What can you change? Not much, really. Unless you know a PC very well and can stand using DEBUG's U command to unassemble and observe how a program works, patching is a limited art form. However, one thing that can be readily changed are the text prompts in a COM or EXE file.

Text strings in a program are "static," displaying information or prompting for input. They don't change, nor are their contents examined. The program displays the string by specifying its offset and then printing all the text characters one at a time until a specific byte is encountered. You can change those strings by replacing the string in memory with one of equal or shorter length and ending it with the same zero byte. This is similar to what was done in the last chapter to change the message in the boot sector.

▶ *Tip:* The byte that ends strings in most programs is typically 00 hex, although some DOS programs use byte 24 hex — the dollar sign ($) — to mark the end of a string. Either way, as long as the new string is equal to or shorter than the original's length, and it ends in that byte, you can freely patch away.

To test this idea, select a good program as a candidate for patching. A small COM file would be nice, although DOS doesn't really come with any good COM files anymore. Instead, consider the innocuous LABEL.EXE program: it's short, does something minor and inconsequential, and the program can't really damage your system if it messes up. It's perfect.

Your first step is to copy LABEL.EXE to a BIN file for editing in DEBUG. I recommend copying the file to a RAM drive or a subdirectory not on the path. For example, my RAM drive is G:

```
G:\> COPY C:\DOS\LABEL.EXE LABEL.BIN
```

Here, LABEL.EXE is copied to RAM drive G and renamed LABEL.BIN. Your next step is to edit LABEL.BIN in DEBUG:

```
G:\> DEBUG LABEL.BIN
-
```

Use the D command to page through the file and scan for any text strings. They will probably be lumped together, usually near the end of the file. With DOS 5.0's version of the LABEL command, I found the strings starting at offset 1F00 in DEBUG, which you can see in Figure 17-1.

Note which character ends the strings. In Figure 17-1, you see that the zero byte, 00 hex, is used. Continue to page through memory to examine each of the strings.

```
-D1F00
25A4:1F00  B4 00 8B 5E 04 89 07 33-C0 5D C3 00 00 00 00 00   ...^...3.]......
25A4:1F10  00 00 00 00 00 00 00 00-4D 53 20 52 75 6E 2D 54   ........MS Run-T
25A4:1F20  69 6D 65 20 4C 69 62 72-61 72 79 20 2D 20 43 6F   ime Library - Co
25A4:1F30  70 79 72 69 67 68 74 20-28 63 29 20 31 39 38 38   pyright (c) 1988
25A4:1F40  2C 20 4D 69 63 72 6F 73-6F 66 74 20 43 6F 72 70   , Microsoft Corp
25A4:1F50  11 00 00 49 6E 63 6F 72-72 65 63 74 20 44 4F 53   ...Incorrect DOS
25A4:1F60  20 76 65 72 73 69 6F 6E-0D 0A 00 43 61 6E 6E 6F    version...Canno
25A4:1F70  74 20 6C 61 62 65 6C 20-61 20 4A 4F 49 4E 65 64   t label a JOINed
```

Figure 17-1 The start of the strings in the LABEL command

If you're familiar with the LABEL command, you should recognize a few of them. Some of them will be error messages you may not have seen before.

The hard part comes after you locate the strings: You need to find each string's starting address and length in memory. The starting address tells you where to patch in a new string, the length tells you how long the new string can be. You'll also need to see which characters start and end the string and keep your new string similar. For example, some strings end with the space character, 20 hex. Others may add a carriage return/line feed, 0D hex and 0A hex. And others may start with a space character. Be observant! You'll need to patch in your replacement strings with those same characters or you'll goof up the display.

> *Tip:* Important characters to watch for at the start and end of a text string are: 20 hex, the space; 09 hex, a tab character; 07 hex, the "beep"; 0D 0A, a carriage return/line feed; 2E, the period; 2A and 2B, the colon and semicolon; and 2C, the comma. You get the idea.

Because I'm in a good mood today, I've already gone through LABEL.BIN in memory and mapped out all the vital strings and their offsets in DEBUG and lengths. Everything is stuck into Table 17-1 for your convenience.

> *Note:* The statistics in Table 17-1, as well as all the patching commands in this section are to the LABEL command that comes with DOS version 5.0. The original LABEL.EXE file is 9,390 bytes long and its date is 4-09-91 at 5:00a. If the numbers don't match up on your screen, you'll need to locate the specific offsets and lengths yourself. Do not blindly patch a program unless you confirm those addresses!

We could patch in silly messages all over, replacing error messages with nondescriptive expletives and just have a good ol' time. Instead, try a few subtle modifications this first time around. For example, consider changing the "has no label" at offset 1FD1 to "is labelless." I know, *labelless* is not a word, but it's cute. That way, when the program runs, it will say "Volume in drive X is labelless" instead of "has no label." Use the following command to patch in the new string:

```
-E 1FC3 " is labelless" 0
```

Table 17-1 The LABEL Command's String Offsets and Lengths

Offset	Size	String/Contents
1F53	18	"Incorrect DOS version" 0D 0A 00
1F6B	33	"Cannot label a JOINed, SUBSTed or ASSIGNed drive" 0D 0A 00
1F9E	25	"Invalid characters in volume label" 0D 0A 00
1FC3	0E	"has no label" 00
1FD1	11	"Volume in drive " 00
1FE2	05	"is " 00
1FE7	2F	"Volume label (11 characters, ENTER for none)? " 00
2016	19	"Volume Serial Number is " 00
202F	02	"-" 00
2031	24	"Delete current volume label (Y/N)? " 00
2055	3A	"Creates, changes, or deletes the volume label of a disk" 0D 0A 00
2090	18	"LABEL [drive:][label]" 0D 0A 00
20A8	1D	"Cannot label a network drive" 00
20C5	1C	"Invalid drive specification" 00
20E1	1A	"Incorrect drive syntax - " 00
20FB	1C	"Cannot make directory entry" 00
2117	17	"Unexpected End of File" 00
212E	21	"Multiple drive letters specified" 00
214F	26	"Too many characters in volume label" 0D 0A 00
2174	2B	"Drive letter cannot be inside volume label" 00

Note that there is a space before the "is" above. The new string ends with a null byte, and it's exactly the same size as the original. Confirm this with the following D command:

```
-D1FC3 LE
```

You should see only the string you patched, and the last byte displayed — at offset 1FD0, should be 00 hex. If so, you've successfully patched in the string.

> **Tip:** Always verify that the string you entered is poked into the proper place. Do this by using the D command followed by the string's offset and maximum length. As long as you see a zero byte marking the end of your string, you're okay.
>
> If the new string doesn't fit, quit DEBUG. Restart it by reloading your file and continue to edit. Nothing is damaged as long as you don't write the file to disk. (Even if you did, damage is done to the backup file, not the original.)

File Editing in DEBUG 329

How about that horrid prompt, "Volume label (11 characters, ENTER for none)?" Try making it a bit more descriptive by patching in the following:

```
-E1FE7 "Type new label; 11 chars. max; Enter deletes: " 00
```

Note that the string ends with a space character after the colon. Type the following D command to confirm that the string fits:

```
-D1FE7 L2F
```

▶ ***Tip:*** I'm using the offset and length values from Table 17-1 to confirm that the new string fits. Those values were obtained when I first loaded the file for patching. It took a while to locate and catalog them all, however, in the real world you'll only need to keep track of the strings you'll be replacing.

When you catalog strings in a program file, use the D command in DEBUG with the offset and length values *before* you patch in a new string. This will confirm that you have the offset and length down properly before you proceed.

Here's a chance for some wit. Replace the humorless "Too many characters in volume label" error message with the following:

```
-E214F "Is that a volume label or a novel?" 0D 0A 00
```

Use the following D command to make sure that it fits:

```
-D214F L26
```

This is an example of a patched string that's less than its original. You'll see two zero hex bytes at offset 2174 hex. That's okay; the program only needs the starting offset and a zero to end the string. By all means, shorter strings work fine. Just remember to cap them with a space, or a carriage return/line feed, as was done above.

Three patches are enough for a single session. (Actually, one patch is enough.) Write the file back to disk and quit:

```
-W
Writing 024AE bytes
-Q
```

In order to test the new version of the LABEL command, you'll need to rename it back to an EXE file. Continue to do this on your RAM drive or in a test subdirectory. Do not replace the original LABEL.EXE file until you're sure the patched version works.

```
G:\> REN LABEL.BIN LABEL.EXE
```

Now type the LABEL command. You'll see something like the following:

```
Volume in drive G is RAM
Type new label; 11 chars. max; Enter deletes:
```

There is your first prompt. Hopefully it worked on your system and displayed exactly as you intended. (If not, recopy LABEL.EXE from your DOS subdirectory and start over.)

Delete the label by pressing Enter and then Y at the next prompt. Then use the LABEL command again:

```
Volume in drive G is labelless
Type new label; 11 chars. max; Enter deletes:
```

If you see "is labelless," then the second patch worked. To confirm the third patch, you'll need to specify a long label name at the DOS prompt. Press Ctrl-C, then at the DOS prompt enter the following:

```
G:\> LABEL I JUST CAN'T THINK OF ANYTHING SHORTER
Is that a volume label or a novel?

Volume in drive G is labelless
Type new label; 11 chars. max; Enter deletes:
```

If everything works, then you have successfully patched a program file. Feel free to select another file or continue to work with LABEL. Remember the rule about renaming EXE files to BIN. Also, only work with backup files and confirm that they work before writing them back to your main directories.

▶ *Tip:* Even if your patched file works, keep the original around "just in case." I rename my original DOS files to *.ORG for safekeeping.

Patching COMMAND.COM

Patching COMMAND.COM is a bad idea. It's just too important a file to mess with. Some intrepid users will come up with interesting patches: a patch that forces DOS to start all batch files with the ECHO OFF condition; a patch that causes DOS to come up in a specific color; patches to modify DOS for operation with certain hardware; a patch to remove the Ctrl-P, echo-to-printer command; and so on.

Most of the patches are provided as script files. Essentially, all the necessary commands are written in a text file that's redirected into DEBUG. The script files are tested to eliminate the possibility of typos that would really wreak havoc in COMMAND.COM

The problems with patching COMMAND.COM are many. Primarily, there are so many different versions of DOS that writing a definitive COMMAND.COM patch is dangerous. And Compaq DOS, Tandy DOS, and other "OEM" versions may have different COMMAND.COM files within even a single release of DOS.

Individually, you can still patch your own copy of COMMAND.COM. Poking in dirty words or insults over the common error messages is a practical use of your time and enjoyable by all. I'll leave that exercise up to you to complete (or wait until the unabridged version of this book appears). However, one thing I will step you through is patching the run order for COM, EXE, and BAT files.

When faced with three program files, named *something*.COM, *something*.EXE, and *something*.BAT, DOS will only run the COM file. When the EXE and BAT files exist, the EXE file wins the fistfight. This is because of a string of text in COMMAND.COM, ".COM.EXE.BAT," which tells COMMAND.COM how to run program files.

If you want to patch the order in which program files are run, copy COMMAND.COM to a backup file, COMMAND.BIN. Load the backup file into DEBUG, then locate ".COM.EXE.BAT" with the following command:

```
-S100 FFFF ".COM.EXE.BAT"
```

✎ *Note:* The S command searches from offset 100 hex up through offset FFFF hex. There is no L command since you're only dealing with an offset address.

On my system, DEBUG shot back with the offset address AA56 hex. If I wanted to patch COMMAND.COM to run BAT files first, the following E command could be used:

```
-EAA56 ".BAT.COM.EXE"
```

Writing that change back to disk patches COMMAND.BIN. Renaming that file to COMMAND.COM means that the run order for program files has been changed.

This is only a minor example of patching COMMAND.COM. Patching COMMAND.COM is generally risky; however, feel free to experiment on your own carefully though. (My joke copy of COMMAND.COM, renamed CMD.COM, contains all sorts of insults instead of error messages. People get a kick out of it, and it really wasn't that much work to put together.)

Document Rescue and Recovery

DEBUG's W command will write any swath of memory out to disk. You give the chunk of memory a name with the N command, put the size into the CX register (and use BX if the file is more than 64K in length), and specify its starting address with W. Zap! The file's on disk. But what is there in memory worth saving? A lot, especially if you're just "bombed out" of a program.

This isn't anything I can readily demonstrate. Unfortunately (or fortunately, if it ever happens), DEBUG is usually best at rescuing very large documents in memory. You can't just demonstrate this by typing in a quick file in EDLIN and then bailing out. The file has to be hefty enough to cover a large expanse of RAM. If not, then DEBUG will probably overwrite most of it when it's loaded into memory.

✎ *Note:* Nothing can save your program in memory if you reset or have to turn the PC off. This usually zeroes out all of RAM. I've heard of some computers that may not erase the contents of RAM after a reset, but personal experience has shown me that (sadly) it's just not true.

If you do have something large looming in memory, or even if you don't and you want to save anything left there, then follow these steps:

1. Enter DEBUG.

2. Use the S command to search for some keyword in your text. For example, suppose this chapter flew off into bit ether while I was writing. Suddenly, the DOS prompt stared me in the face. I could curse that I didn't save the file or back it up. That wouldn't do any good. However, the program did save most of the document in RAM, where I may be able to find a bit or piece. The key is to search for a piece of text unique to what you've lost. For this example, that would be "Chapter 17," which is how I started this document:

   ```
   -S1000:0 LFFFF "Chapter 17"
   ```

   This command searches all of bank 1 in memory for the "Chapter 17" text. The text must match *exactly* what you're looking for; DEBUG won't match "C" with "c"; it's case sensitive.

   After you press Enter, you may see a few instances of your text — especially if DEBUG is also loaded into bank 1. For example:

   ```
   1000:1207
   1000:1E77
   1000:1E86
   ```

   You should check out the above addresses. The odds are pretty good, however, they'll be DEBUG's internal text storage buffers and not the start of Chapter 17. Thus begins your search through all of memory.

3. Type each of the following S commands to scan all of conventional memory for your text:

   ```
   -S2000:0 LFFFF "Chapter 17"
   -S3000:0 LFFFF "Chapter 17"
   -S4000:0 LFFFF "Chapter 17"
   -S5000:0 LFFFF "Chapter 17"
   -S6000:0 LFFFF "Chapter 17"
   -S7000:0 LFFFF "Chapter 17"
   -S8000:0 LFFFF "Chapter 17"
   -S9000:0 LFFFF "Chapter 17"
   ```

▸ ***Tip:*** Just type S and the bank number, then press the F3 key. That repeats the entire command and avoids typos.

You only need to search from banks 1 through 9. Your program probably wouldn't store anything in upper or expanded memory.

Bank zero need not be searched since it contains mostly DOS and BIOS information and, if your program was loaded there, it probably didn't store any information that low in memory.

File Editing in DEBUG   333

Hopefully, the text will be located. If so, you'll see a *segment:address* pop up. Make a note of it, but continue to search through all of memory.

If your text isn't found, try searching for something else, preferably something shorter. Some word processors (or any software) may store special characters between words instead of the space character. Be specific, brief, and try again. If nothing is found the second time around, you can try looking all through memory with the D command:

```
-D1000 LFFFFF
```

This avenue is slower and will blur your eyeballs like nothing else. Use it as a last resort to locate the text. If the text isn't found, then you're stuck out of luck.

4. Take any addresses that popped up and examine them using the D command. For example, suppose the text was located in bank 5000 at offset 625C hex. You'd see the following:

```
-S5000:0 LFFFF "Chapter 17"
5000:625C
```

After scanning the rest of memory, go back and use the D command to look at your "hits." You may see something similar to that shown in Figure 17-2. Now you know the starting address.

5. Continue to use the D command to find the ending address.

As you scan the text, you'll notice that it's fairly intact. If not, then at least it's there. I've seen some text sequestered in memory where every other byte looks corrupted. Restoring it to its original form takes time, but that's a choice you need to make.

6. After locating the end of the text with the D command, note the address. Use that address with the H command to calculate the size. Plug the starting and ending addresses for the text into the following formula:

```
H ending starting
```

```
-d5000:6250

5000:6250  00 00 00 3C 00 FE 00 00-00 00 25 43 68 61 70   .........%Chap
5000:6260  74 65 72 20 31 37 0D 0A-0D 0A 49 74 20 77 61 73   ter 17....It was
5000:6270  20 61 20 64 61 72 6B 20-61 6E 64 20 73 74 6F 72    a dark and stor
5000:6280  6D 79 20 6E 69 67 68 74-2E 20 20 53 75 64 64 65   my night.  Sudde
5000:6290  6E 6C 79 2C 74 68 65 20-64 6F 6F 72 62 65 6C 6C   nly,the doorbell
5000:62A0  20 72 61 6E 67 2E 20 49-74 20 77 61 73 20 74 68    rang. It was th
5000:62B0  65 20 70 69 7A 7A 61 20-67 75 79 2C 20 62 75 74   e pizza guy, but
5000:62C0  20 68 65 20 73 6D 65 6C-6C 65 64 20 6C 69 6B 65    he smelled like
-q
```

Figure 17-2   The text is found in memory

DEBUG will spit out two values; the first is the sum and the second is the difference. You want the difference.

> **Tip:** Suppose the chunk of memory you want spans a bank of memory? No problem: simply calculate the absolute memory address. For example, suppose your text starts address 3000:F810. That equals absolute address 3F810. Reset the DS register to that segment — the first four digits:
>
> ```
> -RDS
> DS xxxx
> :3F81
> ```
>
> Then use the D command starting at offset zero and then refind the end of the block.

7. Take the difference of the two addresses and plug that value into the CX register. For example, suppose the file started at offset 62C0 hex in bank 5 and ends at offset 917D hex. Here is the H command to calculate the size of the block:

    ```
    -H 917D 62C5
    F442 2EB8
    ```

    The difference is 2EB8 hex. But be safe: specify 2EC0 hex or even 2F00 hex in the CX register:

    ```
    -RCX
    CX xxxx
    :2F00
    ```

8. Give the file a name — not the original name. For example, name it RESCUE.BIN:

    ```
    -N RESCUE.BIN
    ```

9. Specify the block's exact starting address with the W command. For example:

    ```
    -W5000:62C5
    ```

    The W command will write the block to disk.

10. Use a text editor to edit the block. A text editor is a much more flexible thing than your word processor. The idea here is to create a text file with all the content of your document intact. If you try a word processor, it may stumble on some stray byte in memory and not load the file. Of course, there is an off chance that it may load the file perfectly. If so, consider popping open a fresh carbonated beverage of your choice and celebrating.

This technique for fishing lost files out of RAM is an old, time-honored tradition. Obviously, it works best with text files that you can readily read. Data base files can also be rescued, although maybe not in the perfect data base format. And spreadsheet and other files, they're a bit riskier to rescue. If you're really good, you may pull it off. I wish you the best of luck.

> ***Tip:*** The best way to rescue a document locked in RAM? Backup! Many applications offer a timed backup feature. *WordPerfect* is set to back up a document every five minutes on my system. The most text I've ever lost is a page. Even so, I was thankful for that timed backup.

18

Programming in DEBUG

At last, it's come to this. If you're this far in this book and haven't yet realized what a useful and needlessly neglected tool DEBUG is, then I have one more trick to show you: programming. Although I can't fully describe the art of programming in a single chapter, I can shed some light on using DEBUG as a programming tool. This starts with a thorough discussion of DEBUG scripts, how they create programs, and how to create them. Then you'll see a few scripts firsthand and discover how they program the computer to do interesting and useful things.

Hip Deep in Scripts

Only the very best PC programmers can sit down and compose a little utility in DEBUG. You have to be very, very good. Programs written in DEBUG are written "top-down." You start at offset 100 hex and work down the screen writing one line after the other. You have no idea where text strings will be located; where jump, loop or call address will be; or any other offsets that may occur later in the program. You can fake it for a while, but that gets tedious.

The solution is to compose the program in an assembler, compile it, then disassemble it in DEBUG. That's how most of the pros write their script files, and that's how I've written them in the past:

1. Create the program (write it, test it, debug it, etc.)
2. Load the program into DEBUG.
3. Create the script file.
4. Test the script file.

Once you have a program written and working, turning it into a script file for DEBUG is a snap. The hardest part is creating the program and getting it to work. Also, only a special kind of program works as a DEBUG script. At over 2 megabytes, no one would want to type in the script for EXCEL.EXE. Most magazines I work with want scripts less than 20 lines, although I've often seen 50 line scripts. Whatever, the end result should be something quick to type and useful.

Creating the Program

DEBUG scripts begin their lives as a thought. The programmer will dream up something useful. I did that for Chapter 5. I needed an example of a filter other than DOS's SORT, MORE, and FIND. What I came up with was 2UPPER, a filter that converts lowercase into uppercase. It's a short program, useful but not crucial, and it makes an excellent DEBUG script.

2UPPER began its life like all assembly language programs. It went through the following steps:

1. 2UPPER.ASM, the "source code" was composed in a text editor (see Figure 18-1).

2. 2UPPER.ASM was compiled into an "object file" using Borland's *Turbo Assembler* program, TASM. The resulting file was 2UPPER.OBJ.

3. 2UPPER.OBJ was converted to an EXE file by the TASM assembler, which was immediately converted into 2UPPER.COM.

Figure 18-1 shows the source code for 2UPPER.COM. With the assembler, I was able to create a program using comments, labels, and procedures — each of them an advantage over composing the entire program in DEBUG. Also, I wasn't hindered by having to work in hexadecimal.

2UPPER.COM contains three routines or procedures: Main, Get, and Put. Get and Put are two parts of the filter: they read and write bytes to and from DOS's standard input and output devices. That way the filter can be used with I/O redirection and the pipe, as you saw in Chapter 5. The Main routine provides the engine that modifies the bytes moving from standard input to standard output.

Note: Figure 5-5 contained the basic layout for a filter. "The machine" in 2UPPER is in the Main procedure. Get and Put are named exactly as they appear in the flow chart.

In Figure 18-1, you'll see how the CALL command is used with GET and PUT in the main section. Also, notice how the CMP, compare, command is used with 'a' and 'z' to select lowercase letters only. These are luxuries you have only in an assembler; it will translate 'a' into the hexadecimal code for the letter "a" for you.

Tip: The key to the 2UPPER filter is the AND AL,'_' instruction right up front. The underline character is used to represent the byte value 5F hex. When that byte is logically ANDed with a lowercase letter, bit 5 in the byte is reset to zero. From Appendix A, you'll see all that separates lowercase from uppercase in ASCII is bit 5.

```
;To Upper case (C) 1992 Dan Gookin
;Written by Dan Gookin, April 11, 1992
;This is Turbo Assembler from Borland

      NAME UPPER2

COMMENT *

This is an example of a filter program.  It reads in a character
from standard input, modifies it, then spits it back out through
standard output.

The main routine is called "keep_reading."  It's also the
"engine" by which the filter works: A character is converted
from lowercase to uppercase.

The GET routine reads a single character from standard input.

The PUT routine sends a character to standard output.

Both GET and PUT handle limited errors that may crop up.

* (end of comment)

      .MODEL small
      .CODE
      Org 100h                  ;This is a COM file
      IDEAL

proc Main
Start:

keep_reading:
      call get                  ;read in the data
      cmp al,'a'                ;narrow search to
      jl skip                   ; alphabetic chars.
      cmp al,'z'
      jg skip
      and al,'_'                ;make uppercase
skip:
      call put
      cmp al,eof                ;done?
      jnz keep_reading

      mov ax,4c00h              ;return
      int 21h

endp Main
```

Figure 18-1 The assembly language source code for 2UPPER.COM

```
;--------------------------------------;
; The PUT routine, display a character
; to standard output
;--------------------------------------;
proc PUT
     mov [buffer],al
     mov bx,1               ;standard output handle
     mov cx,1               ;write one char
     mov dx,offset buffer
     mov ah,40h             ;write
     int 21h
     jnc sucess

bad_error:
     pop bx                 ;adjust stack
     mov dx,offset msg_err  ;error message
     mov cx,me_len
     mov bx,2               ;standard error device
     mov ah,40h             ;write to it
     int 21h
     mov ax,4c01h           ;return w/error code
     int 21h

sucess:
     cmp ax,0               ;was one character written?
     mov al,[buffer]        ;reload
     jz disk_full
ok_2_ret:
     ret

disk_full:
     cmp al,eof
     jz ok_2_ret

     mov dx,offset no_room
     mov ah,9
     int 21h
     pop bx                 ;adjust stack
     mov ax,4c01h           ;return w/error code
     int 21h
endp PUT


;--------------------------------------;
: The GET routine, grab a character
; from standard input.
;--------------------------------------;
proc GET
     mov bx,0               ;standard input
     mov cx,1               ;one char
     mov dx,offset buffer
     mov ah,3fh             ;read
```

Figure 18-1 *(cont.)* The assembly language source code for 2UPPER.COM

```
        int 21h
        cmp ax,0                ;nothing read
        jz nothing_read

        mov al,[buffer]         ;get character
        ret

nothing_read:
    jc bad_error

        mov al,eof              ;set end of file
        ret
endp GET

;------------------------------------;
; Data and string storage
;------------------------------------;

buffer      db ?

eof         equ 26              ;end of file

no_room:    db 0dh,0ah,07,'Insufficient disk space',0ah,0ah,'$'

msg_err     db 0dh,0ah,07,'Some kind of error!',0dh,0ah

me_len      equ $-msg_err

end   Start
```

Figure 18-1 *(cont.)* The assembly language source code for 2UPPER.COM

The PUT function uses DOS Interrupt 21 hex, function 40 hex to write a byte to standard output. The standard output file "handle," stored in register BX, is 1. You can cross reference this with Table 2-4.

If there is an error, the instructions at the "bad_error" label are executed. Note that the error message is written to the standard error device, not just displayed on the screen; register BX is loaded with 2, the file handle for the standard error device (per Table 2-4).

In the GET function, DOS Interrupt 21 hex, function 3F hex is used to read a byte from the standard input device. With both this function and the previous write function (in the PUT procedure), there is no need to open or close the file. Working with files in assembler is perhaps the worst part about the programming language (and why I recommend C instead). However, when you work with standard input and output, you only need to write or read; those "files" are always considered open by DOS.

There's no need to go into any more detail on the program since this book isn't about teaching assembly language. After the program was written and compiled into a COM file, it was tested and run in DEBUG. Once everything proved worthy, the task of creating a script file was undertaken.

Script Strategy

There are two ways to roll a script in DEBUG. The first is to use the E command to poke in a program. The second and less desirable method is to use the A command and assemble it. My recommendation is to use the E command. That usually produces the shortest script with the least possibility of typos.

Everything starts with moving the program in question into DEBUG:

```
C:\> DEBUG 2UPPER.COM
-
```

This command loads 2UPPER.COM into DEBUG. The first step is to figure out the file's size in hexadecimal. This is done with the R command. The size of the file will be in the CX register, which turns out to be AC hex for 2UPPER.COM. This is plugged into the standard script formula, which appears in Figure 18-2. You need four items to make a basic script:

1. The N command to name the file
2. The RCX command, followed by the file's size on the next line
3. The W command to write the file to disk
4. The Q command to quit DEBUG and return control to DOS.

Whether the N command comes first or last isn't crucial. I put it first since it names the script's output file right away and helps identify the text that follows.

You need to follow the RCX command with the file's size. The R*rr* command does not accept a parameter (which is sad), so the hexadecimal file size needs to follow RCX on the next line.

The W command must follow RCX for the proper number of bytes to write to disk. And the Q command needs to be last. Without it, DEBUG would sit and wait for more input from the script file. And wait. And wait. You have to reset to get out of that one.

Using either the A or E scripting method meets with certain quirks: the E command requires an address followed by a parade of bytes. I specify only eight bytes after the E command since that's easier for the eye to follow on a page. The A command starts at offset 100 hex and the last assembly language instruction must

```
N filename.COM
...
E or A commands go here
...
If A is used, a blank line is required here
RCX
filesize
W
Q
```

Figure 18-2 The standard script formula

be followed by a blank line. That blank line — the Enter key — is what exits the mini-assembler and returns to DEBUG's hyphen prompt. Don't forget it!

IIII▶ *Tip:* A good argument to favor the E command over A to assemble a program is that some users may neglect the blank line to exit the mini-assembler.

How you get the bulk of the commands into the script requires a little trickery. Whether the E or A scripting method is used, you'll need to know the file's size in the CX register. Use that value with the D command for creating an E script; use it with the U command when building an A script. The following sections elaborate how this is done.

Creating an E Script

To create an E "poke 'em in" 2UPPER script file, you need to dump out all the hex bytes in DEBUG using the D command. Since the file size is known to be AC hex for 2UPPPER.COM, the following command is used:

```
-D100 LAC
```

That displays all the bytes in the program. The Q command is then typed to exit DEBUG and a special "dump" script file is created. DUMP.SCR is a simple script file used to display all the bytes in the file and then quit DEBUG. It can be quickly created with the COPY CON text editor:

```
C:\> COPY CON DUMP.SCR
D100 LAC
Q
^Z
```

IIII▶ *Tip:* I name all script files with an SCR extension. They can be anything, really: DAT, TXT, DBG, whatever. Consistency is nice.

In this command, the script file DUMP.SCR will issue DEBUG commands that display all the bytes in 2UPPER.COM and then quit. To make that happen — and to save the output in an editable text file, the following command is issued:

```
C:\> DEBUG 2UPPER.COM <DUMP.SCR >2UPPER.SCR
```

DEBUG will load 2UPPER.COM into memory. Standard input will come from the file DUMP.SCR, output is redirected to the file 2UPPER.SCR, which will eventually become the script file. This will all happen in a flash.

Editing proceeds on the file 2UPPER.SCR to remove the excess "junk." You only want offset addresses and byte values. First to be deleted is the ASCII column along with all the segment addresses and the colon that follows them. I'll leave that up to your nimble text-editing fingers to figure out.

Your next task is to change the raw bytes and offset address into the E command format. For example:

344   Dan Gookin's Guide to Underground DOS 6.0

```
0100 E8 57 00 3C 61 7C 06 3C-7A 7F 02 24 5F E8 09 00
0110 3C 1A 75 EC B8 00 4C CD-21 2E A2 76 01 BB 01 00
```

These bytes need to be translated into E commands as follows:

```
E 100 E8 57 00 3C 61 7C 06 3C
E 108 7A 7F 02 24 5F E8 09 00
E 110 3C 1A 75 EC B8 00 4C CD
E 118 21 2E A2 76 01 BB 01 00
```

First, any leading zeros are removed from the offset address. Then each line needs to be split in half. I use the hyphen as the handy spot to split each line. The byte after the hyphen is at offset 8, so the next address is the same as the previous one, plus 8 hex. This is simple to do in a text editor.

Every line in the text file needs to be split and groomed into an appropriate E command. The last E command line may be shorter than the others; it's okay, as long as the value in the CX register is proper it won't matter.

▶ *Tip:* Double-check your E commands! I often make the mistake of forgetting to put E in front of the offset address. Or, when I type in the *xx*8 offset addresses, I'll transpose two values. Review the E commands visually to make sure they all fit.

Once each line is converted, you need to insert your edited E commands into the standard script formula, as shown in Figure 18-2. Remember to specify the proper value for the CX register. The final resulting script for 2UPPER.SCR is shown in Figure 18-3. But the script isn't ready to be run yet. It first needs to be tested, which is covered in the section "Testing the Script" below.

▶ *Tip:* I confess! The script file in Figure 18-3 is not the same as the original 2UPPER.SCR file in Figure 5-4. In the first figure, I took advantage of the E command's ability to poke in text strings. This makes the script file easier to deal with than poking in meaningless hex bytes. This technique is demonstrated in the next section.

Creating an A Script

You create an "A" script in the same way as an "E" script is created. Start with the length of the file; 2UPPER.COM is AC hex bytes long. But instead of using the D command to display bytes in memory, you'll be using the U command to unassemble the program. This change needs to be made in the DUMP.SCR script file, as follows:

```
C:\> COPY CON DUMP.SCR
U 100 LAC
Q
^Z
```

```
N 2UPPER.COM
E100 E8 57 00 3C 61 7C 06 3C
E108 7A 7F 02 24 5F E8 09 00
E110 3C 1A 75 EC B8 00 4C CD
E118 21 2E A2 76 01 BB 01 00
E120 B9 01 00 BA 76 01 B4 40
E128 CD 21 73 13 5B BA 94 01
E130 B9 9C FF BB 02 00 B4 40
E138 CD 21 B8 01 4C CD 21 3D
E140 00 00 2E A0 76 01 74 01
E148 C3 3C 1A 74 FB BA 77 01
E150 B4 09 CD 21 5B B8 01 4C
E158 CD 21 BB 00 00 B9 01 00
E160 BA 76 01 B4 3F CD 21 3D
E168 00 00 74 05 2E A0 76 01
E170 C3 72 B9 B0 1A C3 00 0D
E178 0A 07 49 6E 73 75 66 66
E180 69 63 69 65 6E 74 20 64
E188 69 73 6B 20 73 70 61 63
E190 65 0A 0A 24 0D 0A 07 53
E198 6F 6D 65 20 6B 69 6E 64
E1A0 20 6F 66 20 65 72 72 6F
E1A8 72 21 0D 0A
RCX
AC
W
Q
```

Figure 18-3 The 2UPPER.SCR "E" script

To save the unassembled program output into an editable text file on disk, start DEBUG with the following command:

```
C:\> DEBUG 2UPPER.COM <DUMP.SCR >2UPPER.SCR
```

DEBUG loads 2UPPER.COM into memory. Input is redirected from the DUMP.SCR file, which causes the entire program to be unassembled. Output is redirected to the 2UPPER.SCR file, which will eventually become the script file.

As you may expect, the 2UPPER.SCR file will require a bit of editing. The *segment:offset* address needs to be removed, along with the machine language bytes. You can also clean up the extra spaces DEBUG inserts between the assembly language mnemonics and any leading zeros in the numbers.

```
xxxx:0100  E85700        CALL      015A
xxxx:0103  3C61          CMP       AL,61
```

```
xxxx:0105 7C06        JL       010D
xxxx:0107 3C7A        CMP      AL,7A
xxxx:0109 7F02        JG       010D
```

This output needs to be edited to look more like this:

```
CALL   15A
CMP    AL,61
JL     10D
CMP    AL,7A
JG     10D
```

If you want to keep the columns lined up, fine. It makes the script file easier to read when you're typing it in.

▶ *Tip:* Some A script files may even add comments after the assembly language commands:

```
CALL   15A        ;Call the GET routine
CMP    AL,61      ;Compare the input with "a"
JL     10D        ;Ignore if it's lower
CMP    AL,7A      ;Compare input with "z"
JG     10D        ;Ignore if it's greater
```

This is really optional. From an earlier chapter, remember that while the comments are allowed, they aren't saved to disk nor will they reappear when the program is loaded and unassembled.

One problem you encounter with an "A" script that the other type lacks is dealing with strings. For example, it's much easier to use the following in your script file:

```
E17A "Insufficient disk space"
```

When the above string is "unassembled," DEBUG interprets it as assembly commands — and really confusing ones at that:

```
DEC    CX
DB     6E
JNB    01F3
DB     66
etc.
```

To solve this problem, you need to go back and create another DUMP.SCR script file — but this one for the E command. Append the new, E script to the end of the A script file 2UPPER.SCR:

```
C:\> DEBUG 2UPPER.COM <DUMP.SCR >>2UPPER.SCR
```

The two greater-than signs append the E command to your script file. Use the ASCII column to fish out the strings and their offsets. Then stick those E commands in your script as appropriate, deleting the now unnecessary disassembled text.

> **Tip:** If you do halt the A command and switch over to E, remember to put a blank line after the last assembly language instruction. That's required as the Enter keystroke that exits the mini-assembler.

Figure 18-4 contains the completed script, 2UPPER.SCR. It's much longer than the E script, and was more involved to create. A magazine reader would probably skip over such a script instead of typing it in. But not all A scripts are bad. Figure 3-8 was short and sweet and made a nice A script. So for short files, it is appropriate. But most of the time, you'll be using E-type scripts.

```
N 2UPPER.COM
A100
CALL    015A
CMP     AL,61
JL      010D
CMP     AL,7A
JG      010D
AND     AL,5F
CALL    0119
CMP     AL,1A
JNZ     0100
MOV     AX,4C00
INT     21
CS:
MOV     [0176],AL
MOV     BX,0001
MOV     CX,0001
MOV     DX,0176
MOV     AH,40
INT     21
JNB     013F
POP     BX
MOV     DX,0194
MOV     CX,FF9C
MOV     BX,0002
MOV     AH,40
INT     21
MOV     AX,4C01
INT     21
CMP     AX,0000
CS:
```

Figure 18-4 The completed "A" script, 2UPPER.SCR

```
MOV      AL,[0176]
JZ       0149
RET
CMP      AL,1A
JZ       0148
MOV      DX,0177
MOV      AH,09
INT      21
POP      BX
MOV      AX,4C01
INT      21
MOV      BX,0000
MOV      CX,0001
MOV      DX,0176
MOV      AH,3F
INT      21
CMP      AX,0000
JZ       0171
CS:
MOV      AL,[0176]
RET
JB       012C
MOV      AL,1A
RET

E176 00 0D 0A 07
E17A "Insufficient disk space"
E191 0A 0A 24 0D 0A 07
E197 "Some kind of error!"
E1AA 0D 0A
RCX
AC
W
Q
```

Figure 18-4 *(cont.)* The completed "A" script, 2UPPER.SCR

Testing the Script

Before you know a script is perfect you need to compare its output with the original. I always work in a separate directory, keeping the original safe and sound in a subdirectory on my programming drive. A copy of the original COM (or EXE) file exists on the working directory, which I use to compare with the script file's output.

Since the script file will be creating a COM file (hopefully) identical to the original, I rename the duplicated original to *.BIN for comparison purposes. That way DEBUG's output doesn't overwrite the original file. With 2UPPER, I renamed 2UPPER.COM (the copy in the working directory) to 2UPPER.BIN. Then the script is run:

```
D:\> DEBUG <2UPPER.SCR
```

Using either scripting method, the commands are fed into DEBUG and the file 2UPPER.COM is produced. That file is then compared with the original using DOS's COMP command:

```
D:\> COMP 2UPPER.BIN 2UPPER.COM
```

The COMP command won't point out any specific differences, but it will give you a general thumbs-up or thumbs-down:

```
Comparing 2UPPER.BIN and 2UPPER.COM
Files compare OK
```

Or:

```
Comparing 2UPPER.BIN and 2UPPER.COM
Compare error at OFFSET xx
file1 = xx
file2 = xx
```

If the files are different, then you will be given the offset plus the first several bytes that are different. This will help you patch up your script file and also tell you which bytes to replace. Since the COMP command may fail after 10 compares, you may have to go through the process a few times to get the files exact.

> **Tip:** Before massively restructuring your script file, check all the E commands and make sure they're followed by proper addresses.
>
> The best file comparison utility is Michael Mefford's COMP, a *PC Magazine* utility you can get from one of the many on-line services. Mefford's COMP will display the differences between two files on a byte-by-byte basis. This is the best way to locate differences between what your script file produced and the original file.

So what can you do with all these scripts? Scripts provide a means of distributing small, useful programs. They can be printed in newsletters or magazines or distributed on disks or on-line services as patch files. They also allow nontechnical users to create programs without having to know an ounce of a programming language. Finally, scripts provide yet another reason for using DEBUG, one that applies to everyone: you can create programs with nothing more than a text file.

Programs under DOS

I'm finishing this chapter with four script examples. These were chosen because they're short, quick, and useful — as all scripts should be. They also illustrate some programming techniques you may see used in other scripts. The four programs are described in Table 18-1.

A Good Greeting

The GREET.COM program works like ECHO; it displays a string of text. The text displayed, however, is prefixed by "Good Morning," "Good Afternoon," or "Good Evening," depending on the time of day. The script file is shown in Figure 18-5.

This file works similarly to the SAY.COM program introduced in a previous chapter. There are two major differences: this program uses DOS's Get Time function to tell what time of day it is and this program quits using the preferred DOS quit function, Interrupt 21 hex, function 4C hex. Build GREET.COM using the following DOS command:

```
C:\> DEBUG <GREET.SCR
```

Watch the screen as DEBUG builds GREET.COM using the commands stored in GREET.SCR. It will write the program out to disk and neatly quit to DOS.

Note: The above prompt is C:\>, meaning the root directory of drive C. In practice, you should create these files and put them into a UTIL, BIN, or BATCH directory. That will give you and your batch files access to these handy commands from any location on your hard drive.

Load GREET.COM into DEBUG after you create it. The DOS time function is being called at offset 130 hex. It's function 2C hex, which is loaded into the AX register. Use the RIP command to reset the instruction pointer to offset 103 hex. Then type the *P2* command.

Table 18-1 Four Programs Converted into Script Files

Program Name	Description
GREET.COM	Displays a greeting pertaining to the time of day: Good Morning, Good Afternoon, or Good Evening, followed by optional text.
ASK.COM	Asks a Y/N question, waits for either Y or N to be pressed, then returns a corresponding ERRORLEVEL value for a batch file to examine.
CPU.COM	Tells you which microprocessor you have.
ZIPPY.COM	Manipulates the PC's speaker and plays a tune.

```
N GREET.COM
E100 EB 27 90
E103 "Good $Morning,$Evening,$Afternoon,$"
E126 0D 0A
E128 24 BA 03 01 B4 09 CD 21
E130 B4 2C CD 21 80 FD 0C 73
E138 06 BA 09 01 EB 0F 90 80
E140 FD 11 73 06 BA 1B 01 EB
E148 04 90 BA 12 01 B4 09 CD
E150 21 A0 80 00 3C 00 74 11
E158 98 8B C8 BB 81 00 8A 07
E160 8A D0 B4 02 CD 21 43 E2
E168 F5 BA 26 01 B4 09 CD 21
E170 B8 00 4C CD 21
RCX
75
W
Q
```

Figure 18-5 The script file GREET.SCR

```
CX=0E16 DX=2308
```

DOS returns the time in the CX and DX register pairs, which are listed above as they appeared on my PC. Here's how to read what you see:

CH = hours in 24-hour format = 0E hex = 14 = 2 p.m.
CL = minutes = 16 hex = 22 minutes
DH = seconds = 23 hex = 35 seconds
DL = hundredth seconds = 8 hex = .08 seconds

According to those two registers, I typed the P3 command at 2:22 in the afternoon — which is right according to the clock on my wall.

What GREET.COM does is to examine the contents of the CH register, the hours. If it's before 0C hex — noon — then the PC says "Good Morning." If the time is between noon and five o'clock, 11 hex, then GREET says "Good Afternoon." By process of elimination, what remains is "Good Evening." That's followed by whatever string you type:

```
C:\> GREET DAN!
Good Morning, DAN!
```

This really makes a cute addition to some batch files. For some reason, it really amazes a few users who can't figure out how the computer knows whether it's morning, afternoon, or evening!

The second thing this program does is to quit "properly." Instead of ending with INT 20, it ends with Interrupt 21, function 4C at offset 170 hex. You'll see how much more useful this method of ending a program is in the next example, ASK.COM.

The ASK Program

ASK is a time-honored batch file helper. It has many versions. The version created by the script file in Figure 18-6 displays a string of text then waits for the Y or N key to be pressed (or Ctrl-C to cancel). If the user presses N, upper- or lowercase, an ERRORLEVEL value of 1 is set. If the user presses Y, upper- or lowercase, an ERRORLEVEL of 0 is set. This way your batch file can ask a question:

ASK Proceed with formatting the hard drive (Y/N)?
IF ERRORLEVEL 1 GOTO THANKGOD

Here, ASK is used to pose the question *Proceed with formatting the hard drive*. It's followed by a Y/N prompt. The string and the prompt will be displayed and wait for input while the batch file runs. If the user press N, then an ERRORLEVEL of 1 is returned. The following IF command will then be executed and the program will sanely branch to the THANKGOD label. Otherwise, Y was pressed and who-knows-what will happen to the hard drive.

> **Tip:** ASK ERRORLEVEL values:
>
> 1 = N was pressed.
> 0 = Y was pressed.

To create this ASK.COM program, feed the script file in Figure 18-6 into DEBUG with the following command:

```
C:\> DEBUG <ASK.SCR
```

```
N ASK.COM
E100 A0 80 00 3C 00 74 26 98
E108 8B C8 BB 82 00 E8 33 00
E110 B4 08 CD 21 24 5F 3C 59
E118 74 0E 3C 4E 75 F2 8A D0
E120 E8 0F 00 B8 01 4C CD 21
E128 8A D0 E8 05 00 B8 00 4C
E130 CD 21 B4 02 CD 21 B2 0D
E138 B4 02 CD 21 B2 0A B4 02
E140 CD 21 C3 8A 17 80 FA 0D
E148 74 07 B4 02 CD 21 43 E2
E150 F2 B2 20 B4 02 CD 21 C3
RCX
58
W
Q
```

Figure 18-6 The script file ASK.SCR

Programming in DEBUG

Internally this program doesn't do anything new that you haven't seen in GREET.COM or SAY.COM before that. To see how the ERRORLEVEL returns work, load ASK.COM into DEBUG, and type the following Unassemble command:

```
-U 116 L1B
```

Offset 116 tests the character typed with "Y," ASCII 59 hex. If there's a match, the JMP 128 instruction moves the microprocessor up to offset 128. On your screen, the MOV DL,AL and CALL 0132 commands set things up so the Y is displayed on the screen. Then, at offset 12D, Interrupt 21 hex function 4C hex is called. The AL register is loaded with 00 hex, which is the ERRORLEVEL/return value when you type Y.

The ERRORLEVEL/return value for N is shown at offset 123. There the AX register is loaded with 4C01 hex: 4C hex in AH for the DOS function call, and 01 hex in AL for the ERRORLEVEL value.

Which CPU Is This?

The script in Figure 18-7 is for a cute little program called CPU.COM. It reports which CPU your system has based on a series of microprocessor tests. These tests meet with certain results depending on which microprocessor you have. Also note how the script takes advantage of the E command to poke in strings.

Create CPU.COM by feeding the script file into DEBUG as follows:

```
C:\> DEBUG <CPU.SCR
```

When you run the program, it will report which level of microprocessor you have: 8088/8086, 80286 or '386 "family." There is no distinction made between the 386, 386SX, 486, etc. (although it's possible to make one).

```
N CPU.COM
E100 BA 36 01 E8 29 00 B0 01
E108 72 1C BA 64 01 50 55 8B
E110 EC C7 46 02 00 F0 5D 9D
E118 9C 58 25 00 F0 B0 02 74
E120 05 BA 8E 01 B0 03 B4 09
E128 CD 21 B8 4C 00 CD 21 50
E130 54 58 2B C4 58 C3
E136 "This machine has an 8088/8086 microprocessor.$"
E164 "This machine has an 80286 microprocessor.$"
E18E "This machine has a '386-level microprocessor.$"
RCX
BC
W
Q
```

Figure 18-7 The script file CPU.SCR

Tip: CPU.COM also returns an ERRORLEVEL code representing your microprocessor:

ERRORLEVEL 3 = '386 family
ERRORLEVEL 2 = 80286
ERRORLEVEL 1 = 8088/8086

This program has one major drawback with DEBUG: while you can use a script file to create it, you cannot unassemble, nor can you create the program using DEBUG's mini-assembler. The reason is that DEBUG is an 8088/8086-only debugger. While it understands and will run the program, it misinterprets the 80286 and '386-level instructions contained in the program.

The program still works, and works on all PCs, since DEBUG merely misinterprets the advanced microprocessor's instructions. Unfortunately, DEBUG won't display those routines properly. If you're curious, the individual routines used by CPU.COM are shown in Figure 18-8. Note that assembly language format was used, hence the leading zeros and H's on the hexadecimal figures.

Making the PC Sing

The PC has one, cheap, tinny speaker. About the only thing the BIOS can "play" over that speaker is the Ctrl-G character:

```
;--------------------------------------------------------
; Test to see if the CPU is an 8088/8086 or is higher
;     NC=processor is an 80286 or higher
;     CY=processor is an 8086, 8088, v20, or v30
;--------------------------------------------------------
        push  ax            ;save register used
        push  sp            ;8088/8086 pushes post-push sp
        pop   ax            ;get it back
        sub   ax,sp         ;check for same
        pop   ax            ;restore register used
                            ;Carry flag is set or reset here
;--------------------------------------------------------
; Test to see if the CPU is an 80286 or higher
;       NZ=80286 CPU
;       Z='386-level CPU
;--------------------------------------------------------
        push  0F000h        ;Save F000 hex on the stack
        popf                ;Pop it into the flags register
        pushf               ;Push the flags register
        pop   ax            ;Pop it back into AX
        and   ax,0f000h     ;See if it's the same
                            ;ZR is only true on '386-level PCs
```

Figure 18-8 Two assembly language tests for the microprocessor

```
ECHO ^G
```

This is more annoying than having a kid learning the violin move into your brain. But the PC can be programmed to squawk and sing, albeit stupidly. This is done by manipulating the *outport* lines from the microprocessor that directly connect with the speaker.

By toggling a bit over these outport lines, you can change the pitch of the note played. This is a complex thing to do; otherwise I would have demonstrated it earlier in the book. The note's duration is controlled by reading the PC's internal clock and counting off one second. This is preferable to doing a simple loop, which means that on faster PCs the sound would run too fast.

Note: Programming the PC's speaker is done at a very low, low level. You need to send specific bytes to outports 43 hex and 42 hex, as well as inport 61 hex. Sadly, there is no handy BIOS routine for programming the speaker. The PCjr has such a routine, and some of the fancier clones may. But there never seemed to be a great demand for the obnoxious tones a PC can produce.

The script file for ZIPPY.COM, a program that plays a scale over your PC's speaker, is shown in Figure 18-9. This is a long, involved program and will take some time to type in, but you may find the end result worth it. Once the script file is created, build ZIPPY.COM with the following command:

```
C:\> DEBUG <ZIPPY.SCR
```

You'll notice that ZIPPY.SCR is divided into three sections. I've done this for illustration purposes only; it's all one program and the spaces between each section aren't required. The first set of E commands contains the raw code for programming the speaker. The second set is a "table" of values. The values represented are the notes from C two octaves below middle C to the C one octave above it. The values in this table are used by ZIPPY.COM to play notes.

The final set of values is the "song" that ZIPPY.COM plays. Each value is a byte indicating a specific note to play. (The notes come from the table in the middle section.) In ZIPPY.COM, the notes represent only a scale: bytes 00 hex through 0C hex play the first octave, then the byte value 80 hex indicates a pause. Then bytes 0D hex through 19 hex play the next scale, then another 80 hex byte pause. Finally, bytes 1A hex through 24 hex play the final scale. Byte value FF hex marks the end of the table.

Run ZIPPY at the DOS prompt to hear the three scales and the pause. After confirming that it works, and having a nearby Macintosh owner point out that his machine makes much more beautiful "four voice" music than your cheaper and more useful PC clone, load ZIPPY.COM into DEBUG.

One of the reasons I programmed ZIPPY.COM with tables is to allow you to poke in your own songs! All you need to do is use the E command to punch in a ditty at offset 1A9 hex. The bytes and their note counterparts are listed in Table 18-2. The duration cannot change, though you can insert a pause by adding byte

```
N ZIPPY.COM
E100 BE A9 01 8A 04 46 3C FF
E108 74 17 3C 80 75 15 B4 00
E110 CD 1A 83 C2 01 8B DA B4
E118 00 CD 1A 3B D3 75 F8 EB
E120 E2 CD 20 D0 E0 98 8B D8
E128 B8 00 00 BA 12 00 F7 B7
E130 5F 01 8B D8 B0 B6 E6 43
E138 8B C3 E6 42 8A C4 E6 42
E140 E4 61 0C 03 E6 61 B4 00
E148 CD 1A 83 C2 02 8B DA B4
E150 00 CD 1A 3B D3 75 F8 E4
E158 61 24 FC E6 61 EB A4 83

E15F 83
E160 00 8B 00 93 00 9C 00 A5
E168 00 AF 00 B9 00 C4 00 D0
E170 00 DC 00 E9 00 F7 00 06
E178 01 15 01 26 01 37 01 4A
E180 01 5D 01 72 01 88 01 9F
E188 01 B8 01 D2 01 EE 01 0B
E190 02 2A 02 4B 02 6E 02 93
E198 02 BA 02 E4 02 10 03 3F
E1A0 03 70 03 A4 03 DC 03 17
E1A8 04

E1A9 00 02 03 04 05 06 07
E1B0 08 09 0A 0B 0C 80 0D 0E
E1B8 0F 10 11 12 13 14 15 16
E1C0 17 18 19 80 1A 1B 1C 1D
E1C8 1E 1F 20 21 22 23 24 FF
RCX
D0
W
Q
```

Figure 18-9 The script file ZIPPY.SCR

80 hex. The bytes must end with FF hex, which ZIPPY.COM recognizes as the end of the table.

For example, type in the following E commands:

```
-E 1A9 04 02 00 02 04 04 04
-E 1B0 80 02 02 02 80 04 07 07
-E 1B8 80 04 02 00 02 04 04 04
-E 1C0 04 02 02 04 02 00 FF
```

Type the *G* command and let 'er rip. What you hear over the PC's speaker is, more or less, a rendition of "Mary Had a Little Lamb," rather low. The byte values in the example were taken from the notes in Table 18-2; 80 hex is used to pause and FF hex ends the table.

Table 18-2 ZIPPY.COM Note Values

Note	Value	Note	Value	Note	Value	Note	Value
C	00 hex	C	0C hex	C*	18 hex	C	24 hex
C#	01 hex	C#	0D hex	C#	19 hex	Pause	80 hex
D	02 hex	D	0E hex	D	1A hex	End	FF hex
D#	03 hex	D#	0F hex	D#	1B hex		
E	04 hex	E	10 hex	E	1D hex		
F	05 hex	F	11 hex	F	1C hex		
F#	06 hex	F#	12 hex	F#	1E hex		
G	07 hex	G	13 hex	G	1F hex		
G#	08 hex	G#	14 hex	G#	20 hex		
A	09 hex	A	15 hex	A	21 hex		
A#	0A hex	A#	16 hex	A#	22 hex		
B	0B hex	B	17 hex	B	23 hex		

You can write your customized songs to a specific COM file on disk if you like. Just note the offset of the FF hex character that ends the song, plug it into CX, use the N command to give the file a specific name, and W does the rest.

Where to Go Next?

There are several marvelous books available on learning how to program a PC. If you're adept with DEBUG, you'll probably be curious about assembly language. Several good tutorials exist on the topic, though I'm not certain what the current titles are. Personally, I learned PC Assembly language using Robert Lafore's *Assembly Language Primer* from the Waite Group. I also feel that the assembly language programming book by Peter Norton and John Socha is an excellent beginner's text.

Assembly language isn't the best way to program a PC, although it works well with all the goodies you've seen and it's fun as witnessed in the last two parts of this book. If you really want to flex the PC's muscle, I recommend getting a good C language compiler. The C language is a cross between BASIC and assembler. It offers a convenient way to do some things that would take weeks to do in assembly language (file access, for on), and it lets you manipulate bits and bytes quite easily. There are dozens of "learning" and "how-to" books available, although I'm not really fond of any of them.

▶ *Tip:* Ray Duncan's *Advanced MS-DOS* book is perhaps the best, single source for information on programming in C, Assembler, and DEBUG under DOS. It also contains a full BIOS and DOS programming reference. This book isn't really a beginner's text, but with what you've learned here, you could probably make a good start at it.

For Windows, the best programming environment is Microsoft's *Visual BASIC*. The manual is pretty good, but you'll want to supplement it with a good tutorial. Again, I have no recommendations, although John Socha promises me that his *Visual BASIC* book will be the best (or "is" the best, if he's finished it by the time you read this!). You lose some of the byte-specifics when you program Windows; the PSP becomes useless and Windows rewrites the BIOS Data Area, filling in values according to how you configure your "DOS sessions." But that kind of monkeying around isn't what Windows is all about.

To discover what additional goodies lurk inside your PC's memory or on disk, pick up the latest edition of the *Microsoft MS-DOS Programmer's Reference*. It also completely documents DOS with regards to programming (more than I was capable of here in Appendix E). Peter Norton's *Programmer's Guide to the IBM PC & PS/2* is a good, descriptive reference as well. It goes into more detail about the BIOS than does the *Programmer's Reference*.

If messing with your video system intrigues you, check out Richard Wilton's *Programmer's Guide to PC & PS/2 Video Systems*. The book describes everything about monochrome, Hercules, CGA, EGA, and VGA video — more than you'll ever need to know.

I hope these books will help you continue your exploration of the PC. DEBUG is always available as a handy tool, although I still need to emphasize that it shouldn't be used carelessly.

Knowing how your computer works and peering into its guts help you understand why things are done the way they are in a PC. The end result of this quest is that you're a more knowledgeable computer user; nay, shall I say it — a *power user*! Take the knowledge you've gained and apply it well.

Appendix A

ASCII Table

ASCII Codes and Characters

0	^@	18	^R	36	$	54	6
1	^A	19	^S	37	%	55	7
2	^B	20	^T	38	&	56	8
3	^C	21	^U	39	'	57	9
4	^D	22	^V	40	(	58	:
5	^E	23	^W	41	)	59	;
6	^F	24	^X	42	*	60	<
7	^G	25	^Y	43	+	61	=
8	^H	26	^Z	44	,	62	>
9	^I	27	^[	45	-	63	?
10	^J	28	^\	46	.	64	@
11	^K	29	^]	47	/	65	A
12	^L	30	^^	48	0	66	B
13	^M	31	^_	49	1	67	C
14	^N	32		50	2	68	D
15	^O	33	!	51	3	69	E
16	^P	34	"	52	4	70	F
17	^Q	35	#	53	5	71	G

(continued)

72	H	86	V	100	d	114	r
73	I	87	W	101	e	115	s
74	J	88	X	102	f	116	t
75	K	89	Y	103	g	117	u
76	L	90	Z	104	h	118	v
77	M	91	[	105	i	119	w
78	N	92	\	106	j	120	x
79	O	93	]	107	k	121	y
80	P	94	^	108	l	122	z
81	Q	95	_	109	m	123	{
82	R	96	`	110	n	124	|
83	S	97	a	111	o	125	}
84	T	98	b	112	p	126	~
85	U	99	c	113	q	127	

Extended ASCII Codes and Characters

128	Ç	146	Æ	164	ñ	182	╢
129	ü	147	ô	165	Ñ	183	╖
130	é	148	ö	166	ª	184	╕
131	â	149	ò	167	º	185	╣
132	ä	150	û	168	¿	186	║
133	à	151	ù	169	⌐	187	╗
134	å	152	ÿ	170	¬	188	╝
135	ç	153	Ö	171	½	189	╜
136	ê	154	Ü	172	¼	190	╛
137	ë	155	¢	173	¡	191	┐
138	è	156	£	174	«	192	└
139	ï	157	¥	175	»	193	┴
140	î	158	₧	176	░	194	┬
141	ì	159	ƒ	177	▒	195	├
142	Ä	160	á	178	▓	196	─
143	Å	161	í	179	│	197	┼
144	É	162	ó	180	┤	198	╞
145	æ	163	ú	181	╡	199	╟

(continued)

Appendix A: ASCII Table 361

200	╚	214	╓	228	Σ	242	≥
201	╔	215	╫	229	σ	243	≤
202	╩	216	╪	230	μ	244	⌠
203	╦	217	┘	231	τ	245	⌡
204	╠	218	┌	232	Φ	246	÷
205	═	219	█	233	Θ	247	≈
206	╬	220	▄	234	Ω	248	°
207	╧	221	▌	235	δ	249	·
208	╨	222	▐	236	∞	250	-
209	╤	223	▀	237	φ	251	√
210	╥	224	α	238	ε	252	ⁿ
211	╙	225	ß	239	∩	253	²
212	╘	226	Γ	240	≡	254	■
213	╒	227	π	241	±	255	

ASCII/Hex/Binary Character Codes

Binary	Hex	Decimal	ASCII
0000-0000	00	0	^@
0000-0001	01	1	^A
0000-0010	02	2	^B
0000-0011	03	3	^C
0000-0100	04	4	^D
0000-0101	05	5	^E
0000-0110	06	6	^F
0000-0111	07	7	^G
0000-1000	08	8	^H
0000-1001	09	9	^I
0000-1010	0A	10	^J
0000-1011	0B	11	^K
0000-1100	0C	12	^L
0000-1101	0D	13	^M
0000-1110	0E	14	^N

(continued)

Binary	Hex	Decimal	ASCII
0000-1111	0F	15	^O
0001-0000	10	16	^P
0001-0001	11	17	^Q
0001-0010	12	18	^R
0001-0011	13	19	^S
0001-0100	14	20	^T
0001-0101	15	21	^U
0001-0110	16	22	^V
0001-0111	17	23	^W
0001-1000	18	24	^X
0001-1001	19	25	^Y
0001-1010	1A	26	^Z
0001-1011	1B	27	^[
0001-1100	1C	28	^\
0001-1101	1D	29	^]
0001-1110	1E	30	^^
0001-1111	1F	31	^_
0010-0000	20	32	
0010-0001	21	33	!
0010-0010	22	34	"
0010-0011	23	35	#
0010-0100	24	36	$
0010-0101	25	37	%
0010-0110	26	38	&
0010-0111	27	39	'
0010-1000	28	40	(
0010-1001	29	41	)
0010-1010	2A	42	*
0010-1011	2B	43	+
0010-1100	2C	44	,
0010-1101	2D	45	-
0010-1110	2E	46	.
0010-1111	2F	47	/

(continued)

Appendix A: ASCII Table 363

Binary	Hex	Decimal	ASCII
0011-0000	30	48	0
0011-0001	31	49	1
0011-0010	32	50	2
0011-0011	33	51	3
0011-0100	34	52	4
0011-0101	35	53	5
0011-0110	36	54	6
0011-0111	37	55	7
0011-1000	38	56	8
0011-1001	39	57	9
0011-1010	3A	58	:
0011-1011	3B	59	;
0011-1100	3C	60	<
0011-1101	3D	61	=
0011-1110	3E	62	>
0011-1111	3F	63	?
0100-0000	40	64	@
0100-0001	41	65	A
0100-0010	42	66	B
0100-0011	43	67	C
0100-0100	44	68	D
0100-0101	45	69	E
0100-0110	46	70	F
0100-0111	47	71	G
0100-1000	48	72	H
0100-1001	49	73	I
0100-1010	4A	74	J
0100-1011	4B	75	K
0100-1100	4C	76	L
0100-1101	4D	77	M
0100-1110	4E	78	N
0100-1111	4F	79	O
0101-0000	50	80	P

(continued)

Binary	Hex	Decimal	ASCII
0101-0001	51	81	Q
0101-0010	52	82	R
0101-0011	53	83	S
0101-0100	54	84	T
0101-0101	55	85	U
0101-0110	56	86	V
0101-0111	57	87	W
0101-1000	58	88	X
0101-1001	59	89	Y
0101-1010	5A	90	Z
0101-1011	5B	91	[
0101-1100	5C	92	\
0101-1101	5D	93	]
0101-1110	5E	94	^
0101-1111	5F	95	_
0110-0000	60	96	`
0110-0001	61	97	a
0110-0010	62	98	b
0110-0011	63	99	c
0110-0100	64	100	d
0110-0101	65	101	e
0110-0110	66	102	f
0110-0111	67	103	g
0110-1000	68	104	h
0110-1001	69	105	i
0110-1010	6A	106	j
0110-1011	6B	107	k
0110-1100	6C	108	l
0110-1101	6D	109	m
0110-1110	6E	110	n
0110-1111	6F	111	o
0111-0000	70	112	p
0111-0001	71	113	q

(continued)

Appendix A: ASCII Table 365

Binary	Hex	Decimal	ASCII
0111-0010	72	114	r
0111-0011	73	115	s
0111-0100	74	116	t
0111-0101	75	117	u
0111-0110	76	118	v
0111-0111	77	119	w
0111-1000	78	120	x
0111-1001	79	121	y
0111-1010	7A	122	z
0111-1011	7B	123	{
0111-1100	7C	124	|
0111-1101	7D	125	}
0111-1110	7E	126	~
0111-1111	7F	127	⌂
1000-0000	80	128	Ç
1000-0001	81	129	ü
1000-0010	82	130	é
1000-0011	83	131	â
1000-0100	84	132	ä
1000-0101	85	133	à
1000-0110	86	134	å
1000-0111	87	135	ç
1000-1000	88	136	ê
1000-1001	89	137	ë
1000-1010	8A	138	è
1000-1011	8B	139	ï
1000-1100	8C	140	î
1000-1101	8D	141	ì
1000-1110	8E	142	Ä
1000-1111	8F	143	Å
1001-0000	90	144	É
1001-0001	91	145	æ
1001-0010	92	146	Æ

(continued)

Binary	Hex	Decimal	ASCII
1001-0011	93	147	ô
1001-0100	94	148	ö
1001-0101	95	149	ò
1001-0110	96	150	û
1001-0111	97	151	ù
1001-1000	98	152	ÿ
1001-1001	99	153	Ö
1001-1010	9A	154	Ü
1001-1011	9B	155	¢
1001-1100	9C	156	£
1001-1101	9D	157	¥
1001-1110	9E	158	₧
1001-1111	9F	159	ƒ
1010-0000	A0	160	á
1010-0001	A1	161	í
1010-0010	A2	162	ó
1010-0011	A3	163	ú
1010-0100	A4	164	ñ
1010-0101	A5	165	Ñ
1010-0110	A6	166	ª
1010-0111	A7	167	º
1010-1000	A8	168	¿
1010-1001	A9	169	⌐
1010-1010	AA	170	¬
1010-1011	AB	171	½
1010-1100	AC	172	¼
1010-1101	AD	173	¡
1010-1110	AE	174	«
1010-1111	AF	175	»
1011-0000	B0	176	░
1011-0001	B1	177	▒
1011-0010	B2	178	▓
1011-0011	B3	179	│

(continued)

Appendix A: ASCII Table 367

Binary	Hex	Decimal	ASCII
1011-0100	B4	180	┤
1011-0101	B5	181	╡
1011-0110	B6	182	╢
1011-0111	B7	183	╖
1011-1000	B8	184	╕
1011-1001	B9	185	╣
1011-1010	BA	186	║
1011-1011	BB	187	╗
1011-1100	BC	188	╝
1011-1101	BD	189	╜
1011-1110	BE	190	╛
1011-1111	BF	191	┐
1100-0000	C0	192	└
1100-0001	C1	193	┴
1100-0010	C2	194	┬
1100-0011	C3	195	├
1100-0100	C4	196	─
1100-0101	C5	197	┼
1100-0110	C6	198	╞
1100-0111	C7	199	╟
1100-1000	C8	200	╚
1100-1001	C9	201	╔
1100-1010	CA	202	╩
1100-1011	CB	203	╦
1100-1100	CC	204	╠
1100-1101	CD	205	═
1100-1110	CE	206	╬
1100-1111	CF	207	╧
1101-0000	D0	208	╨
1101-0001	D1	209	╤
1101-0010	D2	210	╥
1101-0011	D3	211	╙
1101-0100	D4	212	╘

(continued)

Binary	Hex	Decimal	ASCII
1101-0101	D5	213	╒
1101-0110	D6	214	╓
1101-0111	D7	215	╫
1101-1000	D8	216	╪
1101-1001	D9	217	┘
1101-1010	DA	218	┌
1101-1011	DB	219	█
1101-1100	DC	220	▄
1101-1101	DD	221	▌
1101-1110	DE	222	▐
1101-1111	DF	223	▀
1110-0000	E0	224	α
1110-0001	E1	225	ß
1110-0010	E2	226	Γ
1110-0011	E3	227	π
1110-0100	E4	228	Σ
1110-0101	E5	229	σ
1110-0110	E6	230	µ
1110-0111	E7	231	τ
1110-1000	E8	232	Φ
1110-1001	E9	233	Θ
1110-1010	EA	234	Ω
1110-1011	EB	235	δ
1110-1100	EC	236	∞
1110-1101	ED	237	φ
1110-1110	EE	238	ε
1110-1111	EF	239	∩
1111-0000	F0	240	≡
1111-0001	F1	241	±
1111-0010	F2	242	≥
1111-0011	F3	243	≤
1111-0100	F4	244	⌠
1111-0101	F5	245	⌡

(continued)

Binary	Hex	Decimal	ASCII
1111-0110	F6	246	÷
1111-0111	F7	247	≈
1111-1000	F8	248	°
1111-1001	F9	249	·
1111-1010	FA	250	·
1111-1011	FB	251	√
1111-1100	FC	252	n
1111-1101	FD	253	²
1111-1110	FE	254	■
1111-1111	FF	255	

Appendix B

Line Drawing Characters

Single Line Characters

179	│
180	┤
191	┐
192	└
193	┴
194	┬
195	├
196	─
197	┼
217	┘
218	┌

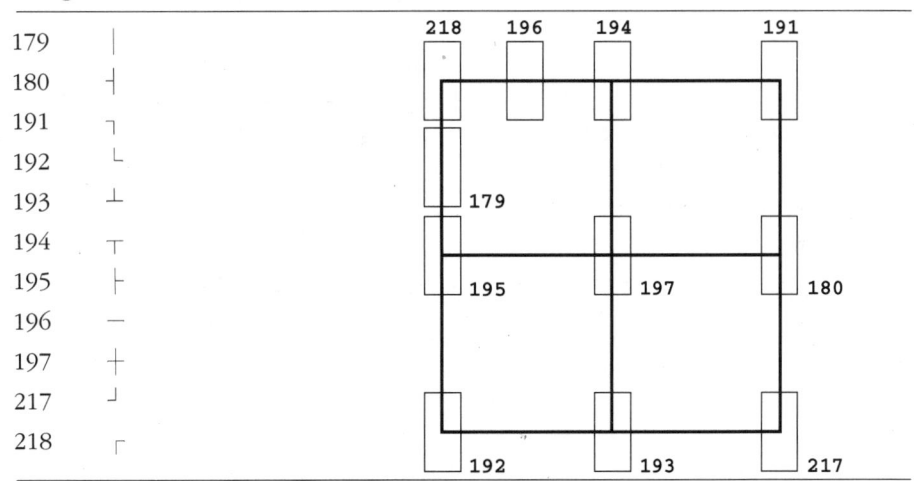

Double Line Characters

185	╣
186	║
187	╗
188	╝
200	╚
201	╔
202	╩
203	╦
204	╠
205	═
206	╬

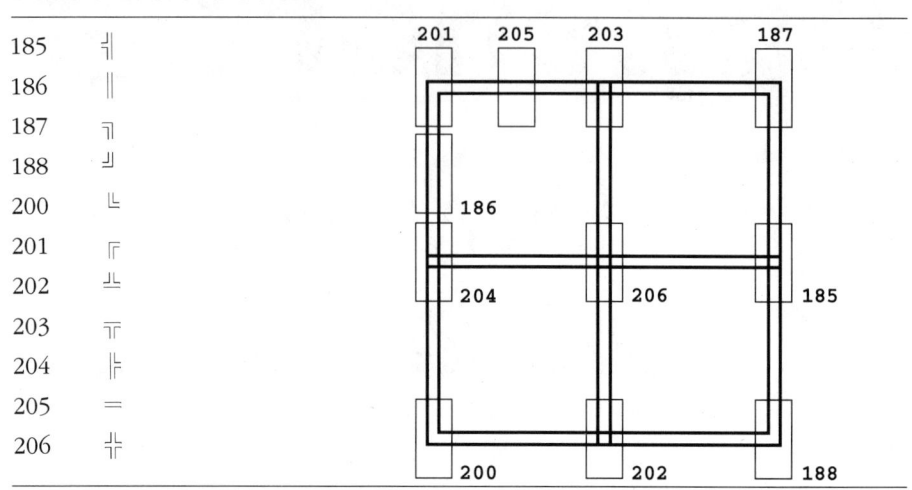

Mixed Line, Single Vertical Characters

181	╡
184	╕
190	╛
198	╞
207	╧
209	╤
212	╘
213	╒
216	╪

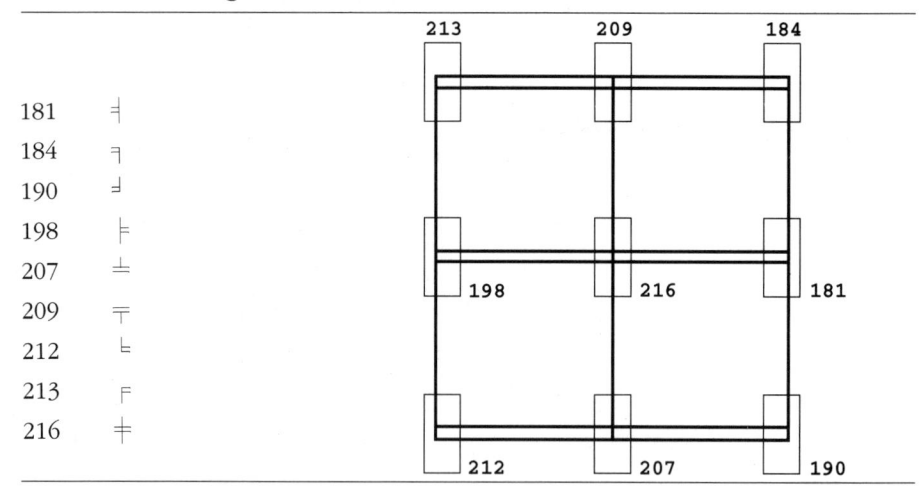

Appendix B: Line Drawing Characters 373

Mixed Line, Double Vertical Characters

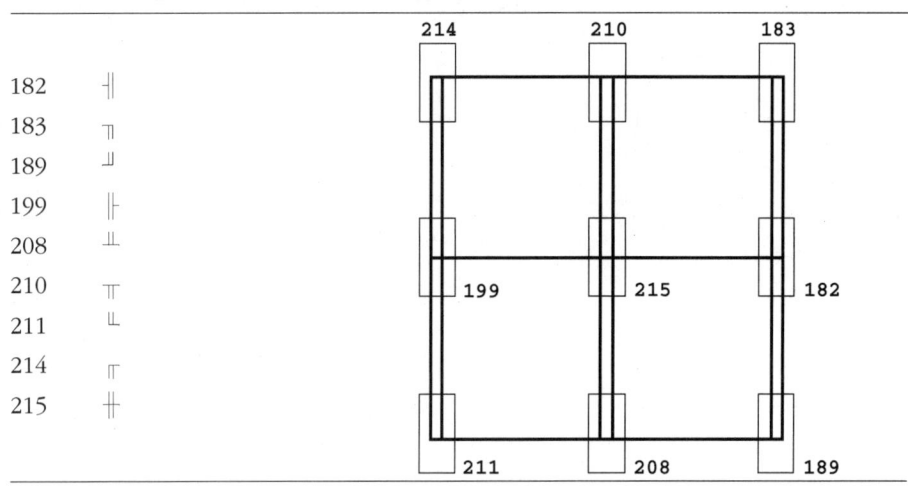

182	╡
183	╖
189	╜
199	╟
208	╨
210	╥
211	╙
214	╓
215	╫

Shade and Solid Characters

176	░
177	▒
178	▓
219	█
220	▄
221	▌
222	▐
223	▀

Appendix C
ANSI Commands

LOCATE CURSOR

←[*n1*;*n2*H

Positions the cursor to row *n1* and column *n2*. Values for *n1* represent row numbers ranging from 1 to 25. Values for *n2* represent column numbers ranging from 1 to 80.

POSITION CURSOR

←[*n1*;*n2*f

This command is identical to Locate Cursor.

MOVE CURSOR UP

←[*n*A

Moves the cursor up *n* rows or one row when *n* is omitted. This command will not scroll the screen if the cursor is on the top row.

MOVE CURSOR DOWN

←[*n*B

Moves the cursor down *n* rows or one row if *n* is omitted. This command will not scroll the screen if the cursor is on the bottom row.

375

MOVE CURSOR RIGHT

←[nC

Moves the cursor right *n* columns or one column if *n* is omitted. The cursor will not "wrap" to the next row if it's at the far right column.

MOVE CURSOR LEFT

←[nD

Moves the cursor left *n* columns or one column if *n* is omitted. The cursor will not "wrap" to the previous row if it's at the far left column.

SAVE CURSOR POSITION

←[s

Saves the current cursor position. The cursor is restored with the Restore Cursor Position escape sequence.

RESTORE CURSOR POSITION

←[u

Restores the cursor to its position as saved by the Save Cursor Position escape sequence.

ERASE DISPLAY

←[2J

Clears the screen and homes the cursor.

ERASE LINE

←[K

Erases the cursor current line, from the cursor's position to the end of the line.

SET GRAPHICS RENDITION

←[nm

Changes the colors of the text foreground and background. Values for *n* are listed below:

0	Normal text
1	High-intensity
2	Low-intensity
4	Underline on (monochrome displays only)
5	Blinking on

Appendix C: ANSI Commands 377

7	Inverse video on
8	Invisible text
30	Black foreground
31	Red foreground
32	Green foreground
33	Yellow foreground
34	Blue foreground
35	Magenta foreground
36	Cyan foreground
37	White foreground
40	Black background
41	Red background
42	Green background
43	Yellow background
44	Blue background
45	Magenta background
46	Cyan background
47	White background

Two or more attributes can be combined using the following format:

←[*n1*;*n2*;...m

SET/RESET MODE

←[=*n*h

Sets the screen resolution. Values for *n* are:

0	Monochrome text, 40 × 25
1	Color text, 40 × 25
2	Monochrome text, 80 × 25
3	Color text, 80 × 25
4	Medium resolution graphics (four color), 320 × 200
5	Same as 4, but with color burst disabled
6	High resolution graphics (two color), 640 × 200
14	Color graphics, 640 × 200
15	Monochrome graphics, 640 × 350
16	Color graphics, 640 × 350
17	Color graphics, 640 × 480
18	Color graphics, 640 × 480
19	Color graphics, 320 × 200

CHARACTER WRAP ON

←[=7h

Sets the character wrap mode to on. This directs ANSI.SYS to display characters printed after the 80th column on the next row.

CHARACTER WRAP OFF

←[=7l

Disables character wrap, setting the wrap mode to off. The command ends in a lowercase L, not the number 1.

KEYBOARD KEY REASSIGNMENT

←[n1;n2p

Reassigns one key to another character: *n1* is the ASCII code for a key to redefine. *n2* is the ASCII code that will be produced when *n1* is pressed.

←[0;n;"string"p

Reassigns a single key to a string of characters.

Appendix D

Counting Systems

Also refer to Chapter 8.

Binary:

Digit	Power	Decimal Value
1	2^0	1
2	2^1	2
3	2^2	4
4	2^3	8
5	2^4	16
6	2^5	32
7	2^6	64
8	2^7	128
9	2^8	256
10	2^9	512
11	2^{10}	1,024
12	2^{11}	2,048
13	2^{12}	4,096
14	2^{13}	8,192
15	2^{14}	16,384
16	2^{15}	32,768

Hexadecimal:

Digit	Power	Decimal Value
1	16^0	1
2	16^1	16
3	16^2	256
4	16^3	4,096
5	16^4	65,536
6	16^5	1,048,576

Decimal, Hexadecimal, and Binary Conversions:

Dec.	Hex.	Bin.	Dec.	Hex.	Bin.
0	0	0000	8	8	1000
1	1	0001	9	9	1001
2	2	0010	10	A	1010
3	3	0011	11	B	1011
4	4	0100	12	C	1100
5	5	0101	13	D	1101
6	6	0110	14	E	1110
7	7	0111	15	F	1111

Second Digit Hexadecimal Values:

Hex.	Decimal	Hex.	Decimal
00	0	80	128
10	16	90	144
20	32	A0	160
30	48	B0	176
40	64	C0	192
50	80	D0	208
60	96	E0	224
70	112	F0	240

Appendix E

Common DOS Function Calls

This appendix lists common Interrupts used in DOS programs. For a complete list, refer to your local bookstore for a DOS reference in the programming language of your choice.

INT 10 — The Video Interrupt

Interrupt:	10 hex
Function:	2 hex
Name:	Set Cursor Position
Call:	AH=2 hex
	BH=Video page number (typically zero)
	DH=Row position (vertical)
	DL=Column position (horizontal)
Return:	Nothing
Description:	The cursor is moved to the locations specified in the DH and DL registers. Position 0,0 is the upper-left corner of the screen. The lower-right corner is position 79,24, which is achieved by loading DH and DL as follows in DEBUG:
	MOV DH,18
	MOV DL,4F

Interrupt:	10 hex
Function:	3 hex
Name:	Get Cursor Position
Call:	AH=3 hex
	BH=Video page number (typically zero)
Return:	DH=Row position (vertical)
	DL=Column position (horizontal)
Description:	The cursor position is returned in the DH and DL registers. The upper-left corner of the screen is position 0,0; the lower-right corner is row 24, column 79.

Interrupt:	10 hex
Function:	5 hex
Name:	Select display page
Call:	AH=5 hex
	AL=page number
Return:	Nothing
Description:	The page number ranges from zero through 3 for the 80-column color text mode; zero through 7 for the 40-column mode. This command only works with color text systems. The standard page number is zero and should be used with all the "display page" values required by other Interrupt 10 hex calls.

Interrupt:	10 hex
Function:	6 hex
Name:	Initialize window and scroll up
Call:	AH=6 hex
	AL=Lines to scroll
	BH=Attribute for blank area
	CH=Row position, upper-left corner of window
	CL=Column position, upper-left corner of window
	DH=Row position, lower-right corner of window
	DL=Column position, lower-right corner of window
Return:	Nothing

Appendix E: Common DOS Function Calls 383

Description:	This command scrolls a "window" of text on the screen. AL contains the number of lines to scroll. When AL is zero, the window is cleared (which is how the screen is cleared). The coordinates in CH,CL and DH,DL define the window on the screen. Position 0,0 is in the upper-left corner of the screen.
Interrupt:	10 hex
Function:	7 hex
Name:	Initialize window and scroll down
Call:	AH=7 hex
	AL=Lines to scroll
	BH=Attribute for blank area
	CH=Row position, upper-left corner of window
	CL=Column position, upper-left corner of window
	DH=Row position, lower-right corner of window
	DL=Column position, lower-right corner of window
Return:	Nothing
Description:	This command works exactly as function 6 hex, but the contents of the window are scrolled down.
Interrupt:	10 hex
Function:	9 hex
Name:	Write attribute and character
Call:	AH=9 hex
	AL=ASCII character code
	BH=Display page (typically zero)
	BL=Attribute code
	CX=Replication factor
Return:	Nothing
Description:	This function puts the character specified in AL on the screen at the cursor's current position. It does not move the cursor forward (refer to function E hex for that). The character is written using the color attributes stored in register BL. Register CX indicates the number of times to write the character. For example, by putting 50 hex into CX you'll write the character 80 times.

Interrupt:	10 hex
Function:	E hex
Name:	Write text in TTY mode
Call:	AH=E hex
	AL=ASCII character code
	BH=Display page (typically zero)
	BL=Foreground color
Return:	Nothing
Description:	This is the "write character to the screen" function. Almost all the text you see on the screen is written there using Interrupt 10, function E. AL contains the character code. After the character is written to the screen, the cursor will move to the next character position.

INT 16 — The Keyboard Interrupt

Interrupt:	16 hex
Function:	0 hex
Name:	Read character
Call:	AH=00 hex
Return:	AH=keyboard scan code
	AL=ASCII character code
Description:	This function reads a character from the keyboard. It will wait until a key is pressed. Shift keys and some odd key combinations are not readable by this function.

INT 20 — DOS Program Terminate Interrupt

Interrupt:	20 hex
Function:	None
Name:	Program Terminate
Call:	CS=Program segment (PSP segment)
Return:	Nothing
Description:	This is the traditional way to end a DOS program, and it's quite convenient. The DOS programming manual recommends, however, that you use Interrupt 21, function 4C hex instead.

INT 21—General DOS Services Interrupt

Interrupt:	21 hex
Function:	1 hex
Name:	Character input with echo
Call:	AH=1 hex
Return:	AL=ASCII character entered
Description:	This function reads a character from DOS's standard input device, normally the keyboard. The character entered will be displayed on the screen. Function keys can be read as well, but you must call this function twice to read their extended ASCII values.

Interrupt:	21 hex
Function:	2 hex
Name:	Character output
Call:	AH=2 hex
	DL=ASCII character code to display
Return:	Nothing
Description:	This function displays a character on the standard output device. Note that the character is stored in the DL register.

Interrupt:	21 hex
Function:	5 hex
Name:	Printer output
Call:	AH=5 hex
	DL=ASCII character to print
Return:	Nothing
Description:	This function sends a character to the printer. There is no way to tell if the printer is on or "busy" using this function.

Interrupt:	21 hex
Function:	8 hex
Name:	Character input without echo
Call:	AH=8 hex
Return:	AL=ASCII character entered

Description:	This function works like function 1, although the character typed isn't displayed on the screen.
Interrupt:	21 hex
Function:	9
Name:	Display string
Call:	AH=9 hex
	DS:DX=address of string ending in 24 hex ($ character)
Return:	Nothing
Description:	DOS will display the string starting at memory address DS:DX. The string consists of ASCII characters, and it must end with a dollar sign. The string will be displayed on the standard output device, normally the screen.
Interrupt:	21 hex
Function:	A hex
Name:	Buffered input
Call:	AH=A hex
	DS:DX=string storage buffer
Return:	Nothing
Description:	This function allows you to input a string of characters. It's the same function used by DOS and DEBUG's prompts. The string storage buffer has a special format:
	Byte offset 0 = Maximum number of characters that can be entered, from 1 to 255.
	Byte offset 1 = zero
	Byte offset 2 = The string entered
	After Enter is pressed, the string will be found at offset 2 from address DS:DX. The byte at offset 1 will contain the number of characters entered—the length of the string.
Interrupt:	21 hex
Function:	2C hex
Name:	Get Time
Call:	AX=30 hex

Appendix E: Common DOS Function Calls 387

Return:	CH=hour, 0 for midnight through 23 for 11:00 P.M.
	CL=minutes, 0 through 59
	DH=seconds, 0 through 59
	DL=hundredths of seconds, 0 through 99
Description:	This function returns the time as kept internally by DOS. Note that the hours are returned in 24-hour "military" format in the CH register. A value of zero equals midnight.
Interrupt:	21 hex
Function:	30 hex
Name:	Get Version Number
Call:	AX=30 hex
Return:	AL=DOS major version number
	AH=DOS minor version number
Description:	This function returns the current DOS version. For DOS 5.0, register AL would contain 05 hex and register AH would contain 00 hex.
Interrupt:	21 hex
Function:	3C hex
Name:	Create File with Handle
Call:	AH=3C hex
	CX=File attributes
	DS:DX=ASCIIZ Filename string
Return:	NC=success, AX=file handle number
	CY=failure, AX=error code: 3, path not found; 4, too many open files; 5, access denied.
Description:	The ASCIIZ Filename string is the name of the file, including a pathname if necessary. The text string must end with a zero hex byte.
	Register CX contains the attributes of the file created. Normally, CX=zero. However, if you want to create a file with unique attributes, set the bits in the CX register according to Table 16-9.
	If the file is successfully opened, AX will contain a file handle number, which is used with functions 3E hex, 3F hex, and 40 hex when reading, writing, and closing the file.

Interrupt:	21 hex
Function:	3D hex
Name:	Open File with Handle
Call:	AH=3D hex
	AL=file access: 0=read-only; 1=write-only; 2=read and write
	DS:DX=ASCIIZ Filename string
Return:	NC=success, AX=file handle number
	CY=failure, AX=error code: 2, file not found; 3, path not found; 4, too many open files; 5, access denied; 6, invalid access.
Description:	The ASCIIZ Filename string is the full or partial pathname of the file ending in a zero hex byte. There are more file access values than the three described above, used primarily for file sharing and networking.
	If the file is successfully opened, AX will contain a file handle number. That number is used with functions 3E hex, 3F hex, and 40 hex when reading, writing, and closing the file.
	There is no need to open the standard devices (see Table 2-4).
Interrupt:	21 hex
Function:	3E hex
Name:	Close File with Handle
Call:	AH=3E hex
	BX=file handle
Return:	NC=success, file closed
	CY=failure, AX=error code (usually 6, invalid file handle)
Description:	This function closes a file opened with function 3D hex. There is no need to close the standard devices (handles zero through 4).
Interrupt:	21 hex
Function:	3F hex
Name:	Read File or Device
Call:	AH=3F hex

	BX=file or device handle
	CX=bytes to read from file or device
	DS:DX=buffer to store input
Return:	NC=success, AX=number of bytes read from file/device
	CY=failure, AX=error code: 5=access denied, 6=invalid file handle
Description:	The file read from must already be opened, although you can always read from DOS's standard devices without opening them (handles 0 through 4, as seen in Table 2-4).
Interrupt:	21 hex
Function:	40 hex
Name:	Write File or Device
Call:	AH=40 hex
	BX=file or device handle
	CX=bytes to write to file or device
	DS:DX=buffer containing bytes to write
Return:	NC=success, AX=number of bytes written
	CY=failure, AX=error code (see function 3F hex)
Description:	The file must already be open for writing, although this is unnecessary for DOS's standard devices. (This is the same as for function 3F hex above.)
Interrupt:	21 hex
Function:	43 hex, subfunction 0
Name:	Get File Attributes
Call:	AH=43 hex
	AL=00 hex
	DS:DX=ASCIIZ filename
Return:	NC=success, CX=attributes
	CY=failure, AX=error code: 1=invalid function; 2=file not found; 3=path not found; 4=access denied.
Description:	The file attributes returned are the same as those listed in Table 16-9. You change attributes with Function 43, subfunction 1.

Interrupt:	21 hex
Function:	43 hex, subfunction 1
Name:	Set File Attributes
Call:	AH=43 hex
	AL=01 hex
	CX=attributes
	DS:DX=ASCIIZ filename
Return:	NC=success
	CY=failure, AX=error code (see Function 43 hex, subfunction 0).
Description:	The attributes in the CX register are set according to the bit patterns found in Table 16-9.

Interrupt:	21 hex
Function:	47 hex
Name:	Get Current Directory
Call:	AH=47 hex
	DS:SI=buffer to hold directory
Return:	NC=success
	CY=failure, AX=error code: 0F hex=Invalid drive.
Description:	The directory string is placed in memory at the offset pointed at by the SI register in the DS register's segment. That buffer must be 64 bytes long. The string returned will end with a zero hex byte.

Interrupt:	21 hex
Function:	48 hex
Name:	Allocate Memory
Call:	AX=48 hex
	BX=number of paragraphs to allocate
Return:	NC=success, AX=allocated block segment
	CY=failure.
Description:	If the CY flag is up, AX will contain an error code describing why memory couldn't be allocated. If AX=7, memory blocks were destroyed or corrupted and memory couldn't be allocated. If AX=8, there wasn't enough memory for the paragraphs

specified in BX. If so, the amount of memory available (paragraphs) will be returned in the BX register.

Remember that BX specifies paragraphs, or 16-byte values. If you want to allocate 1K of memory, that's 64 paragraphs; $64 \times 16 = 1,024$.

Interrupt:	21 hex
Function:	4C hex
Name:	End Program
Call:	AH=4C hex
	AL=return value
Return:	Nothing
Description:	This is the "proper" way to quit a program, rather than INT 20 hex. The value returned in the AL register is made available to batch files as the ERRORLEVEL value.

Appendix F

Keyboard Scan Codes

Keyboard Scan Code Values

	Normal	Shift	Control	Alt
ESC	1	—	—	—
1	2	—	—	0;120
2	3	—	—	0;121
3	4	—	—	0;122
4	5	—	—	0;123
5	6	—	—	0;124
6	7	—	—	0;125
7	8	—	—	0;126
8	9	—	—	0;127
9	10	—	—	0;128
0	11	—	—	0;129
-	12	—	—	0;130
=	13	—	—	0;131

(continued)

Keyboard Scan Code Values

	Normal	Shift	Control	Alt
Backspace	14	—	—	—
Tab	15	0;15	0;148	0;165
q	16	—	—	0;16
w	17	—	—	0;17
e	18	—	—	0;18
r	19	—	—	0;19
t	20	—	—	0;20
y	21	—	—	0;21
u	22	—	—	0;22
i	23	—	—	0;23
o	24	—	—	0;24
p	25	—	—	0;25
[	26	—	—	—
]	27	—	—	—
Enter	28	—	—	0;166
Ctrl	29	—	—	—
a	30	—	—	0;30
s	31	—	—	0;31
d	32	—	—	0;32
f	33	—	—	0;33
g	34	—	—	0;34
h	35	—	—	0;35
j	36	—	—	0;36
k	37	—	—	0;37
l	38	—	—	0;38
;	39	—	—	—
"	40	—	—	—
Left shift	42	—	—	—
\	43	—	—	—
z	44	—	—	0;44
x	45	—	—	0;45
c	46	—	—	0;46

(continued)

Keyboard Scan Code Values

	Normal	Shift	Control	Alt
v	47	—	—	0;47
b	48	—	—	0;48
n	49	—	—	0;49
m	50	—	—	0;50
,	51	—	—	—
.	52	—	—	—
/	53	—	0;149	0;164
Right shift	54	—	—	—
PrtSc	55	—	0;150	0;114
Alt	56	—	—	—
Spacebar	57	—	—	—
Caps Lock	58	—	—	—
F1	0;59	0;84	0;94	0;104
F2	0;60	0;85	0;95	0;105
F3	0;61	0;86	0;96	0;106
F4	0;62	0;87	0;97	0;107
F5	0;63	0;88	0;98	0;108
F6	0;64	0;89	0;99	0;109
F7	0;65	0;90	0;100	0;110
F8	0;66	0;91	0;101	0;111
F9	0;67	0;92	0;102	0;112
F10	0;68	0;93	0;103	0;113
F11	0;133	0;135	0;137	0;139
F12	0;134	0;136	0;138	0;140
Num Lock	69	—	—	—
Scroll Lock	70	—	—	—
Home	0;71	55	0;119	—
Up	0;72	56	0;141	—
PgUp	0;73	57	0;132	—
Gray -	0;74	—	0;142	—
Left	0;75	52	0;115	—
Keypad 5	0;76	—	0;143	—

(continued)

Keyboard Scan Code Values

	Normal	Shift	Control	Alt
Right	0;77	54	0;116	—
Gray +	0;78	—	0;144	—
End	0;79	49	0;117	—
Down	0;80	50	0;145	—
PgDn	0;81	51	0;118	—
Ins	0;82	48	0;146	—
Del	0;83	46	0;147	—

Gray keys:

	Normal	Shift	Control	Alt
Home	224;71	224;71	224;119	224;151
Up	224;72	224;72	224;141	224;152
PgUp	224;73	224;73	224;132	224;153
Left	224;75	224;75	224;115	224;155
Right	224;77	224;77	224;116	224;157
End	224;79	224;79	224;117	224;159
Down	224;80	224;80	224;145	224;154
PgDn	224;81	224;81	224;118	224;161
Ins	224;82	224;82	224;146	224;162
Del	224;83	224;83	224;147	224;163

Index

A

Absolute address, 160–161
Accumulator registers, 207, 210–214
   changing value of, 210
   duality of registers, 213–214
   functions of, 207
   functions of individual registers, 212–213
   working with files, 210–212
Address, meaning of, 167
Addressing scheme, bytes, 156
Address space, 154
AH register, 244
AL register, 283
Alt keys, scan code values, 113
ANSI commands
   format for, 109–110
   listing of, 110, 375–378
ANSI Set Graphic Mode command, 107
ANSI.SYS, 100, 109–120
   alternatives to, 109
   in CONFIG.SYS, 109
   and *DESQview*, 109
   function of, 26, 109
   keyboard reassignment, 110–113, 117–120
      in DEBUG, 115–117
      DISCOM.BAT, 118–119
      with DOS Editor, 113–115
      QUICKDIR.BAT, 119–120
      reversal of, 111–112
   and Windows, 109
Arena header, 275–277
   contents of, 275–276
   parent block of memory block, 276–277
   viewing of, 275
ASCII, 103–109
   ASCII characters
      ALT–keypad access to, 108–109
      characteristics of, 104–105
      control codes, 105
      extended characters, 104, 108
      listing of, 106
   ASCII table, 359–370
   nature/function of, 103–104
A script, 344–347
ASK, and memory-resident programs, 77
ASK program, creating, 352–353
Assembly
   with DEBUG, 132
   See also DEBUG mini-assembler
Assembly language, 222, 223
   call and return instructions, 242
   compiler, 234
   labels in, 234–236
   nature of, 132, 222
   reading instructions, 233
   source code, 234
Attribute bytes
   bit values in, 286
   foreground and background values, 288
   nature of, 281–282, 284–287
   video memory, 282–288
Attributes, 241
Attribute values, video memory, 281–282

397

Index

ATZ, 93
AUTOEXEC.BAT
　basis of, 65–66
　to build PATH, 65, 69–72
　calling batch files from, 77
　to create environment variables, 72–74
　to create prompt, 65, 67–69
　DATE and TIME in, 75–76
　file management functions, 75
　function of, 13–14
　and loading memory-resident programs, 77–78
　and multitasking environment, 57–61
　order of commands, 78
　run by COMMAND.COM, 63–65
　to run startup programs, 76–78
　to run virus scanner, 74
　set up for RAM drives, 74–75
　for system configuration, 74
AUX device, 84, 87
　function of, 84
AX register, 210, 213, 233, 245
　function of, 212

B

Baker's Dozen, 186
BASIC, 222
Batch files, calling from AUTOEXEC.BAT, 77
Binary counting system, 139–140, 379
　nature of, 139–141
　translation of binary to hex, 143–144
BIOS
　extended BIOS, 271
　location of, 271
　nature of, 83
　in upper memory, 269–271
　viewing with DEBUG, 7–8
BIOS Character Generator Interface, 293
BIOS Data Area, 262–269
　deciphering bytes to read contents, 263–264
　equipment list information, 264–265
　Intra-Application Communication Area, 269
　keyboard status information, 265–266
　video mode information, 266–268
　viewing, 263
Bits, 130
　in a byte, 144
BLANK.BAT, 196
Block devices, 30
Blocks, copying blocks of memory, 177–179
Boot filenames, 305
Booting computer, 3–14
　cautions about, 5–6
　cold boot, 4
　with DEBUG, 7–10
　DOS boot process, events of, 10–14
　meaning of, 3
　mechanical aspects, 7
　reasons for, 3–4
　side effects of, 6–7
　time to boot, 5–6
　versus leaving computer on, 4
　warm boot, 5
Boot sector, 298–308
　altering nonsystem disk error message, 306–307
　contents of, 299–306
　creating boot disk, 298
　hard drive boot sector, 306
　partition table sector, 306
　viewing of, 298
Boot sector program, 11
Bootstrap routine, 305
BREAK, function of, 22–23
BUFFERS, 23–24
　and disk-caching software, 24
　format for, 24
　function of, 21, 23–24
　number of buffers needed, 23–24
BX register, 210, 211–212, 213, 260–261, 283
　function of, 212
Bytes
　addressing scheme, 156
　bits in, 144, 151
　bytes per sector in boot sector, 299–300
　count byte, 258
　DEBUG memory activities, 168
　finding byte on screen, 281

hexadecimal value of, 144–145
locating in memory, 159–163, 169–170

C

Cache value, BUFFERS, 24
Calculations, in DEBUG, 148–149
Calculator, programmer's, 148
CALL, 47, 338
   use of, 242
Carry flag, functions of, 219
Character bitmaps, 293, 295
Character bytes, 284
Character I/O, 22
Character sets, video, 292–295
CHCP, foreign language support, 25
CHKDSK
   for checking File Allocation Table (FAT), 314
   for fixing lost clusters, 6
C language, 222
CLOCK$ device, 88
   caution about, 88
Clock, master clock count, 268
CL register, 261
Clusters
   loading onto diskette, 323
   lost
      CHKDSK for, 6
      and resetting computer, 6
   sectors per cluster, calculation of, 322
CMOS, 264
CODEPAGE, foreign language support, 25
Code page commands, 25, 108
CodeView, 130
Cold boot, 4
   method of, 4
Colors of monitor, 284–288
   and attribute values, 285–288
COM1, 84, 93
COM file, 250–251
   as binary image file, 250
   characteristics of, 251
   compared to EXE file, 251, 253, 254
   memory locations in, 251
COMMAND.BIN, 331
COMMAND.COM
   alternatives to, 13
   command format for, 50–51
   command line format, 54–55
   and COMSPEC, 46, 49
   /E switch, 14
   initialization module, 44–45
   /K switch, 57–58
   patching of, 330–331
   as program, 51–52
   /P switch, 14, 50–51, 54–55
   relocating, 13
   resident module, 44, 46
   to run AUTOEXEC.BAT, 63–65
   running under *DESQview*, 58–61
   running under Windows, 55–57
   and shell, 52–54
   size of, 44
   in subdirectory, 49
   transient module, 45–48
   viewing with DEBUG, 47–48
Commander 80, 130
Command history, accessing, 122–124
Command interpreter
   function of, 13, 43–44
   loading of, 48–49
   running computer without, 43–44
   SHELL command, 35, 43, 44, 49
Command line editing, 121–124
   DEBUG, 168
   DOSKEY for, 122–124
   function keys for, 121
Commands, internal commands, 47
Command tail
   format of, 259
   program segment prefix, 255, 258
   storage of strings, 259
COMMENT, 18
Comments
   entering in DEBUG mini-assembler, 235–236
   usefulness of, 235
COMP, 349
Compiler, for assembly language, 234
COMSPEC, and COMMAND.COM, 46, 49
Concatenation, COPY, 90–91
CON device, 50, 84, 87, 88
   function of, 84

400 Index

CONFIG.SYS
  and ANSI.SYS, 109
  and booting PC, 12–13
  BUFFERS, 21
  and DOS 6.0, 37–41
  configuration menu commands, 39–41
  editing of, 19–20
  FILES command, 21
  function of, 15, 17–18, 21–22, 22–37
  loading into memory with DEBUG, 191–192
  location of, 16–19
  STACKS, 22
  suggestions for set up of, 21–22
  and SysInit, 16–19
Configuration commands, 17–18, 22–37
  BREAK, 22–23
  BUFFERS, 23–24
  COUNTRY, 24–25
  DEVICE, 25–27
  DEVICEHIGH, 27–28
  DOS, 29–30
  DRIVPARM, 30
  FCBS, 31
  FILES, 31–32
  format for, 22
  INCLUDE, 39
  INSTALL, 33
  LASTDRIVE, 33–34
  MENUCOLOR, 39
  MENUDEFAULT, 39
  MENUITEM, 39
  NUMLOCK, 34
  REM, 34–35
  SET, 35
  SHELL, 35
  STACKS, 35–36
  SUBMENU, 39
  SWITCHES, 36–37
Control characters, method of entering, 107–108
Control codes, 105
Control keys
  Ctrl-C, 105
  Ctrl-G, 105
  Ctrl-S, 105
  Ctrl-Z, 105
  Esc, 105, 107
  See also specific keys
Conventional memory, 152, 194
COPY
  concatenation, 90–91
  and devices, 89–91
COPY CON, 95, 343
  use of, 89–90
Count byte, 18, 258
Counting systems
  binary counting system, 139–140, 379
  hexadecimal counting system, 141–143, 380
  historical view, 137–138
COUNTRY
  format for, 25
  function of, 24–25
COUNTRY.SYS, 26
CPU.COM, creating program, 353–354
CS register, 283
  functions of, 218
Ctrl-Alt-Delete, for warm boot, 5, 10
Ctrl-Break, action of, 22
Ctrl-C, function of, 22–23, 89, 105
Ctrl-G, function of, 105
Ctrl-L, function of, 90
Ctrl-P, function of, 92
Ctrl-S, function of, 105
Ctrl-Z, function of, 90, 105
CX register, 210–212
  function of, 213

D

DATE, 95
  in AUTOEXEC.BAT, 75–76
DBLSPACE.BIN, 12
DBLSPACE.SYS, function of, 26
DEBUG, 192
  booting computer with, 8–10
  cautions about, 135–136, 186, 200
  command line editing, 168
  commands
    A command, 135, 226
    C command, 180–181
    D command, 147–148, 167, 170–173, 173, 176–177, 183–184, 199, 333–334

Index

E command, 10, 173–176, 176, 187
F command, 173, 176, 177
G command, 9
H command, 148–149
L command, 186, 192, 194, 198, 201
  listing of, 133, 134
M command, 177–179
N command, 186, 188–189, 192
Q command, 190, 194, 195
R command, 209
S command, 134–135, 182–183, 332
U command, 8
  viewing, 133
W command, 186, 190, 200–201, 202, 334
development of, 130
disk activities
  loading file from disk, 191–192
  reading disk directly, 197–200
  saving memory to disk, 186–191
  saving/restoring screen, 192–197
  writing raw sectors to disk, 200–203
error message, 135
examples of use, 134–136
exiting, 8, 136
file editing, program file editing, 326–330
functions of, 130–132
  building/disassembling programs, 132
  debugging programs, 185
  disk transfer, 131
  microprocessor control, 131
  viewing and changing memory, 131
and hexadecimals, 146–149
  calculation of hexadecimals, 148–149
  important numbers to know, 146–147
  memory display, 148
and input redirection, 95–96
and IO.SYS, 16–18
keyboard shortcuts in, 115–117
memory activities
  changing memory, 173–177
  comparing memory, 180–181
  copying blocks of memory, 177–179
  memory display, 148, 168–170
  memory dump, 170–171
  memory manipulation commands, 168
  searching memory, 182–184
mini-assembler of, 132, 135
programming with. *See* DEBUG mini-assembler; DEBUG script files
RCX command, 186, 190, 193
recovery of document, 331–334
running of, 8, 132–134
viewing BIOS, 7–8
viewing boot sector, 298
viewing COMMAND.COM, 47–48
viewing machine language, 16–17
viewing registers, 208–209
Debuggers, types of powerful debuggers, 130
DEBUG mini-assembler, 132
  building program, 226–228
  comments, entering of, 235–236
  loading instruction pointer, 232–234
  running program, step-by-step, 228–230
  saving program to disk, 231
DEBUG script files
  A script, 344–347
  ASK program, 352–353
  CPU.COM, 353–354
  creating program, 338–341
  E script, 343–344
  GREET.COM program, 350–352
  programming sequence, 337–338
  programming speaker of PC, 354–357
  rolling script into DEBUG, 342–343
  testing script, 348–349
DESQview, 34
  and ANSI.SYS, 109
  running COMMAND.COM under, 58–61
DEVICE
  and ANSI.SYS, 109
  format for, 27
  function of, 25–27
Device drivers, 11–12, 87
  and CONFIG.SYS, 22
  DEVICE command, 25–27
  extension for, 26

Index

function of, 25
listing of, 26
order for, 27
resident drivers, 11, 14
types of devices driven by, 25–26
DEVICEHIGH, 78
  format for, 28
  function of, 27–28
Devices
  AUX device, 84, 87
  CLOCK$ device, 88
  CON device, 84, 87
  and COPY command, 89–91
  listing of all devices, 87
  naming convention, 88
  nature of, 83–84
  NUL device, 85–86
  PRN device, 84
  redirected input and output. *See* Input/output redirection
DIR, functions of, 314–315
Directory, 314–320
  directory entry contents, 317–320
  entry map, 317
  function of, 315
  size of root directory, 316
  starting sector of root directory, 315–316
DI register, 214, 215, 217
Disassembly, with DEBUG, 132
DISCOM.BAT, keyboard reassignment, 118–119
Disk activities
  and DEBUG
    loading file from disk, 191–192
    reading disk information directly, 197–200
    saving memory to disk, 186–191
    saving program to disk, 231
    saving/restoring screen, 192–197
    writing raw sectors to disk, 200–203
Disk caches, 25
Disk-caching software, and BUFFERS, 24
Disk-doubling device driver, 27
Disks
  sectors, 198–200
  sectors-per-track values, 302, 303
  tracks of, 197

  volume of, 197
Disk-scanning program, 314
Disk Technician Advanced, 314
Disk transfer, with DEBUG, 131
DISPLAY.SYS, function of, 26
DOS 6.0
  and COMMAND.COM, /K switch, 57–58
  and CONFIG.SYS, 37–41
  configuration menu commands, 39–41
DOS
  function of, 29–30
  interrupts
    DOS services interrupts, 385–391
    keyboard interrupt, 384
    program terminate interrupt, 384
    video interrupt, 381–384
  and memory
    arena header, 275–277
    DOS allocation of memory, 274–275
    environment memory block, 278–280
    finding blocks with MEM, 277–278
    memory and operation of DOS, 273–274
  operation of programs under, 250
DOSEDIT, 168
DOS Editor, ANSI commands for keyboard shortcuts, 113–115
DOSKEY, 8, 56, 77
  for command history, 122–124
  command line editing, 122–124
  editing commands, 123
  macros for shortening DOS commands, 124–125
  macro-building batch file for, 126
  removing macro, 126
  special characters for, 125
DOSOFF.BAT, 119
DOS version, in boot sector, 299
Double word value, 303–304, 320
  meaning of, 320
Drive number, 304
DRIVER.SYS, function of, 26, 30
DRIVPARM
  function of, 30
  versus DRIVER.SYS, 30
DS register, 283
  functions of, 218

Index 403

Dump
  memory dump, 170–171
  screen dump, 170
DVANSI.COM, 109
DX register, 210
  function of, 213

E

ECHO, 92, 93, 97
Editing
  CONFIG.SYS, 19–20
  EDIT, 20
  EDLIN, 20
EDLIN, 20
  entering control characters, 107
EGA.SYS, function of, 26
EMM386.EXE, 154
  function of, 26
Environment memory block, 278–280
Environment variables
  creating with AUTOEXEC.BAT, 72–74
  SET command, 35
Equipment list information, BIOS Data Area, 264–265
Esc
  entering character, methods of, 107
  function of, 105, 107
E script, 343–344
ES register, functions of, 218
EXE file, 251–254
  compared to COM file, 251, 253, 254
  editing image of, 254
  file header, 252
  segments of, 252
  size of, 251–252
  SORT.EXE as example, 252–253
Extended boot signature, 304
Extended characters, access to, Alt-keypad access, 108–109
Extended character set, 104, 108
Extended memory, 165
External drives, 25

F

FASTOPEN, 81
FCBS

  format for, 31
  function of, 31
File Allocation Table (FAT), 301, 309–314
  alternative file systems, 311
  CHKDSK for checking of, 314
  cluster values in, 313
  handling of large files, 311
  map of disk space, 310
  sectors in, 302
  sizes for common disk formats, 310
  structure of, 312–313
  12- and 16-bit tables, 305
  and undelete programs, 314
  viewing of, 311
  and writing file to disk, 310
File comparison utility, 349
File control block, 257–258
  contents of, 258
File editing, in DEBUG, program file editing, 326–330
File handles, listing of, 32
Filenames, forbidden characters in, 202
FILES
  format for, 32
  function of, 21, 31–32
  loading from disk, 191–192
  management with AUTOEXEC.BAT, 75
Filters, 97–102
  FIND filter, 101–102
  formats for, 98, 98–99
  functions of, 97
  MORE filter, 99–100
  SORT filter, 101
  2UPPER.COM, 97–99
FIND filter, 101–102
  function of, 101–102
  switches of, 102
Flags register, 219–220
  carry flag, 219
  changing flags, 220
  functions of, 219
  zero flag, 219
Floppy drives, creating logical drives, 30
Flow control, meaning of, 232
Fonts, writing fonts, 293
Foreign languages
  CHCP command, 25
  CODEPAGE command, 25

404 Index

COUNTRY, 24–25
  KEYB command, 25
  NLSFUNC command, 25
Formatting programs, boot messages, 308
4DOS, 13, 44
Function keys, scan code values, 114

G

GET, 338, 341
GOTO, 232, 242
GREET.COM program, creating, 350–352

H

Hard disk, partition table, 308–309
Hard disk controller, location of, 270–271
Hexadecimal counting system,
    141–149, 380
  byte values, 144–145
  and DEBUG, 146–149
    calculation of hexadecimals,
      148–149
    important numbers to know, 146–147
    memory display, 148
  nature of, 141–143
  translation of binary to hex, 143–144
HEXCALC, 148, 201
High memory area, 29, 165
  viewing, 172–173
High Performance File System, 311
HIMEM.SYS, 8, 27, 29, 165, 172
  function of, 26

I

IBMBIO.COM, 11–12, 15, 305
IBMDOS.COM, 12, 43, 305
IF-EXIST test, 86
INCLUDE, 17
  function of, 39
Index registers, 207, 214–217
  changing contents of, 214–215
  Destination Index register, 214,
    215, 217
  functions of, 207
  moving block of memory, 216

Source Index register, 214, 216, 217
Input, redirection of, 95–96
Input device, CON device, 84
Input/output redirection, 9, 88–102
  and COPY command, 88–91
  filters for, 97–102
  input redirection, 95–96
  output redirection, 91–94
  pipe for, 96–97
  and SORT filter, 101
INSTALL
  format for, 33
  function of, 33
INSTALLHIGH, 18
Instruction pointer
  function of, 232
  loading during programming, 232–234
Internal commands, 47–48
  commands, external commands, 47
  listing of, 48
Interrupts, 243–244
  DOS services interrupts, 385–391
  interrupt number, 243
  keyboard interrupts, 384
  program terminate interrupt, 384
  use by microprocessor, 243–245
  video interrupt, 381–384
Intra-Application Communication Area,
    BIOS Data Area, 269
IO.SYS, 11, 14
  and DEBUG, 16–18
  error messages in, 19
  and system initialization process, 15–19
IP register, 233, 234

J

Jumping
  assembly language jump
    commands, 235
  program jumping, purpose of, 234
Jump instruction, 9, 232, 299, 305

K

Kernel, function of, 12
KEYB, foreign language support, 25
Keyboard

Index 405

enhanced keyboard, 265
keyboard buffer, 265–266
keyboard status information, BIOS Data Area, 265–266
scan code values, 393–396
Keyboard interrupt, 384
Keyboard reassignment, 110–113, 117–120
   ANSI command for, 110–111
   in DEBUG, 115–117
   and DISCOM.BAT, 118–119
   and DOS Editor, 113–115
   examples of, 111, 112–113
   reversal of, 111–112
   and scan codes, 112–113
KEYBOARD.SYS, 26
Kilobyte, 156, 157
Kluge, 158

L

LABEL, 186
Labels, in assembly language, 234–236
LASTDRIVE
   function of, 33–34
   setting for, 33
Line drawing characters, listing of, 371–374
LINK, 254
List program, 16, 19
Literal characters, method of entering, 107–108
LOADHIGH, 29, 78
Logo, 222
LOOP, 262, 283
LPT1, 84

M

Mace Utilities, 186
Machine language, 131
   instructions to microprocessor, 223–226
   nature of, 222
      viewing with DEBUG, 16–17
Master clock count, 268
Master environment, 278–279
   locating in memory, 278–280
Media Descriptor Byte, 301–302

for DOS disks, 302
Megabyte, 152, 153, 156
MEM, 11
   to find memory blocks, 277–278
   output of C command, 28–29
   viewing COMMAND.COM, 51
Memory
   blocks
      allocation of, 274–275
      arena header, 275–277
      comparing blocks, 180–181
      copying blocks, 216
      locating blocks, 277–278
   conventional memory, 152, 194
   DEBUG activities
      changing memory, 173–177
      comparing blocks of memory, 180–181
      comparing memory, 180–181
      memory display, 148, 168–170
      memory dump, 170–171
      memory manipulation commands, 168
      searching memory, 182–184
   and DOS
      arena header, 275–277
      DOS allocation of memory, 274–275
      environment memory block, 278–280
      finding blocks with MEM, 277–278
      memory and operation of DOS, 273–274
   extended memory, 165
   high memory area, 165
   locating bytes in, 159–163, 169–170
   memory banks, 153–154
   paragraphs, 274
   PC memory map, 152–154
   program segment prefix, 249, 254–258
   random access memory (RAM), 155
   range, 168, 171
   read-only memory (ROM), 155
   saving to disk, 186–191
   and segmented architecture, 156–158
   upper memory, 152
   viewing and changing with DEBUG, 131
   viewing block, 275

406 Index

Memory address, 167
　absolute address, 160–161
　location of, 17
Memory dump, with DEBUG, 170–171
Memory managers, 25
　and CONFIG.SYS, 21
Memory-resident programs
　and ASK command, 77
　and INSTALL command, 33
　loading in upper memory, 78
MENUCOLOR, 17
　function of, 39
Menu commands, DOS 6.0 function of, 38–41
MENUDEFAULT, 17
　function of, 39
MENUITEM, 17
　function of, 39, 40
Microprocessor
　checking with DEBUG, 131
　interrupts, 243–245
　machine language instructions to, 223–226
　registers, 206–220
　　accumulator registers, 207, 210–214
　　flags register, 219–220
　　functions of registers, 206–207
　　index registers, 207, 214–217
　　registers/names, listing of, 208
　　segment registers, 207–208, 217–219
　　viewing with DEBUG, 208–209
　and subroutines, 242
　and turning on PC, 7
MIRROR, 308
Mnemonics, 222, 235
MODE, 93
Modem, sending output to, 93–94
MORE filter, 28, 99–100
Most significant byte, 213
Mouse, 26
MSDOS.SYS, 12, 15, 43
Multimedia equipment, 26
Multitasking
　and AUTOEXEC.BAT, 57–61
　and FCBS command, 31
MULTITRACK, 18
Muse, 324

N

NDOS, 13, 44
NDOSEDIT, 168
Networks, and FCBS command, 31
NLSFUNC, foreign language support, 25
Norton Desktop for DOS, 293
Norton Format, 308
Norton Utilities, 186, 293, 324
NUL device, 85–86, 93
　function of, 85
NUMLOCK
　format for, 34
　function of, 17, 34
NUMOFF.COM, 265
　creation of, 75–76

O

Octal, 141
Offset, 157, 158, 160
Output
　pausing with MORE filter, 99–100
　redirecting, 91–94
Output device, CON device, 84

P

Paragraphs, of memory, 146, 274
Partition table, 303, 308–309
　function of, 11
　loading for viewing, 308
　purposes of, 308
　and viruses, 309
Pascal, 222
Patching
　cautions about, 325, 331
　COMMAND.COM, 330–331
　editing program file, 326–330
　meaning of, 325
PATH, 50
　building with AUTOEXEC.BAT, 65, 69–72
Pathname, 37, 79
PAUSE, 196
PC Tools, 186, 293

Pipe
    for input/output redirection, 96–97
    to modify output of DOS command, 100
    to stack multiple commands, 97
Power-on self test (POST), 10, 263
Power supply, nature of, 7
Printers
    PRN device, 84
    sending output to, 92–93
PRINTER.SYS, function of, 26
PRN device, 84
    function of, 84
Program file, editing of, 326–330
Programming
    assembly language, labels in, 234–236
    call and return instructions, assembly language, 242
    DEBUG mini-assembler
        building program, 226–228
        loading instruction pointer, 232–234
        running program, 228–230
        saving program to disk, 231
        and stack pointer, 236–242
    DEBUG script files
        A script, 344–347
        E script, 343–344
        program creation, 338–341
        programming sequence, 337–338
        rolling script into DEBUG, 342–343
    flow control, 232
    information sources on, 357–358
    and interrupts, 243–245
    jumping, 234
    nature of, 221–222
Programming languages
    assembly language, 222, 223
    high-level languages, 222–223
    machine language, 222
Program segment prefix, 249, 254–258
    command tail, 255, 258
    contents of, 254–258
    location of, 255
    viewing, 255
Prompt, creating with AUTOEXEC.BAT, 67–69
PUT, 338, 341

Q

QBASIC.EXE, 212
QEdit, 20
QEMM, 32, 34
QRAM, 32, 34
QUICKDIR.BAT, 120
    keyboard reassignment, 119–120
QUICKOFF.BAT, 120

R

RAM disk software, 25, 26
RAM drives, 26
    losing in reboot, 6–7
    set up in AUTOEXEC.BAT, 74–75
RAMDRIVE.SYS, function of, 26
Random access memory (RAM), 155
    nature of, 155
Range
    meaning of, 168
    specifying range, 171
RCX, 76
Read-only memory (ROM), 155
    nature, 155
REBOOT.BAT, 10, 268, 271
Recovery of document, 331–335
    DEBUG for, 331–334
    steps in, 332–334
Registers
    microprocessor, 131, 206–220
        accumulator registers, 207, 210–214
        flags register, 219–220
        functions of registers, 206–207
        index registers, 207, 214–217
        registers/names, 208
        segment registers, 207–208, 217–219
        viewing with DEBUG, 208–209
REM
    and DOS 6.0, 35
    format for, 34
    function of, 34–35
REPZ MOVSB, 215, 216, 222
Reserved memory. See Upper memory
Reserved sectors, 300
RESET.BAT, 271
    function of, 9–10

Reset button, for warm boot, 5
Resident drivers, 11
RESTORE.SCR, 194, 195, 196
RESTSCRN.BAT, 194, 196
RETURN, 242
ROM, and booting PC, 7, 8, 10–11
ROM BASIC, 11
Root directory sectors, 201
RUNDOS.BAT, 56

S

SAVE.SCR, 194, 195, 196
SAVESCRN.BAT, 194
SAY.COM, 258–262
  writing SAY program, 259–262
Scan codes, 111
  and keyboard reassignment, 112–113
  nature of, 112
  scan code values, 393–396
  values for Alt keys, 113
  values for function keys, 114
Scanners, 26
Screen
  as block of memory, 192–193
  creating larger screen, 100
  saving and restoring with DEBUG, 192–197
  size of, 281
Screen blanking, program for, 290–291
SCREEN.DAT, 194, 195, 196
Screen dump, 170
Script files. *See* DEBUG script files
Searches, DEBUG memory search, 182–184
Sectors
  of disk, 198–200
  per cluster
    in boot sector, 300
    calculation of, 322
  root directory sectors, 201
  sector offsets in memory, 200
  sectors-per-track values, 302, 303
  writing raw sectors to disk, 200–203
Segmented architecture, 156–158
Segment registers, 207–208, 217–219
  functions of, 207–208, 217–218
  functions of individual registers, 218

Serial communications, AUX device, 84
SET
  format for, 35
  function of, 17, 35
SETVER.EXE, function of, 26
SHARE.EXE, 31
Shell, 52–54
  and COMMAND.COM, 52–53
  shelling, meaning of, 53–54
  and command interpreter, 35, 43, 44, 49
  function of, 35, 52
SideKick, 148
Signature, of boot sector, 306
SI register, 214, 216, 217
SMARTDrive, 24
  development of, 26
SMARTDRV.SYS, function of, 26
SORT.EXE, 252–253
SORT filter, 101
  and I/O redirection, 101
  order of sorting, types of, 101
  switches for, 101
Sound, programming speaker of PC, 354–357
Source code, 234–235
SP register, 237
SS register, functions of, 218
Stacker, 27
Stacks, 236–242
  examples of use, 239–242
  nature of, 36
  stack pointer
    error message, 239
    operation of, 237–239
    value of, 237
  format for, 36
  function of, 22, 35–36, 236–237
Standard error device, 84
STARTNET, 242
Startup programs, running from AUTOEXEC.BAT, 76–78
Strings, storage in command tail, 259
Subdirectory, 320–324
  converting to disk drives, 79–80
  creating subdirectory, 321
  loading cluster on diskette, 323
  locating subdirectory, 320–324
  sectors per cluster, calculation of, 322

SUBMENU, 17
    function of, 39
Subroutines, and microprocessor, 242
SUBST, 79–81
    format of, 79
    function of, 79–80
    problems related to, 80–81
SWITCHES
    format for, 36–37
    function of, 36–37
System initialization (SysInit), 12–13
    and CONFIG.SYS, 16–19

T

Text, locating with FIND filter, 101–102
TIME, 95
    in AUTOEXEC.BAT, 75–76
Time Mark, 269
Token value, 18
Tracks, of disks, 197
TSRs. *See* Memory-resident programs
Turbo Assembler, 234
TurboDebug, 130
2UPPER.COM, 96, 97–99
    A script, 344–347
    creating program, 338–341
    E script, 343–344

U

Undelete programs, and File Allocation Table (FAT), 314
Upper memory, 152
    BIOS found in, 269–271
    hard disk controller, 270–271
    loading memory-resident programs in, 78
    map of, 270
    as RAM memory storage, 155
    upper memory blocks, 29, 155
    video memory, 269–270

V

Video
    character sets, 292–295
    information source about, 295
    screen blanking program, 290–291
    video mode information, BIOS Data Area, 266–268
    video pages, 288–292
        number for, 288
        number of available pages, 289
        switching pages, 289–292
Video interrupt, 381–384
Video memory, 280–284
    attribute bytes, 282–288
    attribute values, 281–282
    bytes of, 281
    location of, 269–270, 280
Viruses
    affecting partition table, 309
    running scanner from AUTOEXEC.BAT, 74
Volume, of disks, 197
Volume label, 202
    changing, 202–203
Volume serial number, 304

W

Warm boot, 5
    methods of, 5
WINA.386, 36
Windows
    and ANSI.SYS, 109
    running COMMAND.COM under, 55–57
Word processors, to edit CONFIG.SYS, 19–20
Word values
    deciphering bytes for, 300
    double word value, 303–304, 320
    at offset, 300, 301

X

XMS driver, 172, 173

Z

ZANSI.SYS, 109
Zero flag, functions of, 219
ZIPPY.CON, creating program, 355–357